T0154797

On the Path of the Prophet

Fethullah Gülen's Understanding of Sunnah

Dr. Mustafa Erdil

Copyright © 2020 by Tughra Books

23 22 21 20   1 2 3 4

All rights reserved. No part of this book may be reproduced or transmitted in any form or by any means, electronic or mechanical, including photocopying, recording or by any information storage and retrieval system without permission in writing from the Publisher.

Published by Tughra Books

335 Clifton Ave.

Clifton, NJ, 07011, USA

www.tughrabooks.com

978-1-68206-026-1

ON THE PATH
OF THE PROPHET

Fethullah Gülen's Understanding of Sunnah

Dr. Mustafa Erdil

TUGHRA
BOOKS
New Jersey

Contents

Introduction

Discussing the importance and high status of Hadith in Islam and its direct relevance to the Sunnah, this work expounds the Hadith-Sunnah understandings and works of Hadith scholars in the contemporary Muslim and Western worlds, paying particular attention to the Sunnah understanding of Fethullah Gülen, who has spent his entire life studying and teaching the Sunnah and who is well-known to closely follow the current issues and opposing thoughts concerning the Sunnah, along with his methods and considerations in defense of Sunnah. Exploring the holistic approach of this contemporary Muslim scholar who does not contend himself with defending the Sunnah, it looks further into how he puts his focus on practical interpretations of the Sunnah with his Sunnah-centered solutions to today's problems. The work thus investigates Gülen's holistic approach to understanding the Sunnah providing solutions to the problems at the individual, familial and social levels if it is studied in detail and interpreted within the context of the current era.

An involved work requires some background information on Hadith as a prelude to the topic. Therefore, before delving into the details of the issue, the work first analyzes the position and importance of Hadith in Islam, its close relationship with the concept of Sunnah, and its nature, origin and historical development in Chapter One. Before examining the definitions and understanding of Hadith in the West in the next chapter, here it looks into the meaning and definition of the term "Hadith" within the traditional Islamic context and highlights that the term is reserved by the scholars of theology and the traditionalists specifically for the totality of words, actions and tacit approvals of the Noble Prophet. Within this specific definition of "Hadith," its meaning, as an Islamic term, becomes synonymous with the word "Sunnah," which is translated broadly as the Prophetic traditions as well as the Prophetic discourse, actions, observations and tacit approvals.

Exploring the recordings of hadiths[1] in the time of Prophet Muhammad, upon whom be peace and blessings, while specifically drawing attention to the fact that they were written down under his direct

---

[1] In this work, the word "hadith," when not capitalized, refers to a single, specific hadith of the Noble Prophet while the Hadith, which is identical to the concept of Sunnah, refers to the collection of the words, actions and the tacit approvals of the Noble Prophet.

supervision, the work highlights the reasons behind the prohibition of recording the hadiths in its initial stage as well as their writing with the authorization of recording them at a later time. The private pages of Hadith recordings kept by the Companions are sourced and explored as to how these pages served as prototypes for Hadith compilations of later generations.

Limiting this background information with the early history and development of Hadith literature in Chapter One, the work then analyzes various views and discussions on the Prophetic Traditions that have taken place in contemporary times. Considering the dissimilar views of contemporary scholars on Hadith, the work takes a close look at these different perspectives in Chapter Two. In this regard, it examines the researches carried out in the West about Islamic disciplines which are generally focused on the Qur'an and the Hadith. While examining the Western scholars' approach to Hadith in some detail, it underlines that their perception of Hadith is quite different compared to the Muslim scholars' approach to the discipline.

In doing so, the work takes into consideration the critical approach to religion among the Western scholars which emerged since the Age of Enlightenment in Europe, prompting these scholars to formulate some overly critical views and perceptions on Judeo-Christian faith traditions. These Western scholars have later chosen to subject Islam to the same process of criticism and investigation like their own respective religions. Therefore, these Western scholars' approaches have differed fundamentally from the more traditionally accepted perceptions of Hadith held by Muslims. The primary focus in this chapter is, therefore, on the thoughts and assessments on Hadith in contemporary times, such as historical research done on Hadith in the West, the epistemological differences between Muslim and non-Muslim scholars, and some detrimental effects of modernism on Muslim scholars.

In Chapter Three, the teachings and written works of Fethullah Gülen are analyzed and brought into the spectrum to counter the discourse. Here, it analyzes how Gülen views the differing perspectives of modern-contemporary scholars in the issue of Sunnah/Hadith literature, its authenticity, and its interpretations. It expounds Gülen's responses to criticisms and doubts about the compilation of Hadith recordings during the period of the Noble Prophet's life-time and his interaction with the Companions. When *Gülen's understanding of Sunnah* is analyzed with specific references to his works, it is clearly seen that the Quranic verses decreeing obedience to the Noble Prophet constitute the basis for his approach to the emulation of Noble Prophet's example, practicing and adopting his Sunnah as a way of life. Therefore, Gülen's understanding of Sunnah and the relationship of the Hadith with the Qur'an are discussed extensively in this chapter. Gülen argues that, despite all the strong evidence, there is an attempt to underestimate the Sunnah, and even negate it, in order to leave the Qur'an alone and open to freehand interpretations, ultimately generating a vacuum of faith, a fertile environment for the spread of diverse ideologies. Thus, he reiterates that the Qur'an and the Sunnah exist as integral parts complementing each other.

Considering that Hadith provides the impetus for the interpretation of the Qur'an, the work examines here the Revelation-Hadith correlation, with an emphasis upon the interpretation of the Qur'an by the Hadith. In a Quranic verse, often quoted by Muslim scholars, God Almighty draws our attention to this important role of the Noble Prophet as interpreter:[2] *"[A]nd if you are to dispute among yourselves about anything, refer it to God and the Messenger, if indeed you believe in God and the Last Day."*[3] In this regard, this chapter focuses further on the law-making characteristic of the Hadith after the Qur'an, as the second primary source of Islam. Essentially, the Qur'an did not go into specifics on many issues as detailed explanations were made by Prophet Muhammad, upon whom be peace and blessings. Conforming to this conventional wisdom and Islamic tradition, Gülen displays a similar approach and draws our attention to the functions of the Sunnah as clarifying what is ambiguous in certain verses of the Qur'an, explicating what is implicit, specifying what is general, and making conditional what is unconditional.[4] According to Gülen, the Noble Prophet's exemplary behavior was nothing else than the manifestation of the Quranic value

---

[2] The English interpretations of the Quranic verses in this work are quoted from Ali Unal's *"The Qur'an with Annotated Interpretation in Modern English,"* (New Jersey: Tughra Books, 2008).

[3] Qur'an 4:59.

[4] Ibrahim Canan, *Fethullah Gülen'in Sunnet Anlayisi ("Fethullah Gülen's Understanding of the Sunnah,"* Istanbul: Ufuk Kitap Publishing, 2007), p. 108.

system in practical life. Therefore, interpretation of the Qur'an by the Sunnah should not be confined to a limited number of hadiths mentioned only in those sections of classical Hadith collections titled, "Kitab al-Tafsir" (Book of Quranic Exegesis). He persistently emphasizes in his works that the Noble Prophet's entire life should thus be analyzed day by day carefully. Gülen puts Sunnah in the center of all Islamic disciplines, emphasizing that the Quranic exegesis (*Tafsir*), Islamic jurisprudence (*Fiqh*), and the studies on the Life of the Noble Prophet (*Siyar*) are all developed under the light of Sunnah. He constantly highlights that the Sunnah represents the Divine Revelation's practical aspect and that the Noble Prophet, through his Practice (*Sunnah*), is not only the conveyor and commentator of the Qur'an, but also the true representative of the Divine Word. He further stresses that the Noble Prophet gave priority to the representation of the Quranic verses over their delivery; that is, put "representation" (*tabligh*) one step ahead of "presentation" (*tamthil*). Therefore, Gülen exposes his own self-accountability by putting his focus on representation. He concentrates on the questions of "how" and "why" with regard to the failure in representing Islam. He presents the way out of the problem and the means of achieving the aim by inculcating his interlocutor with inner accountability along with the representation. For Gülen, understanding of Sunnah, internalizing the values in it and finally practicing it is a project of civilization.

As a contemporary writer and scholar with a large worldwide following, some of Gülen's works have been translated into various world languages. Thus, one can easily face, through his extensive works in major world languages, a balanced thinker who has a deep understanding of both the past and present issues, providing answers to the problems stemming from the hardcore salafi approaches as well as the critiques of the rejecters of Hadith both in the contemporary Islamic world and the greater modern-secular world. The work hence analyzes how Gülen looks at both the challenges and criticism of traditional Islamic sources through the Sunnah perspective and offers solutions and answers from his contemporary perspective. In this regard, Gülen's appeal to the Noble Prophet's Companions and the Prophetic Traditions is strikingly different from the interpretation of the modern-day salafis. With the main difference lying in their contextualization of the early Islamic period, Gülen takes the early history and modern society into consideration while the salafis look at the issue quite a historical manner. The hardcore salafi approaches try to take contemporary Muslims to the early period of Islam without any change while Gülen tries to bring the understanding of the early period with some amendments to today. He focuses on the universality of the Sunnah, and keeps links between the periods sound and strong, trying to establish a healthy chain of transmission from the early period of Islam to the present day, and from here to the future. According to him, the architects of the future need to reinterpret the Book, the Sunnah and the legal opinions of the pious predecessors (*salaf al-salihin*) in a manner consistent with the perception, style and understanding of the time by taking the advantage of the flexibility and universality of the religious-societal dynamics. Essentially, at the foundation of historical dynamics, a healthy society, and scientific progress lays the proper reading of religious principles in accordance with the spirit of the time.

In addition, while Gülen's views on Hadith understandings in the Western world are discussed here in length, a special focus is given to his assessments along with his stance vis-à-vis skeptical western approaches to the transmitters of hadiths. His position in the face of modern critical thinking sweeping the Muslim world—which resulted in the emergence of skepticism about this important discipline of Islamic knowledge—is also explored in this chapter. This is mainly because of the fact that all these skeptical approaches and critical works on Hadith have naturally affected some Muslim intellectuals and researchers. This skeptical approach developed in the West, especially toward the narrators of hadiths, has contributed to the negative approach toward hadiths among some Muslims. The focus in this section is, therefore, to seek answers to questions such as, "Does Gülen agree with the new critical approaches? If so, to what extent?" and "If he stands against certain tendencies in the Muslim world, how does he challenge the unorthodox observations?" In this regard, it is very significant to analyze how Gülen counteracts the negative moves and trends in the modern contemporary world for the offsetting of negative and detrimental perspectives and outlooks about Islam and the Muslims.

In Chapter Four, Gülen's usage and interpretation of Sunnah are explored in relation to various contemporary issues. Gülen's personal interpretations of and perspectives on Hadith studies and how he deals with the modern contemporary issues are investigated in this chapter. For this reason, the teachings and written works of Gülen are analyzed and brought into the spectrum. In his works, Gülen focuses on the necessity of understanding what he coined "the *Sirah* philosophy"—the very philosophy behind the Practices (*Sunnah*) of the Noble Prophet in relation to the solutions to the problems of our contemporary age. Gülen's dynamic evaluations of the Sirah with his distinctive approach to link the lessons learnt through the incidents that took place in the Noble Prophet's lifetime to the problems of the contemporary age, provide an alternative perspective for further inquiries into the Sirah and Hadith disciplines of the contemporary age.

The leader of a movement, Fethullah Gülen is a scholar and intellectual who has endeavored to cultivate a peaceful new generation equipped with a range of modern skills and a positive approach to the present-day problems. Obviously, his teachings are based on the Qur'an and the Sunnah with a particular focus on the contemporary interpretations of hadiths and understanding "the philosophy behind the Practice of the Noble Prophet" in order to better see the current problems and serve the people of our contemporary age.

According to Gülen, it is necessary to have a comprehensive acquaintance with both the Age of Bliss and the contemporary age we're living in. This way, people of this age will be able to act upon the Prophetic Practice consciously and better fulfill the requirements of their own age. With this new concept of "the *Sirah* philosophy," Gülen tries to raise people's awareness for doing whatever is expected of them "here-and-now" by knowing, and acting upon, the methods and practice of the Noble Prophet in every situation of our daily life. This new approach to, and fresh interpretations of, the Sunnah have placed Gülen amongst a new group of contemporary scholars. This is the primary reason why this work focuses upon Gülen's understanding of Sunnah. Indeed, his thoughts and ideas on the issue have now drawn the interest of scholars and researchers from many parts of the world.

Gülen's teaching of Hadith is another major topic utilized as a source and reference point in this work. While Gülen's views about the discipline of Hadith are given, his contributions to the discipline are investigated quite in detail in Chapter Five. Muslim scholars, by convention, bring evidence from the Qur'an and the Sunnah, and emphasize the importance of the Prophetic Traditions since the early period of Islam. In this regard, the scholars from the traditional Islamic colleges (*madrasa*s) teach and utilize the Hadith discipline as a major source and reference point. Gülen's Hadith teaching methods are analyzed and compared with the methods used in these traditional colleges. Unlike what has been prescribed in the *madrasa*s, Gülen's outstanding perspectives and contributions to the discipline of Hadith, and the new methods he introduced, are analyzed in this chapter. The work looks further into Gülen's teaching of Hadith in his private circle and his reflections on certain academic areas. Although it is open to subjective evaluations, it devotes lengthy discussions to the question of how Gülen internalizes the principle of Sunnah in his own life and to his personal interpretation of Hadith and Sunnah according to various contemporary developments and changes.

Introduction to Hadith in Historical Perspective

Early History of Hadith Collections

Before anything else, it is of great importance to know the thoughts and works of the early generation Muslims in order to clearly understand the matters of authenticating, recording, and compiling the hadiths. The lack of a thorough and complete knowledge in these matters leave today's Muslims rather exposed to the influence of the works and excessive critical comments of the Hadith critics—thus raising uncertainties in their minds and causing the emergence of views that take only the Qur'an into consideration, disregarding the Hadith (Prophetic Reports) and hence discrediting the Sunnah (Prophetic Practice). Such questioning of the primary religious sources other than the Qur'an eventually means leaving the Qur'an as the only reference that is exposed to free-hand interpretations.

Primarily known as "the period of *salaf* (the predecessors)," the historical era of the registration, revision and codification of the hadiths as well as the formation of reliable knowledge and corpus of these Prophetic reports by the Prophet's Companions and the following early Muslim generations, is considered an important time-frame of the Islamic tradition. Considering the significance and function of the Prophetic Traditions (Hadith and Sunnah) among the primary Islamic sources, it is necessary to draw attention initially to the works carried out on the reliability, recording, safeguarding and compilation of these Prophetic Traditions during the early period of Islam.

According to Islamic sources, Prophet Muhammad, upon whom be peace and blessings, encouraged his Companions to memorize and study the Hadith alongside the Qur'an.[5] As the Companions' reports clearly demonstrate, the Prophetic reports and practices (Hadith and Sunnah) have been rigorously learned, safeguarded and transmitted since the time of the Noble Prophet. For this reason, while the Prophetic

---

[5]   See Abu Dawud, *'Ilm,* 10; Tirmidhi, *'Ilm,* 7; Ibn Majah, *Muqaddimah,* 18; Ibn Hanbal, *al-Musnad,* 4, 82.

reports (hadiths) were recorded on whatever material was available at the time, such as leather, wood and date leaves, by some of the Companions, other Companions collected and compiled these Prophetic reports in the form of booklets, called *sahifah*. Among these booklets, the two most famous ones are Abdu'llah ibn 'Amr ibn al-As' (684 CE) collection, called *Sahifah al-Sadiqah* (*The Truthful Script*), and Abu Hurayrah's (681CE) *Sahihah* (*Authentic Traditions*).[6]

Following these early works, the intensive process of comprehensive Hadith compilations began at the end of the first century AH.[7] The first comprehensive compilation in this area was achieved by Abu Hurayrah's student, Hammam ibn Munabbih (719 CE). He compiled the Noble Prophet's reports and traditions from the Companions. Besides other works beginning to emerge at this early period, the works on the classification of the hadiths gained greater care and attention at the beginning of the mid-second century AH. Also authored during this early period were the Prophetic Biography works (*Sirah*), the biographies of the Companions (*Tabaqat*),[8] and various kinds of Hadith collections, such as *sunan* (plural of "sunnah," meaning "Prophetic traditions"), *jami'* (large collections of authentic hadiths) and *musannaf* (Hadith collections with content arranged according to topics).

The Hadith works collected by Muslim scholars in the second century after Hijrah could be classified in five groups: the books of *sirah wa maghazi*—works on the Noble Prophet's life and the early period of Islam, *sunan, jami', musannaf* as well as those works assigned specifically for some significant topics. The books of *sirah* and *maghazi* are about the life of Prophet Muhammad, upon whom be peace and blessings, and the early

---

6 Talat Kocyigit, *Hadis Tarihi* (*The History of Hadith*), (Ankara: Ankara University Publications, 1988), p. 199.

7 AH is short for "After Hijrah." The Islamic calendar starts from the day the Noble Prophet emigrated from Mecca to Medina in 622 CE, the event known as the *Hijrah* (literally meaning "Immigration").

8 The biographical entries in the Islamic Tabaqat literature offer evaluations of the personal, religious and intellectual quality of their subjects. These collections of *Tabaqat* works are typically used as tools to assist the scholars of the Hadith science in their efforts to classify the hadith transmitters and determine the quality of particular chain of transmission (*isnad*) accompanying each and every hadith. The *Tabaqat* genre is thus used for authenticating the Prophetic reports narrated by those righteous, honest, and competent transmitters in the early Muslim generations.

period of Islam. These works also recorded the Noble Prophet's worship and his moral values. The *sunan* books contain the hadiths that classified topics according to the discipline of Islamic jurisprudence (*fiqh*) such as cleanliness, the Prayer, Prescribed Purifying Alms, Fasting, Pilgrimage, family life, lawful and unlawful. The comprehensive *jami'* works are similar to the *sunan* works but a *jami'* contains extra knowledge different from *sunan*, such as the creation of the human being, the universe and other issues. It also contains the history of bygone nations and their Prophets, the virtues of the Last Prophet's Companions and so on.[9]

By the third century of Islam, the most famous *muhaddiths* (traditionists)[10] completed their six major authentic Hadith collections, called *al-Kutub al-Sittah* (*The Six Books of Hadith*) that are considered the most important reference sources in Islam after the Qur'an.[11] These "Six Books of Hadith" contain 33,132 hadiths in total, including those that are repeated. Some Hadith scholars recompiled in one book all the hadiths contained in *al-Kutub al-Sittah* by excluding the repeated ones. Ibn al-Dayba's (d. 1537 CE) *Taysir al-Wusul ila Jami' al-'Usul*, which contains 10,490 hadiths, is considered to represent *al-Kutub al-Sittah* in terms of datum, an authority as it includes all of the hadiths included in these six famous collections.[12] The works and methods of the first Muslim generations were observed by the scholars of the following generations and were thus adopted as a norm in the discipline of Hadith.

According to Sunni Muslims, the six major Hadith collections of *Kutub al-Sittah* contain the authentic hadiths. These six Hadith books are as follows:

- *Sahih al-Bukhari*: This collection contains 7,275 authentic hadiths. The work is divided into nine volumes and collected by Abu Abdullah Muhammad ibn Ismail ibn al-Mughirah al-Bukhari (d. 870 CE).

- *Sahih Muslim*: This collection contains 9,200 hadiths and is

---

9   Kocyigit, *Hadis Tarihi (The History of Hadith)*, pp. 207-212.
10   *Muhaddith* is a Hadith scholar who knows the hadiths with their chain of transmissions, the names of narrators and the various wordings in their narrations. Technically, the term *muhaddith* can refer to either a transmitter of hadiths or a collector or compiler of hadiths.
11   Kocyigit, *Hadis Tarihi (The History of Hadith)*, pp, 200-231.
12   Ibrahim Canan, *Fethullah Gülen'in Sunnet Anlayisi* (Istanbul: Ufuk Kitap Publishing, 2007), p. 8.

divided into seven volumes. This source is the most authentic book of Hadith after *Sahih al-Bukhari* in Islam and was collected by Muslim ibn al-Hajjaj (d. 875 CE).

- *Sunan Abu Dawud*: As the third main source in Hadith collection, *Sunan Abu Dawud* is divided into five volumes. This source contains 4,800 sound hadiths collected by Abu Dawud Sulayman ibn al-Ash'ath al-Azdi as-Sijistani (d. 888 CE).
- *Jami' al-Tirmidhi*: This collection contains 3,956 hadiths and is divided into fifty chapters. This Hadith source was collected by Abu 'Isa Muhammad ibn 'Isa al-Tirmidhi (d. 892 C.E). It is classified according to the topics of hadiths, such as Purification, Prayer, Charity and Fasting.
- *Sunan al-Nasa'i* (aka. *Sunan al-Sughra*): Collected by Abu Abdu'r-Rahman Ahmad ibn Shu'ayb ibn Ali ibn Sinan al-Nasa'i (d. 915 CE), this collection contains 5,270 hadiths, including repeated narrations, and is divided into 6 volumes.
- *Sunan ibn Majah*: Collected by Ibn Majah (Imam Muhammad ibn Yazid Ibn Majah al-Qazvini) (d. 887 CE), this source contains over 4,000 hadiths in 32 books divided into 1,500 chapters.

Muslim Approaches to Hadith in Contemporary Times

In the last few centuries, Muslim intellectuals, who use the examples of non-Muslim scholars' works and their approaches to the Hadith, have been exposed to reading the Prophetic Traditions (Hadith and Sunnah) skeptically and critically. This has resulted in the emergence of different ideas about the Hadith and the Sunnah inside and outside of the Islamic world.

Although the non-Muslim scholars' investigation of the primary Islamic sources has been going on since the mid-twelfth century in the Western world, their Qur'an and Sunnah-oriented researches began to intensify at the beginning of the eighteenth century, mostly heading towards criticizing the hadiths and questioning their authenticity. This criticism and questioning continued periodically onto the later centuries and has influenced the Muslim scholars.[13]

---

[13]   M. Said Hatiboğlu, *Hadis Tedkikleri (Hadith Researches)*, (Ankara: Ozkan Matbaacilik,

Looking at the works produced in this area in a chronological framework, it is clear that this kind of criticism has been alive in the Muslim world since then. It is, therefore, important to focus on the history of the ongoing criticisms of Hadith. Obviously, the Western scholars' skeptical approaches and critical works on the religious values have affected Muslim intellectuals and researchers. Many Muslim intellectuals have then focused on the Hadith and the Sunnah due to this influence.

However, it is of great benefit to know the thoughts and works of the early generation Muslims in order to clearly understand the matters of authenticating, recording, and compiling the hadiths. The lack of a thorough and complete knowledge in these matters leave today's Muslims rather exposed to the influence of the works and excessive critical comments of the Hadith critics—thus raising uncertainties in their minds and causing the emergence of views that take only the Qur'an into consideration, disregarding the Prophetic Traditions. This viewing of the Qur'an as the only reference can be seen as the main reason for the critical approach to the Hadith and the Sunnah increasingly coming to the forefront.

In this regard, Albayrak asserts that both the secular-minded and devout Muslims of the contemporary period assert the need to interpret the Qur'an in the light of contemporary issues and contexts. He summarizes the typical approach of the modern era emerging in this area as follows:

> Modern understanding of Islam is Qur'an-centered; religious matters are regarded to be solved primarily with references to the Qur'an alone. In view of this understanding, a skeptical approach to religious sources other than Qur'an has emerged. The first element of the target of the said skepticism and criticism is none other than the Hadith and the Sunnah.[14]

There are many scholars who point to the skeptical approach developed in the Western scholarship of Islam towards the transmitters of hadiths, constituting a cause for the rejection of Hadith as a primary source of Is-

---

2009), pp. 47-54.

[14] Ismail Albayrak, *Fethullah Gülen Hocaefendi'nin Tefsir Anlayisi (Fethullah Gülen's Understanding of the Quranic Exegesis)*, (Istanbul: Nil Publishing, 2010), p. 26.

lam. Under the influence of such a tendency, a new class of contemporary Muslim intellectuals, who are quite distanced from their own value system and trapped between tradition and modernism, has emerged in the Islamic world. As a result, those who could not remain indifferent to the skeptical and critical thoughts have authored books in defense of the Hadith and the Sunnah. Muhammad Abu Shahbah (b. 1914) authored his *Difa'un 'an al-Sunnah* (*Defense of the Sunnah*), considered as the first of its kind, as a refutation to this emerging thought stemming from the non-Muslim scholars' efforts to discredit the Hadith. Besides this, there are countless articles and rebuttals published in various parts of the Muslim world, especially in Egypt, in defense of the Hadith and the Sunnah. According to Gormez and Ozafsar,[15] refutations of disparaging views on Hadith began to appear only after the 1950s in Turkey. This was mainly due to the fact that no serious work in this contemporary age was carried out in the discipline of Hadith until this time.[16]

  Among the first scholars who raised the issues of Hadith criticism and rejection within the Muslim world were Sayyid Ahmad Khan (d.1898), Mawlawi Charagh Ali (d.1895), Abdu'llah Chakralwi (d.1930), Mawlawi Ahmad al-Din Amritsari (d. 1948) and Muhammad Abduh (d. 1905). According to Sayyid Ahmad Khan,[17] who seems to have been seriously affected by the Hadith criticisms, the nature of Hadith can be summarized as follows:

> Not all speeches of the Prophet are revelation. He executed many works in his life as a statesman, not as a Prophet. The six most famous hadith collections (*al-Kutub al-Sittah*) contain many forged hadiths. Words in hadith collections belong to narrators, and they mainly represent the accounts of daily lives and views of the first few generations of Muslims. All hadiths contradictory to Qur'an, human intellect and experience must be rejected.[18]

---

[15] Mehmet Gormez and M. Emin Ozafsar expressed these views in the preface of their translation of Muhammad Abu Shahbah's work, *Difa'un 'an al-Sunnah,* into Turkish as *Hadis Mudafaasi (Defense of the Hadith).*

[16] Muhammed Abu Shahbah, *Hadis Mudafaasi 1 (Defense of the Hadith, Vol. 1),* trans. by Mehmet Gormez, M. Emin Ozafsar, Preface (Ankara: Rehber Publishing, 1990), pp. 23–33.

[17] Daniel W. Brown, *Rethinking Tradition in Modern Islamic Thought,* vol. 1 (Cambridge: Cambridge University Press, 1996), pp. 34-54.

[18] Mustafa Donmez, "Islam Dunyasinda Hadis Inkarcilari ve Gorusleri" (Deniers of Hadith

Mawlawi Charagh Ali holds similar views and explains his understanding of Hadith this way:

> The orders and guidance of the Prophet are of temporary nature. Most of the words attributed to the Prophet in *al-Kutub al-Sittah* are fabricated. Practicing according to these hadiths, is, in fact, acting contrary to reason and conscience. The Prophet did neither leave behind a legal system nor any suggestion in that regard. He wanted Muslims to establish their own civil laws and the basis of their religion according to the needs of the time.[19]

Muslim thinkers began reflecting on Hadith along the same line as modern revisionist scholars. While some of them accepted their thoughts and skepticism without questioning, others added them to their repertoire of thinking after a rigorous process of explaining. In this sense, the effect of positivist-rationalist logic is apparent in the thoughts of Muhammad Abduh, who holds a relatively rationalist approach and argues for the Qur'an to be taken as the sole source (which has to be interpreted according to the needs of the time) and that conceivable principles ought to be brought to the forefront. He offers a rationale similar to those displayed by Sayyid Ahmad Khan and others.[20]

There are also modern-day Muslims who hold the same or similar views: Ahmad Din (d. 1908), Tawfiq Sidqi (d. 1920), Ahmad Amin (d. 1954), Hafiz Muhammad Aslam Jarajpuri (d. 1955), Ahmad Parwiz (d. 1964), Abu Rayyah (d. 1970), Fazlur Rahman (d. 1982), Ghulam Ahmad Parwiz (d. 1985), Mahmud M. Taha (d. 1985) and Muhammad Ghazzali (d. 1996). For example, regarding the Hadith and the Shari'ah, Mahmud M. Taha says, "The Prophet's words and approvals are not *sunnah*, but they constitute *shari'ah*, which is limited by time; and, *shari'ah* is only applicable during his time."[21] Further, Ahmad Amin says, "The

---

in the Islamic World and Their Views), https://dusuncetarihi.files.wordpress.com/2010/01/islam-dunyasinda-hadis-inkarcilari-ve-gorusleri.pdf.

19   Ibid.

20   Zohair Hussain, "Muhammed Abduh (1849-1905) Kimdir" in "M. Hilmi Bas" (2015), http://www.islamdusuncesi.net/muhammed-abduh-1849-1905-187h.htm.

21   Mustafa Donmez, "Islam Dunyasinda Hadis Inkarcilari ve Gorusleri" (Deniers of Hadith in the Islamic World and Their Views), https://dusuncetarihi.files.wordpress.com/2010/01/islam-dunyasinda-hadis-inkarcilari-ve-gorusleri.pdf.

number of *mutawatir* (soundest) hadiths is no more than seven. Hadiths are not reliable as they were kept in memories for a long time without written records. Hadiths were fabricated even during the early centuries of Islam."[22] Similarly, Abu Rayyah states, "Sunnah was not written during the early centuries of Islam and Abu Hurayrah is a character who forged hadiths," and gives the following explanation, "Hadiths have no sanction on an individual for taking or giving up something, no sin is committed by such an action."[23] An important point is that most of these views present similarities in terms of condescending Hadith approaches—almost like copycats of each other or their non-Muslim counterparts. For instance, Fazlur Rahman, who is considered one of the pioneers of the reformist school in contemporary Islamic thought, exhibits a structure of thought similar to Goldziher's and Schacht's. One can perceive his opinion of the Hadith through the following statement:

> Because there were only a few prophetic hadiths in the early period, the great majority of them originated from later generations rather than the Prophet himself. That is, most of the hadiths were formulated after the time of the Prophet; therefore, the textual contents of hadiths cannot be attributed to the Prophet.[24]

Clearly, there is a strong tendency among Muslims whose approaches to the Hadith are very critical. Nevertheless, it is almost impossible to claim that majority of Muslims' view is in tune with this revisionist approach.

Here, in summary, it is necessary to draw attention to the ideas of Muslim scholars who do not accept the adverse criticism of Hadith. Well-versed in Hadith studies in the West, Muhammad Mustafa al-Azami, who is an eminent researcher in the field has made an important contribution to the Hadith science and the defending of the Hadith. Al-Azami rebutted Schacht's criticisms on Hadith in his work, titled *On Schacht's Origins of Muhammadan Jurisprudence* (Cambridge, 1996). With his profound knowledge and using the major Islamic sources, he

---

[22] Ibid.
[23] Ibid.
[24] Fazlur Rahman, *Tarih Boyunca Islami Metodoloji Sorunu* (Trans. by Salih Akdemir; originally published as *Islamic Methodology in History)*, (Ankara: Ankara School's Publications, 1995), p. 47.

exposed the falsity of the claims Schacht made about the Sunnah in his *The Origins of Muhammadan Jurisprudence.* Along with that, Pakistani Ahmad Hasan also wrote a refutation, titled *The Early Development of Islamic Jurisprudence* (Islamabad, 1988) against Schacht's work. Also, upon the criticism of Hadith in the West, Ali Osman Ates authored *Oryantalistlerin Hz. Peygamber'le Ilgili Iddialarina Cevaplar (Answers to the Orientalists' Allegations about the Noble Prophet)* (Istanbul, 1996) while Ali Dere wrote *Oryantalistlerin Hadis'e Yaklasimlari (Orientalists' Approach to Hadith)* (Ankara, 1999). Among numerous others, Mehmed Said Hatiboglu wrote an extensive article on the issue, titled *Batidaki Hadis Calismalari Uzerine (On the Hadith Studies in the West)* (Ankara, 1992).[25]

As an answer to the indexed criticisms of the Qur'an and the Hadith, Muhammad Asad (1900-1992) wrote two works, titled *Islam at the Crossroads* (1934) and *The Road to Mecca* (1954). Acknowledging Muhammad Asad's thoughts, Sayyid Qutb (1906-1966) emphasizes that the works on Hadith criticism are scathing criticisms, aiming to inflict damage to the religion. Similarly, Hussein Nasr (b.1933) considers these Hadith criticisms as a distortion of the original Islamic establishment.[26]

After this brief introduction to the history of Hadith, a special focus will be given to the significance of Hadith in Islam and the Hadith-Sunnah understandings and works of both the modernist intellectuals and the contemporary Muslim scholars who follow the ideas of the predecessors (*salaf*)[27] in the first two chapters on "Hadith in Islam" and "The Contemporary Western Approaches to Hadith Science" respectively. Then, the work will pay particular attention to Gülen's understanding of the Prophetic Traditions, his interpretation in respect of *salaf* along with his approaches to and assessment of the modernist thought of the Prophetic Traditions, and the terminology he has used in relation to the Prophetic practice and reports (Sunnah and Hadith) in his close

---

[25]   G.H.A. Juynboll, *Oryantalistik Hadis Arastirmalari (Orientalistic Studies on Hadith)*, vol. 1 (Ankara: Ankara School Publishing, 2001), pp. 21-22.

[26]   Robert Irwin, *Oryantalistler Ve Dusmanlari (trans. by* Bahar Tirnakci; originally published as *The Orientalists and Their Enemies),* (Istanbul: Yapi Kredi Publishing, 2007), pp. 315-318.

[27]   *Salaf* (Early Muslim) in traditional Islamic scholarship means someone who died within the first four centuries after the Noble Prophet, including scholars such as Abu Hanifa, Malik, Shafi'i, and Ibn Hanbal.

circle and his writings. Since the work also pays particular attention to the analysis of Gülen's approaches to, and assessment of, the modernist thought of Sunnah, it will review any convincing answers in his writings in the face of their new critical approaches. Therefore, Gülen's responses to criticisms and doubts about the compilation of Prophetic traditions and Hadith recordings and his attitudes and views about the Western and modern Muslim scholars' opinions on the relationship between Revelation and Hadith will later be discussed in detail.

CHAPTER ONE

HADITH IN ISLAM

Prophetic Traditions as a Primary Source of Islam

Islam is based on two fundamental sources. The first is the Qur'an, which consists of verses (*ayah*s) and chapters (*surah*s) of various lengths. According to Muslims, Quranic texts are the direct, unaltered and final revelation of God's words that were sent down in 23 years to the Noble Prophet, who taught and dictated them to his Companions. The Prophetic Traditions (Hadith and Sunnah) are the second primary source in Islamic legislation after the Qur'an.[28] The Prophetic Traditions have been accepted as the second primary source of Islam since the early period in terms of reference and interpretation and for legal rulings (*hukm*) and interpersonal transactions and dealings (*mu'amalat*). One of the key reasons for this classification lies in the well-known words of the Noble Prophet: "I have left two things with you. As long as you hold fast to them, you will not go the wrong way. They are the Book of God (Qur'an) and the Practice (Sunnah) of His Messenger."[29]

In addition, the primary source of Islam, the Qur'an, also contains numerous proofs and evidence (*dalil*) in determining the Hadith and the Sunnah as legal sources as in the following verse (which means): "*If you are to dispute among yourselves about anything, refer it to God and the Messenger, if indeed you believe in God and the last day.*"[30] According to Muslim scholars, this particular verse of the Qur'an, in terms of determining and solving a problem, ordains primarily God and, immediately after that, the Noble Prophet as the main points of reference. There are a number of similar verses in the Qur'an establishing the Prophetic Traditions as the second primary source in Islam.[31]

Regarding the notion of Prophethood, there are two very important concepts employed in the Qur'an: *nabi* (prophet) and *rasul* (messenger).[32] A close examination of the Quranic usage of these two terms will make clear the relation of the Hadith and the Prophetic mission toward

---

[28] Kocyigit, *Hadis Tarihi (History of the Hadith)*, p, 11.

[29] Malik ibn Anas, *Muwatta*, Book 46, Number 46.1.3.

[30] Qur'an 4:59.

[31] Qur'an 5:92.

[32] In Islamic terminology "Rasul" was used for the Messenger who brought a new *Shariah* (Codes of law) while those Prophets who did not bring any new *Shariah* but followed the *Shariah* of a previous "Rasul" were called "Nabi." That`s why "Rasul" is higher than "Nabi."

humankind. A Prophet's duty as a *nabi* is to invite people to believe in the fundamental religious principles.[33] From the Quranic perspective, this is cited under three main topics: *tabligh* (conveying the Divine message), *tabyin* (making clear, explaining) and *tatbiq* (practicing).[34] Clearly, the understanding of Quranic verses, their teaching and implementation would be realized by the representation and explanation of Prophet Muhammad, upon whom be peace and blessings. While some figurative verses dictate belief in the Unseen (*Ghayb*), other verses[35] enjoin more concrete issues such as interpersonal transactions and dealings. In other words, in terms of implementation, some *mujmal* (unclear/ambiguous) verses necessitate clarification. Verses that relate to the Prayer (*Salah*) are very good illustrations of this ambiguous form. In the related Quranic verses,[36] times of the Prayers and numbers of bowings and prostration are not mentioned explicitly. Other similarly ambiguous verses[37] require the explanation and actions of the Noble Prophet. At this point, Prophetic Practice (Sunnah) comes to the fore to play an expository and applied role.

Definition of Hadith

Hadith, which is an Arabic word derived from the word *hadatha*, literally means "a new one." The word "hadith" as a noun means narrative or news while its infinitive form of *tahdith* means to inform or talk about something.

The word "hadith" has been mentioned in the Qur'an, in multiple senses, in 23 different verses. The word "hadith" (announcement) in this verse of the Qur'an, *"[t]hen maybe you will kill yourself with grief, sorrowing after them, if they do not believe in this announcement (hadith),"*[38] has been used in the sense of announcement or news referring to the Qur'an itself.[39] In the verse, *"God sends down in parts the best of the words as a*

---

[33] Kocyigit, *Hadis Tarihi*, p. 12.

[34] Suat Yildirim, *Kuran-i Hakim Ve Aciklamalı Meali (The Wise Qur'an and Its Annotated Interpretation)*, (Istanbul: Isik Publications, 2006), p. 87.

[35] Qur'an 2:3, 2:33, 3:44, 3:179, 6:50, 10:20, 11:123.

[36] Qur'an 2:238, 2:177, 2:110, 4:55, 6:72, 7:170.

[37] Qur'an 19:31, 20:132, 33:33.

[38] Qur'an 46:6.

[39] Kocyigit, *Hadis Tarihi* (The History of Hadith), p. 9. In another verse, the word *tahdith* has been used: *"and as for the favour of your Lord, proclaim it"* (Qur'an 93:11).

Book fully consistent in itself,[40] the word "hadith" means message, words, and book. The word "hadith" in the verse, *"[w]hen you meet such [people (O Messenger)] as indulge in (blasphemous or derisive) talk about our revelations, turn away from them until they engage in some other talk,"*[41] is used in the sense of subject matter or discourse.[42]

According to Arabic linguistic sources, the word "hadith" carries the meaning of "new" as opposed to "old." The word also refers to "narrative" and "report," and was often used by the pre-Islamic era (*jahiliyyah*) Arab poets in reference to these meanings. With the advent of Islam, this word has been used in relation to the words and actions of the Noble Prophet.[43] The Companions and early period Muslim scholars have reserved this word for this specific context.[44]

The usage of the word "hadith" by the Noble Prophet in reference to his own speeches specifies its meaning. A hadith narrated by Abu Hurayrah provides an example:

> I asked: "O God's Messenger! Who will be the luckiest person, who will gain your intercession on the Day of Resurrection?" God's Messenger said: "O Abu Hurayrah! I have thought that none will ask me about it before you as I know your longing for hadiths (i.e. for learning "my words"). The luckiest person who will have my intercession on the Day of Resurrection will be the one who said sincerely from the bottom of his heart 'La ilaha illa'llah' (There is no deity but God)."[45]

In Islamic terminology, although Hadith generally refers to the words of the Noble Prophet, some Muslim scholars have ascribed meanings to this term in the context of different Islamic disciplines. According to the scholars of 'Usul (juristic methodologies), Hadith refers exclusively to the speeches, actions and declarations of the Noble Prophet. With this usage, the word *hadith* becomes synonymous with the term *sunnah*. On the other hand, some scholars of Hadith also use the term for all the news

---

[40] Qur'an 39:23.
[41] Qur'an 6:68.
[42] M. Mustafa al-Azami, *Studies in Hadith Methodology and Literature* (Plainfield, USA: American Trust Publications, 1997), p. 30.
[43] Zubayr, *Hadith Literature, Its Origin, Development and Special Features*, p. 52.
[44] Ibid, p. 51.
[45] Bukhari, *'Ilm*, 34, hadith no. 98.

(*khabar*) about the Noble Prophet as well as the narrations attributed to a Companion (*mawquf*) or a successor from the second Muslim generation (*maqtu'*). When assessed from this point of view, the term *hadith* carries the meaning of "reports" from or about the Noble Prophet. Yet, other scholars of Hadith restrict the term "hadith" to refer exclusively to the traditions of the Noble Prophet while they define all other narrations that are attributed to the Companions or their successors from the following generation as "reports" concerning the Noble Prophet.

Taking into account these various meanings attributed to the term "hadith," the specialists engaged in the field of Hadith are called *muhaddith* while those who are engaged in the field of the transmission of historical reports and factual events are given the title *akhbari* (one who gives *khabar*—news that include hadiths).[46]

Looking at Islamic literature in general, it can easily be observed that the term *hadith* has been used exclusively to refer to the speeches, actions and declarations of the Noble Prophet.[47] While scholars of methodology and scholars of Hadith differ to some extent in defining the term *hadith*, nevertheless they agree on a similar purpose. However, a glance into the views and opinions expressed by non-Muslim researchers in Hadith studies and some contemporary Muslims—e.g. Fazlur Rahman is known to have this opinion—will reveal that Hadith is not only employed to refer to the sayings and actions of the Noble Prophet, but also to designate customs and traditions. For example, G. H. A. Juynboll uses the word "hadith" to refer to "customs and traditions" in general terms.[48]

Relationship between Hadith and Sunnah

An accurate determination of the relationship between Hadith and Sunnah necessitates a clear understanding of the meanings of each of these two terms independently. It is only through this method that the meanings in common can be correctly understood.

---

[46]   Kocyigit, *Hadis Tarihi (The History of Hadith)*, p. 10.
[47]   Ibn al-Salah al-Shahrazuri, *An Introduction to the Science of the Hadith*, trans. Eerik Dickinson (UK: Garnet Publishing Limited, 2006).
[48]   G. H. A. Juynboll, *The Authenticity of the Tradition Literature* (Leiden: Brill Archive, 1969), p. 17.

The word *sunnah* is derived from the Arabic root "*snn*," which is normally used to refer to an issue gaining certainty, absolute accuracy of news, its continuity and advancement in that direction. It is also understood that the derivation is from another Arabic word, *sanan*, which is used in the sense of "an open, straight path without hindrance." Hence, with this meaning, the word *sanan* is used synonymously with *sunnah*. Another meaning attributed to the word *sunnah* is "behavior."[49] Along with these meanings, the word *sunnah* also refers to "a way—in the sense of both good and bad—that is followed, *sirah* (biography), and community."[50] Here, the usage of "bad" in discourses refers directly to the actions that are regarded as unacceptable by the Noble Prophet and thus frowned upon by Muslims, as any negative or non-beneficial deed would never be considered as a sunnah act in the first instance. As one of the qualities of Prophethood in Islam is "immunity from sin" (*'ismah*), Prophet Muhammad and all other Prophets of God, peace be upon them all, are regarded as protected and free from sins. In al-Fayumi's (d. 770 AH) work, *al-Misbah al-Munir*, and al-Jawhari's (d. 1002 or 1008 AH) *al-Sihah*, the word "sunnah" was mentioned as being used among pre-Islamic Arabs synonymously with "hadith" in reference to "traditions, courses and customs of the forefathers."[51] According to these explanations, *hadith* and *sunnah* are therefore derived from root words that have close meanings with different nuances. With the advent of Islam, the usage of these two words—which Arabs had been using synonymously since the Age of Ignorance—has been reserved for the utterances, actions and approvals of the Noble Prophet, and the acceptance of this usage by the majority of Muslim scholars, since the early days of Islam, strengthens the claims of their synonymity.

In the Qur'an, the word *sunnah* is used in various verses in the form of "*sunnah of Allah*" (God's Way),[52] "*sunnah al-awwalin*"[53] and "*su-*

---

49 Yusuf, *The Sunnah: Its Development and Revision, Hadith and Sunnah*, p. 103.
50 Mustafa Genc, "Vahiy Sunnet Iliskisi" (The Relation between Revelation and Sunnah), (Konya: Selcuk University, Theology Faculty, 2005), p.11.
51 Ahmad ibn Muhammad al-Muqri al-Fayyumi, "Al-Misbah al-Munir fi Gharib al-Sharh al-Kabir," (2009), http://art.thewalters.org/files/pdf/W590.pdf.
52 Qur'an 33:38; 48:23; 17:77.
53 Qur'an 35:43.

nan"[54] in reference to "law, ruling, wisdom, obedience and method."[55] Similarly, it occurs in the Qur'an in the sense of "invariable laws, commandments and clear facts." In this connection, the use of the term *sunnah* by scholars of Hadith and Fiqh in reference to a "path to follow, law, custom, safe and secure way" is noteworthy. Imam al-Shafi'i[56] also accepted the Sunnah as the words and actions of the Noble Prophet.[57] When considered in terms of these definitions and views, Sunnah consists of all actions and avoidances of the Noble Prophet that were transmitted and demonstrated regardless of their legal basis for transactions. According to Hanafites, *fardh* (obligatory), *wajib* (necessary), *sunnah*, *mustahab* (recommended) and *adab* (ethical norms) are inclusive of all, and Sunnah consists of the Noble Prophet's character (*shama'il*), lifestyle and biography (*sirah*).[58]

When taking all this into consideration, the close relationship of the meanings of Hadith and Sunnah is remarkable. For example, Kockuzu says, "Hadith, in the terminology of Hadith scholars, is the written form of words, actions, affirmations and qualities ascribed and attributed to the Noble Prophet."[59] Muhammad Abd al-Azim al-Zarqani's and Husayn al-Qudsi's use of Hadith and Sunnah interchangeably is also significant.[60] Further, Talat Kocyigit elucidates this unity of meaning between Hadith and Sunnah as follows: "In the early period, everything stemming from the Noble Prophet, in the form of speech, action and approval, was established as his Sunnah."

Looking at the understanding and definitions of Hadith and Sunnah among the later period scholars shows that they use the term Sunnah synonymously with Hadith, while jurists assert that Sunnah consists solely of the words, actions and affirmations transmitted from

---

54   Qur'an 3:137; 4:26.

55   Genc, "Vahiy Sunnet Iliskisi" (The Relation between Revelation and Sunnah), pp. 11–12.

56   Abu 'Abdillah Muhammad ibn Idris al-Shafi'i was a Muslim jurist and scholar (150-204 AH). Imam al-Shafi'i was active in *fiqh* (Islamic jurisprudence) and his teaching eventually led to the Shafi'i School of *fiqh* named after he passed away.

57   al-Sarakhsi, *'Usul al-Fiqh*, I, 113

58   Canan, *Fethullah Gülen'in Sunnet Anlayisi*, p. 111.

59   Ali Osman Kockuzu, *Rivayet Ilimlerinde Haber-i Vahitlerin Itikat Ve Tesri Yonlerinden Degeri* (Ankara: Religious Affairs Directorate Publications, 1988), p. 19.

60   Ash-Shaykh Muhammad 'Abd al-'Azim al-Zarqani, *Manahil al-Irfan fi Ulum al-Qur'an*, vol. 2 (Beirut: Dar al-Ma'rifah, 2001).

the Noble Prophet. However, according to scholars of Hadith, Sunnah has a terminological meaning more comprehensive than that which is accepted by scholars of 'Usul (Methodology), in which Sunnah encompasses all speeches and actions of the Noble Prophet, including those before his Prophethood. Thus, the term *sunnah* is equivalent to *hadith*.[61]

In light of all these explanations, it can be asserted that the terms *hadith* and *sunnah* are generally used synonymously, but in some cases, *sunnah* gains more weight in reference to actions (Prophetic practice), while *hadith* is used to refer to verbal narrations (Prophetic reports). This is among the strongest views.[62]

From this perspective, Hadith, or Sunnah, are classified under three categories: verbal, practical and tacit approval. According to the scholars of 'Usul and Hadith, verbal Sunnah is a statement uttered by the Noble Prophet on any subject. Thus, all hadiths beginning with "The Messenger of God said" (*Qala Rasul Allah*) fall under this category.[63] With these hadiths, the Noble Prophet mostly explains some *mujmal* (ambiguous) or *mughlaq* (obscure) verses from the Qur'an, providing their full meaning and purpose, making them easier to understand and facilitating their application in practical life. Hence, all these explanations together are his verbal statements (hadiths) that form an integral part of Quranic exegesis (*Tafsir*).

Practical Sunnah, or Hadith, comprises the actions of the Noble Prophet, conducted privately or in the presence of others, to show practical examples to his followers of how to perform their religious duties. These news or traditions have been transmitted by the Companions through narratives. For example, the news and narratives like "God's Messenger used to perform his Prayers in this particular way," "He used to make ritual ablution using these actions," "He used to pay alms at this rate and give charity in this amount using this method" and "During this particular Prayer, he used to recite these chapters from the Qur'an" indicate the practical Sunnah of the Noble Prophet.[64]

---

61 Talat Kocyigit, *Hadis Usulu (Hadith Methodology)*, (Ankara: Ankara University Publishing House, 1987), p. 15.
62 Mahmut Aveder, "Hadis Ilmi" *(Hadith Science)*, (2008), p. 1.
63 Kocyigit, *Hadis Usulu (Hadith Methodology)*, p. 16.
64 Ibid.

From time to time the Noble Prophet was asked for his opinion about certain deeds of his family members and Companions. He sometimes approved these actions and allowed them to be practiced by keeping silent or corrected them and showed another way; at other times he disapproved of them by way of his instructions or actions. The Noble Prophet's manner of approval or rejection of some actions in this way is called *Taqriri Sunnah* (Sunnah by tacit approval). Derived from this meaning, the legal decisions of the Companions on matters with no clear ruling in both the Qur'an and the Sunnah are also defined as *Taqriri Sunnah*.[65] This view is accepted by scholars of Hadith and 'Usul alike.

As a result, it is clear that Sunnah—as the Noble Prophet's words, actions and tacit approvals—has become another form of the expression of *Hadith* so long as it is transmitted from the Noble Prophet. The assessments of the scholars of Hadith and jurists point towards the integrity of meaning, which developed around the notions of Hadith and Sunnah since the early period of Islam. With these assessments, it can be concluded that Hadith and Sunnah refer to the same meaning (i.e. Prophetic traditions), and can, therefore, be used interchangeably. In some instances, however, Hadith can be used to refer to the verbal traditions while Sunnah is confined to the actions. In respect of meaning and representation, both words present a unique system of life that was demonstrated by the Noble Prophet. Hence, all the meanings of the Qur'an, clear and obscure, can be read in the light of Sunnah.

Hadith as the Second Primary Source

A Prophetic tradition is an inspiration revealed by God to His Prophet: "*He does not speak on his own, out of his own desire; that (which he conveys to you) is but a revelation that is revealed to him.*"[66] The Noble Prophet's Sunnah is one of the sound primary sources of the religion of Islam and has an extremely important place in the foundation and development of different Islamic disciplines. Accordance to Muslim scholars, by decreeing in this verse, "*[w]hoever disobeys God and His Messenger has evidently gone astray,*"[67] God makes it clear that the authority of es-

---

[65]   Ibid. 15–16.
[66]   Qur'an 53:3.
[67]   Qur'an 33:36.

tablishing any legal canon belongs exclusively to God and His Messenger.[68] Muslims believe that the boundaries of *halal* and *haram* (lawful and unlawful) have been established by God and explained in detail by His Prophet.

Muslims hold that keeping these sensitivities in mind and acting accordingly will not only help individuals and societies to avoid deviation from fundamental laws of life, but also to uphold the integrity of the Islamic disciplines. By weighing their thoughts and theories on this scale of sensitivity, human beings can freely express themselves and embark upon a wide range of quests without the risk of transgressing boundaries. This can open up new horizons for those who ponder, thus facilitating development of new theories and syntheses in disciplines of physical and religious realms. It can be safely said that, in Islam, the discipline of Hadith—after the Qur'an—constitutes the foundation layer of the science of jurisprudence and all other secular and religious disciplines.

With the advent of Islam, the understanding and development of jurisprudence was formulated due to the norms and practices of the Prophet's Companions, especially those who were close around the presence of the Noble Prophet on a daily basis. In this manner, the family members around him as well as his foremost Companions could observe him and formulate in their memories how the Noble Prophet went about the daily chores in his life.

The fundamental issues, as well as controversial ones, that become the subject of Islamic jurisprudence have been resolved and clarified in light of the Noble Prophet's statements. Some of these rulings have manifested themselves as matters in direct relation to individuals, families and the wider community. For example, knowledge and rulings on questions related to family life, such as women's rights, respect for women and women's issues, have been explained to Muslim women by the Prophet's wives, thus becoming norms of life. It is noteworthy to mention the Prophet's beloved wife A'isha, who occupies an exceptional place in Islam in terms of her understanding of the Qur'an and transmis-

---

[68]   Muhammad Abu Zahw, *Hadis Ve Hadisciler (The Hadith and the Traditionists*, originally published as *Al-Hadith wa'l-Muhaddithun),* (Istanbul: Ensar Publications, 2007), p. 31.

sion of the Prophetic traditions on matters concerning the family and women.[69]

The love, respect and tolerance that constitute the base of the family unit are just as important as jurisprudence and family rights in Islam. At the same time, it is clearly pointed out that there is no place for hatred in a family environment. In fact, hatred between couples is a major cause for divorce, which is a permissible but disliked act in Islam.[70] Furthermore, the Qur'an and the Prophetic traditions have put the family in place as the cornerstone of a stable Islamic societal structure.

Further, the duties and responsibilities of officers and administrators employed by the state are explained in the light of Sunnah, and rules and regulations are established accordingly. Hence, it can be observed that most rights and responsibilities at individual, family and state level have been established by means of Sunnah, which fundamentally stems from the Qur'an, paving the way for an Islamic social system and governance.

The fundamental bases of the discipline of jurisprudence, such as *ijtihad* (legal decision), *qiyas* (analogy) and *ijma'* (consensus), have also been developed by means of the Noble Prophet's teachings and training, and a multitude of ambiguous legal issues have been solved in the light of the Qur'an and the Sunnah. The training examples provided by the Noble Prophet have been liberally used by Muslim scholars as needs arose, thus becoming instrumental in the formulation of many legal rulings. For example, concerning a person eating or drinking as a result of forgetfulness while fasting, Abu Hanifah (d. 772 CE), alluding to *qiyas* (analogy), said: "If there did not exist any Prophetic report, I would rule by means of analogy."[71] Nevertheless, he referred to the hadith related to this issue and based his *fatwa* (legal opinion) on that hadith. The narration Abu Hanifah was referring to is a hadith related by Abu Hurayrah, in which the Noble Prophet is reported as saying: "If

[69]   Saliha Akgul, *Ezvac-i Tahirat (The Pure Wives of the Prophet)*, (Istanbul: Gul Yurdu Publishing, 2007), p. 53.

[70]   Abu Dawud, *Kitab al-Talaq*, Hadith no. 2172-73.

[71]   Abdullah Kahraman, "Fikhi Hadislerin Dogru Anlasilip Yorumlanmasi Hususunda Bazi Esaslar" ("Certain Principles regarding the Correct Understanding and Interpretation of the Hadiths on Judicial Matters"), *Eski Dergi* (n.d), http://eskidergi.cumhuriyet.edu.tr/makale/316.pdf.

anyone forgets that he is fasting and eats or drinks, he should complete his fast (of the day), for it is only God Who has fed him and given him drink."[72] This hadith clarifies an issue that was not mentioned clearly in the Qur'an. While explaining the role of Hadith and Sunnah in legislative process, Imam Shafi'i purports that matters that are not clearly mentioned in the Qur'an are adjudged by means of the Noble Prophet's deductions (*ijtihad*). While this type of Sunnah is considered a matter of controversy among a number of Muslim scholars, according to the majority of scholars, and particularly the scholars of Hadith, the Sunnah, having originated from a Godly source, can have a legislative power under certain circumstances. As a result, Sunnah also has been accepted as an independent source of law.[73]

In view of these opinions of Muslim scholars and Hadith authorities, the Sunnah becomes an integral part of physical and spiritual life in Islam. Adherence to the Sunnah, particularly in the individual, family and social spheres, plays an effective corrective role. Muslims believe it is only in this way that a healthy society, as it was in the time of the Noble Prophet, can be achieved. Undoubtedly, following the Prophetic traditions is most valuable, especially at times when innovations in religion are prevalent. In a time when the society is corrupt, complying with even a small matter of Prophetic traditions signifies a powerful faith (*iman*) and piety (*taqwa'*) because following the Sunnah directly recalls the Noble Prophet and, ultimately, that recollection and remembrance is transformed into recollection of the Almighty God. Emulating the Noble Prophet's conduct even in the least significant dealings—i.e. his manner of eating, drinking, sleeping or similar habitual, natural acts—becomes a meritorious act of worship in compliance with Islam. For a Muslim, such commonplace actions are nothing less than adherence to the Prophet's Practice and considered as conduct of the Islamic way of life. With the satisfaction of following the Sunnah and turning their heart to God, the True Lawgiver, a believer gains a perpetual sense of God and worship.[74]

---

[72] Bukhari, *Sawm* 26; Muslim, *Siyam* 171; Tirmidhi, *Sawm* 26; Abu Dawud, *Sawm* 39.
[73] Kahraman, "Fikhi Hadislerin Dogru Anlasilip Yorumlanmasi Hususunda Bazi Esaslar," p. 4.
[74] Bediüzzaman Said Nursi, *Lemalar* (Istanbul: Sahdamar Publishing, 2007), p. 63.

Basic Terms for Various Types of Hadiths

In order to properly understand Hadith and its status, it is necessary to briefly mention certain terms used in the classification of hadiths. The term *mutawatir* (consecutive) hadith refers to a successive narration that is transmitted by a significant number of narrators where it is inconceivable they could have agreed upon a falsehood. This condition must be accrued at every level. Because of the very high standards of authenticity required, only a limited number of *mutawatir* hadiths exist. Being considered as definitely authentic, the rejection of a *mutawatir* (consecutive) hadith is regarded as unreasonable and its acceptance becomes a necessity.

 Sahih (authentic) hadith refers to the soundest hadith, which has no missing links in its chain of narrators, all of whom are absolutely trustworthy (*thiqah*), and it contains no defect or irregularities. In other words, from a technical point of view, this is a hadith that belongs to the Noble Prophet beyond any reasonable doubt.

 A *sanad* (narrator chain) that contains one or more narrators who have the qualities of *'adl* (integrity and reliability), but have some weaknesses in their ability of retention and thus transmission of the hadith word for word (*dabt*), would lower the rank of the hadith to *hasan*.[75] If a hadith has a continuous chain of narrators (*sanad*), going back from the last *rawi'* to the first, reaching a well-known Companion and then the Noble Prophet, it is classified as *musnad* (supported).[76]

 A hadith by narrators who do not have the qualities of those who narrated *sahih* or *hasan* (good) hadith is classified as *da'if* (weak).

---

[75] *Hasan* is a term used to describe a hadith whose authenticity is not as well-established as that of a *sahih* hadith, but it is used as evidence in Islamic sciences.

[76] The early scholar of Hadith, Muhammad ibn Abdullah al-Hakim, defines a *musnad* (supported) hadith as follows: A hadith which a scholar of Hadith reports from his *shaikh* whom he has apparently heard the hadith from at an age conducive to that, and likewise each *shaikh* having heard from his *shaikh* until the chain of transmisssion (*isnad*) reaches a well known Companion.

The *musnad* hadith refers, therefore, to a narration reported from those early period *shaikhs* (elder scholars) who actually met and reported the hadith to the next generation in person, mostly in a student-teacher relationship, for the purpose of narrating the hadith precisely. Hence, the documentation of the *musnad* (supported) hadiths puts utmost emphasis on the authentic hadiths' chain of transmission which linked the hadiths directly to the Noble Prophet through the reports of reliable narrators.

A hadith reported by a weaker *rawi'* (narrator) in contradiction of a *sahih* hadith narrated by *thiqah rawi'* is called *munkar*. Finally, a fake or fabricated saying attributed to the Prophet is called *mawdu'*, which, according to some scholars, is the lowest degree of *da'if* hadith. According to another view, different from the *mutawatir* hadiths, the *mawdu'* ones are not subject to study for the simple reason that the former are definite and the latter fabricated. There are many other technical terms used in the Hadith science, but will not be focused on as they're not the topic of this work.

Development of Hadith Literature

Recording of Hadith in the Time of the Noble Prophet

Looking at historical documentation, it is evident that the recording of the hadiths dates back to the time of the Noble Prophet, although serious efforts for the compilation of hadiths were not started until the beginning of the 2nd century AH. Furthermore, Islam being a way of life, all deeds and words of the Noble Prophet were taken into account by the Companions and practiced in their daily lives.

Besides the group of people called *'Ahl al-Suffah*, who dedicated their life to learning and teaching Islam, many other Companions memorized the Hadith and Sunnah of the Noble Prophet and committed them to writing as much as they could, even with limited resources. Memorization was more prominent than writing due to Arab literature, well-established in the Arabian Peninsula, which helped the Companions build a strong memory.[77] The literate ones of the Companions recorded the hadiths they learned on any material they could find which included a piece of leather, wood or date leaf. Some of the Companions safeguarded these recorded materials and compiled them into small booklets called *sahifah*. *Al-Sahifah al-Sadiqah* of Abdullah ibn 'Amr ibn al-'As and *al-Sahifah* of Hammam ibn Munabbih comprising *al-Sahifah al-Sahihah* of Abu Hurayrah are the most famous among them.[78] The Companions' learning and teaching of Hadith was encouraged by the

---

[77] Kocyigit, *Hadis Tarihi (The History of Hadith)*, p. 20.
[78] Ibid., p. 199.

Noble Prophet. In a hadith, the Noble Prophet said, "May God brightens a man who hears a tradition from us, gets it by heart, and passes it on to others."[79] This hadith and many others of similar[80] import may have been amongst those that served as a legal source of reference for the Companions—and the generations to come—for safeguarding and conveying the Prophetic traditions.

In the time of the Noble Prophet, the Prophetic traditions were open to discussion among the Companions, who had the opportunity to approach the Prophet directly and clarify any matters. Or if a Companion erred while reporting a hadith, he would be corrected immediately by another. In this way, Hadith and Sunnah were continuously checked and confirmed. Even the Companions who lived outside Medina, upon experiencing difficulties in terms of understanding a hadith, used to travel long distances to come to Medina and see the Noble Prophet for clarification.[81] This case set a precedent, in the centuries to come, for undertaking months-long journeys in the pursuit of collection of authentic and sound hadiths from reliable transmitters.

However, many different arguments have been put forth, especially during the last few centuries, in relation to the prohibition of writing down hadiths during the time of the Noble Prophet. Nevertheless, Ahmad Muhammad Shakir (d. 1958), a well-known Egyptian Muslim traditionalist, asserts that the hadiths prohibiting writing down the traditions were abrogated by those permitting writing.[82]

One of the strongest pieces of evidence of the Prophetic traditions being recorded in writing during the time of the Noble Prophet can be found in al-Ramahurmuzi's (d. 362) work titled *al-Muhaddith al-Fasl*

---

[79] Abu Dawud, *'Ilm*, 10; Tirmidhi, *'Ilm*, 7; Ibn Majah, *Muqaddimah*, 18; Ibn Hanbal, *al-Musnad*, 4/82.

[80] In another hadith, he said, "May God bless a person who heard some discourse from us and then passed it on to others. How many persons to whom our message is conveyed are there, who have more retaining faculty than those who receive it." Abu Dawud, *Sunan*, II, 289; Ibn Majah, *Sunan*, 1.104.

[81] For example, 'Uqbah ibn al-Harith married the daughter of Abu Ihab ibn Aziz and soon after learned that he and his wife were suckled by the same woman. 'Uqbah travelled from Mecca to Medina to clarify the matter and asked for a verdict directly from the Noble Prophet. After obtaining the ruling about milk kinship preventing marriage, he returned to Mecca and divorced his wife (Al-Bukhari, *Sahih*, 1.30–31).

[82] Canan, *Fethullah Gülen'in Sunnet Anlayisi (Fethullah Gülen's Understanding of Sunnah)*, pp. 99-104.

Bayn al-Rawi wa al-Wa'i, which is considered one of the most important and comprehensive works on the subjects of Hadith methodology and Hadith history. In this work, al-Ramahurmuzi includes forty-eight narrations permitting the recording of Prophetic traditions in writing during the time of the Noble Prophet, while he mentions only eight narrations that are related to the prohibition of writing down hadiths. Tirmidhi compiled narrations related to the permission and prohibition of writing hadiths under separate topics.[83]

On the basis of all the documented and authentic evidence, Muslims have no doubt that Prophetic traditions have been recorded, memorized and safeguarded since the time of the Companions, their followers and the third generation following them; these records have been transmitted from one generation to the next, and compiled into corpus.[84]

Prohibition on Writing Hadiths

The main motive behind the early generations' Endeavour for learning and safeguarding the traditions of the Noble Prophet was that the Hadith and the Sunnah were their only guide in putting the Word of God into practice. However, the first and foremost reason for safeguarding the Sunnah was the Qur'an's—as well as the Prophet's—encouragement to follow his example.[85] The following verse constitutes strong evidence for this:

> Whatever the Messenger gives you accept it willingly, and whatever he forbids you, refrain from it. Keep from disobedience to God in reverence for Him and piety. Surely God is severe in retribution.86

Because of the clear instructions in this verse and many others of this import, the Companions considered the Sunnah as an invaluable trust and did not want to lose any part of it; thus, they wrote it down or committed it to memory.

---

[83] Ibid., p. 102.

[84] M. Fethullah Gülen, *Sonsuz Nur (Muhammad: Messenger of God)*, *Sunnetin Tespiti ve Tesrideki Yeri* (Izmir: Nil Publications, 1994), p. 135.

[85] Muhammad Ajjaj al-Khatib, "Sunnetin Tespiti," in "Harun Karipcin," (2010), http://www.herkul.org/kitap-ozetleri/suennetin-tesbiti/.

[86] Qur'an 59:7.

There are also some reports that the Noble Prophet prohibited his Companions from writing the traditions down while they were so deeply committed to recording the Qur'an. The most eminent hadith is transmitted by Abu Sa'id al-Khudri (d. 63/682 or 64/683), who reported the Noble Prophet as saying:

> Do not write anything from me except the Qur'an, and whoever has written something from me except the Qur'an, he should erase it. Narrate to others (what you hear) from me; and whoever deliberately attributes a lie to me, he should prepare his seat in the Fire.[87]

Following these narrations, Companions who wanted to write down hadiths were prevented from doing so by these reports. The case of Zayd ibn Thabit (d.660 CE) preventing Mu'awiyyah (d. 680 CE) from writing down hadiths is a good example of this.

The majority of the scholars who studied the reports of banning the writing of hadiths, and tried to reconcile the arguments, came up with this result: Writing down hadiths was banned only in the early period of Islam due to the fear that the Hadith could be mixed up with the Qur'an, and that people would incline more towards Hadith and neglect the Qur'an.[88] The main objective was the preservation and publication of the Qur'an and keeping it clear from all kinds of doubts and confusion. Pages and booklets of Hadith (*sahifah*) had been written by the Companions since the early days, and these pages posed a real risk of being mixed up with the Qur'an.

Moreover, after mentioning the reports for and against the compilations coming from the Companions and their successors, al-Khatib al-Baghdadi (d. 1071 CE) states the lack of juristic qualification among the majority of Arabs, their inability of distinguishing Quranic words from others, and their risk of taking any word that may creep into the

---

[87] Muslim, *al-Zuhd wa'l-Raqaa'iq*, 5326. In another hadith, Abu Hurayrah narrates, "God's Messenger came to us while we were writing Hadith and asked, 'What are you writing?' We replied, 'Hadith that we heard from you.' He said, 'A book other than the Book of God! The nations before you deviated because they wrote other books alongside the Book of God.' We asked, 'Can we narrate from you?' He said, 'Yes, you may narrate from me; that is fine. However, those who knowingly lie about me should prepare their abode in the Fire." Ibn Hanbal, *al-Musnad*, vol.17, p. 156.

[88] Ajjaj al-Khatib, "Sunnetin Tesbiti."

Book as the Word of God as the main reasons for the prohibition of writing down hadiths.[89] Ibn Qutaybah (889 CE), on the other hand, stresses that the banning of Hadith compilation was specifically for those who could not write well, as the written form of the Arabic language was not sufficiently developed in the early days of Islam. Therefore, those who could not write well or whose religious knowledge was limited could not be considered free from the risk of making mistakes when writing down hadiths, causing confusion and weakening interest in the Qur'an. This is why the Noble Prophet prohibited these people from writing down hadiths while permitting those who could write well.[90]

Taking these comments into account, prohibition of those who did not possess good writing skills from writing down hadiths, may bring to mind the question of why writing down the verses of the Qur'an was permitted. This point further strengthens the argument of the likelihood of mixing up the Hadith with the Qur'an, if the simultaneous writing down of the hadiths was permitted.

Permission for Writing Hadiths

Following the prohibition of writing down hadiths, there are numerous reports regarding the permission given by the Noble Prophet to keep records of his Sunnah in writing. The number of narrations giving permission to write down hadiths is much greater than the narrations that prohibited it, and in fact, it can be said they abrogated the banning reports. It appears the banning of writing down hadiths was only temporary, due to the fear of the words of men creeping into the Qur'an, and, as soon as this risk was removed, the Noble Prophet granted permission to his Companions to record his traditions. This is supported by a number of authentic narrations. However, Goldziher and some other Western scholars, basing their arguments on the prohibition of compilation of hadiths, assert that hadiths were written under the decree of 'Umar ibn 'Abd al-Aziz, (d. 682 CE) 100 years after the death of the Noble Prophet.[91] 'Abd Allah ibn 'Amr narrates this instance:

---

[89]   Al-Khatib, *Taqyid al-'Ilm*, 57.
[90]   Ibn Qutaybah, *Ta'wil al-Mukhtalif al-Hadith*, 365.
[91]   Ghulam Nabi Falahi, "Development of Hadith: A Concise Introduction of Early Hadith Literature," (n.d), http://muqith.files.wordpress.com/2010/10/development-of-hadith.pdf.

I used to write everything which I heard from God's Messenger. I intended (by it) to memories it. The Quraysh prohibited me saying: "Do you write everything that you hear from him while the Messenger is a human being: he speaks in anger and pleasure?" So I stopped writing, and mentioned it to God's Messenger. He signaled with his finger to his mouth and said: "Write, by Him in Whose hand my soul lies, only right comes out from it."92

There are also many other reports which support the views of those who say the Noble Prophet permitted his Companions to write down the Hadith.[93]

As mentioned earlier, some of the Companions and their successors kept records of hadiths in small booklets called *sahifah* (pages). Others like Hammam used to spend most of his time with Abu Hurayrah and write down every hadith this close Companion of the Prophet narrated. According to Muslim sources, once he narrated a hadith to Abu Hurayrah, but he said: "I do not remember this one now." Hammam then brought the book where the hadith was recorded and persuaded Abu Hurayrah. These pages were published by the late Muhammad Hamidullah (d. 2002). Scrutinies and carbon analysis of these pages proved them to be thirteen centuries old. This fact is considered by majority of Muslims as one of the proofs of the hadiths being recorded in a sound and healthy manner. The hadiths on these pages are included in the *Musnad* of Ahmad ibn Hanbal (d. 855 CE) and in the reputable Hadith collections of *Sahih al-Bukhari* and *Sahih Muslim*.[94]

The two prominent Companions and the first two caliphs, Abu Bakr (d. 634 CE) and 'Umar ibn al-Khattab, (d. 644 CE) are also known

---

[92] Sunan Abi Dawud, 3646, in Book 26, Hadith 6.

[93] Someone from among the Ansar came to the Noble Prophet and said: "O Messenger of God! I hear a word from you; I like it, but I cannot memories it." The Noble Prophet, signaling his hand, said: "Get help from your right hand (write)" (al-Khatib, *Taqyid al-'Ilm*, 65–66); Anas ibn Malik reports from the Noble Prophet as saying: "Record knowledge by writing." (Imam Zayn al-Din Ahmad ibn Ahmad al-Sharji al-Zubaydi (d. 893 CE), *(Tajrid al-Sarih*, 1/44). When the Noble Prophet was delivering his speech on the day of victory over Mecca, Abu Shah, a Yemenite, stood up and said, "O Messenger of God, get it [your speech] written for me, please." The Noble Prophet said, "Write it for Abu Shah." (Bukhari, *'Ilm*, 39; idem, *Luqatah*, 7; Abu Da'wud, *Manasiq*, 89; idem, *Diyyah*, 4; Tirmidhi, *'Ilm*, 12.).

[94] Nurullah Agitoglu, "Hadislerin Tedvini" (The Recording of Hadiths), *Yeni Umit*, Issue 85 (2009).

for their Endeavour to write down hadiths. Indeed, there are reports that Abu Bakr wrote down 500 hadiths, which he heard directly from the Noble Prophet and later on destroyed for fearing to be mistaken.[95] 'Umar ibn al-Khattab consulted the Companions on the subject of the compilation of hadiths and reached the conclusion that it was a reasonable idea. Later, he abandoned this idea due to some concerns.[96]

Besides all these examples, letters from the Noble Prophet to the kings, emperors and other rulers of the neighboring states are well known historical diplomatic documents. These letters are also acknowledged as a written form of hadiths. Furthermore, there exist hundreds of written texts, invitations, treaties, appointments of state officials, job descriptions, land records, land revenues, safety and security, and reference letters, most of which were recorded during the Medina period.[97] A close look into these documents makes it clear that there is no doubt on the accuracy of the writing, compiling and transmitting of the Prophetic traditions.

Veracity of the Companions in Recording Hadiths

Understanding the Quranic messages perfectly was an extremely important matter for the Companions. It was for this reason that every word and action of the Noble Prophet was discussed among the Companions and written down on any medium available to them at that time. This is how Anas ibn Malik (d. 711 CE) describes the Companions' fastidiousness on this subject: "We used to hear a speech from the Messenger of God whilst we were sitting with him, and as soon as we left him, we used to talk about and discuss it among us."[98] This report clearly indicates that there were always some people around the Noble Prophet observing and recording his words and deeds. Thus, hadiths were subject to discussion and recorded for safekeeping. Those which were doubtful and those which were not understood properly were vigorously discussed among them and confirmed through sound and reliable witnesses. If clear un-

---

[95]   Al-Dhahabi, *Tadhkirah al-Huffaz*, I.5.
[96]   Ibn Sa'd, *Tabaqat*, III.1, 206; al-Khatib, *Takyid al-'Ilm*, 50; Ibn 'Abd al-Barr, *Jami' al-Bayan al-'Ilm*, I.64; Al-Suyuti, *Tanwir al-Hawalik Sharh 'ala Muwatta' Malik*, 6.
[97]   Kocyigit, *Hadis Tarihi*, pp. 32–33.
[98]   Muhammad 'Ajjaj al-Khatib, *al-Sunnah Qabl al-Tadwin*, p. 160.

derstanding was not possible, the Noble Prophet was approached for clarification. Because of this sensitivity of the Companions, the preservation and transmission of the Prophetic traditions in their original form—to minute details—represented the most important task in their minds. It seems that they paid utmost attention to eliminate the risk of any incorrect word or false interpretation on their part blemishing the authenticity of the traditions.

The Companions were a group of people who understood very well the meaning of the severe punishment for reporting a false statement from the Noble Prophet, as well as the reward of a sound and healthy transmission. Thus, the seriousness of the study, safekeeping and narrating of the hadiths raised concerns among the Companions regarding the transmission of traditions from the Noble Prophet. The risk of being condemned to eternal loss because of a distortion or alteration was the main reason for this reluctance.[99] It was due to these hesitations and concerns that Zubayr ibn al-'Awwam (d. 656 CE) reported only a limited number of hadiths. When his son asked him why he reported only a few hadiths from the Noble Prophet, he replied, "I was always with him (the Messenger of God) and I heard him saying, 'Whoever tells a lie against me (intentionally), then (surely) let him occupy his seat in Hell-Fire.'"[100] 'Ali ibn Abu Talib, (d. 661 CE) who acted cautiously with regards to these hadiths, said, "Whenever I tell you a narration from the Messenger, by God, I would rather fall down from the sky than ascribe a false statement to him."[101]

Anas ibn Malik, who had been in the service of the Noble Prophet for a long time, dedicated himself to the memorization of the words of the Noble Prophet. "Out of fear of committing error, I would have narrated more hadiths from the Messenger."[102] Presented to the Noble Prophet as a house aid by his mother at an early age, Anas was brought up in the Prophet's household and served him for ten years. He

---

[99] Gülen, *Sonsuz Nur (Muhammad: The Messenger of God), Sunnetin Tespiti Ve Tesrideki Yeri*, p. 63.

[100] Bukhari, *'Ilm*, 38; In another hadith, which supports the content and meaning of this hadith, the Noble Prophet said, "Whoever narrated a hadith from me which is seen as a lie, then he is one of the liars." (Muslim, *Muqaddimah*, 1).

[101] Bukhari, *al-Istitabah*, 6; Abu Dawud, *Sunnah*, 28.

[102] al-Darimi, *Muqaddimah*, 25.

did his best to commit as many hadiths as he could to memory, paying attention—with extreme proficiency—to *Prophetic wisdoms* with the
same fervor shown by the Companions to memories the verses of the
Qur'an during their revelation. That is to say, due to the fear of forget-
ting the verses while receiving them from Archangel Gabriel, the Noble
Prophet was repeating with his tongue after him. Due to the action of
the Noble Prophet using his tongue to memories the verses, a verse was
revealed in the Qur'an: *"(O Messenger!) Move not your tongue to hasten
it (for safekeeping in your heart)."*[103] Then, this is explained in detail in
another verse: *"(for the guidance of humankind,) We will establish the
Qur'an in your heart and have you recite (it to others), so you will not forget (anything of it)."*[104] It is safe to assume that the attention and extreme
care displayed by the Noble Prophet to the verses of the Qur'an set an
example for the Companions—who realized the importance of Hadith
and Sunnah in Islam—to preserve the Prophetic traditions.

The Companions' fear of committing mistakes gave rise to prefer
each other for hadith narration. The anecdote which is noted by 'Abd
al-Rahman ibn Abi Layla (d. 702 CE) is worth quoting:

> I met and knew one hundred and twenty Companions; they all could
> sit in a mosque together; when they were asked something they knew,
> they would look at one another's face; while talking, with the fear of
> confusing God's Messenger's words, they would wait for someone to
> answer; when no one replies, one of them grits his teeth and by taking
> refuge in God narrates something with a warning like Ibn Mas'ud's
> words: "Look! I am transmitting something from my memory but you
> must know that the Messenger of God uttered something approxi-
> mately in the same meaning or in close meaning or similar to what I
> told you."105

Besides the transmission of verbal traditions, the Sunnah, which also
required practical demonstration, were taught in detail with great care.
The Companions did their best in terms of diffusion of the practical Sun-

---

[103]   Qur'an 75:16.
[104]   Qur'an 87:6.
[105]   Imam Shamsudin Muhammad ibn Ahmad al-Dhahabi, *Siyar A'lam al-Nubala*, vol. 12 (Bei-
       rut: Mu'assassat al-Risalah, 2014), vol. 4, p. 263.

nah in its authenticity.[106] For example, while performing ablution when he was in Kufah, 'Ali ibn Abu Talib said, "Anyone who would be pleased to see the ablution of God's Messenger should watch this. Even as you were watching this, I saw God's Messenger. Showing this to you—in detail—pleased me."[107] There are numerous examples regarding this kind of reports.[108]

Historically, the great efforts exerted by the Prophet's Companions and the following generations in terms of reporting a hadith verbatim, instead of reporting by meaning, cannot be denied. Yet, reporting a hadith by meaning (*riwaya al-hadith bi al-ma'na*) was permitted under certain conditions, such as within the whole context of a word (*sibaq* and *siyaq*).[109] However, when confronted with a hadith reported by meaning, the Companions used to discuss it among themselves over and over again to ensure its accuracy.

Concerning this matter, Qatadah ibn Di'amah (d. 736 CE) reported that Abu Hilal, Shu'bah and Sa'id ibn Abi Sadaqah used to go to Hisham al-Dastawa'i for arbitration when they fell into hesitation about a wording and would ask: "Did he say this or did he say that?" Similarly, when Shu'bah and Sawri hesitated on something, they would approach to Mis'ar ibn Kudam.[110] The narrators' high level of cautiousness was—at the same time—helping to prevent lies from creeping into Hadith.

To ensure the sound and healthy transmission of hadiths, the Companions and the following generations investigated the lives of the hadith narrators in detail, and issued warnings about those with defect or doubtful background. For example, Zayd ibn Abi Unaysah (d. 737 CE) said: "Do not accept any hadith narration from my brother."[111]

---

[106] Aynur Uraler, "Sahabe Uygulamasi Olarak Sunnete Baglilik" (Adharence to the Sunnah as the Practice of the Companions), *Yeni Umit,* Issue 51 (2001), p. 247.

[107] 'Abd al-Razzaq, *Musannaf* I, 38-39; Ahmad ibn Hanbal I, 158; Darimi, *Taharah,* 31; Abu Dawud, *Taharah,* 51; al-Nasa'i, *Taharah,* 75.

[108] Again, Abu Ayyub al-Ansari, a well-known Companion of the Noble Prophet, when people asked about the Prophet's way of washing his head while in the consecrated state of *ihram* during the pilgrimage, showed to them how to do it by washing his head and said, "I saw the Messenger of God doing it like this" (Muwatta', *Hajj,* 4; Bukhari, *Jaza' al-Sayd,* 14; Muslim, *Hajj,* 91; Ibn Majah, *Manasiq,* 22; Abu Dawud, *Manasiq,* 37; Nasa'i, *Manasiq,* 27).

[109] Gülen, *Sonsuz Nur (Muhammad: The Messenger of God), Sunnetin Tespiti ve Tesrideki Yeri,* p. 65.

[110] Ibn Hajar, *Tahzib al-Tahzib,* 2/395; Ramhurmuzi, *al-Muhaddith al-Fasil,* 395.

[111] *Sahih Muslim bi Sharh al-Nawawi,* Yahya ibn Sharaf al-Din al-Nawawi, v. I, 12.

Likewise, Bukhari, who authored the first book about the Companions, asked Ali ibn al-Madini (d. 849 CE) —a man who is seen as the imam of the great traditionists like Muslim—"How is your father?" He replied: "Don't ask me, ask others about him." When questioned further, he said: "Hadith is religion, but my father is weak."[112] *Rijal* works are full of this kind of anecdotes.

While strict criteria were applied in writing and transmitting hadiths, when confronted with difficulties, rigorous research and investigations were also carried out. From this point of view, the Companions and followers are acknowledged as expert investigators. For example, during the caliphate of Abu Bakr, an old woman applied to the caliph for a share on the inheritance of her late grandson. The caliph said: "I do not see a verse in the Book of God about your entitlement to a share, and also, I do not remember the Messenger saying anything on this." Then, Mughirah ibn Shu'bah stood up and said: "The Messenger would give one-sixth share to the grandmother." When Abu Bakr asked if there was anyone else who knew about this, Muhammad ibn Maslamah (d. 666 CE) confirmed Mughirah ibn Shu'bah's statement, saying: "I also heard the same thing from the Messenger." Abu Bakr gave the woman her share.[113]

Besides investigation, discussion, sensitivity against lies and authority in representation of verbal and practical traditions of the Noble Prophet, criteria such as memorization, style and truthfulness constituted a solid basis for recording and narrating hadiths.

Qualities Sought in Hadith Narrators

The meaning of *rawi'* in Hadith terminology is a person—man or woman—who narrates a Prophetic tradition together with its chain of transmitters.[114] The discipline of *al-Jarh wa al-Ta'dil* (injure and adjust)—which is associated with the narration and the narrator—is a discipline that seeks the best and perfect conditions in hadith transmitters. In other words, it is a branch of science that deals with and determines the necessary criteria for the sound transmission of hadiths.

---

112 Ibn Hajar, *Tahzib al-Tahzib*, 5/153; Ibn Hibban, *al-Majruhin*, 2/15.
113 Dhahabi, *Tazkirah al-Huffaz*, 1/2; Tirmidhi, *Fara'idh*, 10.
114 Al-Khatib al-Baghdadi, *al-Kifayah*, 97.

In the period of the Noble Prophet, there was no doubt about the accuracy of the teaching and transmitting of the Prophetic traditions. The control of the narrations' health did not present any problem because the Noble Prophet was alive and among the Companions. However, the events of sedition—which started soon after the Noble Prophet's death and particularly after the assassination of Caliph 'Uthman ibn 'Affan (d. 656 CE)—raised concerns among the Companions and followers who were engaged in the discipline of Hadith. It was during this period that fraudulent hadiths began spreading among the public. These false traditions, which were fabricated to cause turmoil, alarmed the Companions and the early Muslims from the following generation, and became the main factor in raising their sensitivity in the narration and teaching of hadiths.

Under these circumstances, constituting a serious danger for the safeguarding of the Prophetic traditions, the Companions and their followers undertook extra precautions and opted to accept hadiths transmitted only by well-known chains of narrators. At the same time, they began scrutinizing the narrators' reliability. As related by Muslim in the *Muqaddimah* to his *Sahih*, Ibn Sirin confirms this:

> Previously, they did not ask about the chain of narrators, but after the sedition started they began asking us the names of the transmitters in the chain. This way they were accepting hadiths transmitted by *ahl al-Sunnah* (the people of the Prophetic tradition), and rejected the ones by *ahl al-bid'ah* (the people of innovation).[115]

These safety measures, adopted to protect the authenticity of the Prophetic traditions, led to the birth of the discipline of "al-Jarh wa al-Ta'dil," a branch of knowledge accepted as the criticism of hadith narrators. By means of certain rules and principles established under this discipline, hadith narrators were subject to reliability tests.

Where a narrator fails to meet these criteria, the traditionists conclude they are not reliable and the hadith reported by them is not healthy. When a narrator is subjected to scrutiny under such strict conditions and accepted, their truthfulness and reliability, and the hadith they re-

---

[115]   Kocyigit, *Hadis Tarihi (The History of Hadith)*, pp. 167–168.

ported being free from lies, errors and negligence becomes evident. All those who do not meet these criteria—no matter how many hadiths they memorized—are not qualified to narrate a hadith. They can listen to and learn hadiths, and practice them in their private lives, but they are not authorized to transmit them to others. The important point here is the ascertaining (*tathbit*) and recording (*dabt*) of the Prophetic traditions in a sound and healthy way. Ascertainment and recording constitute the first stage in this process, and are an important step in establishing trust for the authenticity of the Prophetic tradition.[116]

The first quality sought in a narrator is to be a Muslim who has accepted Islam in their heart and mind. This necessitates belief in God, His angels and the Books, all the Prophets sent by God, the Day of Judgment, and the Divine Destiny and Decree. A person who fails to meet this criterion cannot qualify for hadith narration.[117]

The second important matter is that the narrator must have reached the age of obligation (*mukallaf*). A child who has not reached the age of obligation is not subject to religious responsibility (*taklif*) and there is nothing to prevent that child from lying. However, there is no harm for an adult narrating a hadith they learned in childhood. The Companions' consensus on the acceptance of narrations from certain youth, i.e. Ibn 'Abbas, Ibn al-Zubayr and Mahmud ibn Rabi, constitutes evidence for this. They based their acceptance on the following hadith narrated by Mahmud ibn Rabi: "When I was five years old, I remember the Messenger of God taking water into his mouth and throwing on my face."[118]

The third important quality required in narrators is justice (*'adalah*). This means a person who has never lied in their life and is trusted by everyone. The Prophet's Companions can be given as a good example of this. For a narrator, the quality of justice is more important than any other criterion. In the history of Hadith, there are many people who had the quality of justice and narrated hundreds of hadiths like Zayd ibn Harithah (d. 629 CE), who was an emancipated slave, and Umm Maktum (d. 636 CE), who was blind.[119]

---

[116] Canan, *Fethullah Gülen'in Sunnet Anlayisi* (Fethullah Gülen's Understanding of Sunnah), p. 100.

[117] Abu Shahbah, *Hadis Mudafaasi 1 (In Defence of the Hadith)*, p. 75.

[118] Bukhari, *Kitab al-Da'wat*, 31; Ibn al-Hajar, *Fath al-Bari*, v.1, 189.

[119] Abu Shahbah, *Hadis Mudafaasi 1* (In Defence of the Hadith), p. 76.

Another quality sought in a narrator to qualify them as acceptable is their ability to preserve the information safely. This is done in two ways. The first method is commitment to memory and is called *dabt al-sadr* (memorization by heart). This is the narrator's ability of repeating a hadith with its chain of transmitters exactly as they learned from their mentor. The traditionists refused to accept any hadith from narrators with a weak memory. They accepted hadiths from only intelligent and trustworthy people, and rejected those with failing memory and who erred or expressed suspicion.[120]

The second method is the recording of hadiths by writing them down, which is called *dabt al-kitab* (recording in a book). When transmitting a hadith, the narrator must be able to present their book containing the hadith in its originality. However, scholars like Abu Hanifah and Imam Malik are opposed to transmission by writing.[121] Suleyman ibn Musa said: "The traditionists used to say, 'Do not accept knowledge from people who narrate from recorded pages rather than memory. This is mainly because of the fact that they do not have the knowledge to differentiate the hadiths from the fraudulent ones; they make errors in writing words; and they make too many mistakes."[122]

Along with these criteria, other conditions, such as endurance, mien, homeland, family, birth and death dates, are required in a narrator to qualify. Naturally, hadiths narrated by a person whose birth and death dates do not match the lifetime of the person from whom they narrate, or succeed in the chain of narrators, were rejected. Similarly, narrations by two people, placed successively in a chain of narrators, but geographically lived too far away from each other—the distance between them not permitting to see each other face to face—are not accepted.

In the light of these explanations, it becomes evident that many traditionists—from the Companions to the *muta'akhkhirin* (the later ones)—made vigorous criticisms within the discipline of al-Jarh wa al-Ta'dil. Ibn 'Abbas and Anas ibn Malik, from among the Companions, and al-Sha'bi and Ibn Sirin, from among their followers, are the most famous of them. There are numerous works in the discipline of al-Jarh

---

[120] Ibn Athir *Jami' al-'Usul*, v.1, 72.
[121] Ibn al-Salah, *Muqaddimah*, 185.
[122] Ibn al-Muflih, *al-Adab al-Shar'iyyah*, v. 2, p. 155.

wa al-Ta'dil. Ibn al-Sa'd's (d. 791 CE) 15 volumes work, titled *al-Tabaqat*, is one of them. Al-Suyuti (d. 1505 CE) abridged and published this work under the name of *'Ijaz al-wa'd al-Muntaqa min Tabaqat ibn al-Sa'd*. 'Ali ibn al-Madini (d. 848 CE)'s *Tarikh ibn Hibban* is another book in this field, consisting of ten chapters (*juz'*) on the suspicions of the historians. Also, Bukhari's *Tarikh* and Ibn Kathir's *At-Takmil fi Ma'rifat at-Thiqat wa Dhu'afa' wa al-Majahil* are considered the leading works in this field.[123]

Interpreting the Qur'an by Prophetic Traditions

One of the qualities of God's Prophets in Islamic theology is *fatanah*. Besides its literal meaning of "intelligence" or "shrewdness," in Islamic terminology this refers to the faculty of shedding light—with the aid of the heart and mind open to inspiration—on matters that are too difficult to grasp by ordinary human intellect and require detailed explanation. From one of its aspects, the word can be defined as Prophetic reasoning and intuition. It is by means of this attribute that the Prophets of God comprehended the contents and meaning of the Divine Revelations, and explained them to their people in detail. This Quranic verse sums up the duties of Prophet Muhammad, upon whom be peace and blessings, while pointing to his special ability of annotating the Qur'an:

> As We have sent among you a Messenger of your own, reciting to you Our Revelations, and purifying you (of false beliefs and doctrines, and sins and all kinds of uncleanness), and instructing you in the Book and the Wisdom, and instructing you in whatever you do not know.[124]

When explaining the duties and responsibilities of the Prophetic office in light of the above verse, al-Ghazzali (d. 1111 CE) stresses that the job of the Noble Prophet is to understand and explain in detail the provisions—stipulated in the Qur'an and pertaining to individual lives, social and state structures—that are rules combining wisdom and correctness within themselves.[125]

Quranic verses are generally categorized under several groups: some verses are *mujmal* (indistinct with more than one meaning, thus

---

[123] Al-Salih, *Kitab al-Suluk*, pp. 82–83.
[124] Qur'an 2:151.
[125] Al-Ghazzali, *Tafsir on the Qur'an* 2007, p. 145.

requiring explanation), some *mubayyan* (distinct with one particular meaning and without ambiguity), *sarih* (clear in meaning) or *mufassar* (unequivocal), and some others *muhkam* (explicit/law-giving) or *mutashabih* (allegorical/ambiguous). The *muhkam* (explicit) and *mutashabih* (allegorical) verses are explained in the Qur'an:

> It is He Who has sent down on you this (glorious) Book, wherein are verses absolutely explicit and firm: they are the core of the Book, others being allegorical. Those in whose hearts is swerving pursue what is allegorical in it, seeking (to cause) dissension, and seeking to make it open to arbitrary interpretation, although none knows its interpretation save God. And those firmly rooted in knowledge say: "We believe in it (in the entirety of its verses, both explicit and allegorical); all is from our Lord"; yet none derives admonition except the people of discernment.[126]

What is understood from "*seeking (to cause) dissension*" and "*seeking to make it open to arbitrary interpretation*" in this verse is that the judgment of God's verses and decisions on unclear matters should be left to the Noble Prophet.

Verses with clear-cut meaning do not normally require further explanation for understanding or making judgment. For instance, the verse, "*Those (the God-revering, pious) pray: 'Our Lord, we do indeed believe, so forgive us our sins and guard us against the punishment of the Fire,'*"[127] has a clear meaning and plainly refers to the state of truly pious people. However, *mujmal* (indistinct with more than one meaning) and *mutashabih* (allegorical/ambiguous) verses are not easy to comprehend; they give only concise or ambiguous information, and are referred to the Noble Prophet for detailed explanations. Only God and those who are firmly rooted in knowledge and wisdom can know the meaning of the ambiguous verses (*mutashabihat*).

The traditions of the Noble Prophet fulfill various functions such as delivering, clarifying and interpreting the commands in the Qur'an; they expand and explain (*tafsir*) what is implicit (*mubham*),

---

[126] Qur'an 3:7.
[127] Qur'an 3:16.

and particularize or specify (*takhsis*) what is general (*'am*). At the same time, they confirm (*ta'yid*), strengthen (*ta'kid*) and complement (*it-mam*) some of the provisions in the Qur'an and make judgments on behalf of the Qur'an. When the Qur'an and the Prophetic traditions are evaluated as a whole, the ordinances' confirmation—rather than contradicting—of each other becomes plainly evident. In addition, according to Hanafite jurists, under certain circumstances, the Prophetic traditions may abrogate some rulings in the Qur'an[128] For example, the following verse commands the believers to perform ritual ablution each time they stand up for the Prayer: "*O you who believe! When you rise up for the Prayer, wash your faces and your hands up to the elbows, and lightly rub your heads and your feet up to the ankles.*"[129] This may sometimes present Muslims some difficulties. Nevertheless, the religion gives preference to ease, and at the same time, recommends to simplify and ease matters. The following Prophetic tradition, which clarifies the issue, minimizes the ruling to a level almost akin to abrogation:

> Sulayman ibn Buraydah reported on the authority of his father who said: "The Messenger of God offered the Prayers with one ablution on the day of the conquest (of Mecca) and wiped over the socks (instead of washing his feet). 'Umar said to him: 'You have today done something that you have not been accustomed to before.' He (the Noble Prophet) said: 'O 'Umar, I have done that on purpose.'"[130]

The Prophet's office as promulgator and enforcement of law is significant and relevant here. Based on the Revelation, the Noble Prophet as leader and excellent model for believers explains the requirements of the law at hand and practices it in view of his followers. This function is alluded to in the following verse: "*He does not speak on his own, out of his own desire; that (which he conveys to you) is but a Revelation that is revealed to him,*"[131] clearly asserts the source of his tradition. Another verse refers to the same

---

[128] Ajjaj al-Khatib, "Sunnetin Tesbiti".
[129] Qur'an 5:6.
[130] Muslim, *Taharah*, 86/277.
[131] Qur'an 53:3-4.

issue from a different perspective: "*We have never sent a Messenger but that he should be obeyed by God's leave.*"[132]

According to Imam Abu Hanifah's understanding, the Prophetic tradition does not embody any opposition to the Qur'an nor does it give rules or detailed explanations contradicting the Qur'an, because the Qur'an and the Sunnah are two sources sustained by Divine Revelation. This discernment of Abu Hanifah, i.e. submitting the Prophetic tradition to the Qur'an for approval, was the way of the Companions. When making textual criticism of a new hadith they heard, they used to scrutinize its relation to the Qur'an. In his book, titled *al-'Alim wa al-Muta'allim*, Abu Hanifah stated on this subject:

> If someone says, "I believe everything the Noble Prophet said. The Noble Prophet would never command wrong, and never instruct anything that contradicts the Qur'an," these words would prove his affirmation of the Qur'an and the Noble Prophet, and also mean that the Noble Prophet would never go up against the Qur'an because, if the Noble Prophet ever acts in opposition to the Qur'an, or says anything on behalf of God that He did not command, God would prevent him from doing so. The Noble Prophet would not decree something which God prohibited, and he would not prohibit something which God permitted. He would not attribute any quality to anything other than what God attributed.[133]

---

[132] Qur'an 4:64. It is also important to note that when the verse, "*Those who have believed and not obscured their belief with any wrongdoing (of which, associating partners with God is the most grave, unforgivable kind)—they are the ones for whom there is true security, and they are rightly guided*" (Qur'an 6:82), was revealed, the word *zulm* (wrong-doing) in the verse caused some concerns and hesitation among the Companions. This was because of the fact that, in the Arabic language, this word is used in reference to "wrong," "transgression" and "deviation from the truth and justice," and people did not know in which sense it was used in the verse. In a broad sense, this word would implicate almost everyone in the community. The matter needed to be resolved. They went to the Noble Prophet and said, "Who amongst us has not mixed his belief with wrong?" He replied: "The verse does not mean this. But that (wrong) means to associate others in worship to God. Don't you listen to what Luqman said to his son when he was advising him, 'O my son! Join not others in worship with God. Verily, joining others in worship with God is a great wrong (*zulm*) indeed'" (Qur'an 31:13; Bukhari, *Tafsir*, 31, 1). The explanation of the Noble Prophet clarified that the word *zulm* in this verse was used in the sense of associating partners with God. This hadith is a good example of clarification of a Quranic verse by the Noble Prophet and making sure that its purpose is understood properly.

[133] M. G. Dumayni, *Hadis'te Metin Tenkidi Metodlari* (Methods of Textual Critique in the Hadith Science), (Istanbul: Kitabevi Publications, 1997), p. 247.

Imam Abu Hanifah's view can be summarized by the verse: *"He who obeys the Messenger (thereby) obeys God"* (Qur'an 4:80). Furthermore, the fact the Qur'an and the Prophetic traditions would not contradict each other is highlighted by this hadith:

> You will encounter many hadiths after me. When a hadith is narrated to you from me, submit it to the Book of God. If it is in conformity with the Book, accept it, and know that it is from me. If it falls in contradiction with it, reject it, and know that it does not belong to me.[134]

With this tradition, the Noble Prophet showed a method for the textual criticism of hadiths and, at the same time, he indicated the fact of interpreting the Qur'an by the Prophetic traditions.

The prescribed Prayer is an important form of worship and the second pillar in Islam. The Qur'an points to the importance of the Prayer, *"Be ever mindful and protective of the prescribed Prayers, and the middle Prayer, and stand in the presence of God in utmost devotion and obedience,"*[135] and makes specific emphasis about *al-salah al-wusta'* (the middle Prayer). The Prophet's wife 'A'ishah and Ibn Mas'ud from among the Companions believed the middle Prayer referred to the Late Afternoon Prayer (*al-Salah al-'Asr*), and they commented as such. 'A'ishah asked her servant to write a copy of the Qur'an for her personal use, and when they come to this verse she instructed to write it as the Late Afternoon Prayer, and said: "This is what I heard from the Messenger of God."[136] Despite the various interpretations of this verse, 'A'ishah and Ibn Mas'ud maintained their conviction that the middle Prayer referred to the Late Afternoon Prayer.

Generally, the Noble Prophet's words (hadiths) would further elucidate verses of the Holy Qur'an, through his physical presence and practice, verbal or actual demonstration, guidance or approval. Prophetic traditions also expand and interpret the concise Quranic verses by deduction and conclusion. Despite being the primary worship, none of the verses described the Prayers either quantitatively or qualitatively. Quranic exegetes (*Mufassirin*) deduced five times prayer a day from the verse below:

---

[134] 'Abd al-'Aziz al-Bukhari, *Kashf al-Asrar*, III, 10.
[135] Qur'an 2:238.
[136] Tirmidhi, *Tafsir al-Qur'an*, 3.

Establish the Prayer (O Messenger) at the beginning and the end of the day, and in the watches of the night near to the day. Surely good deeds wipe out evil deeds. This is advice and a reminder for the mindful who reflect.[137]

However, the specific timing of the Prayers was fixed through revelation: "*The Prayer is prescribed for the believers at fixed times.*"[138] Archangel Gabriel guided the Noble Prophet towards the specific times of the prescribed Prayers. After this, the Noble Prophet stood up for the Prayer in front of his Companions and said: "Pray as you see me praying."[139] Furthermore, the Noble Prophet taught—quantitatively and qualitatively—the details of the prescribed Prayers, i.e. *fard* (obligatory), *wajib* (necessary), *sunnah* (the prophetic tradition), *mustahab* (recommended), *ruku'* (bowing) and *sujud* (prostration).[140]

Another case in point would be the Quranic verse with regard to inheritance. In Islam, heritage is a right and relatives are entitled to certain shares on the inheritance of the deceased. As indicated in the following verse, there are provisions for inheritance in the Qur'an:

> For the male heirs is a share out of what parents and near kindred leave behind, and for the female heirs is a share of what parents and near kindred leave behind, whether it (the inheritance) be little or much—a share ordained by God.[141]

As can be seen, the verse mentions entitlements to inheritance only in general terms. Although the inferred meaning in the verse still constitutes a basis for jurists' rulings, a hadith, reported from the Noble Prophet in relation to this verse, brings another perspective. On the entitlement to inheritance for a murderer, the Noble Prophet said: "There is nothing for the murderer."[142] The general ruling in the verse has been clarified by the tradition of the Prophet, stating that a murderer cannot inherit.

---

[137] Qur'an 11:114.
[138] Qur'an 4:103.
[139] Bukhari, *Adhan*, 18; Musnad, 5/53.
[140] Gülen, *Sonsuz Nur (Muhammad: The Messenger of God), Sunnetin Tespiti Ve Tesrideki Yeri,* p. 28.
[141] Qur'an 4:7.
[142] Tirmidhi, *Fara'idh*, 17; Abu Dawud, *Diyat*, 18.

In relation to provisions of this tradition, Hanafite jurists highlight this point: "Killings punishable by retaliation (*qisas*) or atonement (*kaffarah*) preclude the killer from inheritance. Premeditated, intentional and accidental killings are of this nature."[143] By the particularization and commentary in the hadith, the Noble Prophet highlighted the security and sanctity of life as the main factor in terms of relations between relatives. The Noble Prophet also builds a family structure upon a solid and secure foundation by fostering the security of life and property among individual members of the family.

Quranic verses have been proclaimed and interpreted—as the circumstances arise—by the Prophetic traditions. This means the Qur'an and the Prophetic tradition complement each other. Looking into this from another point of view, by leaving the proclamation and detailed explanation of the Quranic verses to the Noble Prophet, God Almighty presents His Messenger as a practical role model.

Prophetic Traditions: the True Commentator of the Qur'an

The Qur'an and the Prophetic Traditions (Hadith and Sunnah) constitute two fundamental sources of Islam. The first source, the Qur'an, is the direct Word of God, and the Prophetic traditions, as the second source, represent the words, actions and tacit approvals of the Noble Prophet. The term "Prophetic Traditions" has been used throughout this work in reference to Hadith and Sunnah because these two terms are used interchangeably by the traditionists. However, according to the general acceptance, the term *Hadith* refers to verbal traditions and *Sunnah* to the actions, guidance and approvals or more comprehensively, the lifestyle of the Noble Prophet.

In the light of this, the Prophetic Traditions thus expand and explain the Qur'an. It also clarifies the practical and legal matters enjoined in the Qur'an. The Qur'an commands that, once a matter has been decided by God and His Messenger, that should be final and there is no other option for believers. As understood from all these, the Prophetic Traditions offer a complete lifestyle for Muslims.

---

[143]   al-Sarakhsi, *al-Mabsut*, XXVI, 59; al-Kasani, *Bada'i' al-Sana'i'*, VII, 234, 254.

As the literacy of the Companions improved, the system of living established in the time of the Noble Prophet increased the desire among them toward the study of the Prophetic Traditions. From that period onward, hadiths have been recorded in writing or committed to memory—and narrated—by the *Ahl al-Suffah* and most of the Companions. The sensitivity displayed by the Companions and their followers on the issue of recording and safeguarding of the Prophetic Traditions is a well-known fact among scholars. However, when confronted with uncertainty, the Companions used to approach the Noble Prophet for clarification. This means direct control and observation of the Noble Prophet over the conservation of his traditions.

Although the Noble Prophet initially prohibited recording of his traditions in writing, later on, he allowed his Companions to write them down and encouraged them to do so. The main reason behind the prohibition was the risk of mixing up hadiths with Quranic verses. Once this concern ceased to exist, the recording of traditions in writing was allowed.

Learning traditions directly from the Noble Prophet, recording them in writing and committing them to memory continued ceaselessly until the death of the Noble Prophet. After the Prophet's death, beginning from the end of the first century AH, serious works were undertaken in the field of Hadith, and a robust system was established by the third century AH. During that time, the process of codification of hadiths continued and authentic traditions were compiled into large books. Within the context of these scholarly works, the traditionists established certain selection criteria for the hadiths and founded the discipline of biographical evaluation, thus making sound and healthy transmission of traditions possible.

Despite all these criteria and sensitivity for safeguarding the authenticity of hadiths, the last few centuries witnessed efforts and views spreading doubts on the Prophetic Traditions. A number of Western scholars, as well as some Muslim scholars with modernist ideas, published works questioning the authenticity of hadiths and criticizing the position of the Prophetic Traditions as a reference source. They claimed that the Quranic verses are clear enough and do not need any explanation or interpretation by the Prophetic Traditions. As asserted in this work, the Prophetic Traditions are supported and approved by Divine Revelation; it has been carefully recorded and transmitted through reliable chains of narrators, whose reliability has been checked and confirmed by painstaking works and efforts of traditionists. In all aspects, the Prophetic Traditions are the true commentator of the Qur'an.

CHAPTER TWO

CONTEMPORARY WESTERN APPROACHES TO
THE HADITH SCIENCE

Thoughts and Assessments on Hadith in
Contemporary Times

The focus of this chapter will be on questions like "What is hadith?", "What is not hadith?" and "What is the Hadith's status as a religious fundamental in Islam?" according to Western scholars, rather than Muslims scholars, and their approaches will be critically analyzed. Also, certain points on the beginning of Hadith studies in the Western world and its historical course will be discussed. What are the motives urging Western scholars to study Islamic sciences and particularly the Hadith discipline: a genuine desire to learn or destructive criticism? This work will attempt to establish whether these efforts stem from a premeditated goal or the sheer love of acquiring knowledge. Answers to questions of this nature will be sought in this chapter.

Furthermore, the various doubts expressed by Western scholars on the recordings and authenticity of hadiths since the early period together with critical approaches to the compilations of hadiths during the period that followed the death of the Noble Prophet, and the emergence of Hadith corpuses, will be assessed from different perspectives.

From the outset, it is important to make it clear that, while thoughts and theories can be discussed and criticized freely, their strength and validity can be analyzed profoundly. What is paramount is ascertaining claims through objective rationale and traditional evidences. Only views free from prejudice can be commonly regarded as correct, and disparaging thoughts and views, which do not meet these criteria and which are motivated by destructive intentions, are doomed to oblivion.

Recent times have witnessed similar debates and controversies on the subject of Hadith within the Islamic world, due to the influence of critical approaches exhibited in the West. Starting from this point, the present work will assess how the contemporary Muslim understanding has been influenced by Western thought and consider both its positive and negative aspects.

Finally, contemporary Muslim scholars' approaches regarding the status of Hadith as a fundamental source in Islam will be critically discussed.

Western and Muslim Worlds from Scholarly, Religious and Philosophical Perspectives

In Islamic literature, the Qur'an, the Prophetic traditions (Hadith and Sunnah) are considered the primary sources not only for Islamic sciences, but also for natural sciences. If religion is regarded as a whole, it is reasonable for it to point to natural sciences as well as metaphysical sciences. If the Qur'an focused only on the physical aspects of humankind and ignored their inner world, it would constitute a serious deficiency.[144] With its material and spiritual educational elements, the functionality of religion provides guidance to humankind in both realms. However, attempting to associate every religious value with physical sciences would not be appropriate, since not all religious standards may conform to the scientific data available in a given time. Essentially religion is based on "belief in the unseen" (*ghayb*) as the Qur'an ordains: "*Those [God-revering, pious] who believe in the Unseen...*"[145] By submitting to this Divine decree, human beings commit themselves to accept or believe in what they are unable to see through their physical eyes.

In terms of dealing with scientific progress, the Qur'an and the Hadith draw man's attention to the study of the natural sciences, while emphasizing this as an integral part of faith. The following Quranic verse is a good example of urging man to introspection through investigating and exploring scientific data: "*[O Prophet!] Read in and with the Name of your Lord, Who has created—created human from a clot clinging (to the wall of the womb).*"[146] Thus, in the Islamic world, a faith-based thought and research system has become a point of departure for all scientific and scholarly activities, opening new doors to acquire correct and healthy knowledge while simultaneously nurturing scientific and religious progress. It must also be said that, in every age, it is inevitable that the interactions between the followers of a religion and the members of other socio-religious systems will mutually affect each other with their new ideas and discoveries. Considered from this point of view, the mutual relations between the Islamic and non-Muslim worlds can be

---

[144] Gülen, *Kur'an'nin Altin Ikliminde (In the Light of the Qur'an's Golden Climate)*, (Istanbul: Nil Publication, 2010), p. 297.

[145] Qur'an 2:3.

[146] Qur'an 96:1–2.

traced back to the early days of Islam. Beginning with interchanges in the fields of sciences, these relations spread over time into the area of thoughts and gained a different dimension when philosophy came into the equation. Philosophy-oriented interaction between the Western and Islamic worlds began in the tenth century and continued uninterrupted until the beginning of the Age of Enlightenment. Within the framework of cultural interactions, such as Islamic philosophy being influenced by ancient philosophy, Western philosophy was influenced by Islamic philosophy; this is an accepted historical fact. The impact of this influence manifested itself as the revival of humanist movements in the West and the recognition of scientific methodology alongside ancient sciences.[147]

The questioning of religious values triggered by the influence of philosophy caused the beginning of great changes in the West. By distancing itself from religious values and trying to develop a humanist and secular thought system, the Western world unavoidably found itself face to face with a series of problems in the spheres of faith. Viewed from this point, the embracing character of the Qur'an and the Hadith vis-à-vis natural sciences did not escape the attention of non-Muslim philosophers and researchers. With this backdrop of Islamic culture where mutual relations between science and thought were vibrant, the non-Muslim thinkers felt the need to study the Qur'an and the Sunnah. However, the reformist thought that criticizes some religious values in the West adopted an approach that was prejudiced and entrenched with deep suspicions toward the logic of faith and the scientific data in the Islamic world. The prevalence of a positivist approach, and the criticism of religious values from this viewpoint, resulted in Islamic sciences being criticized within the same framework. Thus, some Islamic sciences, including the Hadith disciplines, received more than their share of subjective criticisms. These thoughts and attitudes developing in the West, unsurprisingly found a place of reflection in the Islamic world over time, unavoidably due to the impact of age-old relations between the two worlds.

The most interesting situation during this period in the Islamic world was the emergence of secular and atheistic intellectuals, along-

---

[147] Enver Demirpolat, "Islam Felsefesinin Bati Dusuncesine Etkisi" (The Influence of Islamic Philosophy in the West), (Konya: Selcuk University, *Journal of Institute of Social Science,* Issue 9 (2003), pp. 431–432.

side the religious scholars and academics, taking their place in modern debates on the fundamental sources of the religion of Islam. Albayrak draws our attention to the skeptical attitude developed in the West towards the chains of transmissions (*isnad*), forming the basis for the rejection of Hadith.[148] The most important concern here is the manipulation of the principle of referring to the Qur'an as the first primary source—a method that is characterized with the traditional Islam—and, under the pretence of "revering the Qur'an," promoting the questioning of the legitimacy and health of authentic Islamic sources. Distanced from their own values, and trapped between tradition and modernism by the influence of aforementioned views originating from the West, a new breed of modernist Muslim intellectuals, who exerted themselves to reinterpret Islam, emerged.

Developing in the West and over time spreading to the Islamic world, it has been a subject of wonder how this dialectic critical and reformist thinking emerged in the Western world. First of all, there is a need to focus on the perception of Hadith within the framework of these thought movements, concentrating on the Qur'an and the Hadith. So, how does the Western world see and weight Hadith?

I must emphasize this important point here: the Western researchers familiarizing with the Islamic culture, with the determination of Mgr. Armand Olichon, needed a detailed understanding and research of Islamic sciences. First, for the understanding of Islamic sources, the scholars were educated to learn the Arabic language. Their first scientific researches focused on the Qur'an, later on, since the eighteenth century, they moved onto Hadith-based researches.[149]

Western Literary Works of Hadith Studies

After the Renaissance and the birth of reform movements which encouraged open thought and freedom of speech in Europe, eastern religions and faith traditions increasingly came under investigation and scrutiny. The first independent works on Hadith and Sunnah in the West were pioneered by Alois Sprenger (d. 1893). These efforts continued in later

---

[148]   Albayrak, *Fethullah Gülen Hocaefendi'nin Tefsir Anlayisi*, p. 26.
[149]   Hatiboglu, *Hadis Tedkikleri*, pp. 46-52.

periods by the intensive studies[150] of William Muir (d. 1905), C. Snouck Hurgronce (d. 1936) and Ignaz Goldziher (d. 1921).[151] Goldziher is one of the first Western scholars who started attacking and critiquing outright the institution of Hadith, whilst describing Sunnah as "a tradition forged by the Prophet with his companions into the generations that followed them." Conversely, these customs and traditions, in the presence of and sanctioned by the Noble Prophet, had already been sanctified as habits practiced by the early Muslims. As understood from this, Goldziher accepts Hadith and Sunnah as a collection of habits sanctified out of reverence to the Prophet within the community, rather than a religious principle and source.[152] He also says he sees Hadith as verbal expression of the Sunnah. This perception shows some resemblance to Muslim traditionists' observations about the relation between Hadith and Sunnah. Goldziher, with his definition of Hadith to that effect, asserts that hadiths are a source of reference in Islam employed to solve complex problems and issues.

Contrary to negative Orientalist[153] perspectives, Goldziher comes out in support of the Islamic world-view on the origin of hadiths and evolution of their memorization and recording and categorization. On the issue of recording of Hadith and Sunnah, he highlights the possibility of safeguarding them with great respect since the time of the Prophet.[154] Judging by these views, it can be said that Goldziher is contradicting himself in a number of ways. Instead of placing Hadith on sound foundations as a source of reference, he raises doubts by classifying Hadith among customs and practices, which can be changed or cancelled at any time in the course of history in a society. In this way, he

---

[150] For more detailed information on this see Zubayr, *Hadith Literature: Its Origin, Development and Special Features.*

[151] Hatiboglu, *Hadis Tedkikleri,* p. 51.

[152] Mehmet Gormez, "Klasik Oryantalizmi Hadis Arastirmalarina Sevk Eden Temel Faktorler," *Islamiyat,* III, 1 (2000).

[153] The concept of Orientalism, especially formed in the 18th and 19th centuries, is a term being used to refer to scientific studies of Western scholars about Islam.
Erkan Dikici, "Dogu-Bati Ayrimi Ekseninde Oryantalizm ve Emperyalizm " *Tarih Kultur ve Sanat Arastirmalari Dergisi* (Journal of History, Culture and Art Research), Karabuk University, Issue 3, (June 2014).

[154] Mehmet Gormez, "Klasik Oryantalizmi Hadis Arastirmalarına Sevk Eden Temel Faktorler," *Islamiyat, III,* 1 (2000).

is also obfuscating the Qur'an's clear reference to the Prophetic Practice (Sunnah) in such a manner that can open ways leading to doubts and hesitations. At the same time, he also fashions a situation in which the abolition of other significant functions of Hadith and Sunnah, such as the interpretation of the Qur'an, can occur. In my opinion, Goldziher is attempting to sever the organic tie between the Qur'an and the Hadith, and weaken the Hadith's most important role, which was established in Islamic literature.

Goldziher devoted the majority of the second volume of his work, titled *Muhammedanishe Studien*, to his views about Hadith. After the publication of this work, patchy studies on Hadith in the West became an independent subject of research. This work constituted a source of reference for many non-Muslim scholars that followed him.[155]

Goldziher accepts Hadith as a norm for practical application for a particular period of time, as well as an authoritative medium in the interpretation of the Qur'an, he also argues that, during later periods, Hadith lost its authenticity. When providing a definition, he explains that Hadith attributed to the Prophet and his Companions "are not authentic reports of these persons but rather reflect the doctrinal and political developments of the first two centuries of Islam."[156] According to this, hadiths do not have a direct relation to the Noble Prophet. In his opinion, hadiths are important media to access information related to the Prophet and his time. For Goldziher, the majority of hadiths reported from the Prophet, which took their honorable place in *al-Kutub al-Sittah*, are lies and fabrications. If hadiths are considered as fabricated during the two centuries that followed the death of the Noble Prophet, an important point, which Goldziher disregards or even deems non-existent, draws our attention – the established criteria of reporting and the discipline of *rijal* (biographical evaluation of narrators), a subject treated by the Companions, the generation that followed them and the scholars of Hadith with utmost care and respect. He not only tends to ignore the

---

[155] Fatma Kizil, "Oryantalistlerin Hadis Literaturu Hakkindaki Gorusleri" (Orientalists' Views on Hadith Literature), (2009), http://sonpeygamber.info/oryantalistlerin-hadis-literaturu-hakkindaki-gorusleri.

[156] Falahi, "Development of Hadith: A Concise Introduction of Early Hadith Literature," p. 2.

criteria scholars of Hadith mentioned in *'Ilm al-Rijal*, and even treats the *mutawatir* hadiths as fabricated.[157]

Given his views and style, Goldziher's still a pioneer in reviewing and investigating the Islamic primary sources, his method of studying Hadith and sources of reference must be taken into consideration to determine his starting point. When he asserts his opinions about Hadith and Sunnah, and provides his supporting evidence, he draws heavily on specific and unorthodox sources such as *Mu'tazilah* and *Shi'ah*.[158]

From a literary perspective, Leone Caetani, an Italian scholar and historian of the Middle-East, also known for his work on the history of Islam, produces views about Hadith and Sunnah similar to Goldziher's. His thoughts echo Goldziher's "sanctified habits and customs" whilst for him, Hadith and Sunnah represent no more than a simple perception of memories of the Prophet preserved by the Companions, which fell into oblivion after his death. Drawing attention to his statement about the Noble Prophet's "Farewell Sermon" is also fitting. In his view, "[T]his might have stemmed from a desire to perform the hajj devotion—only with Muslims—in front of a community of thousands of Muslims, all of them recently converted and submitted themselves to his now absolute power and authority."[159] Treating the Farewell Sermon—a speech covering topics like women's status, importance of faith, usury, and a charter for social justice based on important legal principles[160]— as nothing but a simple memory is, in simplest terms, an injustice to academia. Completely overlooking the well-established transmission of narration (*riwayat aqli* and *naqli*), non-Muslim scholars seem to ignore the intense documentation recording the chains of narrators. The Companions, their followers and third generation of Muslims following them did not consider Hadith and Sunnah as a collection of memories; on the contrary, they acknowledged and preserved them as a fundamental

---

[157] Seyfullah Kara, "Hz.Peygamber'e Karsi Oryantalist Bakis ve Bu Bakisin Kirilmasinda Metodolojik Yaklasimin Onemi," *Ataturk University, Journal of Theology Faculty* 23 (2005), p. 26.

[158] Bekir Ezer, "Alman Oryantalistlerin Hz. Muhammed Sunnet ve Hadis Hakkindaki Calismalari (1900–1950)" (Master Thesis, Erciyes University, 2007), p. 42.

[159] M. Asim Koksal, *Mustesrik Caetani'nin Yazdigi Islam Tarihindeki Isnad Ve Iftiralara Reddiye* (Ankara: Diyanet Isleri Baskanligi Publications, 1986), p. 30.

[160] The Farewell Sermon was delivered to an audience numbering 110,000 and its details were confirmed by a large number of Companions who attended the speech.

source of the religion, second after the Qur'an, and as detailed explanations of the religion provided personally by Prophet Muhammad, upon whom be peace and blessings.

Joseph Schacht (d. 1969) was a leading Western scholar on Islamic law. Looking into his research reveals a theory or model that assumes Hadith and Sunnah do not constitute a basis in Islamic literature and, therefore, have no association with the Prophet. Hadith, in his view, is a phenomenon invented and attributed to the Prophet by the scholars from the second and third centuries AH in order to support their arguments. In presenting his views he follows a reverse chronological order, and says:

> If we must say in general terms, first emerged the living traditions of old schools of law, to a great extent based on individual cases, then at the second phase, these have been advanced, and attributed to the companions [narrating them as hadiths].

He continues with his argument and arrives to this point:

> We learn that the majority of the hadiths attributed to the Prophet have emerged at the time of the generation that followed him, that is during the second quarter of the second century. However, we do not come across any legal sunnah transmitted from the Prophet that can be considered authentic.[161]

Looking from Schacht's viewpoint, Hadith and Sunnah are lies fabricated in the name of the Prophet rather than being his genuine deeds and words. Schacht also claims that historical data has been constructed upon lies and fabrications. He draws attention to a situation in which lies were attributed to all scholars and jurists among the lineage of people, starting from the Companions through to the generations that followed them, and their valuable works were considered null and void. There is also a case of false accusation on the Noble Prophet, who permitted—and encouraged—the writing down of Hadith and Sunnah. Schacht's

---

[161] Ezer, "Alman Oryantalistlerin Hz. Muhammed, Sunnet Ve Hadis Hakkındaki Calismalari (1900–1950)" (German Orientalists' Studies on Prophet Muhammad, the Sunnah and the Hadith), p. 48.

approach mostly resembles Goldziher's views on Hadith and this gives the impression they share the same basic viewpoint. Schacht's views also attempt to ascertain that Hadith and Sunnah are just a collection of habits and customs. He mentions the claim by Ibn al-Muqaffa' that the term *sunnah* was forged within the Umayyad state administrative system during the second century AH.[162]

Another leading name on the research of Islam in the West is Hurgronje. Hurgronje regards the majority of hadiths as an expression of views and ideas during the first three centuries AH.[163] Beside this, Hurgronje makes reference to Goldziher, and stresses that hadiths cannot be used for Quranic exegesis. He reckons, when rumors and narratives are eliminated, what is left as the oldest news can only provide some information about the first century AH, and establishing a tangible connection between this data and the Prophet is not possible.[164]

Looking into Hadith from the viewpoint of Western scholars, such as Alois Sprenger, Snouck Hurgronje, Ignaz Goldziher and Joseph Schacht, who published books and articles on Hadith, biographies and other Islamic sciences, certainly some doubts arise.

Alongside those who criticize hadiths, and fall just short of declaring them non-existent, other Western scholars have chosen to mitigate the atmosphere. Some of them admit that reproachful criticisms of Hadith are exaggerated and unjust. For example, J. Fück, one of the leading Western scholars of the last century on Islam, says, "The logic of considering every legal sunnah fake until proven otherwise is feeding a skepticism based on an ego without boundaries."[165] As can be seen from this kind of assessment in the West, a relative softening of rigidity on approaches toward Islam in general, and Hadith in particular, becomes evident. For example, Daniel W. Brown states his views on Hadith and Sunnah in *Encyclopedia of Islam*: "During Muhammad's lifetime and immediately after that, when faced with problems to solve, people reminded each other in their discourse (*hadith*) of how the Prophet and his first faithful followers had acted under particular circumstances. This

---

[162] A'zami, *Islam Fikhi (Islamic Jurisprudence)*, p. 144; Schacht, *Origins*, pp. 58–59.
[163] Kizil, "Oryantalistlerin Hadis Literaturu Hakkindaki Gorusleri," p. 54.
[164] ibid.
[165] J. Fück, *The Role of Traditional in Islam, Studies in Islam* (New York, 1981), pp. 99–122.

resulted in an as yet unstructured, oral transmission of more or less correctly remembered practices and customs, *sunnas*. Towards the end of the 1st century, when the need thereto arose, these memories began to be transmitted in a more standardized manner after the introduction of a newly-developed authentication device, the *isnad*."[166]

In explaining his views on the Noble Prophet's receiving of the Divine Revelations, Maxime Rodinson asserts that he was not suffering from an illness, such as an epileptic fit as was claimed by the early period critics.[167] He explains his views on the Noble Prophet as follows:

> The Christian theologians who looked upon Muhammad as a liar as well as the eighteenth century philosophers are now left behind. The advancement in the sciences of psychology and psychiatry subdued these stumpy statements. The concept of subconsciousness has made us easily understand this kind of events.[168]

However, he views the Hadith as the sayings of the Prophet that were not written in the life of the Prophet and if written, they were not cultivated by the Prophet during his life personally.[169]

It is important to understand these rational approaches to Hadith in recent times alongside the earlier Western critical approach to the relationship between the Hadith and the Qur'an.

Motives Urging the West to Study Islamic Sciences and the Hadith

A proper understanding of the motives urging and encouraging studies and research on Hadith and other Islamic sciences in the West requires analysis and interpretation of the available historical data in a rigorous manner. Keeping in mind that only correct data can lead to the truth and realistic interpretations, research carried out and theories construed that do not reflect the truth can, besides damaging his-

---

[166] D. W. Brown, "Sunna," *The Encyclopaedia of Islam*, (Leiden: E J Brill, 1986), p. 878.

[167] Kara, "Hz.Peygamber'e Karsi Oryantalist Bakis Ve Bu Bakisin Kirilmasinda Metodolojik Yaklasimin Onemi," pp. 153–156.

[168] M. Rodinson, *Hz.Muhammed, Yeni Bir Dunyanin, Dinin Ve Silahlı Bir Peygamberin Dogusu*, trans. Attila Tokatli (Istanbul: Gocebe Publication, 1968), pp. 87–88.

[169] Muhammad Akram Sajid and Muhammad Abdullah, "'Muhammad' by Maxime Rodinson (An Analytical Study)," *Jihat al-Islam*, Lahore, 4, no. 1-2 (July-December 2010/January-June 2011).

torical facts, also cause science to lose its trustworthiness and blemish academia's reputation.

It is possible to make a list of the motives urging Western scholars to study this field. Showing one single reason or pointing to one single possibility is not realistic. Reasons varied during the course of the historical research process. What is essential is the presence of historical records and documents supporting the arguments. This is the reason why it is necessary to assess the subject matter with its different aspects since the early periods. Historical relations between Muslim and non-Muslim states date back to the time of the Noble Prophet. These relations were developed in cultural, religious, scientific and other areas with the passages of time.

For example, the presence of Andalusian Muslims in this multicultural geography for centuries paved the way for a rich variety of religious and cultural dialogues and interpretations. When Ibn Jubayr (d.1217), a Muslim traveler, visited Sicily in 1185, he noted that King William II (d.1189) could read and write in Arabic, and the Christians of Palermo spoke Arabic and dressed like Muslims. Norman kings in Sicily used Arabic writing and the Islamic (*Hijri*) calendar. According to Philip Hitti (d. 1978), during the caliphate of Abdurrahman II (d. 852 CE) in Andalusia, the majority of the Christian population living in cities had a lifestyle similar to Muslims' due to the influence of language, literature and social institutions.[170]

It is a well-known fact that the first serious works on Islam in the West began by translating the meaning of the Qur'an into Latin in 1143 CE. That is, the twelfth century is when the influence of Islam on the West was truly felt. This is, in a way, also known as the first period of Western encounter of Islam. The advancement of Muslims in scientific works in this period attracted the attention of the Western world. This may have encouraged Western scholars to study Islamic sciences as a challenge. However, apprehensions raised in the West caused concern for the Eastern Christians and the protection of their faith became an objective. Thus, missionary works started for this purpose became ev-

---

[170]   Philip K. Hitti, *Islam Tarihi (History of Islam)*, vol. I, p. ii, trans. Salih Tug (Istanbul: Kitap Yurdu Publication, 2011), p. 811.

ident. Here, it is paramount to emphasize this point: the basis of missionary works was to protect the faith of the Christian population, not to convert Muslims from their religion.[171]

During this period, Western scholars did not possess sufficient knowledge on Islamic sciences, and there was a serious need for studies to be carried out in this field. Therefore, they considered debates with Muslim scholars to be very risky. This may also be seen as a reason for the prohibition enforced on the publication of the Qur'an during the Cromwell era in England.[172] During the course of matters that followed, working groups—composed of clergymen and using resources provided by them—were implemented to carry out research on Hadith along with other Islamic sciences, thus works began. The real intention of this research was to collect the material they would need to criticize Islam, not to increase their knowledge or enrich their culture by learning about one of the major world religions. Core issues such as the life of the Noble Prophet and the rise of Islam were used to serve this purpose.[173] Research on the life of the Noble Prophet, focusing especially on the correlation between him and the Qur'an, was a work-in-progress during the centuries that followed. For this reason, the proper understanding of the Qur'an and the Sunnah was crucial for them. What can be construed from this information, the real purpose of all these efforts, were the safeguarding of the Christian faith and the strengthening of ties between Eastern and Western Christianity.

In other words, preserving the unity within Christianity, while trying to develop a type of defense mechanism against Islam, may be shown as one of the reasons for this research. A close scrutiny of these works clearly reveals that a critical approach was adopted for the purpose of the research on Islam and the Hadith.

In the meantime, the intellectuals became alienated against Christianity. As a result of questioning the religion with the influence of philosophy and rationalist thought currents, Christianity suffered a se-

---

[171] R. Irwin, *Oryantalistler Ve Dusmanlari, (For Lust of Knowing: The Orientalists and Their Enemies)*, trans. Bahar Tirnakci (Istanbul: Yapı Kredi Publications, 2008), p. 91.

[172] Nabil Matar, *Islam in Britain, 1558-1685*, vol. 1 (Cambridge University Press, 2008), p. 76.

[173] Irwin, *Oryantalistler Ve Dusmanlari (For Lust of Knowing: The Orientalists and Their Enemies)*, p. 90.

rious decline in the West. Without doubt, influenced by these thought currents, Islam had also been subjected to questioning. This rationale, which questions and criticizes any religious principle it comes across, also led the way to start works to criticize and disparage Islamic values. This structure of thought especially focused on the truth of the Qur'an and the reliability of Hadith. Therefore, it may be possible to say that another reason for research on the Qur'an and the Hadith is this philosophical trend. This is what Cerrahoglu writes in this connection:

> In the West, works on Islam and its sources were carried out—in the past to some extent, and in our times exclusively—by Orientalist circles and similarly minded scholars. These works have been authored with a hostile intention rather than the noble cause of learning more about or serving Islam. Therefore, they have to be carefully studied before being referred to as a source although they contain some scientific elements.[174]

Bringing Cerrahoglu's assertion of "hostile intention" together with Irwin's views reveals very important data on the starting point and motives of these works.

Bernard Lewis points out the psychological background of the works, and says:

> Some Western scholars, motivated by their own nationalist agendas, are labeling Muslims with qualities such as backwardness, weakness and ignorance. With this approach, they are aiming particularly at Muslim readers to drive them into a psychology of losing their self-confidence.[175]

Considering these assessments made by Lewis together with discussions that took place in the first part, the West's reactionary and competitive approach to Islamic culture exposes itself very clearly. Hence, sowing the seeds of suspicion in the minds among the Muslim populace and creating an upheaval in their thought system is in question. In a community

---

[174] Ismail Cerrahoglu, "Oryantalizm Ve Batida Kur'an Ve Kur'an Ilimleri Uzerine Arastirmalar" (Orientalism and the Researches on the Qur'an and Quranic Sciences in the West), *Ankara University, Journal of Faculty of Theology,* XXXI (1989), p.115.

[175] Bernard Lewis, *Islamin Siyasal Soylemi (The Political Language of Islam),* trans. Fatih Tasar (Istanbul: Phoenix Publication, 1992), p. 20.

whose thought system was turned upside-down with minds preoccupied with doubts and hesitations, achieving healthy results with such a scientific and scholarly methodology would be questionable.

Looking down on others with disdain can be considered a leading motive behind Western scholars' adoption of negative approaches, such as criticism, competitiveness and antagonism. Even the large number of responses given by Muslim scholars to those criticisms and suspicions provide some idea about the quantity of works on Islamic sciences carried out in the West. This again supports Lewis' views. However, extending this assertion over the whole of the Western world would be an injustice to those objective and valuable works also carried out in the same part of the world.

In recent times, one can see a relatively moderate policy of distancing from prejudicial and disparagingly critical approaches on scientific works in order to carry relations to a more favorable ground. The skepticism that developed—through Western thoughts and perspectives—impacted on Muslims toward information originating from the West and gradually became widespread among the Muslim scholars. This situation in the scientific area is also becoming apparent in political as well as commercial areas. The policy of moderation in relations is an effort to overcome this distrust between the two great civilizations.

Western Views on the Recording of Hadiths

An important matter from the viewpoint of historical discourse and soundness of hadiths, in the West, is the prohibition enforced on the writing of hadiths and permission being granted again at a later stage. Muslim and Western scholars have differing views on the recording of hadiths by writing or committing to memory. Primarily, it is useful to know the Companions' approach to Hadith according to Muslim sources. Works written on the subject clearly show that the Prophet's Companions were extremely sensitive about his words. The Companions' regard for Hadith stemmed from the respect they had for the Noble Prophet as well as reverence to the Qur'an. Warnings in Quranic verses caused the Companions to focus on the Noble Prophet and his Practice (Sunnah). A verse decrees: "*And whatever the Messenger gives you, accept it, and from whatever he forbids you, keep back, and be careful of (your duty to) God.*"[176] The Companions' efforts to memorize, protect and preserve Hadith came to the fore because of this verse.

The method of memorization in the Arabian Peninsula was mostly based on the power of memory and strong Arab literature.[177] After the migration (*Hijrah*) to Medina, however, the *Ashab al-Suffah*'s scholarly works can be seen as a good example in regard to the writing down and memorization of hadiths. The Noble Prophet's appointment of Abdu'llah ibn Sa'id ibn al-'As to teach them how to read and write is a well-known historical fact.[178] The Companions who knew how to read and write were writing the hadiths on materials available at that moment, such as leather, wood and date-leaves. The recordings and memorization of hadiths were carried out under the Noble Prophet's supervision.

After a while, however, the scriptural recording of hadiths was prohibited by the Noble Prophet. In compliance with these narrations, the Companions stopped writing down hadiths, and those who tried to write were prevented by reminders of these reports. Zayd ibn Thabit's preventing Mu'awiyyah from writing down hadiths is a good example of this. However, the Noble Prophet permitted his traditions to be memorized and transmitted verbally.[179] To clarify the point, a blanket prohibition of the transmission of hadiths had never been the case.

Some commentaries were made on such hadiths as well as the prohibition imposed by the Noble Prophet. First, looking at Western scholars' comments reveals an interesting picture. Goldziher views a correlation between the prohibition of writing down hadiths and taking another verbal source apart from the Torah as a base in Judaism. He argues that a legislative development of Judaism had a warning effect on the rejection of Hadith—which, according to Muslims, have a Divine origin—and the prohibition of their recording by writing.[180] According to him, the objection against the writing down of hadiths was mainly

---

[176] Qur'an 59:7.
[177] Kocyigit, *Hadis Tarihi*, p. 20.
[178] Ibn al-Athir, *Usd al-Ghabah*, III, 175.
[179] Ibn Hanbal, *al-Musnad*, 758.
[180] Ignaz Goldziher, *Muslim Studies*, trans. C.R. Barber and S.M. Stern (London: Allen and Unwin, 1971).

the concern of Islam being treated in the same way as Judaism. He holds this was the reason the Prophet stopped his Companions writing down hadiths. In this connection, Goldziher gives this example: Abdu'llah ibn al-A'la requested from Abu Bakr's grandson Qasim to have hadiths written down for him. Qasim replied: "The numbers of written hadiths were increased during the time of 'Umar ibn al-Khattab. 'Umar asked people to bring them to him; when he had all of them in his hands, he ordered to burn them, and said this: 'Do you want a duality like the duality of Judaism?'" In Goldziher's view, the duality here refers to the *Mishnah* (Oral Torah) in Judaism.[181]

Goldziher mentions the prohibition of writing down hadiths, but he interprets this ban on the grounds of different reasons. In his later views, he holds as fabricated the part of the aforementioned hadith: "Whoever deliberately attributes a lie to me, he should prepare his seat in the Fire." In regard to this matter, he argues this hadith is not a sound narration and fabricated to prevent people from forging false hadiths. One important point here is that Goldziher contradicts himself by accepting the prohibition of writing down hadiths on the grounds of the first part of the abovementioned hadith—and commenting on the subject—and immediately rejects the other part of the hadith—which is in contextual accord with the first part—as fabricated.

Some Western scholars of recent times further argue that the Noble Prophet copied the Qur'an from texts of the Old and New Testaments. Goldziher, when he was arguing the prohibition of writing down hadiths due to concerns of Islam being treated the same as Judaism, may be alluding to this: the Companions, through the experience of writing down hadiths, may come to learn the structure of *Mishnah*, and consequently may arrive to the truth of the Prophet having drawn heavily on the Torah. He claims, therefore, that the Prophet prohibited the recording of hadiths to prevent this truth from coming out.

These kinds of theories may be construed on the basis of Goldziher's clearly contradictory views. Explaining it in any other way, the acceptance of one part of a hadith and rejection of another part, would

---

[181] Ceyhan, "Alman Mustesrik Ignaz Goldziher'in Islam Hukukunun Kaynaklari Hakkindaki Gorusleri ve Bu Goruslerin Degerlendirilmesi," p. 29.

pose some difficulty. On the other hand, looking from another angle, it is no less than attributing lies to the Noble Prophet.

While Goldziher looks into the prohibition of writing down hadiths and the truth in a moderate manner, it can also be said that he did not opine adversely on the recording of hadiths in writing. He uses, as a basis to his views, the narration by Abu Hurayrah, "There is not anyone, except Abdu'llah ibn 'Amr ibn al-'As, among the Prophet's Companions who reported more hadiths than me. He used to write them down but I didn't write."[182] According to Goldziher, this style of hadiths can be accepted as evidence of the recording of hadiths by writing during the time of the Noble Prophet.[183] In light of these views, he, like Sprenger, may be deemed as coming closer to Muslim scholars' views on the recording of hadiths. However, the meaning Goldziher inferred from *kitabat* (recording, writing in book form) and the meaning Muslim scholars attributed to the term are rather different. He regards these written documents as collections of individual accounts the Muslims heard at different times and recorded for their own use. These recorded notes were obtained without *qira'at* (reciting) or *sama'* (reporting of hadiths by way of direct acquisition from an acceptable authority) of the person involved or their textual contents being considered as if they were received through a proper channel of transmission. Using Abdu'llah ibn Lahia's (d. 790 CE) books as examples to these written notes, Goldziher points to Abdu'llah's loss of his reliability and never gaining back his prestige after the destruction of his notes as a result of a fire.[184] While it is a well-known fact that Muslim scholars base their views, regarding hadiths reported from the Companions, on chains of narrators confirming each other, Abdu'llah's loss of his notes would not mean much had been lost, if another Companion knew and maintained the same hadiths. Yet, there are also verbal narrations alongside written narrations. Reports from the Companions, if their authenticity is verified, are accepted as verbal or written narrations. However, in Goldziher's understanding of recording, an isolated and baseless consideration strikes

---

[182] Bukhari, *al-Jami'u's-Sahih*, "Ilm," 39.
[183] Nimetullah Akin, "Hadislerin Yazili Kaydi Ve Literatur Esasli Bir Disiplin Olma Sureci: A. Sprenger, I. Goldziher Ve G. Schoeler'in Yaklasimlari," *Journal of Hadis Tetkikleri* VI/1(2008), p.54.
[184] ibid., p. 55.

one's attention. That is, he was convinced the Companions had individual written records that did not support each other.

Goldziher's assertions on the prohibition of writing down had-iths have been explained by Muslim scholars in a rather different manner. The Noble Prophet did not allow the recording of hadiths in writing be-cause he wanted nothing but the Word of God, the Qur'an, to be revered and espoused by the Muslims with all its characteristics. He did not view the scholarly procedures of scribing the verses of the Qur'an to be ap-plied to Hadith as fitting. Besides, the prohibition of writing down had-iths in the Medina period brings to mind the period in Mecca. During the Meccan period, the verses revealed were related to the belief of the Oneness of God (*Tawhid*). The false beliefs related to God were exposed by these revelations. Thus, there was not too much to be explained by the Noble Prophet. The principles of the Islamic system were established in later years and the need for the Noble Prophet's explanatory teachings arose mostly in Medina. Therefore, recording hadiths in writing in ear-ly periods was not closely related to the normal historical development of Islam.[185] Also, the huge difference in the numbers of Muslims who could read and write during the Mecca and Medina periods must be em-phasized. Historical records show there were only 24 Companions who could read and write during the Meccan period, while these numbers in the Medina period show a significant increase as a result of the Prophet's encouragement and support.

The prohibition of recording hadiths in writing became espe-cially relevant for the majority of Arabs who were not well-versed in Is-lamic traditions and were unable to differentiate between Quranic verses and other words.[186] Other views by Muslim scholars and traditionists on the prohibition imposed on the writing down of hadiths included: there were only a few people who could read and write, so a written culture was inadequate during the early period;[187] the ban was for those with a powerful memory, but who feared they could only trust written

---

[185] Ismail Lutfi Cakan, *Hadis Edebiyati (Hadith Literature)*, (Istanbul: Marmara University, The Foundation of the Faculty of Theology, 1997), p. 4.

[186] Al-Khatib, *Taqyid al-'Ilm*, 57.

[187] Ismail Cerrahoglu, "Tefsir Ve Hadis Kitabetine Karsi Peygamber Ve Sahabenin Durumu," Ankara: Ankara University, *The Journal of the Faculty of Theology*, 9 (1962), p. 43.

records; on the other hand, the permission for writing was for those who feared they would forget if they did not write things down;[188] writing was banned for the general public, but permission was given for the well-literate;[189] and the prohibition was specific to the period of Quranic revelation to prevent Quranic verses and hadiths being written on the same pages, but they could be written on separate pages.[190]

As can be understood from these explanations, the aim of the Noble Prophet's banning of the recording hadiths in writing is related to protection of the Qur'an. Looking for any other consideration is secondary.

Sprenger does not ignore the ban of writing down hadiths being imposed by the Noble Prophet. According to him, this ban was reported by many Companions. He expresses his opinion this way:

> The author of the book most read, Qur'an, had a prejudice—a prejudice, which was shared by the majority of the Companions—against keeping a written record of hadiths. Ibn Mas'ud, Abu Hurayrah and others hold that there was no permission given for writing.[191]

It is important to highlight this point: the Noble Prophet's unfavorable stance was not against the usage of writing, but was against the process of writing and compiling hadiths into booklets.[192] In this connection, Sprenger opines:

> We have to make a difference between notes kept to help the memory, and corpora and books. Muslims began keeping notes to help their memory since the early period, and, those with more moderate thought are in the opinion that note-taking in writing was allowed.[193]

However, Sprenger's opinions on the banning of recording hadiths during early periods may be viewed as showing some similarities with Islamic literature. He accepts that, from the material point of view, there

---

[188] Al-Suyuti, *Tadribu'r-Rawi fi Sharhi Takribi'n Nawawi*, (Cairo: Daru'l-Hadith, 2004), p. 354.

[189] M. A. M. Ibn Qutaybah, *Ta'wilu Muhtalafi'l-Hadith*, (Beirut: Daru'l-Kutubi'l- Ilmiyya, n.d), p. 266.

[190] Al-Suyuti, *Tadribu'r-Rawi fi Sharhi Takribi'n Nawawi*, p. 354.

[191] Akin, "Hadislerin Yazili Kaydi Ve Literatur Esasli Bir Disiplin Olma Sureci: A. Sprenger, I. Goldziher Ve G. Schoeler'in Yaklasimlari."

[192] ibid., p. 4.

[193] ibid.

was no cause preventing the writing down of hadiths in the early periods, and the practical applications proved this. Nevertheless, Sprenger's favorable approach to the written records of hadiths does not mean he also holds a similar view on the health and soundness of hadiths.[194]

Looking into Sprenger's and Goldziher's views concerning the banning of recording hadiths in writing, it is possible to say they were endeavoring to cast doubts upon the reliability of these sources. On the one hand, there is Goldziher's acceptance of small booklets, like Sprenger's, but on the other hand, there is his emphasis upon the Noble Prophet's negative attitude to the compilation of hadiths into book form. Looking from their perspective, it is possible to construe questions such as: Although the Noble Prophet did not want hadiths being compiled into a book form since the early period, why have Hadith collections been published by traditionists since the second century AH? This could be considered a practice which violates the Prophetic Practice (Sunnah)! Through these kinds of comments, assertions and questions, doors can be opened to doubts and criticisms on hadiths and Hadith collections.

Effects of Modernism on Muslim Scholars' Perception of Hadith

There is a modernist and reformist current of thought in the Muslim world, influenced by both Western critical thinking and Muslim revivalist movements, which demonstrates different approaches to Hadith and argues for new approaches to the tradition within the Islamic world. This current, which began emerging at the beginning of the nineteenth century, continues to show its influence in different aspects and viewpoints. Ahmad Din (d. 1936), Ahmad Parwiz (d. 1953), Ahmad Amin (d. 1954), Hafiz Muhammad Aslam Jairajpuri (d. 1955), Abu Rayyah (d. 1970), Ghulam Ahmad Parwez (d. 1985), Mahmud M. Taha (d. 1985), Fazlur Rahman (d.1988), and Muhammad Ghazali (d. 1996) are some of the scholars within this current of thought. These representatives of modernist thought in the Muslim world have focused their works mostly on Hadith and its associated sciences. It can be said that the emergence of confusion and new criticisms on Hadith among Muslims are the product of thoughts of this kind. Topics like their perceptions of Hadith and their

---

[194] ibid.

stance on the status of Hadith are important, and should be carefully discussed and analyzed.

With his assertion of hadiths being fabricated after the time of the Prophet, Fazlur Rahman declares openly that he disregards all traditional principles and bases in the discipline of Hadith. Or put differently, giving him the benefit of the doubt, one could say that he approaches these sciences with deep suspicion. If the question was one of doubt concerning the authenticity of hadiths, the basis and sources of such hesitation should be made available in scholarly works. His views show some similarities to Goldziher's assertion of hadiths being forged from the second century AH, in accordance with the political views of the time.

Fazlur Rahman, when giving his views on the disciplines of Islamic jurisprudence (*fiqh*) and theology (*kalam*), says that the thoughts and views of scholars have been attributed to the Prophet from the second century AH. In this connection, he says:

> The hadith movement reached an advanced point by the middle of the second century AH. Although most of the hadiths were still attributed to people—to Companions and especially to the generations that followed them—other than the Prophet, some of the legal and theological views of Muslims of the early period were started to be attributed to the Prophet.[195]

Here, there is an ascription of lie and distrust to the Companions. Also, with these statements and through the body of Hadith, questions are being raised about the principal disciplines, such as Islamic law and theology. In his view, if the ideas of early Muslims can be linked to the Prophet, it can only be through the medium of Hadith. Therefore, he claimed that the discipline of Hadith suffers from a serious problem of reliability, as hadiths can be the ideas of ordinary people attributed to the Prophet or fabricated in the second century AH.

It is always necessary to adopt a prudent approach toward the disciplines of Islamic law and theology, which establish their origin with the Noble Prophet. Nevertheless, while some modernist scholars followed the paths of Jamal al-Din Afghani, Muhammad Abduh, Rashid

---

[195] Fazlur Rahman, *Tarih Boyunca Islami Metodoloji Sorunu* (Originally published as *Islamic Methodology in History*), p. 37.

Rida and Fazlur Rahman, others assert they were wrong. Some of them talk about the "historicalness" of the Qur'an and the Sunnah, while others even go to the extent of claiming that the Noble Prophet authored the Qur'an. Some researchers and scholars also reject the status of the Juridicial Consensus and Analogy (*Ijma'* and *Qiyas*) as sources of the Islamic Law. One group talks about the illegality of the judicial schools of thought (*madhhabs*), another one talks about mixing *madhhabs* (which is called *talfiq*, or eclecticism, resulting in "nondenomination"), and yet another one argues that every individual should be allowed to arbitrarily deduce legal rulings directly from the Qur'an.[196] Some writers and scholars, such as Turan Dursun, Yasar Nuri Ozturk, Zekeriya Beyaz, Edip Yuksel and Huseyin Atay, are known to be the followers of this modernist understanding and the secular approach in Turkey.

In his polemical books, Turan Dursun, who holds an ultra-secular stance, concentrates on the probability of the Qur'an being the words of the Prophet. Also known is Dursun's skeptical approach to the early periods of Islam and the efforts of the Companions in the field of Hadith.

Yasar Nuri Ozturk, another modernist scholar, asserts his view on Hadith as follows:

> All hadiths, except thirty or fifty of them, are forged. Accepting any source other than the Qur'an is polytheism (*shirk*) because no source other than the Qur'an has the guaranty of [Divine] protection. The hadiths pertaining to [the event of] *Mi'raj* (the Prophet's Ascension to heavens) are full of contradictions. Narrations attributed to the Prophet, which command the writing [down of hadiths] are fabricated. What were written as hadiths were attributed to the Prophet as if they were his words. Hadiths are not bounding from the legal point of view; they cannot be a source of reference in court rulings because they are full of contradictions.[197]

From his words, it can be understood that the Hadith cannot be used to interpret the Qur'an. According to him, the Hadith cannot constitute a

---

[196] Osman Akyildiz, "Dinde Reformcu Yaklasimlar Veya Dini Modernizmin Yukselisi," *Journal of Akademya*, 1 (September-December 2010), pp. 94–108.

[197] Donmez, Mustafa. "Islam Dunyasinda Hadis Inkarcilari ve Gorusleri" (The Deniers of Hadith in the Muslim World), (1999-2000), http://www.islah.de/sunnet/sun00008.pdf.

source for legal rulings; there are serious doubts about their preservation. Thus, Hadith with an unreliable origin and doubtful authenticity cannot possibly be a source of reference in Islam. With these views, he comes closer to the current of thought that does not accept any source other than the Qur'an. In this thought, what is essential is the Qur'an and there is no need for Sunnah for its understanding. Ozturk continues his statements on hadith, and says:

> Imitators ['*muqallid*'] who are intermediaries of polytheism (*shuraka'*) have formulated a religion outside the Qur'an by making these people [Companions] as well the history lie, and two centuries after his death, attributing to the Prophet the pile of *mishnah* amounting to ten times of the size of the Qur'an.[198]

His assertion of Hadith being forged in the times after the Prophet shows some similarities with views held by Sprenger, Goldziher, Schacht and Hurgronje. This argument also shows a striking resemblance to Goldziher's view of the Mishnah-Hadith correlation.

In explaining his view on the Noble Prophet's legislative authority beside the Qur'an, Ozturk states that he views this as a form of polytheism. Answering a question on the power of the Noble Prophet in laying down legislation, he says:

> The Prophet has no authority to lay down law except [what is mentioned] in the Qur'an; if you say, "Yes, he has," this would constitute polytheism. The Prophet is the servant and prophet of God. A prophet is the messenger [one who delivers the message] of the Power he represents, but not His partner.[199]

It must be noted that mainstream Muslim scholars have no doubt the Noble Prophet had the authority to lay down the law and the Sunnah has the quality to interpret the Qur'an. This is supported by many Quranic verses such as the following:

> (We sent them with) clear proofs of the truth and Scriptures. And on you We have sent down the Reminder (the Qur'an) so that you may

---

[198] Yasar Nuri Ozturk, *Kur'andaki Islam (Islam in the Qur'an)*, (Istanbul: Sidre Publication, 1992), p. 124.

[199] ibid., 656.

make clear to humankind whatever is sent down to them (through you of the truth concerning their present and next life), and that they may reflect.[200]

This verse is one of the strongest evidence showing that the Sunnah is a principal source and the interpreter of the Qur'an.[201]

As for Zekeriya Beyaz, who generally follows the same line of thought as Ozturk, he is known for his ultra-national views. He argues that Hadith emerged after the time of the Prophet, after second century AH, and cannot be attributed to the Prophet. According to him, hadiths have not been recorded and safeguarded since the time of the Prophet.

In summary, modernist logic—in whichever Muslim country it may be—basically exerts the thought structure of Western scholars and acquires a position of being their representative. Unfortunately, after the works endeavoring to create doubts and hesitation about the Qur'an, the direction of studies was changed to focus on the Hadith and the Sunnah. It is a fact that the aim of this was again to raise doubts, but this time mainly on Hadith.

Despite all the critiques and prejudices both in the West and in the post-modern Islamic world against the preservation and documentation of Hadith, we need to record that the non-scribe Arabs' innate ability, though being largely illiterate, to memories and remember the exact words of the Noble Prophet as their experiences unfolded in company with him in their lifetime. This unique legacy of transmission became an integral counseling/learning activity and prized past-time with immediate Companions (*Sahabah*) who lived on for decades after the demise of the Noble Prophet.

Concluding Remarks Concerning the Discussions on Hadith

Old relations between Islam and the West have been instrumental in mutual cultural exchanges and scholarly research. In those researches, perspectives and views focused initially on the translation of the Qur'an into Western languages. Later on, with the expansion of Islam into Eu-

---

[200] Qur'an 16:44.
[201] Yildirim, *Kuran-i Hakim ve Aciklamali Meali (The Wise Qur'an and Its Annotated Interpretation)*, pp. 271–276.

rope and into the countries with Christian and Jewish population, debates and dialogues emerged due to the influence of philosophies and the Renaissance movement in the West. This naturally led to the questioning of the origin of the Qur'an and determining its authenticity. Also, the correlations between God, the Holy Qur'an and the Noble Prophet were put on the table; critical research carried out on the subject from the viewpoint of deist ideology that does not accept a prophetic office in religions. These works on the Qur'an and the Prophet resulted in studying the Hadith discipline. During the course of events that followed, questions like the soundness of Hadith and its position as the second primary source after the Qur'an emerged as a focal point of the works.

In the eyes of most Western scholars, hadiths are not a reality connected to the Prophet. While some of them view hadiths as common usage, habits, customs and traditions, others assert hadiths are a phenomena forged from the second century AH in connection with certain socio-political motivations. Contrary to the approach of Muslims scholars, which argues for the unique correlation between the Qur'an and the Hadith, the vast majority of Western scholars persistently steered away from establishing any kind of link between the two, and focused especially on raising doubts through disparaging criticisms. Works and research carried out in this respect have kept the Western and Muslim worlds busy over many years, and this is still continuing to some extent.

It is a well-known fact that Muslim scholars authored refutations based on historical data against assertions put forth by Western scholars. In this connection, it is necessary to mention the influence of research and thoughts in the West on reformist and modernist Muslim scholars. They are known, in their own countries, for their works, particularly on Hadith, with the influence of Western thoughts. It is possible to say that their efforts resulted, to some extent, in raising a number of doubts in the minds of some Muslims, also in various deviations and deteriorations in certain religious matters. These damaging works done on religion and religious sources have caused certain tensions in political and commercial relations between Muslims and the West, and paved the way for frictions between the two civilizations.

Muslim scholars with strong traditional ties expressed their common view on works on the Qur'an and the Hadith originating from the West, saying they cannot be trusted and warned researchers they should be cautious when making reference to them. It is also a fact that their prejudiced criticisms and assertions on the Qur'an and the Hadith resulted in Muslim scholars returning to scholarly works on Islamic sciences, thus to re-familiarize themselves with their own sources and learn them better.

Another established fact is that some Western scholars, with their new works and theses, made valuable contributions to the softening of tense relations experienced between the East and West. It can also be said that certain political and mutual understanding have played a role in this relative softening in their views and assertions. In addition, the emergence of the profile of modernist and reformist Muslim scholars, and the popular views they came up with becoming defendable—even if it is in a marginal scale—may have had a comforting effect on Western scholars in relaxing their efforts. This can be viewed as another indirect influence in the softening of the tension between civilizations. Dialogue coming to forefront, rather than confrontation or argument, can also be viewed as another factor contributing to this softening.

As a final word, as long as the views and approaches of Muslim and Western scholars are commonsense, unprejudiced and based on scientific sources, mutual contacts and discussions can produce good results for the peace and welfare of members of both civilizations.

Chapter Three

_____

GÜLEN'S UNDERSTANDING OF SUNNAH

Brief Biography of Fethullah Gülen

M. Fethullah Gülen is a Muslim intellectual and a religious scholar. He was born in 1941 in Erzurum, a town in the eastern part of Turkey. Gülen's first teachers were his parents who taught him the Qur'an while he was a young child. He also took his first Arabic lessons from his father. He began his religious studies at a very young age, taking lessons from the well-known scholars in Islamic disciplines. At the same time, he continued his education through private studies and acquired comprehensive knowledge in modern science subjects as well as advanced Arabic grammar, Islamic history and philosophy.

At the age of 20, Gülen was appointed as an imam of a mosque in Edirne, a western border town of Turkey. He continued his career as a Qur'an teacher in the metropolitan city of Izmir located in the west of the country. He visited many towns in the eastern and western parts of Turkey to deliver sermons, lectures and conferences to people from all walks of life. These discourses covered subjects that focused primarily on religion, morality and other social issues. This made Gülen a well-known preacher in Turkey. He was arrested by the military rulers in 1971 and freed six months later without any charges laid against him. Returning to his teaching position, he continued his sermons, lectures and conferences until 1990.[202]

With his concerted efforts in interfaith and intercultural dialogue works, he met with Pope John Paul II in 1998. In 1999, due to increasing medical problems, Gülen moved to the United States. Currently, residing in the US, Gülen continues to teach Quranic exegesis (*tafsir*), Hadith and other Islamic disciplines to students who reside with him.

Gülen is accepted in academic and non-academic circles as a leading expert in Hadith and Sirah (Prophetic biography) studies, especially in the field of the philosophy of Sirah. Gülen is quoted as saying, "I spent my life investigating the Sunnah,"[203] and it becomes apparent he has spent many years studying and researching the Hadith literature.

---

[202] For more details: http://fgulen.com/en/fethullah-gulens-life/about-fethullah-gulen/biography.

[203] Ali Unal, *M. Fethullah Gülen: Bir Portre Denemesi (Fethulah Gülen: A Portrait Essay)*, (Istanbul: Nil Publishing, 2002). p. 307.

As such, this statement, along with his teachers, the subjects he studied and the quality of education he received should be considered in detail. Finally, as mentioned in one of Ali Unal's works, Gülen stands at a point where scholarship, wisdom and intellectuality meet together.[204] While Unal's view of Gülen is somewhat assertive and requires further investigation, the main focus of this work will be limited with Gülen's perception and teaching of Hadith and related matters.

Gülen's Understanding of Sunnah

The preceding chapters discussed the Sunnah and its functions, the Hadith science, the recording and compilation of hadiths from a traditional Islamic perspective along with the critics of Sunnah in the Muslim world as well as the researches carried out and the theories developed by non-Muslim scholars on the concept of Sunnah. In this chapter, Gülen's thoughts on the Sunnah—that is, definitions of Hadith, discipline of Hadith, the process of recording and compiling of Sunnah, Sunnah's function in legislation as well as the depth of Gülen's knowledge of Sunnah, his acceptances, methods he adopted, and his revised and contemporary interpretations of Sunnah—will be examined in light of his works.

Gülen's views on Sunnah are dispersed throughout his works, i.e. books, articles, conferences, sermons and discourses, thus making a study of his observations on the subject rather challenging. However, Gülen's way of dealing with different aspects of Sunnah within the context of many subjects offers researchers an invaluable opportunity to ascertain his views on Sunnah more clearly and encourages them to discover his distinct interpretations within a rich archive. Furthermore, this also provides a firm ground with concrete examples for a contextual analysis to discover the relationship between Sunnah and real-life issues. Nevertheless, the last chapter of Gülen's book, entitled *Sonsuz Nur*, (which is also available in English as "*Muhammad, the Messenger of God: An Analysis of the Prophet's Life*") brings together the outlines of his assessments on various aspects of Sunnah.

What is the position of Sunnah in legislation according to

---

[204] ibid., pp. 307–308.

Gülen vis-à-vis the majority of Muslim scholars? Did Gülen, taking the needs of the contemporary age into account, bring in a new description or interpretation of the Sunnah? Does he has different views on the recording and compilation of the Sunnah or does he just repeat verbatim the classical historical account of *Sunnah*? How much is known—and how sound is this knowledge—about the nature and the depth of Gülen's understanding of Sunnah? To what extent does Gülen use Sunnah in his works and public speeches? What are the exact meanings of Islamic terms, such as *sunnah, hadith, fiqh*, etc., according to Gülen? What are the places and importance of these terms in practical life and also from the doctrinal perspective? Does Gülen merely follow received knowledge generally agreed upon in Islamic history and leave newly-arising matters to respective experts to discuss? According to Gülen, what should be the main point of discussion in the interpretation of Islamic terms and technical issues in our time? These and similar questions are of primary importance and should be fully addressed in order to comprehend Gülen's understanding of Sunnah. Attempting to seek answers to these questions would also reveal useful information on Gülen's methods and practical applications.

Gülen's Description of Sunnah

First of all, it is beneficial to focus on Gülen's approach to Sunnah. It cannot be said that Gülen often mentions and explains in detail classical definitions of Sunnah in his printed works and public discourses, or emphasizes their acceptance, teaching and dissemination. This is understandable, considering Gülen's works target a world-wide populace, emphasizing the notion of *hizmet* (service) rather than pushing a certain doctrine or normative and academic information. Perhaps it is for the same reason that he did not write a specific and systematic book on Sunnah. However, most of his views on Sunnah and its historical development have been collected in his work on the life of the Noble Prophet, titled *Sonsuz Nur*. Drawing heavily on this work, the late Hadith professor Ibrahim Canan states Gülen uses traditional Hadith definitions as his references, and embraces established practices and conventions adopted by a great number of traditional Muslim Hadith scholars in various disciplines, such as discernment of hadiths, Hadith narration, Hadith methodology, and all other related sub-branches.[205]

Hadith, literally meaning "something new" or "talk," is a term used for the traditions attributed to Prophet Muhammad, upon whom be peace and blessings, and includes what he said, did or tacitly approved.[206] According to Gülen, Hadith is a branch of knowledge teaching the Prophet's words (*aqwal*), actions (*af'al*) and spiritual states (*ahwal*). He also affirms that the majority of Muslim scholars consider the tacit approvals of the Noble Prophet as part of his "actions." When it comes to his evaluations of the term of Sunnah, Gülen confirms that this term covers the entirety of all speeches, deeds and silent approvals attributed to the Noble Prophet. It is clear that this definition of *sunnah* is synonymous to the term *hadith* according to Muslim jurists.[207] Gülen, like the majority Muslim scholars, concurs that these two terms are identical in meaning.[208] However, he generally prefers the usage of *sunnah* as a technical term, which is more comprehensive and covers the practical and transactional aspects of Prophetic Traditions. Primarily, *hizmet*-oriented activities, being the aim of the movement he leads, appear to be the most rational explanation of his choice of the term *sunnah* instead of *hadith*. In this work, the term *sunnah* will be used to refer to both Hadith and Sunnah to avoid misunderstanding and confusion.

Canan's assessment of Gülen's acceptance of the traditional *sunnah* definitions of methodologists and jurists proves to be accurate as Gülen uses these definitions in his works in a concise manner when needed. Gülen's referencing these classical sources directly may be interpreted to mean that he deems these definitions sufficient for the purpose of reflecting the true nature of the Sunnah. Gülen made no attempt in his works to come up with a new definition of Sunnah. His words illustrate that he—repeating various terminological connotations of *sunnah*—

---

[205] Canan, *Fethullah Gülen'in Sunnet Anlayisi*, pp. 65, 67.

[206] Calis, *Mastering Knowledge in Modern Times: Fethullah Gülen as an Islamic Scholar.*

[207] M. Fethullah Gülen, *Sonsuz Nur, Vol. 2 (Muhammad: The Messenger of God)*, (Istanbul: Nil Publishing, 2010). pp. 381-382.

[208] For further information, see Zakiyyuddin Shaban, *Islam Hukuk Ilminin Esaslari (originally titled, 'Usul al-Fiqh al-Islami)*, trans. Ibrahim Kafi Dönmez (Ankara: Diyanet Publications, 1996), p. 71.

stands in the same line with the scholars of the classical period, and leaves no space for argument:

> This term [Sunnah] has different terminological connotations according to each group of traditionists, methodologists, and jurists. Traditionists view it as including everything connected to the religious commandments reported from God's Messenger and categorized, according to the Hanafi legal school, as obligations, necessities, practices particular to or encouraged by the Noble Prophet himself as recommended and desirable.
>
> Methodologists consider it to be every word, deed, and approval of God's Messenger as related by his Companions. Jurists, who approach it as the opposite of innovation in religion (*bid'ah*), consider it a synonym for Hadith. They use it for the Noble Prophet's words, deeds, and approvals, all of which provide a basis for legislation and categorizing people's actions.[209]

Gülen's approach is to explore and explain to his followers the safeguarding of Sunnah, its legal status and its position in the daily life of a Muslim. In other words, his method is to elaborate on the practical aspects of Sunnah rather than getting caught up in scholarly arguments about the details of how to define the term *sunnah*; he considers that the arguments put forth by the *salaf* ("predecessor," first three generations of Muslims) would suffice to clarify the issue for an average Muslim. If any further arguments are deemed necessary among scholars, it is a matter for experts in the field of Hadith.[210] What is of primary importance for Gülen is to restudy the resources and terminology related to Sunnah, review their practicability, and prioritize and, if necessary, reinterpret their practical application according to the needs of the contemporary age.

In Gülen's thinking, social life and modern sciences are closely related to Sunnah. Therefore, focusing on this aspect of Sunnah is more important than discussing Sunnah-related classical terms and definitions. He really wants to socialize Sunnah and believes that only in

---

[209] M. Fethullah Gülen, *Muhammad, the Messenger of God: An Analysis of the Prophet's Life*, trans. by Ali Unal (New Jersey: Tughra Books, 2005). p. 315.

[210] Ibid.

this way one can update the content of the Prophetic Traditions. Gülen's works imply the unnecessary nature of focusing on classical definitions of Sunnah or spending time holding discussions on the issue. This is not mentioned in his writings or discourses, most probably out of his respect for the scholars from the early Muslim generations (*salaf*). Looking into the matter from an academic and relevancy perspective, engaging in classical terminology beyond the required level of knowledge would be considered a practice of repeating the existing knowledge rather than stimulating the mind and opening ways to new deductions and theories. This, in turn, may lead to a vicious circle of never-ending scholastic arguments. He primarily believes that satisfactory understanding of the essence of the matter that constitutes the basis for a given discipline of science would save scientific advancement from stagnancy. What is important for this is the willpower and mind to execute their share of tasks.[211] Gülen's thoughts on classical definitions of Sunnah may be read and evaluated along these lines. In other words, according to him, dealing with the essence of a matter is of prime importance.

On the basis of this criterion, according to Canan, in terms of the presentation of the theory and practice of Sunnah according to the needs of the present time, Gülen offers—besides established traditional definitions—certain differences and new approaches with a kind of richness.[212] In other words, being an eloquent and articulate speaker, Gülen introduced a finesse and sublimity into otherwise desiccated scholarly language. This approach of Gülen's may be interpreted as explaining the characteristics of Sunnah through different expressions, rather than providing a new self-contained definition. For instance, Gülen comes up with a rather elegant definition for Sunnah as follows:

> Sunnah is of divine origin and the second primary source in legis-
> lation, which has been accepted and safeguarded by the majority of
> Muslim scholars and referenced in all Islamic scholarly issues since
> the time of the Noble Prophet and his Companions.[213]

---

[211] Gülen, *Asrın Getirdiği Tereddütler*, Vol. 1*(Questions and Answers about Islam)* (Istanbul: Nil Publishing, 2011). p. 19.

[212] Canan, *Fethullah Gülen'in Sunnet Anlayisi.* p. 69.

[213] Gülen, *Sonsuz Nur, Vol. 2 (Muhammad, The Messenger of God)* (Istanbul: Nil Publishing, 2010), p. 382.

With this definition, Gülen puts vitality and vigor into the Sunnah, which has been subjected to suspicion and criticism during the last two centuries.[214] Thus, Gülen emancipates Hadith from the dullness of its classical scholarly definitions—without compromising or challenging established fundamental principles—and, emphasizing its functional aspect, strives for connecting Sunnah with the social sciences of our time and the educational and scientific data available. Making an Endeavour to determine Sunnah's position among other disciplines stands out in this approach. Instead of simply describing Sunnah as the words and deeds of the Noble Prophet, Gülen seeks to thoroughly analyze Sunnah, discover its scientific aspects concealed in its unseen dimension, and to establish a correlation with the modern era. Consequently, and by giving it a new perspective, he highlights the third dimension of Sunnah.

A more rigorous analysis of Gülen's definition yields a more effective and clearer understanding of inferences that have been explained so far. Gülen's atypical interpretations of certain hadiths represent a new aspect to definitions in, and contribution to, Hadith literature. While assigning future educators a mission, he invites them to ponder the following hadith: "People are like mines of gold and silver; those who were excellent in *Jahiliyyah* (during the Days of Ignorance) are [also] excellent in Islam, when they attain knowledge."[215] With the interpretation he brings to this hadith, Gülen advocates character analysis as an important factor and the first stage of human education, thus making a distinct contribution to education methods.[216] He articulates that human physiognomy reflects one's actual inner emotional and mental state, and calls for the development of individual education methods for different human moods. Although Gülen appears to provide a mere interpretation of a hadith, his interpretation of this specific hadith demonstrates his unique portrayal of the hadith with respect to understanding the human character.

By referring to the Noble Prophet's Companions in his definition, Gülen points to the Age of Bliss (*al-'Asr al-Sa'adah*)[217] and draws

---

[214] Canan, *Fethullah Gülen'in Sunnet Anlayisi*. pp. 65, 67.
[215] Bukhari, *Manaqib* 1; Muslim, *Birr* 160.
[216] Gülen, *Sonsuz Nur, Vol. 2 (Muhammad: The Messenger of God)*. p. 396.
[217] The Noble Prophet said: "The people of my generation are the best, then those who follow them, and then those who follow the latter..." Bukhari, *Shahadat*, 9; Muslim, *Fadhail al-Sahabah*, 214.

attention to the fact that the Sunnah has been taken care of with utmost sensitivity alongside the Qur'an ever since the gestation period of Islam. Furthermore, he stresses the attribute of '*adalah* (justice and uprightness) of the Companions. In doing so, he focuses upon the Prophetic Practice-Companions (*Sunnah-Sahabah*) correlations, and ultimately to the authenticity of Sunnah by pointing to the meticulousness of the Companions. Indeed, '*adalah* (justice and uprightness) is considered in Islamic literature as a distinguishing characteristic possessed by the Companions, their followers and the generation that followed them, meaning "justice and uprightness" in terms of transmitting the Sunnah to next generations without any corruption. Besides this, Gülen draws his audience's attention specifically to the Sunnah, which has been mentioned with confidence alongside the Qur'an, and its chain of transmission through the course of history.[218] It is almost impossible to deny the fact that Gülen from time to time prefers to use popular discourse rather than pure academic one. Thus, his reflection on the status of the Companions should be read in the light of this dual reading.

Gülen often supports his thoughts and views with quotations and anecdotes carefully selected from the time of the Companions and their successors. Similarly, when elaborating on Sunnah and its characteristics, his comments are substantiated through the use of examples from the same slice of history. When he needs to use the term "the vast majority of the scholars," he makes sure he illustrates it with an example from that particular era. For example:

> Anas ibn Sirin, from among the successors, mentions, "When I ar-
> rived in Kufah in the middle of the second century AH, there were ap-
> proximately 4,000 qualified Hadith students in Kufah mosques," and
> he reckons that about 400 of them were jurists.[219]

Taking into account the socio-cultural and economic conditions of the era, these figures could represent the substantial number of Hadith students and jurists in one town. Considering that the majority of these students travelled from other populated areas in search of knowledge,

---

[218] Canan, *Fethullah Gülen'in Sunnet Anlayisi*. p. 108.
[219] Gülen, *Sonsuz Nur, Vo. 2 (Muhammad: The Messenger of God)*. p. 498.

it shows the burden undertaken, the earnest commitment and the system employed for the study of Sunnah. While pointing to the care exercised when dealing with the Sunnah, Gülen again highlights the large number of students and teaching staff. Kufah was not the only center of education at that time; it is believed that there were other towns with similar capacities in the area. With this elucidation, Gülen strives to present Sunnah in a functional and interactive position within the society and, while emphasizing the confidence on Hadith collections, he draws attention to careful criticism.[220]

Besides these laborious presentations, Gülen also explains Sunnah within the contexts of positive sciences. Establishing various connections between Sunnah and physical sciences, he attempts to achieve an agreement between them. Accordingly, he rejects the problematic approach advocating "Sunnah is nothing more than a collection of advices exclusive to the morality and worship."[221] In this way, he attempts to prove that the Qur'an and the Sunnah are a comprehensive program of civilization that meets the needs of society. According to Gülen, Sunnah offers believers values and principles on matters such as law, education, economics, morality, politics, international relations, medicine, positive sciences and dress codes.[222] With this approach, he highlights the shortcomings of contemporary thinkers and researchers in their skepticism of Sunnah. He challenges thinkers and researchers to examine Sunnah in more detail, rather than merely accept its classical definitions. Considering his approaches, it is possible to say that Gülen looks into Sunnah from a different and pro-active perspective. What is different is Gülen's part in encouraging fresh approaches and contributions of new interpretations and understanding.

These kinds of interpretations reveal Gülen's definition of Sunnah. His tendency to turn to the core and the practical aspect of Sunnah reflects his views and mission, thereby distinguishing him from his contemporaries. For this reason, it can be said that, according to Gülen, the path to true existence goes through bringing together thought and action; in effect, thoughts and actions are conducive to the

---

[220] Canan, *Fethullah Gülen'in Sunnet Anlayisi.* p. 111.
[221] ibid.
[222] ibid. 112.

change and renewal of society in a positive sense.[223] This presents a new "Gülen theory." According to Gülen's systematic thought, presentation and content are just as important as the container when dealing with religious terminology. Although the container is directly related to what it contains, in most cases its content becomes more prominent.

In conclusion, Gülen approaches to the early Islamic scholars' definition of Sunnah as "words, actions and behaviors of the Noble Prophet" with respect. In essence, he is closely linked to the early Islamic scholars' classical definitions of Hadith; however, when it comes to the presentation, exemplification and explanation of Sunnah, he brings in some novelties with shades of richness in accordance with the conditions and practices of the contemporary times.[224] With this side of him, and in respect to defining the Sunnah, Gülen stands out among others, portraying an active man with strong beliefs who is intimately connected to his roots of moral values. Therefore, he conceptualizes the social and individual fabrics he is weaving as Sunnah-centered structures, and in doing so, he takes Sunnah as his guidance. More particularly, he emphasizes the very values Sunnah contributes to the social structure and reform.

Gülen believes that his thesis of making Sunnah functional and applying it to all spheres of life will result in the whole society being turned into a school environment, and that all modern technical facilities, such as the internet and mass-media, will assume the functionality of knowledge centers.[225] Thus, society will become integrated with its material and moral cultural values. According to Gülen's thought, this is the reunification of the Muslim community—which harbors respect for the Sunnah—with its societal and historical dynamics. At this point, practical Sunnah's function is substantial. The conclusion derived from Gülen's focus on Sunnah in his works and his interpretations is that defining and interpreting the Sunnah in accordance with the perception, style and understanding of the modern era—but always strictly following the rules and bounding with the reasoning (*ijtihad*) of the very well-established traditions—

---

[223] Unal, *M. Fethullah Gülen: Bir Portre Denemesi*, pp. 173-174.
[224] Canan, *Fethullah Gülen'in Sunnet Anlayisi*. p. 69.
[225] Unal, *M. Fethullah Gülen: Bir Portre Denemesi*, p, 175.

is a necessity and responsibility resting on the shoulders of today's Muslims toward future generations.[226]

The Evolution of Hadith and the Other Disciplines According to Gülen

Hadith and Sunnah enjoy considerable importance and effect in Gülen's works. It stands to reason that he must have carefully studied the overall authenticity and reliability of this system, which he has accepted as a basis for his own faith. It is paramount for him to ensure that Sunnah has been safeguarded from errors and tampering, and transmitted to current times in a condition as pure and authentic as possible. Sunnah, according to his view, is one of the two fundamental primary sources of Islam next to the Qur'an, and it is impossible to establish the foundation of Islam without Hadith and Sunnah.[227] He is convinced that the conditions required for establishing the safeguarding and health of Sunnah must be as sound and prudent as the prerequisites for safeguarding the Qur'an. Indeed, Gülen's systematic thought has been shaped by the following hadith shedding light on the issue:

> The best word is the Word of God (Qur'an); the best guidance is the guidance of Muhammad (Sunnah). The most evil of deeds are *bid'ah* (innovations in religion, which are "deviations from Sunnah"). And every *bid'ah* is *dalalah* (deviation).[228]

So, this well-known hadith constitutes the basic starting point of his occupation with the science of Hadith.[229] Gülen established his own rectified criteria to determine the reliability of Hadith, according to which he supports his arguments with references from classical Hadith sources. In fact, to express a view or defend or prove a hypothesis, he derives his paradigms from Sunnah. Highlighting the particular hadith stating, "God likes that when you do anything, you do it excellently,"[230] suggests

---

[226] M. Fethullah Gülen, *Ruhumuzun Heykelini Dikerken (The Statue of Our Souls)*, (Istanbul: Nil Publishing, 2011). pp. 67-68.

[227] Gülen, *Sonsuz Nur, Vol. 2 (Muhammad: The Messenger of God)*. p. 591.

[228] Muslim, *Jumu'a*, 43; Nasai, *Iydayn*, 22; Ibn Maja, *Muqaddimah*, 7.

[229] Gülen, *Sonsuz Nur Vol. 2 (Muhammad: The Messenger of God)*, p. 591.

[230] bu Ya'la, *Musnad*, 7/349; Tabarani, *al-Mu'jam al-Awsat*, 1/275.

Gülen takes it as his guidance in Hadith and other scientific studies.[231] Ensuring all details and sound supportive material, when focusing on a study subject, is the basis of his work principles. Therefore, and in light of the depth of his knowledge in Hadith disciplines, his interpretation of the part of the above hadith "the most evil of deeds" as "deviation from Sunnah" and "increase in innovations" should be considered normal.[232] Starting from this point would normally lead one to a conclusion that he must be a very keen student of Hadith and would take a very cautious approach when investigating the soundness of a tradition. For the above hadith and those others that follow it, which are carefully selected for his works, reflect a strong emphasis on the seriousness of the matter.[233] His way of selecting hadiths reveals lessons and responsibilities he derived from Sunnah. While discharging his responsibilities, Gülen confirms the authenticity of Sunnah, and at the same time, establishes his belief and theories on solid foundations. Otherwise, the possibility of Sunnah being unreliable—considering he founded his belief, thoughts and actions upon Sunnah—would put him face to face with a very awkward situation in his next steps and render his faith very problematic. Defending a theory, project or his actions on the basis of a doubtful source of reference could leave him facing many questions and criticisms. Ultimately, Gülen would be questioned about his understanding of Sunnah, which is his source of inspiration and starting point at individual, social and civilizational levels. Therefore, in his view, this source—which is the foundation of the faith of a community—must be freed from all doubts and the structural soundness of the discipline of Hadith methodology—which is instrumental in transmitting this valuable source to our time—must be confirmed.

Gülen considers following the Sunnah and referencing all his thoughts and actions on Sunnah as an "action."[234] He focuses his intellectual approach on Sunnah-based scholarly and scientific research for, according to him, religion and science always coexisted all along the

---

[231] Gülen, *Sonsuz Nur Vol. 2 (Muhammad: The Messenger of God)*, p. 71.
[232] ibid. pp. 591-594
[233] ibid.
[234] Unal, *M. Fethullah Gülen: Bir Portre Denemesi (M. Fethullah Gülen: A Portrait Essay)*, p. 175.

history of Islam and never collided.[235] Religion and genuine science are the two faces of the truth; religion has been fundamental for science to achieve its objective.[236] As he considers Sunnah the purpose of his life,[237] which also shapes his thoughts, it is only by nature that he adopts Sunnah as a way of life and occupies himself with its soundness and reliability. Therefore, it is inconceivable to imagine Gülen uninterested and keeping himself aloof from the science of Hadith.

Gülen underlines the fact that the early generations of Islam closely followed and benefitted from the scientific progress of their own age while strictly adhering to the Qur'an and the Sunnah. This may be one reason that he often mentions in his works the strenuous efforts exerted by theologians, jurists and scholars of Hadith with regard to recording and safeguarding Sunnah during the times of the Companions, successors and followers of the successors. Therefore, Gülen closely following the Sunnah in such a way discloses some ideas about his sensitivities concerning the discipline of Hadith. Glancing at his views on Hadith science one detects a new perspective in his understanding and interpretation of the discipline.[238] He usually illustrates through anecdotes the early Islamic scholars' works on authentication and codification of hadiths. He studies the meticulousness and practices of the pious predecessors (*salaf*), and finds them healthy and reasonable. Therefore, he does not criticize their applied principles; he does not consider modifying or rejecting them.[239] He is confident that the methodology they developed is reliable although it can be taken further by modern scholarly approaches. He affirms that Sunnah has been—beyond any doubt—recorded, memorized, codified and safeguarded by critical researchers and transmitted to current times since the early days of Islam.[240]

It is necessary to make a brief evaluation of one of the disciplines of Islamic sciences, *'Usul al-Fiqh* (Methodology of Islamic Jurisprudence). According to Islamic sources, *'Usul al-Fiqh* is directly related to the

---

[235] Gülen, *Vuslat Mustusu (Glad Tidings of a Reunion)*, Kirik Testi series, Vol. 8, (Istanbul: Nil Publishing, 2011), p. 202.

[236] Gülen, *Olcu Ve Yoldaki Isiklar (Pearls of Wisdom)* (Istanbul: Nil Publishing, 2011), p. 31.

[237] Latif Erdogan, *Fethullah Gülen Hocaefendi: Kucuk Dunyam (Fethullah Gulen: My Small World)*, (Istanbul: Ufuk Publishing, 2006), p. 45.

[238] Canan, *Fethullah Gülen'in Sunnet Anlayisi*, p. 69.

[239] ibid.

[240] Gülen, *Sonsuz Nur Vol. 2 (Muhammad: The Messenger of God)*, p. 522.

discipline of Hadith. A closer look at Gülen's views about the status of these two disciplines reveals his thoroughness about the discipline of Hadith. For instance, in spite of his deep respect for early Islamic scholars, Gülen maintains the necessity of revising the discipline of *'Usul al-Fiqh*, which involves the scanning of all collected works produced in the past and, ultimately, formulating a new, alternative methodology. He elaborates the necessity of a diligent process of sifting and rearranging all *fiqh* topics—excluding those related to worship—according to the needs of the day. He argues that legal opinions based on customs may be archaic or outdated and no longer relevant to contemporary time. Such legal opinions should be judiciously reviewed by a committee of experts equipped with updated knowledge of the current socio-economic situation. By his statement, "[I]t is important to emphasize once more that all these activities must be executed by an expert committee," Gülen demonstrates his persistence and sensitivity on this issue.[241]

While Gülen exhibits such diligence on the revision of the *fiqh* discipline, what is his standing on Hadith methodology? According to Canan, Gülen does not think that a revision of Hadith methodology is necessary[242] because Hadith literature is generally devoid of juridical issues and free from legal opinions, customs and practices that can be changed according to various influences over time. Zaheed al-Kawthari, argues that early Islamic scholars' evaluations on Hadith deserve to be respected, and says:

> Hadith discipline does not deal with events and issues—as in the *fiqh* discipline—that will keep arising as civilizations progress to the Day of Judgment. Therefore, scholars of Hadith do not need to make *ijti-had* on hadiths. All they need to do is memories and safeguard traditions transmitted from *salaf*.[243]

According to Canan, Gülen's views are similar to Zaheed al-Kawthari's views. Gülen does not see any requirement relevant to the discipline of Hadith, like al-Kawthari. In fact, Gülen's works bear no trace of such a

---

[241] Gülen, *Fasildan Fasila, Vol. 4 (From Chapter to Chapter)* (Istanbul: Nil Publishing, 2001), pp. 140-141.
[242] Canan, *Fethullah Gülen'in Sunnet Anlayisi*, p. 69.
[243] Zaheed al-Kawthari, *Shurut al-A'immah al-Khamsah*, p. 118.

view on Hadith methodology. Gülen affirms that, consistent with Islamic literature, scholarly efforts have continued in succession beginning from the time of the Prophet. The crux of the matter is an unbroken line of recording (technically, an *isnad*), preserving and transmitting hadiths safely to the future. There is no mentioning of verdicts, legal opinions or any other requirements.[244] This confirms that no need has arisen for such scholarly efforts. What is needed from this point onward is to safeguard and disseminate hadiths as much as the available facilities permit.[245] Clearly, for Gülen, Hadith scholars are like pharmacists whereas the jurists are doctors, thus they have the final word for ijtihad on the basis of the curative work done by the pharmacists.

An important point relevant to this matter needs to be mentioned: Hadith is a fundamental source of reference in Islamic jurisprudence, and indeed, its reliability has been a subject of careful study for jurists as well. Legal rulings based on Hadith—which is directly correlated with the Qur'an—constitute a valuable source for Islamic sciences. A jurist involved with this process is a scholar who can use the Qur'an, the Sunnah and the consensus of scholars (*Ijma'*) as sources of reference, and who has the aptitude to deduce religious verdicts from these sources.[246] In other words, there is another class of scholars called "fuqaha" (jurists), who are engaged in Hadith discipline besides the scholars of Hadith. For jurists, the basis for legal rulings is the authentic Sunnah, which is free from any doubt.[247] Otherwise, legitimacy of the verdicts would be under doubt and suspicion. According to Muslim scholars, transactions cannot be based on lies and presumptions, but rather are based on evidence.[248] Lies and presumptions are prohibited by the Qur'an.[249] Given Gülen's perspective, a jurist must know very

---

[244] Gülen, *Sonsuz Nur Vol. 2 (Muhammad: The Messenger of God)*, pp. 518-519.

[245] Gülen, *Yenilenme Cehdi (Endeavor for Renewal), Kirik Testi series, Vol. 12*, (Istanbul: Nil Publishing, 2012), p. 238.

[246] Gülen, *Sonsuz Nur Vol. 2 (Muhammad: The Messenger of God)*, p. 499.

[247] Gülen, *Fikir Atlasi (The Atlas of Ideas)* (Istanbul: Nil Publishing, 2006), p. 140.

[248] ibid.

[249] *O you who believe! Avoid much suspicion, for some suspicion is a grave sin (liable to God's punishment); and do not spy (on one another), nor backbite (against one another). Would any of you love to eat the flesh of his dead brother? You would abhor it! Keep from disobedience to God in reverence for Him and piety. Surely God is One Who truly returns repentance with liberal forgiveness and additional reward, All-Compassionate (particularly towards His believing servants)"* (Qur'an 49:12).

well the particular hadith that he accepts as a basis for a legal ruling, must be convinced about its authenticity and possess the qualities of a Hadith scholar. This is the reason why, in Islamic literature, the criteria that qualifies jurists are the same as the prerequisites for scholars of Hadith. Gülen draws attention to the criteria employed by early Islamic scholars in the qualification of expert jurists and Hadith scholars in the discipline of Hadith, and recognizes their discretions and assessments.[250] According to the early Islamic scholars' criteria, Imam al-A'zam Abu Hanifah (d. 772 CE), Imam Abu Yusuf (d. 798 CE), Imam Muhammad (d. 805 CE), Imam Shafi'i (d. 820 CE) and Imam Malik (d. 795 CE) are all recognized as *fuqaha'*. However, the same cannot be said as easily for Ahmad ibn Hanbal (d. 855 CE),[251] who memorized almost one million hadiths. Abu Ja'far al-Tabari (d. 923 CE)[252] has been criticized by Hanbelites when he said, "Ahmad ibn Hanbal was not a jurist." By saying, "Whether Ahmad ibn Hanbal is a jurist or not, with this statement, al-Tabari is trying to explain to us a reality about the conditions and seriousness of being a jurist,"[253] Gülen points to the seriousness of erudition and reliability of Islamic sciences during that period of time in the history of Islam. According to Gülen, the criteria for qualifying as a jurist are very stringent. Satisfying these criteria and having one's views and legal opinions recognized by other Muslim scholars is a serious stage to accomplish. A very well-known figure like Ahmad ibn Hanbal has been criticized on the basis of traditions he transmitted according to these criteria. Ibn al-Jawzi (d. 1201 CE)—even though Ahmad ibn Hanbal was his imam in the Hanbali School of Thought—conceded that numerous hadiths mentioned in his *Musnad* were either *mawdu'* (fabricated, false), *da'if* (weak) or *matruk* (disregarded).[254] However, Ibn Hajar al-Asqalani (d. 1449 CE) re-examined all the traditions Ibn al-Jawzi found defective, and declared them all sound and healthy, except

---

[250] Gülen, *Sonsuz Nur Vol. 2 (Muhammad: The Messenger of God)*, pp. 499-500.
[251] Ahmed ibn Hanbal (d. 780/855) was born and died in Baghdad. He is reported to have memorised one million hadith. He was a student of Imam al-Shafi'i. His famous work, *Al-Musnad*, contains forty thousand *hadith*. He is the founder of the Hanbelite School of Thought.
[252] Abu Ja'far Muhammad ibn Jarir al-Tabari (838/923 CE) was an Islamic scholar. His most influential and best known work is the Quranic commentary known as *Tafsir al-Tabari*.
[253] Gülen, *Sonsuz Nur Vol. 2 (Muhammad: The Messenger of God)*, p. 499.
[254] ibid. 467.

13 of them. He mentions these 13 traditions in his work, titled *al-Qawl al-Musaddad fi Musnad Ahmad.*[255] In the light of these examples Gülen used as sources of reference in his work, the science of Hadith and other related disciplines have been kept under stringent scrutiny despite the severe conditions of the era.[256] Perhaps, he endeavors to justify firstly his own disposition and then convince his audience. With this approach, Gülen does not only re-examine and justify the soundness of the hadiths he uses, but also draws attention to the reality of Sunnah. According to Gülen's rationale, these events that happened in history constitute evidence to the factuality and recording of the subjects to which they relate. On the other hand, proving the opposite can only be possible by disproving the existence of these historical events, and the onus is on the opponents to prove their case.

Gülen does not limit himself with only textual study of Prophetic Traditions, but also pays serious attention to the linguistic excellence of the text, from which he derives conclusions. For example, he mentions about a famous pre and Islamic woman poet al-Hansa (d. 645 CE), who possessed such a high level of linguistic proficiency that she could detect eight mistakes in a four-verse poem spoken by well-known poet of the Noble Prophet, Hassan ibn Thabit (d. 674 CE).[257] With this example, Gülen emphasizes the linguistic adeptness of the Companions.[258]

Evaluating from a scholarly perspective, each one of these events can be no more than a *khabar al-wahid* ("single person's report") as they were related only by one single authority. However, in Gülen's mind, when their numbers reach certain levels, they gain a quasi-kind of *mutawatir* (successive narration) status from a contextual point of view. At this juncture, Gülen's rationale appears to be in perfect conformity with the principles defining *mutawatir* hadith in Islamic literature. What is also understood from the above assessments is that Gülen has no doubt about the level of expertise of the Companions and the succeeding generation

---

[255] Ibn Hajar, *al-Qawl al-musaddad fi al-dhabb 'an al-Musnad li al-Imam Ahmad*, 1-45.

[256] Gülen, *Sonsuz Nur Vol. 2 (Muhammad: The Messenger of God)*, pp. 467-468.

[257] Hassan ibn Thabit used his poetic talents in the service of his faith. The Noble Prophet once told him, "O Hassan, reply on behalf of God's Messenge" and then prayed for him saying, "O God, support him with *Ruh al-Quds* (Holy Spirit)!" (Bukhari, *Salat*, 68; Muslim, *Fadha'il al-Sahabah*, 151–152).

[258] Gülen, *Sonsuz Nur Vol. 2 (Muhammad: The Messenger of God)*, p. 502.

as well as the scholars of Hadith to determine whether a text was a hadith or not. Companions with these qualities have become role models for future generations, thus leading the way for the emergence of scholars of Hadith with similar expertise and meticulousness. Hence, when people asked, "Fabricated hadiths are widespread [in Muslim world]; what are we going to do [about it]?" 'Abdu'llah ibn Mubarak (d. 181 CE)[259] calmly answered: "No need to panic; to counter that [threat], we have experts to distinguish the authentic hadiths from the fabricated ones."[260] According to Gülen, the scholars of Hadith with such a degree of expertise certainly attained the capability to detect the divine connotation enshrined in an authentic narration, and approve it—even before examining its chain of transmission—or to sense the contradiction in a fabricated saying that is reported as hadith and reject it.[261]

Gülen's insistence on convincing his interlocutor in this regard drives the course of the discussion to different dimensions, and naturally, necessitates more relevant examples to illustrate his point. By bringing examples from the Turkish-Islamic and world literature, he endeavors to bring the issue closer to mind, makes comparisons and puts forward some rational and logical arguments. This is another point demonstrating his confidence in his own views and convictions as well as in his sources of reference. A person who repeatedly read great figures such as Dante (d. 1321), Shakespeare (d. 1616), Molière (d. 1673) and Tolstoy (d. 1910) from world literature, and similarly, Mehmet Akif Ersoy (d. 1936), Nurettin Topcu (d. 1975), Necip Fazil Kisakurek (d. 1983), and Sezai Karakoc (b. 1933) from Turkish-Islamic literature, and who thoroughly studied them, can easily and safely distinguish their words and texts from among piles of other texts. This is possible because of variations in writing style or penmanship. According to Gülen, if this is the situation in literature, the case of Hadith scholars—who are experts in Arabic language, have dedicated

---

[259] Abdullah ibn Mubarak (736/797) was from among the *Taba' al-Tabi'in* (the third generation that followed the successors of the Companions). His full name is 'Abd Allah ibn Mubarak ibn Wadih Hanzali Tamimi; his *kunyah* is Abu 'Abd al-Rahman. He was a scholar of *hadith* and *fiqh*. He was born in Marw during the time of the Umayyad Caliph Hisham ibn 'Abd al-Malik and died in a place called Hit near Baghdad.

[260] Canan, *Fethullah Gülen'in Sünnet Anlayışı*, p. 85.

[261] For further information, see Babanzade, *Tajrid*, 1, 283.

their lives to the study of Hadith and are so closely associated with Sunnah round-the-clock—would not be any different. As they are continually engaged in the Sunnah of the Noble Prophet, they have developed the aptitude to tell if it is a Prophetic Tradition or not as soon as they start uttering the words of a narration.[262] Looking from the perspective of these qualities, it is safe to assume that early Islamic scholars were masters of speech and judges of vocabulary. In addition, Gülen, in contrast to many modern Muslim and non-Muslim critics of Hadith, offers textual analysis rather than limiting himself to the traditionally applied criticism of the chain of *isnad*. Gülen also believes that there were some individual Muslims in the early and classical period of Islam who displayed a similar approach. For example, if Ahmad ibn Muhammad al-Tahawi (d. 933 CE) had appeared in one of the locations where Hadith literature developed, he would have been recognized as more eminent than Imam Bukhari. He was able to sort flimsy words from sound ones, evaluate hadiths and work comfortably like an artisan in this discipline.[263] Evaluating the Companions and their successors in light of Gülen's explanations infers the conclusion they were closely associated with and strictly adhered to the Noble Prophet and his message.

During that period where the language factor was so prominent, narrating a tradition in its original wording represented a different significance. Gülen draws attention to the strict adherence to narration criteria when reciting or discussing a tradition, although reporting a hadith in meaning only instead of its complete original text is permissible. With this approach, he demonstrates his respect and adherence to the views of early Islamic scholars. When discussing the Companions' strictness in this issue, he brings anecdotes from the early period of Islam to clarify the subject.[264] As recorded in Bukhari, the Noble Prophet's Companion al-Bara' ibn 'Azib (d. 690 CE) narrates:

> God's Messenger said to me, "When you want to go to bed, perform ablution as you do for the Prayers, then lie down on your right side

---

[262] Gülen, *Sonsuz Nur, Vol. 2. (Muhammad: The Messenger of God)*, p. 463.

[263] Gülen, *Fasildan Fasila, Vol. 3 (From Chapter to Chapter)* (Istanbul: Nil Publishing, 2011), pp. 205-206.

[264] Gülen, *Sonsuz Nur, Vol. 2 (Muhammad: The Messenger of God)*, pp. 450-451.

and say: (…)" While I was trying to memories it, I repeated it saying, "….in Your Messenger whom You have sent." The Messenger said, "No, but say: 'in Your Prophet whom You have sent.'"[265]

As can be seen in this example, the Noble Prophet—for a reason we can sense intuitively or not—reminds his Companion that he should memorize it verbatim and say "Prophet" instead of "Messenger," and thus sets up a criterion through this narration.[266] Here, at first glance, Gülen may seem to follow a literalist approach. However, to have a clearer picture of the matter, it is useful to pay careful attention to Gülen's academic sensitivities. A closer look at his life story and the whole corpus of his works reveals that his main objective is not literalism, but a burning desire to quest more deeply for the wisdom behind the Prophet's statement, which is of prime importance for him from a theological perspective. In other words, he generally endeavors to penetrate to the deeper meaning by concentrating his focus on the literal meaning. With the word *Nabi* (Prophet), which is mentioned in the above hadith, he denotes its meanings, such as "explanation," "spreading" and "applying/practicing." In this fashion, he presents to his interlocutor lessons that can be taken from Sunnah and practicable injunctions, and emphatically highlights his views on the practical aspect of Sunnah.

According to Gülen, verbatim reporting of the Prophetic Traditions—the way the Companions and their successors reported from the Noble Prophet with their utmost attention and accuracy—constitutes an important principle in the discipline of Hadith. Due to this normative formation, great scholars of Hadith—who paid maximum attention to the nuances in the meanings of words and to textual variations in hadiths—were brought up during later periods, thus resulting in the emergence of the great tradition of *al-rihlah* ("journeying in the pursuit of knowledge").

Gülen also mentions in his works certain principles established by the early generation scholars concerning the narration of hadith by meaning and considers the rationality behind it as permissible.[267] While

---

[265] Bukhari, *Daawat*, 6.
[266] Gülen, *Sonsuz Nur, Vol. 2 (Muhammad: The Messenger of God)*, p. 451.
[267] ibid. 505.

approving this *salaf* method, he draws attention to certain qualities of the narrator, which are also recognized by scholars. He deliberates on qualities such as the narrator's perfect command of the Arabic language, a sound understanding of the full meaning of the hadith, and particularly the choice of word to correspond to the whole context of the word in the original text to such an extent that Hadith experts should not be able to detect any deviation in the meaning. Furthermore, he justifies this method of narration only in a particular situation where the original text of the hadith is lost in its entirety. In accordance with a famous word of wisdom, "A thing cannot be abandoned altogether just because some parts thereof are missing," he advocates benefiting from Sunnah as much as possible.[268] While establishing Hadith on a solid ground—on the basis of these criteria—he acts persistently and cautiously to eliminate any chance of even a smallest part of the hadith being lost.

At this point, it is relevant to highlight another characteristic of Gülen's aptitude in interpreting the narration of hadiths by meaning. Narrating a hadith by meaning is a serious task that requires expertise: competence in Arabic language as much as to be able to differentiate between words that are fully or partly synonymous and competence in Hadith narration, including all details, are the two fundamental requirements. Canan asserts that Gülen possesses these linguistic requirements and presents as supporting evidence the major part of Gülen's prolific works being based on Hadith and Sunnah.[269]

Another important factor in the Hadith discipline is the discussion and testing of traditions thoroughly in terms of chain of transmission and text. As discussed earlier in this work, a hadith has two main parts: *sanad* (the chain of transmitters) and *matn* (the text narrated). The number of transmitters varies from only a few names to some very long chains.[270] In Islamic literature, it is not a healthy approach to speculate doubts about Prophetic Traditions that have been filtered through these criteria and authenticated during the time of the Companions and the period of *salaf* that followed. Considering the case of an authentic tradition, various famous scholars of Hadith reached

---

[268] ibid. pp. 505-506.
[269] Canan, *Fethullah Gülen'in Sünnet Anlayışı*, p. 115.
[270] Calis, *Mastering Knowledge in Modern Times: Fethullah Gülen as an Islamic Scholar.*

the same hadith through different methods and chains of transmission, and had the opportunity to closely examine it for elements that could weaken or injure its authenticity, thus conducting their assessments based on solid justifications. In a way, through academic discussions, they established the identity of the hadith with the Noble Prophet at its roots. Yahya ibn Ma'in (d. 847 CE) clarifies the rationale of this discussion and examination, saying, "We cannot recognize a hadith unless we write it down [at least] fifty times."[271] By virtue of this situation, Ibn Salah (d. 1245 CE), who is considered the founding father of Usul al-Hadith discipline, argued that what was established by the early Islamic scholars concerning the authenticity of a hadith is not permissible to be changed by scholars of later periods.[272] Gülen sees these principles and criteria reasonable, and he acts in accordance with these views regarding following the *salaf*. He also acknowledges the mutual discussion method as a determining factor in the discipline of Hadith. On this issue, he bases his views on the advice given by Abu Sa'id al-Khudri and Ibn 'Abbas to their students: "Memories these hadiths and discuss among yourselves. For some of them will remind you some others. Therefore, you must continuously discuss them among yourselves."[273]

In Islamic literature, the term *al-rihlah* constitutes an important factor with regard to safeguarding the authenticity of Sunnah and its reliable reporting, and has been a subject of serious study in the course of history. *Al-rihlah* is a term denoting a laborious long-distance journey in the pursuit of seeking knowledge to study and confirm the authenticity of hadiths directly from those well-versed narrators during the time of the Companions and centuries that followed. It can also be described as a difficult and painstaking scholarly sensitivity that can give clues about the source, health and method of the narration of Sunnah.[274] According to Gülen, focusing only on this particular term and thoroughness in narrations may lead the way to the emergence of healthy views about Sunnah.

In the course of history, the method represented by this Islamic term can be observed constituting an example for other disciplines in the

---

[271] Al-Dhahabi, *Tadhkirat al-Huffaz*, 2/420.
[272] Ibn Salah, *Mukaddima*, 11–12.
[273] Gülen, *Sonsuz Nur, Vol. 2 (Muhammad: The Messenger of God)*, p. 451.
[274] ibid., p. 455.

Islamic world, such as experimental sciences, medicine, mathematics, literature and philosophy.[275] This lead, in time, to the development of various higher education institutions (*madrasas*) and other education centers in numerous locations, and ultimately, lead the way to increasing research, new discoveries and rapid spread of knowledge to different places, thus laying the foundation for the promotion of learning.[276] Furthermore, it is possible to say it has resulted in inter-civilizational relations in sciences as well as exchange of thoughts and views in the field of philosophy. Gülen presents his views to his interlocutor through the words of a famous Western thinker, Saint Martin, who stated: "Ripe fruits are falling on the West, but the roots of the tree are in Asia,"[277] to highlight all this.

In the discipline of Hadith, establishing the authenticity of every tradition, tracing its chain of transmission back to the Noble Prophet, investigating the narrator's qualities in terms of justice and memory, and verifying its text so strictly to the point where one can see if a single letter has been used in a different position are considered the main principles of *al-rihlah*. The aim of this stringent process is to establish the continuity of the chain of transmission through the second Muslim generation and the Companions back to the Noble Prophet. There are some examples in this regard. Gülen illustrates the phenomena of *al-rihlah* through certain anecdotes he chooses from the time of the Companions and their successors. He affirms that the Companions showed care and solicitude to such an extent that they organized journeys to distant places (*al-rihlah*) to authenticate even one single hadith.[278] As narrated by 'Ata' ibn Abi Rabah (d. 732 CE), a jurist from among the successors, Abu Ayyub al-Ansari (d. 674 CE) travelled to Egypt, where 'Uqbah ibn 'Amir (d. 677 or 678 CE) was living, to investigate the original of a hadith. Immediately after verifying its authenticity, he said, "This was the reason why I came here" and returned home. Gülen emphasizes that, although Abu Ayyub al-Ansari already knew very well that the hadith affirms: "Whosoever

---

[275] Gülen, *Kalb İbresi: Kirik Testi series, Vol. 9, (The Heart's Cursor)* (Istanbul: Nil Publishing, 2010), p. 245.

[276] ibid., pp. 243, 244.

[277] *Gülen, İnsanın Özündeki Sevgi,* (Toward a Global Civilization of Love and Tolerance) O. Faruk Tuncer, (ed.) (Istanbul: Ufuk Publishing, 2004), p. 241.

[278] Gülen, *Sonsuz Nur, Vol. 2 (Muhammad: The Messenger of God),* pp. 455-456.

covers (the sins of) a Muslim, God covers (his or her sins) on the Day of Judgment,"[279] he wanted to remove doubts and verify its authenticity with 'Uqbah ibn 'Amir who was the only Companion who had heard the hadith directly from the Noble Prophet. This was the hadith Abu Ayyub al-Ansari already knew—and he knew it well—however, 'Uqbah ibn 'Amir was the only living Companion, in his town, who had heard it directly from the Noble Prophet; he travelled to confirm its soundness.[280] Gülen usually handles issues broadly, bringing detailed accounts of events from the time of the Companions and their successors to support his views.

This is a method Gülen often employs to persuade his readers. Gülen persistently makes use of historical literature to place emphasis on the importance of and precision in the collection of hadiths. By doing so, he confirms and strengthens his own ideas with similar ones put forward in history while allowing the reader to watch the enlivening of past cases in today's society. According to documented sources, it is known that scholars from among the successors of the Companions also traced the Companions' path, and practiced *al-rihlah* to investigate with other Companions a hadith they come across. Abu al-'Aliyah, from among the successors, says that wherever—be it in Basra, Baghdad, Khorasan or Transoxania—they hear something from the Companions, they would not confine themselves to only one Companion, and would travel to Mecca and Medina to confirm it through other Companions,[281] and only then would feel confident about the health of that hadith.[282] *Al-rihlah* has been practiced under challenging conditions and in all times as a general principle for reaching the truth in the discipline of Hadith, and

[279] Ahmad ibn Hanbal, *al-Musnad*, 4/153, 159; Humaydi, *al-Musnad*, 1/189.
[280] Gülen, *Sonsuz Nur, Vol. 2 (Muhammad: The Messenger of God)*, p. 455. There are also other related anecdotes which are mentioned by Gülen. He presents this event, reported by Bukhari, as evidence to support his views: Jabir ibn 'Abd Allah, from among *Ansar* (Helpers), takes on a journey of one whole month to hear a *hadith* directly from its narrator, 'Abd Allah ibn Unays. Saying, "I come to know that you narrated a *hadith*, which I did not hear directly from the Prophet. I come to you because of the fear of one of us could die before I hear it from you," he receives the *hadith* from 'Abd Allah ibn Unays and returns to Medina. (Ahmad ibn Hanbal, *al-Musnad*, III.495; Bukhari, *al-Adab al-Mufrad*, 337, Hakim, *al-Mustadraq*, II.475).
[281] Darimi, *Muqaddimah*, 47; Ibn Sa'd, *al-Tabaqat al-Kubra*, 7/113; Hatib al-Baghdadi, *al-Rihlah fi Talab al-Hadith*, s.93; Ibn 'Abd al-Barr, *al-Tamhid*, 1/56.
[282] Gülen, *Sonsuz Nur, Vol. 2 (Muhammad: The Messenger of God)*, p. 457.

has been instrumental in producing sound results and development of sciences. This point, which is often mentioned with confidence in Islamic literature, has been confirmed and taken its place in historical documents.

Another essential principle in Hadith literature is the justice (*'adl*) characteristic of narrators. Some of the important factors that can injure or destroy this attribute are: narrator's loss of memory and witnessing them utter a word of untruth, even if it is only once in their life. Gülen accepts this method as an important criterion in transmitting hadiths and deals with it in a bright style in his works. This is a narrative style he adds to the subject.

Gülen explains that liars are well pursued and identified, and no hadith would ever be accepted from one who was detected lying, even only once in their life, or from one who made a deliberate mistake. Furthermore, no hadith would be reported from someone who has fallen into suspicion, even if they were once considered a trustworthy (*thiqah*) narrator.[283] Gülen is concerned that even the smallest deviation from the center would evolve into a more serious aberration as it moves toward the periphery. He asserts that mistakes on narratives have been thoroughly taken care of since the time of the Companions, and any minor fault in a narrator was considered a reason for the rejection of the hadith(s) they reported. In case of the hadith being supported by another hadith, the particular narrator was excluded from the chain of transmission. Gülen illustrates this view through an example from Abu Dawud: Ibn Abi Lahi'ah (d. 709 CE), whose name has been frequently mentioned in his *Sunan*, used to narrate from his books and not from his memory. However, he lost his trustworthiness in Hadith narration after his books were lost. For this reason, receiving narrations from him were linked to strict criteria. For example, Imam Bukhari accepted and recorded from him only narrations supported by other reports and legal rulings.[284] What is understood from Gülen's approach is the narrator's safeguarding of his qualifications for Hadith transmission which comes before his private

---

[283] ibid., pp. 462, 463.
[284] ibid., p. 463.

personality. According to him, sensitivities and disciplines need to be put in place properly. He argues that leading figures in Hadith discipline, such as Amir ibn Sharahil al-Sha'bi (d. 721 CE), Ibn Sirin (d. 728 CE), Qatadah ibn Di'amah (d. 736 CE), Ibn Shihab al-Zuhri (d. 742 CE), Sufyan al-Sawri (d. 778 CE), 'Ibrahim ibn Yazid al-Nakha'i (d. 714 CE), Hisham al-Dastawa'i (d. 771 CE) and Mith'ar ibn Qudam (nd), acted like morality police in the pursuit of those who told any word of untruth. He also maintains that these personalities used to closely follow those infected with ethnic, religious and ideological bigotry for their possible lies and ask, "Who did you hear this hadith from?"[285]

These examples given by Gülen clearly demonstrate he is a faithful follower of the early Islamic scholars in the discipline of Hadith. The reason for his selection of hadiths, especially from the time of the Companions, when defending his views indicates his enthusiasm to emphasize Hadith literature reaching our time without interruption and corruption. In this way, he also highlights the efficacy of the established criteria in Hadith discipline. It is important to pay attention to the two aspects of Gülen giving hadith examples directly from the Companions: one is regarding the Sunnah and the other regarding the Companions. With regard to safeguarding Sunnah, Gülen brings to the forefront the Companions of the Noble Prophet, and explains with anecdotes their endeavors and determination in this regard. In other words, he secures the safety of Hadith and elevates the institution of Sunnah on their shoulders while protecting the integrity of the Companions in relation to Hadith and Sunnah. In Islamic literature, there are many traditions reported from the Noble Prophet elevating the value and status of the Companions.[286] They are presented by the Noble Prophet, in terms of social values, as a community to be emulated[287] and imitated. The great love and respect Gülen harbors for the Noble Prophet and his Companions is clearly manifested here.

---

[285] ibid., p. 459.

[286] "The people of my generation are the best, then those who follow them, and then those who follow the latter..." (Bukhari, *Shahadat*, 9; Muslim, *Fadhail al-Sahabah*, 214).

[287] "My Companions are like the stars, whomever of them you follow, you shall be guided." (*Faidh al-Qadir*, 4,76; *Jami' al-Bayan al-Ilm*, 2/91).

Gülen's methodology in terms of Hadith and biographies is not only pragmatic but also logical in the sense of directing his interlocutor to deep philosophical thinking. He presents a chunk of historical events with a series of illustrative examples and anecdotes, highlights the necessity of pondering on and reconsidering these events, and demonstrates this, saying, "an accumulation [of knowledge] verified and represented by tens of thousands of great scholars in every period of time."[288] While propelling his students to read and contemplate, he argues that the course of history in the sphere of the development of sciences must be dealt with using common sense and fairness.

In conclusion, the examples and anecdotes given by Gülen demonstrate that he shares the same views as very well-established Islamic scholarship with regard to the discipline of Hadith. He presents strong and logical evidence about the fundamentals and historical development of this branch of science. He bases his views on common sense, and cautiously approaches issues that may be incorrect. He minutely and carefully investigates the views that he presents to his interlocutors as a thesis. He exercises extra care to ensure that no void exists in his theses nor gap in logic.

On the face of his available literature, Gülen could be criticized that his approach to the discipline of Hadith does not fully meet academic standards. It is true that Gülen's approach is far from being purely academic, and such a criticism may appear to be legitimate at first glance. However, considering Gülen's mission as the leader of a global movement, and having not written a specific work on the subject, any such argument becomes irrelevant. Besides, his close involvement in Hadith literature is not driven by academic interest, but rather his adoption of Sunnah as a lifestyle. Although he admires and trusts the works produced by early Islamic scholars, Gülen's adherence to their path can never be seen as blind following. He critically studies and verifies any hadith before using it.

---

[288] Gülen, *Sonsuz Nur, Vol. 2 (Muhammad: The Messenger of God)*, pp. 173-175

Gülen's Thoughts on Recording, Ascertaining and Compilation of Sunnah

In Islamic literature, learning and recording hadiths in writing or by committing to memory by the Companions during the time of the Noble Prophet is expressed by the Islamic terms *dabt* and *tathbit* ("recording and writing of hadiths"). According to Muslim scholars, this process was carried out under the watchful eyes of the Noble Prophet.[289] Being rigorously studied and critically examined, the soundness of this process was proven by Muslim scholars according to the established criteria in Hadith discipline. However, this did very little in terms of preventing Hadith collections subsequently becoming the subject of continuous debate.

According to Gülen, the Quranic verse, "*Indeed it is We, We Who send down the Reminder in parts, and it is indeed We Who are its Guardian,*"[290] represents objective evidence to preserve the Qur'an in various means and ways.[291] In his book entitled *Sonsuz Nur*, Gülen uses this verse as the main theme for the introduction to the ascertaining of Sunnah. Immediately, he puts forward a thesis arguing that the Sunnah—like the Qur'an—has been recorded, memorized, safeguarded and transmitted to the present time without changing or alteration.[292] In commenting on this verse, Gülen explains that God's protection also extends to Sunnah, and further elaborates that the Companions of the Noble Prophet exercised the same sensitivity and care in the recording and safeguarding of Sunnah as they did for the Qur'an.[293] Likewise, in

---

[289] Canan, *Fethullah Gülen'in Sunnet Anlayisi*, pp. 100–101.

[290] Qur'an 15:9.

[291] In *The Qur'an with Annotated Interpretation in Modern English*, Ali Ünal states this verse means: "The text of the Qur'an was preserved in four different ways during the lifetime of the Messenger of God, upon him be peace and blessings:

• The Prophet, had the whole text of the Divine Messages, from the beginning to the end, committed to writing by the scribes of Revelations.

• Many of the Companions learned the whole text of the Qur'an, every syllable, by heart.

• All the illustrious Companions, without exception, had memorized at least some portions of the Holy Qur'an, for the simple reason that it was obligatory for them to recite it during worship.

• A considerable number of the literate Companions kept a private record of the text of the Qur'an and satisfied themselves as to the purity of their record by reading it out to the Messenger, upon him be peace and blessings."

[292] Gülen, *Sonsuz Nur, Vol. 2 (Muhammad: The Messenger of God)*, p. 415.

[293] ibid.

drawing attention to Gülen's thoroughness on Sunnah, Canan shares Gülen's thoughts regarding this issue and argues that God's protection of the Qur'an also encompasses Sunnah.[294]

In a way, Gülen's interpretation of the verse attempts to make it a responsibility for Muslims to strive to protect Sunnah. He argues that, although God sent down the Qur'an and will protect it from corruption, Muslims should not fall into the error of exempting themselves from responsibility and leave everything to the care of Divine will.[295] If Divine decrees are sent down through a causal agency—i.e. the Messenger of God—to His servants to practice and adopt them as a way of life, there is nothing unusual about expecting humankind to be responsible for preserving them similarly by means of causal processes. This responsibility also extends to safeguarding the Noble Prophet's commentaries and interpretations of Quranic verses as well as his personal Sunnah. In a way, besides taking up material responsibility to establish and protect the religion, the above verse recommends undertaking scholarly responsibilities to uphold its fundamental principles and sustain its integrity. It is quite reasonable to say from the cause-effect point of view that making these inferences from Gülen's thoughts is possible. In other words, while offering religious arguments for Sunnah being under protection, Gülen rationalizes these arguments and puts the issue into a more plausible framework. This approach is not very common among other Muslim scholars.

Taking into account this verse and related commentaries, it is not too difficult to understand the sensitivity of the Companions, their followers and Muslim scholars that followed them. According to Gülen— like the majority of Muslim scholars—Sunnah was vigorously discussed among the Companions and written in "book" form, and these booklets were handed from generation to generation.[296]

Gülen's way of assertion has an underlying methodology to support his views with evidence drawn firstly from the Qur'an and then from the Sunnah. Quranic verses decreeing obedience to the Noble

---

[294] Canan, *Fethullah Gülen'in Sunnet Anlayisi*, p. 85.

[295] Gülen, *Sonsuz Nur, Vol. 2 (Muhammad: The Messenger of God)*, p. 546.

[296] Gülen, *Zamanın Altın Dilimi (The Golden Realm of Time)*, *Cag Ve Nesil series*, Vol 4 (Istanbul: Nil Publishing, 2011), pp. 184, 186.

Prophet constitute the main basis for this approach of which verses has already been mentioned and quoted. According to him, it would be beneficial to focus on the Companions' care regarding the emulation of Noble Prophet's example (Sunnah). Further, proper understanding of the Companions' prudence and attention reveals the reasons behind their trend and adoption of Sunnah. Therefore, this verse must be carefully analyzed and evaluated from the points of view of cause, occasion and objective. Looking from this perspective, the verse clearly enjoins conformity and obedience to all messages delivered by the Noble Prophet as an obligation (*wajib*). This also means refraining from all acts and deeds the Noble Prophet prohibited—directly by Quranic verses or by his own views, commentaries or interpretations there from.[297] By emphasizing the Islamic concept of *taqwa* ("piety and reverence for God" or "God consciousness"), the clause "*keep from disobedience to God in reverence for Him and piety*" (*wa at-taqu Allah*) in the verse draws attention to the significance of Sunnah and encourages its treatment with utmost care and sensitivity.[298] This is how the Companions interpreted the last phrase of the verse, assuming responsibility to guard and preserve Sunnah together with the Qur'an. Gülen believes, due to the elucidatory and guiding position of the Companions, that piety can be achieved by upholding and adhering to the Prophetic Traditions.[299]

Gülen elucidates that the verse, "*Assuredly you have in God's Messenger an excellent example to follow for whoever looks forward to God and the Last Day, and remembers and mentions God much,*"[300] determines a different task and objective for the Companions. The verse, as they understand it, tells them it is only through strict adherence to Sunnah that true faith and just religious rulings can be achieved. The verse also indicates that objective and subjective problems can be solved and eschatological topics, such as *barzakh* (the intermediary stage between this life and the life in the Hereafter or interval between death and Resurrection), *mahshar* (resurrection), *hisab* (judgment), *shafa'ah* (intercession), *jannah* (paradise), *jahannam* (hell), elucidated

---

[297] Gülen, *Sonsuz Nur, Vol. 2 (Muhammad: The Messenger of God)*, p. 419.
[298] ibid., p. 418.
[299] ibid., p. 419.
[300] Qur'an 33:21.

through the help of Sunnah. This is because the Qur'an and the Sunnah were offering the Companions, within their socio-cultural environment, a new and original worldview and a belief in the afterlife. Hence, they were following the Noble Prophet's footsteps, memorizing, recording, practicing and transmitting all his actions, words, hand signs and facial expressions like smiles and embitterment.[301] Setting his focus on the above verses, Gülen concludes that the Companions assumed upholding Sunnah as their duty. Needless to say, his inference coincides exactly with the majority of the Sunni scholars' views. Although Gülen prefers to expound his views with the help of rational arguments, the fact that his approach to issues—within the framework of Quranic verses—draws a didactic and confessional picture should not be overlooked.

Gülen supports his arguments through examples and evidence selected from within the Sunnah alongside evidence drawn from verses of the Qur'an. Thus, he stresses that he holds his argument because it is supported with Sunnah, which he believes is sound and healthy. He also views Hadith as evidence supporting that the Companions had been encouraged by the Noble Prophet to safeguard and transmit the Sunnah.[302] *Gülen regards the* Noble Prophet's instruction to the delegation of 'Abd al-Qays from Rabi'ah tribe, "Be mindful of these directives and inform those whom you have left behind, about them,[303]" as another encouragement for the learning and spreading of Sunnah. Similarly, the Noble Prophet's instruction, "...and those who are present here should convey this to those who are absent,"[304] at the end of his Farewell Sermon—a speech that highlights important points in Islamic law—is viewed by Gülen as another piece of strong evidence for recording and conveying the Sunnah.[305] *Gülen's citation of this evidence throughout his works brings the study and practical application of* Sunnah to the fore, and at the same time, shows that his preferred method of establishing facts is based and relies on records and resources.

---

[301] Gülen, *Sonsuz Nur, Vol. 2 (Muhammad: The Messenger of God)*, pp. 419–420.
[302] ibid., p. 420.
[303] Bukhari, *faith*, 40; Muslim, *faith*, 24.
[304] Bukhari, *ilm*, 9, 10, 37; Muslim, *hac*, 446; *qasamah*, 29.
[305] Gülen, *Sonsuz Nur, Vol. 2 (Muhammad: The Messenger of God)*, pp. 420–421.

Gülen brings divergent interpretations of the Qur'an's and
Sunnah's persistent encouragement of the Companions for retaining and
recording the Prophetic Traditions. A case in point is that the Companions'
eagerness in recording and reporting Sunnah, as Gülen explains, was
driven by their concern and fear that their lack of action would cause
the truth to become hidden and concealed from other people. Likewise,
Gülen inferred this interpretation from another tradition of the Noble
Prophet: "He who is asked something he knows and conceals it will have
a bridle of fire put on him on the Day of Resurrection."[306] *Gülen explains
that the* Companions well understood this hadith, and were mindful of
the responsibility it placed on them.[307]

In light of above evidence drawn directly from the Qur'an and
the Sunnah, Gülen asserts that the Sunnah has been ascertained as a
result of a long, incessant and meticulous process, based on rigorous
criteria and transmitted from generation to generation with utmost care.

In continuation of his furnishing of evidence, Gülen explains
that the Noble Prophet made the Companions memories certain verses
and supplications, which they discussed among themselves. With this
example, Gülen draws attention to the role of the Noble Prophet in the
process of establishing Sunnah; thus, inferring that the Companions
could not remain exempt of this Endeavour, as it was personally led by
the Noble Prophet. Gülen illustrates his thoughts with various examples,
including the following one reported by Ibn Mas'ud (d. 653 CE): "He
[the Noble Prophet] used to teach us the *tashahhud* supplication (recited
in sitting position during the Prayer) the way he taught us the Qur'an."[308]
Similarly, Gülen presents the hadith, "He (the Noble Prophet) used
to teach us the *istikharah* (seeking guidance from God) in all matters

---

[306] Tirmidhi, *ilm*, 3; Abu Dawud, *ilm*, 9.

[307] Gülen also expounds that the following verse was considered by the Companions as evidence of their duty to safeguard and communicate *sunnah*: *"Those who conceal the truths
and commandments in the Book that God has sent down, and sell them for a trifling price
(such as worldly benefit, status and renown), they eat nothing but fire in their bellies. And God
will not speak to them on the Day of Resurrection (when they will be in dire need to speak to
Him, to implore forgiveness and mercy), nor will He absolve them to pronounce them pure. For
them is a painful punishment"* Qur'an 2:174. Gülen, *Sonsuz Nur, Vol. 2 (Muhammad: The
Messenger of God)*, p. 421.

[308] Bukhari, *isti'dhan*, 28; Muslim, *salat*, 59.

as he would teach us a chapter from the Qur'an,"[309] as an evidence to strengthen his case.[310]

Obviously, the mutual discussion method constitutes an important factor of the Prophet's teaching system. The Noble Prophet employed this method during his time and strongly advised its usage. Dating back to the time of the Noble Prophet, Gülen highlights this method and its reliability, especially in establishing and collecting hadiths, and emphasizes that the Noble Prophet encouraged his Companions to study and mutually discuss everything he taught them.[311] Interestingly enough, by citing numerous individual anecdotes, Gülen implies that if one takes them as a whole, it becomes apparent that there is a collective effort to preserve the Sunnah. At this juncture, Gülen draws attention to this hadith:

> No people gather together in one of the Houses of God, reciting the Book of God and studying it among themselves (*tadarasa*), except that tranquility (*sakinah*) descends upon them, and mercy envelops them, and the angels surround them, and God mentions them amongst those who are with Him.[312]

Semantically speaking, the word *tadarasa* in the hadith has been used in the sense of "mutual discussion" (in the text, rendered "studying it among themselves"), and refers to mutual sharing of knowledge, its confirmation, yielding correct inferences, and drawing sound and rational conclusions. The Companions checked and controlled the degree of soundness of many hadiths using this method; if they encountered any problems, they asked the Noble Prophet for clarification. As can be seen from the above examples, to support his views, Gülen exerts himself to derive evidence not only from the general meaning of hadiths, but also by performing linguistic analysis of keywords within their texts (*matn*).

The discussion up to this point demonstrates that Gülen has convinced himself concerning the reliability of the recording and reporting of the Sunnah. The predominant theme throughout his works is the concern of how to convince others within the context of having

---

[309] Bukhari, *tahajjud,* 25; Tirmidhi, *vitr,* 18; Abu Dawud, *vitr,* 31.
[310] Gülen, *Sonsuz Nur, Vol. 2 (Muhammad: The Messenger of God)*, p. 422.
[311] ibid.
[312] Muslim, *dhikr,* 38; Tirmidhi, *qiraat,* 10; Abu Dawud, *witr,* 14.

evidence both "by transmission" (*naqli*) and "by inference" (*'aqli*). This is the reason why he endeavors to derive various implications from almost every transmission he deals with to justify the soundness of Sunnah. The hadith reported by Anas ibn Malik, "We used to sit with God's Messenger and hear something from him, and when we left his presence, we used to remember and discuss it among ourselves,"[313] is a good example of how Sunnah was established through mutual discussions.[314] Having originated from the hadith, this method is known to be widely used by Muslim scholars to deal with subjects related to the compilation and soundness of Sunnah during later periods.

Noting the Companions' aspiration to learn and teach hadiths, Gülen highlights the effect of the exhortation stemming from the Sunnah. In other words, making his expertise in the discipline of *Sirah* (biographies) conducive to new perspectives in the transmission of hadiths, Gülen draws attention to the Companions' individual and communal state of mind, and attempts to do some psychological analyses—an Endeavour rarely seen among other scholars. He prefers to support his argument by emphasizing the *Ashab al-Suffah*'s (People of the Bench) almost ceaseless efforts to study the Qur'an and the Sunnah. He also notes the presence of instructors (*mudarris*) teaching Hadith periodically to up to 70 Companions. Taking into consideration the high number of female Companions' participation in this teaching campaign, the time of the Noble Prophet emerges as a period of intense Hadith teaching. At this juncture, Gülen points to the fact that female Companions were also taking lessons from the Noble Prophet on certain days of the week, and by asking questions directly to him, receiving also guidance on issues specific to women. This meant religious ruling concerning issues related to women were also memorized and recorded. Likewise, details of the Noble Prophet's private family life were reported and explained by his wives.[315] It is of benefit to note that Muslims are very convinced that the Companions, who knew of life before the advent of Islam, were willing to receive whatever the Noble Prophet taught them. Needless to say, the Noble Prophet's teaching put human beings in

---

[313] Hatib al-Baghdadi, *al-Jami' li Akhlaki'r-Rawi wa Adabi's-Sami'*, Vol. 1, pp. 363-364.

[314] Gülen, *Sonsuz Nur, Vol. 2 (Muhammad: The Messenger of God)*, p. 423.

[315] ibid., pp. 423–424.

the forefront and—with the establishment and spread of Sunnah, which is an important source of code of conduct—satisfied a huge social need. Moreover, continuation of this educational drive, especially after his *Hijrah* (migration to Medina) was conducive to the increase in literacy during the Medinan period.

The events the Companions experienced with God's Messenger were discussed during these classes and confirmed by the Messenger. Gülen presents certain examples to illustrate these events, such as the death of 'Uthman ibn Maz'un (d. 3rd year AH),[316] the announcement of Quzman position—a Companion who was killed during the Battle of Uhud,[317] the declaration of certain Companions who were killed on the Day of Khaybar as martyrs,[318] Dimam ibn Tha'labah's acceptance of Islam,[319] and 'Ubay ibn Ka'b's (d. 643 CE)[320] heralding by the Quranic chapter of *al-Bayyinah*.[321] *Gülen explains that the* Companions witnessed, discussed, recorded and communicated these happenings.[322] Indeed, these are historically accurate occurrences witnessed by a great number of Companions. Gülen deems the silence or admission by the witnessing Companions as substantiation of these historical events. He emphasizes that these events were confirmed at the time of happening and communicated to others without any lies or interpolation. Through these examples, Gülen uses the historical environment to justify the authenticity of Sunnah. Clearly, Gülen uses every single anecdote and opportunity to build a solid foundation for his views by rationalizing the question. On the other hand, in the thinking process of Islam, it is a fact that the inferential (*'aqli*) evidence is also based on the transmitted textual (*naqli*) evidence. That is, disregarding neither of them, Gülen employs both *'aql* (inference and intellect) and *naql* (what is transmitted, i.e. the Qur'an and the Sunnah) by putting them into each other's service.

Drawing on the Islamic "biographical literature" (*tabaqat*) from time to time, Gülen articulates several arguments in order to illustrate

---

[316] Bukhari, *Janaiz*, 3, *Manaqibu'l-ansar*, 46; Ahmad ibn Hanbal, *al-Musnad*, 1/237, 6/436.

[317] Bukhari, *jihad*, 182; Muslim, *faith*, 178.

[318] Muslim, *faith*, 182; Ahmad ibn Hanbal, al-*Musnad*, 1/30, 47.

[319] Bukhari, *ilm*, 6; Nasai, *siyam*, 1.

[320] Bukhari, *tafsir*, (98) 1–3; Muslim, *fadailu's-sahaba*, 121–122.

[321] Qur'an, 98.

[322] Gülen, *Sonsuz Nur, Vol. 2 (Muhammad: The Messenger of God)*, pp. 425–428.

the Companions' yearning desire for learning and safeguarding Sunnah. For example, he explains there were about 40[323] scribes around the Noble Prophet,[324] and there was a serious Endeavour among the Companions to learn how to read and write to be able to better study and understand the Qur'an and the Sunnah. Gülen argues it is because of this reason that the Noble Prophet fostered literacy learning. One of the articles in the peace agreement signed after the Battle of Badr stipulated a ransom for the liberation of each prisoner of war to teach ten Muslims how to read and write.[325] *Gülen uses this condition to justify his argument. Moreover, Gülen views this incentive and yearning desire across the community as a declaration of an educational campaign aiming to learn, record and safeguard* the Sunnah. There was something in front of the Companions they never experienced before—an original phenomenon that was called Sunnah. This was another factor motivating or even forcing them to memories and write this newly found source of guidance.[326] Thus, Sunnah was set for overall official codification.[327] Through the above explanations, Gülen infers that the codification of Sunnah began at the time of the Noble Prophet, although the official process started during the time of the Umayyad Caliph 'Umar ibn 'Abd al-'Aziz (d. 720 CE), and the compilation was modeled on the works of the Companions.

Although recording the Sunnah in writing for its safekeeping—like the Qur'an—was a major task undertaken by the Companions, this also sparked intense debate in Hadith discipline due to an open to interpretation "writing ban" on hadiths during the early years of the Medinan period.[328] This particular hadith constituted the basis for diverse interpretations during later periods and still does in our time.[329]

---

[323] ibid. p. 509.

[324] M. Ajjaj al-Khatîb, *as-Sunnatu Qabla't-Tadwin*, p. 298.

[325] Ibn Sa'd, *at-Tabaqatu'l-Kubra*, 2/22.

[326] Gülen, *Sonsuz Nur, Vol. 2 (Muhammad: The Messenger of God)*, p. 430.

[327] ibid., pp. 509–510.

[328] Muslim, *Kitab Dhuhd;* Ibn Hanbal, *Musnad*, 3/12, 21, 33.

[329] Basing their arguments on this hadith, some researchers claimed that Prophetic Traditions were not written during the time of the Noble Prophet and the *sunnah* was established in later periods, thus are not authentic. Paradoxically, the critics of *sunnah* base their views on this particular source, which is "untrustworthy" in their own terms. Dr. Rasit Kucuk highlighted this contradiction by directing this question to one of his opponents: "How come that you present a Prophetic Tradition you deem 'unreliable' in order to justify your argument? Don't you think this is self-contradictory?" Canan, *Fethullah Gülen'in Sunnet Anlayisi*, pp. 102-103.

Starting from this point, Canan argues that the prohibition of writing anything other than the Qur'an was a "temporary ban," and imposed during the early days of the Medinan period. To support his views, he refers his readers to Khatib al-Baghdadi's *Taqyidu al-Ilm*, a work that brings together all narrations related to the permission of recording hadiths in writing.[330] Here, the following questions may come to mind: If the writing ban was imposed during the Medina period, what is the status of the Prophetic Traditions that were committed to writing during the 13 years of the Mecca period? Were there any hadith recorded and safeguarded during that time? If this was the case, what was the method employed? An important point to be highlighted is that the Mecca period became notable for the memorization of revealed verses of the Qur'an and they were also recorded in writing by scribes. At this juncture, Gülen emphasizes the qualities of the Companions, and argues they were by nature very intelligent and had strong memories; once they committed a Quranic verse or hadith to memory, they would never forget it.[331] The Companions' endeavors to memories Prophetic Traditions and their question as to the permission for writing[332] them during the Medina period indicates that the memorization method prevailed during the Mecca period. After all, there were only 17 Companions[333] who could read and write during the Mecca period, and most of them were appointed as revelation scribes—busy writing down Quranic verses as they were revealed. However, unlettered Companions from within the inner circle of the Noble Prophet chose to memories Prophetic Traditions alongside Quranic verses—the importance of memorization in Arab literature was mentioned earlier in this work. As for the Medina period, it emerges as a transitional period from memorization to the written method thanks to the increase in the Companions' educational level. In one aspect, this period can be seen as the verification of memorization qualities by pen and writing. The Companions asked God's Messenger if writing down hadiths was allowed while they memories them; "Seek help from your hand" he replied.[334]

---

[330] ibid., p. 103.
[331] Gülen, *Sonsuz Nur, Vol. 2 (Muhammad: The Messenger of God)*, p. 431.
[332] Tirmidhi, *ilm*, 12; Tabarani, *al-Mu'jamu'l-awsat*, 3/169.
[333] M. Hanefi Palabiyik, "Cahiliye Donemi ve Islam'in ilk Yillarinda Okuma-Yazma Faaliyetleri "*The Journal of Ataturk University, Theology Faculty, Issue 27*, (2007), pp. 32-33
[334] Gülen, *Sonsuz Nur, Vol. 2 (Muhammad: The Messenger of God)*, p. 513.

Looking into Gülen's comments on the prohibition of writing down hadiths reveals that he focuses on the rationale behind this ban. Gülen asserts that the very narration, "We asked the Prophet if we could write down hadiths but he did not give his permission,"[335] which is widely used as evidence for the prohibition of writing down traditions, is not considered authentic by scholars specialized in the field of Hadith. Hence, Gülen emphasizes that it does not constitute sound evidence for the writing ban.[336]

Again, he puts his focus on the rationale of the ban, which is based on Prophetic Tradition. He observes that the rationale behind the prohibition is a concern that hadiths recorded on the same writing material with the Qur'an would be mingled with the Word of God.[337] The Noble Prophet's apprehension may be stemming from his concern about preserving the authenticity of the Qur'an. Gülen explains that 'Umar also exhibited the same sensitivity on this issue with similar fervor. This was during the early stages of the revelation and the Word of God needed to be learned, understood, and its practical functionality properly grasped. Over time, the Companions become accustomed to the distinct style of the revelation, and developed similar sensitivity and meticulousness for its preservation, so the prohibition on writing down the hadiths was revoked by the Noble Prophet himself. After they developed the aptitude to differentiate between the Qur'an and the Hadith, the Companions were allowed to write down Sunnah in the same way they wrote verses of the Qur'an.[338] *Gülen puts forward the view suggesting* that the ban on writing was subsequently abrogated.[339] As above evaluation shows clearly, Gülen follows general remarks of Muslim traditions in his interpretation of this report.

The narration of writing down with hands draws attention to two factors—memorization and writing—in establishing and recording hadiths. While encouraging his Companions to safeguard

---

[335] Muslim, *dhuhd*, 72; Ahmad ibn Hanbal, *al-Musnad*, 3/12, 21; Darimi, *Muqaddimah*, 42.
[336] Gülen, *Sonsuz Nur, Vol. 2 (Muhammad: The Messenger of God)*, p. 511.
[337] ibid. pp. 511–512.
[338] ibid. pp. 511–512, 519.
[339] ibid. p. 519.

the Sunnah, the Noble Prophet also taught them the methods to be employed in this discipline. The inference Gülen draws from this tradition is the view that writing verifies what is committed to memory. He backs up this view[340] with further evidence drawn from a narration where Rafi' ibn Khadij (d. 63 AH) asked the Noble Prophet if they could write things they hear from him. The Noble Prophet said: 'Write. There is no harm in it.'[341] To provide yet further support for his argument, Gülen draws attention to certain matters mentioned in the works of Imam Darimi (d. 181 AH) and Ibn Hajar (d. 852 AH). According to these two famous scholars, the Noble Prophet reduced to writing certain legal rulings with regard to *sha'a'ir al-Islamiyah* (Islamic symbols and customs), *qisas* (*lex talionis*), and *diyyah* (blood money) and sent them to 'Amr ibn Hazm, the governor of Yemen at that time.[342] Also, the Noble Prophet wrote an agreement for his Companion Wa'il ibn Hujr (narrator of the hadith).[343] As can be seen from the above outline, Gülen selects his sources of reference very carefully, and—due to the sensitivity of the issue—tries to explain the matter as clearly as he can. Presenting a multiplicity of examples further strengthens his argument.

There is another narration that holds an interesting place on the issue of writing down hadiths where the Noble Prophet, on his sick-bed, asked for a pen and paper, allegedly to write or dictate something for his community,[344] a request that could not be met. Some Muslim scholars comment that whatever the Noble Prophet wanted to say remained hidden. However, Gülen has a rather different comment on this tradition, which holds a special place in his mind:

> It is true that something that which God's Messenger had wanted to be written remained hidden, but what is fundamental is the fact that his traditions were written down during his time, and furthermore, he

---

[340] ibid., p. 513.
[341] Hatib al-Baghdadi, *Takyidu'l-Ilm*, s.73. See different narrations: Ahmad ibn Hanbal, *al-Musnad*, 2/215; Haysami, *Majmau'-Dhawaid*, 1/151.
[342] Darimi, *diyah*, 1,3,11,12; Ibn Hajar, *al-Isaba*, 6/228; Ibn Hisham, *as-Siratu'n-Nabawiyyah*, 5/294.
[343] Gülen, *Sonsuz Nur, Vol. 2 (Muhammad: The Messenger of God)*, p. 514.
[344] Bukhari, *Ilm*, 39, *Marda*, 17; Muslim, *Wasiyah*, 22.

himself dictated or wanted something to be recorded in writing.[345]

The request of writing by the Noble Prophet suggests that keeping written records was a routine part of the culture. Therefore, the Noble Prophet did not ask from his Companions something to which they were not accustomed; he, in fact, confirmed and justified a method they had been using for quite some time. With this interpretation, Gülen exhibits a different approach and method of critical analysis of the Prophetic Traditions. His critical approach and comments based on sound rational arguments, through which he draws inferences related to the fundamentals of Sunnah, can be explained most logically by his persistent focus on ascertaining and compilation of Hadith collections. Thus, he draws attention to certain points overlooked in the past.

The First Compilers of Prophetic Traditions in Muslim Community

After the process of memorization and writing down of hadiths as mentioned above, there was another important process that took place in the history of Islam. This is the stage during which vigorous efforts were exerted to compile the Prophetic Traditions.

At this point, Gülen brings forth examples of the Companions such as 'Umar (d. 644 CE), Ibn 'Abbas (d. 688 CE), Abu Musa al-Ash'ari (d. 662 or 672 CE), Abu Sa'id al-Khudri (d. 693 CE) and Zayd ibn Thabit (d. 660 CE), and those like Sha'bi and Nakha'i (d. 682 CE) from among the successors—whom he considers geniuses of memory—who were advocates of memorization and verbal transmission of hadiths. By bringing these great Hadith scholars into the agenda by highlighting the strength of their memory, Gülen calls attention to an intellectual "checks and balances" mechanism that scrutinizes hadith transmission. It is important to remember that these scholars had initially positioned themselves against writing for reasons already mentioned.[346]

According to Gülen, *tadwin* (compilation and recording the Traditions) is a term representing a state of being in an unending brainstorm, intellectual fertility, and researching and structuring basic principles to understand the past, control the present and formulate

---

[345] Gülen, *Sonsuz Nur, Vol. 2 (Muhammad: The Messenger of God)*, p. 515.
[346] ibid., p. 520.

the future.[347] That is to say, *tadwin* is one of the ways to reach new interpretations and legal rulings by preserving the fundamental principles and original data. According to Gülen, *tadwin* is a process that began in the early period when the Companions memorized and recorded the Prophetic Traditions, and still continues today.[348]

However, Gülen stresses that *tadwin* as an official state project was initiated by Umayyad Caliph 'Umar ibn Abd al-Aziz (d.720 AH),[349] whom he considers[350] the first *mujaddid* (reviver of the religion)[351] in Islam.[352] Ibn al-Shihab al-Zuhri was commissioned by 'Umar ibn Abd al-Aziz (d. 720 CE) to collect and compile the Prophetic Traditions. 'Abdullah ibn 'Umar's emancipated slave and Imam Malik's teacher Nafi'—who was also Layth ibn Sa'd's *shaykh*—and Layth ibn Sa'd also collected traditions.[353] The official *tadwin* works initiated by 'Umar ibn Abd al-Aziz were continued by the efforts of 'Abd al-Malik ibn Jurayj (d. 767 CE) in Mecca, Sa'id ibn Abi 'Arubah (d. 157 AH) in Iraq, Awza'i (d. 774 CE) in Damascus, Muhammad ibn 'Abd al-Rahman (nd) in Medina, Za'idah ibn Qudamah (d. 161 AH) and Sufyan al-Thawri (d. 778 CE) in Kufah, Hammad ibn Salamah (d. 783 CE) in Basrah, and Abdullah ibn Mubarak (d. 797 CE) in Khorasan.[354] *Gülen explains that these* Hadith scholars, as a result of their meticulous works, left behind for future generations valuable materials comparable to large libraries.[355] It is understood that knowledge centers were established in most cities during this period, and compilation processes were supervised by committees composed of expert scholars in Hadith discipline. With this elucidation and examples, Gülen displays an Endeavour to convince his interlocutors that there were solid supervisory mechanisms overseeing

---

[347] Gülen, *Gurbet Ufuklari (Horizons of Foreign Land), Kirik Testi series*, Vol. 3 (Istanbul: Nil Publishing, 2011), pp. 185, 186.

[348] Gülen, *Sonsuz Nur, Vol. 2 (Muhammad: The Messenger of God)*, pp. 516–517.

[349] Gülen, *Gurbet Ufuklari (Horizons of Foreign Land), Kirik Testi series*, Vol. 3, p. 191.

[350] Gülen, *Sonsuz Nur, Vol. 2 (Muhammad: The Messenger of God)*, p. 520.

[351] "Umar ibn Abd al-Aziz developed the idea of bringing back a Muhammadan spirit to governments that have lost their original Islamic ruling." Gülen, *Gurbet Ufuklari (Horizons of Foreign Land), Kirik Testi series*, Vol. 3, p. 191.

[352] Gülen, *Sonsuz Nur, Vol. 2 (Muhammad: The Messenger of God)*, pp. 519–520.

[353] Gülen, *Yol Mulahazalari (Contemplating the Journey), Prizma series*, Vol. 6 (Istanbul: Nil Publishing, 2007), pp. 188–189.

[354] Ibn Hajar, *Hadyu's-Sari*, p. 4; M. Ajjaj al-Khatib, *as-Sunna Qabla't-Tadwin*, p. 337.

[355] Gülen, *Sonsuz Nur, Vol. 2 (Muhammad: The Messenger of God)*, p. 521.

the compilation processes. He argues that the huge task of the *tadwin* process, which extends back to the time of the Noble Prophet, stands in front of us as a momentous historical event. Considering the distances between the abovementioned cities and transport facilities available at the time,[356] *Gülen's persistence in arguing about the size and importance of the works undertaken is well-understood.*

If one may say, there is a considerably long time between 'Umar ibn Abd al-Aziz's caliphate and the time of the Noble Prophet, how was this long period of time filled in Gülen's view? How was the Sunnah safeguarded during this long period of time? At this juncture, Gülen puts forth certain views. Basing his argument on evidence derived from Hadith, he asserts that Sunnah was protected individually by Hadith scholars until the caliphate of 'Umar ibn Abd al-Aziz. He derives this conclusion from the Noble Prophet's saying:

> A group of people from my Muslim community (*ummah*) will always remain triumphant on the right path and continue to be triumphant (against their opponents) [They will protect the religion; the religion will never be eradicated from the face of Earth]. He who deserts them shall not be able to do them any harm. They will remain in this position until God's Command is executed (i.e. *qiyamah* is established).[357]

Explaining this hadith, Gülen stresses that, all along Islamic history, there has been no shortage of helpers for the religion and Islam has been protected with all its fundamentals since its inception. According to Muslim scholars, the meaning of "help" is inferred from the word *jama'ah* ("community," translated "a group of people" in the text) in the hadith. In Bukhari's view, "These are the people of Sham (Damascus)"[358] which was a center of Islamic sciences during that time. It is widely known that scholars like Abdu'r-Rahman al-Awza'i (d. 774 CE), Al-Layth ibn Sa'd (d. 791 CE) and Imam Malik used to send their outstanding students to Damascus to further their studies. According to some scholars, the word *jama'ah* in the hadith refers to scholars of Hadith,

---

[356] Gülen, *Fatiha Uzerine Mulahazalar (Al-Fatiha: The Opening, A Commentary on the First Chapter of the Qur'an)*, (Istanbul: Nil Publishing, 2011), p. 33.

[357] Bukhari, *i'tisam*, 10; *tawhid*, 29; Muslim, *imara*, 170.

[358] Bukhari, *tawhid*, 29.

while others argue it denotes the exegetes of the Qur'an. However, Gülen's interpretation is somewhat free from the restrictions of time and location. He argues that Bukhari's interpretation stems from his consideration of Damascus as a center of science. Whether this is true, Gülen views this comment as restricting Prophetic foresight to a time and locality, and stresses that the heralded protection of the religion, as foretold in the narration, is effective until the Day of Judgment. In his view, this *jama'ah* once fulfilled its duties in Damascus and served under 'Umar ibn Abd al-Aziz at another time.[359] Viewing the word *jama'ah* from this perspective, Gülen derives duties—i.e. contributing to the preservation of the religion—from this narration for our time and future generations. What we see is that in Gülen's epistemology, besides the Qur'an and the Sunnah, the consensus of the Muslim community plays a significant role in transmitting and producing knowledge. At first glance, his above mentioned approach to the issue looks like a theological reading of the hadith text, but in reality, it is socio-political reading of the report. By this way, he concludes that early Muslims took active part in the preservation of the Sunnah.

In Gülen's opinion, 'Umar ibn Abd al-Aziz derived duty from the endeavors undertaken up until his caliphate and, assuming the preservation of the Sunnah as a state responsibility, he made a governmental decision to start compilation works officially for the first time. Scholars of Hadith and jurists were officially employed for the compilation and recording of hadiths (*tadwin*) during his caliphate.[360] 'Umar ibn Abd al-Aziz and his policies and practices have been mentioned abundantly in Gülen's works and often used as illustrating examples. His decision to assume the preservation of Prophetic Traditions as a state responsibility provided the highest level of protection for the Sunnah. This policy also demonstrates that besides independent individual efforts, supporting religious scholarship is a state responsibility. Due to some political upheavals during his time, 'Umar ibn Abd al-Aziz made great efforts to return Sunnah to practical life[361] in a more functional manner.[362] *Gülen brings in a different perspective to this*

---

[359] Gülen, *Sonsuz Nur, Vol. 2 (Muhammad: The Messenger of God)*, p. 487.

[360] Gülen, *Gurbet Ufuklari (Horizons of Foreign Land)*, *Kirik Testi series*, Vol. 3, p. 192.

[361] ibid., p. 191.

[362] It could be said that Gülen's approach to practicing *sunnah* has also been influenced by

period of compilation and describes it as a "renaissance in Islam" (or the vivification and revitalization of Islam), as he highlights intense intellectual activities taking place during that time. However, Gülen expresses his disappointment in the failure to maintain in later years the acceleration achieved during this period. He lays the blame on Muslims for this failure and reminds them again and again of their responsibility in the fields of Sunnah and other Islamic sciences.[363] *Gülen views, correctly, the highest status attributed to* Sunnah during 'Umar ibn Abd al-Aziz's caliphate as a precursor to massive social melioration and restructuring.[364] Comparing that period to the present time, Gülen believes that eroded social values can be restored by adopting the principles of Sunnah.[365]

From the onset we note that non-Muslim scholars became critical and skeptic about the Prophetic Traditions – practices and sayings of Prophet Muhammad, upon whom be peace and blessings. Any student of Islam and religion thus deems it crucial and significant to assess and evaluate the views, perspectives and feelings of those who do not consider themselves Muslims. More simply put, any reader or researcher can identify with the difference of opinions and criticism of Islamic principles, fundamentals and terms and terminology.

However, from a Muslim perspective, the research endeavors to balance out the arguments, perspectives and approach by also presenting arguments for and against whilst elucidating and presenting the Muslim point. This is offered here in the approach and views Gülen holds and expresses.

Sunnah's Function according to Gülen

Detailed analyses were made on the status and function of Sunnah in Islam, and certain Muslim scholars' and researchers' views were examined in Chapter One. In this section, Gülen's views will be evaluated thoroughly. Answers will be sought to questions regarding the function Gülen attributes to the Sunnah in comparison to his contemporaries, the

'Umar ibn Abd al-Aziz.

[363] Gülen, *Kirik Testi-1* (The Broken Jug, Vol. 1), (Istanbul: Nil Publishing, 2010), p. 140.

[364] Gülen, *Asrin Getirdigi Tereddutler -2* (Questions and Answers about Islam, Vol. 2), (Istanbul: Nil Publishing, 2010), pp. 256–260.

[365] Gülen, *Enginligi Ile Bizim Dunyamiz, Iktisadi Mulahazalar (Our World in Depth, Economic Contemplations)*, (Istanbul: Nil Publishing, 2011), pp. 142–144.

way he brings it to current times, the way he practices it in his daily life and his final objective. An attempt will be made to clarify these issues through selected passages from his works.

In the section related to the Sunnah's function in his work, titled *Sonsuz Nur* (which is also available in English with the title "*Muhammad: The Messenger of God*"), Gülen confirms and fortifies the *Ahl al-Sunnah* (Sunni Muslims) view on the function of the Sunnah. He emphasizes the invalidity of shallow claims like "The Qur'an is the only source in Islam." "The Sunnah has no mission like interpreting the Qur'an, imposing legal provisions and explaining social problems."[366] As understood, besides being a religious source of reference, Gülen asserts that the Sunnah provides solutions to problems at an individual, familial and social level. He also suggests it fosters scientific research and innovation, throwing light on and preparing ground for medicinal development, chemistry and other scientific realities of the present day. Pointing to the role of scientific realities in subserving the fundamentals of religious truths, Gülen focuses on the thesis that scientific facts do not differ from the facts described in the Qur'an and the Sunnah.[367] He thus attributes a scientific mission to the Sunnah. He defends and proves the guiding status of the Sunnah against those who generate opposing views. It is sufficient to give a single example here: Prophetic Traditions foretold that 20 people will share one pomegranate and eat to their fill, resting under the shade of its tree[368]; this draws a path for the agricultural sector in the future. Gülen comments, "By the advance in genetic technology, or by other ways or means unknown for the time being, it may be possible to produce plants and fruits of the size described in the hadith."[369] He reinforces his comment by highlighting the hormone and gene technologies that are progressing quickly nowadays. Be that as it may, it is safe to assume that Gülen is also under the influence of modern science and scientific approaches to the religious texts. Nevertheless, he is not obsessed with science and does not attempt in excessive scientific interpretation.

---

[366] Canan, *Fethullah Gülen'in Sunnet Anlayisi*, p. 97.
[367] Osman Bakar (ed.), *Sagduyu Cagrisi*, Fethullah Gülen'in Din Ve Bilim Yorumu: Dine Bilimsel Yaklasim, (Istanbul: Isik Publishing, 2005).
[368] Muslim, *Fitan*, 110.
[369] Gülen, *Fikir Atlasi (The Atlas of Ideas), Fasildan Fasila* series, Vol. 5, pp.148-149.

Legislative Aspect of Sunnah

While dealing with Sunnah's function, Gülen does not confine himself to the standard statements by just saying that Sunnah is the second fundamental legal source after the Qur'an. He prefers to elaborate on Sunnah's finer details, its involvement in other Islamic sciences, and verdicts that are not expressly mentioned in the Qur'an.[370] Looking from this perspective, Gülen intends to prove that the Sunnah has many profound and elaborate aspects and functions.

A careful study of the thought structure that Gülen exposes in his works reveals that he invites his interlocutors to analysis and synthesis rather than superficial thinking, and channels them to elaborate thinking. In other words, he advises them to pay attention to the Prophetic Traditions' deep and implied meanings—from which legal deductions can be made—as well as their literal and clear meanings. Gülen's dealing with Sunnah in this way unveils his students' analytical abilities. According to Gülen, if studied in detail and interpreted within the context of the current era, Sunnah can be constituted as an independent source of reference. When dealing with differing views among Muslim scholars on the possibility of the Qur'an and Sunnah being independent sources of reference, Faruk Beser draws attention to Gülen's views and comments on this issue. Reflecting on the generality of the views and comments expressed in Gülen's works, Beser asserts that Gülen tacitly views Sunnah as an independent source of reference.[371] Looking from Gülen's perspective, the Sunnah is not only an independent source of reference, but also, like the Qur'an, a legal source that declares certain things lawful and others unlawful, and sets rules and principles with regards to the Islamic rules (*al-ahkam al-Islamiyyah*). It also has a function in clarifying what is ambiguous in the Qur'an, explaining what is implicit, specifying what is general and limiting what is unconditional.[372] Clearly, Gülen is following classical path of Muslim scholarship in his approach to the legal function of Sunnah.

If Gülen is read in the context of the legal, social and scientific

---

[370] Gülen, *Sonsuz Nur, Vol. 2 (Muhammad: The Messenger of God)*, pp. 382–383.
[371] Beser, Faruk, *Fethullah Gülen Hocaefendinin Fikhini Anlamak*, Vol. 2, (Istanbul: Ufuk Kitap Publishing, 2006), p. 37.
[372] Gülen, *Sonsuz Nur, Vol. 2 (Muhammad: The Messenger of God)*, p. 383.

functions he ascribes to the Sunnah, his overall approach can be better understood. Evaluating him from this perspective helps in accepting that his conclusions and interpretations on Sunnah are correct. For example, when he says that Sunnah makes certain things unlawful,[373] he elaborates this view and presents his comment on the basis of a solid example. He asserts that the Qur'an does not mention certain matters directly or indirectly, and bestows the legislative authority to the Noble Prophet. Such matters are abundant where the Qur'an remains silent. Prohibition of eating from the flesh of domesticated donkeys[374] or predatory animals;[375] or marriage with paternal or maternal aunts are some of the examples of issues the Qur'an does not deal with clearly. However, the Sunnah puts provisions and renders them *haram* (unlawful).[376] Gülen asserts that the Sunnah acts independently in implementing provisions concerning these issues. This approach and the examples he chooses are the same as Sunni Muslims scholars' understanding in classical period. In other words, by not putting forth a different view, Gülen highlights the accuracy of the righteous predecessors (*salaf*) in their views. Thus, Gülen draws evidence therefrom to support his view that the Companions who kept these points in mind viewed the Sunnah as a source of legislation and safeguarded it with a similar sensitivity to the Qur'an.[377]

In fact, the Noble Prophet's approach in exercising such a power is perfectly in line with the Quranic context and he derives his authority from the Holy Qur'an.[378] The Quranic verse, *"They ask you (O Messenger) what is lawful for them (including, in particular, the game caught by trained hunting animals...)"*[379] is considered the source of this authority. Through

---

[373] With such acceptance and ideologies, Gülen shows that he indeed walks parallel to many of the scholars of Sunnah.

[374] Bukhari, *fardu'l-humus*, 20; Muslim, *sayd*, 26.

[375] Bukhari, *niqah*, 27; Muslim, *niqah*, 33–40.

[376] Gülen, *Sonsuz Nur, Vol. 2 (Muhammad: The Messenger of God)*, p. 383.

[377] Ibid., pp. 383–384.

[378] *"They follow the (most illustrious) Messenger, the Prophet who neither reads nor writes (and has, therefore, remained preserved from any traces of the existing written culture and is free from any intellectual and spiritual pollution), whom they find described (with all his distinguishing features) in the Torah and the Gospel (that are) with them. He enjoins upon them what is right and good, and forbids them what is evil; he makes pure, wholesome things lawful for them, and bad, corrupt things unlawful. And he relieves them of their burdens (remaining of their own Law) and the restraints that were upon them"* (Qur'an 7:157).

[379] Qur'an 5:4

this verse, God justifies the legitimacy of the Prophet's rulings. Supposing he erred in his verdicts, the Noble Prophet—who is constantly supported with Divine guidance or revelation—would certainly be warned and his verdicts abrogated. A close study of Islamic literature shows no trace of any Prophetic ruling being repealed. Furthermore, verses in the Qur'an commanding[380] obedience[381] to God's Messenger are well known among Islamic scholars. These particular verses clearly bestow power upon the Prophet to legislate rules.

Gülen's approach is parallel with the majority of Muslim scholars. However, pondering within the context of the hadith, "God shall raise for this ummah at the head of every century a man who shall renew (or revive) His religion,"[382] Gülen displays a different approach. Quoting from Wahil, he says the Noble Prophet has left behind a clear footprint that can easily be followed, i.e. his Sunnah.[383] Thus, Gülen—being a follower of this footprint—believes that solutions to new jurisprudential issues the Muslim community may encounter in present times must be sought along the axis of Sunnah. To facilitate this task, as mentioned earlier, he suggests the establishment of a scholarly consultative council (*shura*) that functions within the sphere of Sunnah.[384] Thus, he stresses that the Sunnah lights the way for progress and solving the problems of the contemporary age. He also argues that innovations (*bid'ah*) and superstitions (*batil*) that crept into the community (*'ummah*) can be purged by way of adherence to the Sunnah.[385] He describes the characteristics of the representatives of such a mission as "being able to analyze and synthesize the signs of God both in the (horizons of) the universe (*afaq*) and in their own selves (*anfus*)..."[386]

[380] Qur'an 3:31; 4:65, 80; 5:92; 24:54; 59:7.
[381] "*O you who believe! Obey God and obey the Messenger, and those from among you who are invested with authority; and if you are to dispute among yourselves about anything, refer it to God and the Messenger, if indeed you believe in God and the Last Day. This is the best (for you), and fairest in the end*" (Qur'an 4:59).
[382] Abu Dawud, *Malahim*, 1.
[383] Gülen, *Sonsuz Nur, Vol. 2 (Muhammad: The Messenger of God)*, p. 65.
[384] Gülen, *Fasildan Fasila series, Vol. 4, (From Chapter to Chapter)*, (Istanbul: Nil Publishing, 2010), p. 167.
[385] Canan, *Fethullah Gülen'in Sunnet Anlayisi*, p. 217.
[386] Gülen, *Irsad Ekseni (The Ideal Human)*, (Istanbul: Nil Publishing, 2011), pp. 125–126

Sunnah's Interpretations of the Qur'an

Evaluating Gülen's views from above-mentioned perspective shows he directs his focus on the two main functions of Sunnah. Firstly, Sunnah defines certain lawful and unlawful deeds not mentioned in the Qur'an; secondly, it interprets the Qur'an.[387] According to Muslim exegetes, the Noble Prophet appears to have literally interpreted only a limited number of Quranic verses.[388] However, it is important to study the Prophet's daily life—which was a living Qur'an in practice—rather than the limited number of hadiths that literally interpreted the Qur'an. His behavior was nothing else than the manifestation of the Quranic value system in practical life. Therefore, interpretation of the Qur'an by the Sunnah should not be confined only to those hadiths mentioned in those sections of classical Hadith collections that are usually titled, "Book of Quranic Interpretation" (*Kitab al-Tafsir*).[389] Therefore, Gülen persistently emphasizes in his works that the Noble Prophet's entire life should be analyzed day by day carefully.

Albayrak draws attention to the importance given by Gülen to the functions of the Sunnah from several aspects. According to him, Gülen employs Hadith in interpreting Quranic verses, delivering important messages, for guidance (*irshad*) purpose, and in explaining and elaborating on keywords mentioned in many Quranic verses.[390] Thus, Gülen uses Sunnah as a source of reference in almost all subjects, with which he substantiates his views and theories. Hence, he remains very determined to explain Sunnah's key role to his audiences.

After these explanations, illustrating with some examples is important for better understanding of the subject. Gülen explains that the Companions asked God's Messenger directly when there was something they could not understand in a verse, and as soon as the Prophet answered and the issue was clarified, they put it into practice. Gülen supports his view with examples from the Sunnah. For example (as given in the part

---

[387] Albayrak, *Fethullah Gülen Hocaefendi'nin Tefsir Anlayisi*, p. 80.

[388] See for details M. Akif Koc, *Isnad Verileri Cercevesinde Erken Donem Tefsir Faaliyetleri: Ibn Abi Hatim (d.327/939) Tefsiri Orneginde bir Literatur Denemesi,* Ankara: Kitabiyat Publishing, 2003.

[389] Albayrak, *Fethullah Gülen Hocaefendi'nin Tefsir Anlayisi,* p. 80.

[390] ibid., pp. 80–81

of "Interpreting the Qur'an by Prophetic Traditions"), God mentioned "*zulm*" in the Quranic verse (6:82) and the Noble Prophet explained the meaning of the *zulm* in the verse as associating partners with God. Gülen most appropriately gives this explanation: "If the word *zulm* was not explained by the Noble Prophet as 'associating partners with God' (*shirk*), the true intent of the verse would not be understood."[391] Therefore, these misinterpretations would cause confusion and damage to Muslims' creed, and even lead to heresy; proper understanding and practicing of Islam could face most serious difficulties. Evidently, this would be inconsistent with the Qur'an's delivery and guidance rationale. Gülen continues and says, "Thanks to the Companions' question, the Sunnah stepped in at a critical stage, clarified the true objective of the verse and prevented Muslims from construing unnecessary misconceptions."

At this point, this question may come to mind: "Why does Gülen concentrate on the same examples, knowing that majority of the Muslim scholars used similar examples and achieved the same results?" By concentrating on these illustrations, Gülen demonstrates he shares the same views with the early period Muslim scholars. Simply by directing our attention once again towards the Age of Bliss – the time of the Noble Prophet, he highlights the authenticity of the source and soundness of its chains of transmission. He explains the Sunnah like a multi-lane motorway, keeping in mind that Sunnah offers solutions to problems of all ages as it did during the early period of Islam. In other words, as the problems encountered during the early stage of Islam revisit the present day populace—although in different versions—they undoubtedly will resurface again in the future. Gülen focuses on the universality of the Sunnah and its aspect that encompasses all ages. Thus, he refutes answers to arguments like "Sunnah has accomplished its mission during a set period; it has no functionality today." To put it in another way, Gülen attempts to put forward a different understanding of Sunnah with examples manifesting from his own life. Keeping links between periods sound and strong, he is trying to establish a healthy chain of transmission from the early period of Islam to the present day, and from here to the future. He takes assessments of the early period, compares them with the

---

[391]   Gülen, *Sonsuz Nur, Vol. 2 (Muhammad: The Messenger of God)*, p. 406.

present day values and demonstrates similarities in between.

Gülen presents hadiths according to subjects mentioned in Quranic verses or their relevance to the message he would like to deliver. Often using this method, he puts forth new comments about Sunnah. In other words, this is a presentation of Hadith by Gülen in an extraneous mode.[392] For example, in explaining the Quranic phrase "*[God] will assign for them love*," which is mentioned in the following verse, he points out the love and grace of God:

> Assuredly, those who believe and do good, righteous deeds, the All-Merciful will assign for them love (in the hearts of the inhabitants of the heaven and many on the earth, so that they will receive welcome throughout creation, no matter if they are weak and small in number now).[393]

For this reason, he interprets this verse with the help of a hadith: "When God loves someone, He calls Gabriel, 'I love so-and-so. So love him too.' And Gabriel announces this amongst the inhabitants of the heavens and earth…"[394]

Gülen's explanation of the above verse in light of this hadith has been mentioned in the past by Fakhr al-Din al-Razi (1149-1210), Ibn Kathir (1301-1373), and Sayyid Qutb (1906-1966). This demonstrates that Gülen's approach coincides with these famous exegetes' works. With this interpretation, *Gülen stresses that those Muslims who put themselves into the service of others will be granted Divine appreciation.*[395] In a way, elaborating on the meaning of the verse in the light of the hadith, Gülen gives messages to the current generation. Further, the encouragement he gives to the participants of the Hizmet Movement under his leadership should not be overlooked.

By presenting hadiths in an extraneous mode, Gülen handpicks the hadiths relevant to the messages he wants to give. As explained before, this demonstrates his preference for practical Prophetic

---

[392] Albayrak, *Fethullah Gülen Hocaefendi'nin Tefsir Anlayisi*, p. 81.
[393] Qur'an 19:96.
[394] Bukhari, *bad al-halq*, 6; *adab, 41; tawhid*, 33; Muslim, *birr*, 157; Tirmidhi, *tafsir* (19), 6
[395] Gülen, *Kur'andan Idrake Yansiyanlar (Reflections on the Qur'an)*, (Istanbul: Nil Publishing, 2009), p. 269.

Traditions. Gülen is convinced that faith that is not applied in practical life cannot be strong enough. This is perfectly consistent with the essence of the Sunnah. While Qur'an draws the theoretical structure, the Sunnah applies it into daily life. The Qur'an is a set of Divine rules sent down to regulate worldly life, whereby the canonical injunctions are lived to the full in a practical sense. Therefore, if the Qur'an is a corpus of guidance and laws for nations and communities, it must be reflected in their practical life. The way and method to realize this can only be found in the Noble Prophet's Sunnah.

Gülen chooses another Quranic verse to substantiate his views. To illustrate, he uses the following verse as an example:

> (The hypocrites have deceived them) just like Satan, when he says to human, "Disbelieve (in God)!" Then when he disbelieves, he says (to human): "Surely I am quit of you, for surely I fear God, the Lord of the worlds!"[396]

Gülen points out Satan's "fear of God" despite his rebellion and rebellious nature. He brings an explanation from the Sunnah to caution believers against slipping out and falling at a critical point, just like Satan: "Woe unto me, the son of Adam was commanded to prostrate, and he prostrated and Paradise was entitled to him and I was commanded to prostrate, but I refused and am doomed to Hell."[397] As understood from this verse and hadith, human beings are ontologically susceptible to rebellion, and due to this weakness, can find themselves on the verge of losing their faith at any time. Starting from this point, Gülen points to a correlation between the rebellion mentioned in the verse and the commandment of prostration mentioned in the hadith.[398] With this comment, he draws attention to the truth that prostration acts as breaks against denial that comes from a lack of faith. Thus, deeds build immunity to sins by filling in any doors to denial and act as conductors.

Sunnah Explains Ambiguities in the Revelation

Besides these approaches, Gülen points out a different function of

---

[396] Qur'an 59:16.
[397] Muslim, *faith*, 133; Ibn Maja, *iqama*, 70; Ahmad ibn Hanbal, *al-Musnad*, 2/443.
[398] Gülen, *Kur'andan Idrake Yansiyanlar* (Reflections on the Qur'an), pp. 402–403.

Sunnah. According to him, Sunnah clarifies what is ambiguous in the Qur'an. This view represents a function of Sunnah that is generally accepted by Muslim scholars. That is, Gülen shares the same view with the majority of Muslim scholars without adding a diverse annotation. There are various ambiguous expressions without explicit details in the Qur'an concerning the obligatory Daily Prayers, which is one of the most important pillars of Islam. For example, the following Quranic verses refer to the obligation of the Prayer: '...*And establish the Prayer in conformity with its conditions.*'[399] These and many other verses in the Holy Qur'an have a bearing on the continuing nature of the Prayer in its appropriate times.

However, the exact times and details of the Daily Prayers are not explained.[400] *Gülen stresses that, even if the times of the* Prayers were established, the other important acts of the Prayer, such as *fard* (obligatory), *wajib* (necessary), *mustahab* (recommended, but not necessary), *makruh* (undesirable, abominable), *mufsid* (any act that spoils a worship that started properly), *ruku'* (bowing), *sujud* (prostration), *qira'ah* (recitation of the Qur'an), *tahiyyah* (supplication) and *salam* (to end the prayer), could not be known unless the Noble Prophet explained them. The interpreter and clarifier of this ambiguous Divine command '...*And establish the Prayer in conformity with its conditions...*'[401] is the Sunnah. Furthermore, to teach them how to pray correctly, the Noble Prophet said to his Companions, "Pray as you see me praying."[402] Based on this, Gülen asserts that the Qur'an and the Sunnah act like factors to intrinsically complement each other.[403] If the Qur'an had to deal with all disciplines in detail, it would be bloated to such a gigantic size that its study would be far beyond human power, causing serious difficulties in understanding and practicing the Divine commandments. Hence, the Qur'an might have not been understood and found itself in a position outside the sphere of practical life. This is the reason why the Qur'an deals with the essence of matters, and leaves the details and practical

---

[399] Qur'an 33:33.
[400] Gülen, *Sonsuz Nur, Vol. 2 (Muhammad: The Messenger of God)*, pp. 406–407.
[401] Qur'an 33:33.
[402] Bukhari, *adhan*, 18; Ahmad ibn Hanbal, *al-Musnad*, 5/53.
[403] Gülen, *Sonsuz Nur, Vol. 2 (Muhammad: The Messenger of God)*, pp. 407–408.

aspects to the Sunnah.

While the situation is as such with the Prayer, it is not much different with *Hajj* (pilgrimage to Mecca), which is another pillar of Islam. According to Gülen, it is the Sunnah that explains the details of the rituals of pilgrimage. During his Farewell Hajj, the Noble Prophet explained it in practice and in more detail than what is described in the Qur'an.[404] In accordance with the hadith, "Learn your rituals (of hajj) from me,"[405] the rites of pilgrimage are established with all the details by Sunnah.[406] Analyzing the Farewell Hajj which was the only Hajj performed by the Noble Prophet—in this way would be more plausible.

Sunnah Specifically Delimits Verses

Another function of the Sunnah—besides clarifying the ambiguous verses—is to particularise or specify certain Quranic verdicts. Certain issues of the laws of inheritance in Islam have, for instance, been stipulated by Qur'an but further enhanced and elucidated by the detailed explanations of the Noble Prophet.

According to Gülen, the scope of some verses encompasses everybody including the Noble Prophet. However, he interprets a particular issue here in light of evidence he derives from the Sunnah. After the death of the Noble Prophet, his daughter Fatimah approaches Caliph Abu Bakr to collect her inheritance from her father. Upon this, Abu Bakr narrates a hadith he heard directly from the Noble Prophet: "We Prophets do not leave inheritance, whatever we leave is for charity."[407] According to Gülen, this hadith limited the generality of the above verse.

In a way, Gülen holds Sunnah as an important legislator in the Islamic legal system concerning overall public safety and welfare. Through these kinds of examples, he highlights the Sunnah's various aspects looking towards nurturing individuals, families and societies. He endeavors to strengthen cordial relationships, eradicate enmity and safeguard the social structure by creating a solid bond of love and

---

[404] "The Hajj is in the months well-known. Whoever undertakes the duty of Hajj in them, there is no sensual indulgence, nor wicked conduct, nor disputing during the Hajj..." (Qur'an 2:197)

[405] Nasai, *Manasiq*, 220; Ahmad ibn Hanbal, *al-Musnad*, 3/318, 366.

[406] Gülen, *Sonsuz Nur*, Vol. 2 (Muhammad: The Messenger of God), pp. 408–409.

[407] Bukhari, *i'tisam*, 5, *humus*, 1; Muslim, *jihad*, 49-52; Ahmad ibn Hanbal, *al-Musnad*, 2/463.

respect between individuals, families and the wider society. Thus, Gülen assigns a much lower priority to disputes over material expectations. Furthermore, to hold this bond together and ward off disintegration, he reminds people of the Quranic and Prophetic verdicts that debar from inheritance. Gülen, in a way, assumes the role of a social engineer. By playing a functional role in certain Quranic verses, Sunnah imposes conditions on the application of their verdicts.

Sunnah Sets Conditions for the Injunctions of Verses

According to Gülen, for example, the following verse stipulates general rules and principles of commerce:

> O you who believe! Do not consume one another's wealth in wrongful ways (such as theft, extortion, bribery, usury, and gambling), except it be dealing by mutual agreement; and do not destroy yourselves (individually or collectively by following wrongful ways like extreme asceticism and idleness. Be ever mindful that) God has surely been All-Compassionate toward you (particularly as believers).[408]

However, the Noble Prophet imposed some further conditions to the agreement mentioned in the verse by this principle: "Do not sell fruits of dates till they are in good condition."[409] According to Gülen's approach, the Quranic verses impose a verdict in general terms without much detail. However, the Noble Prophet attached conditions to agreements in order to protect both the buyer and the seller in the produce market. Gülen illustrates this through examples. A wholesale price agreement can be made on the basis of an estimated amount of produce while trees are at blossoming time. However, this agreement holds risks as well as opportunities of excessive profit for both parties. Due to natural disasters, trees may be affected while blossoming and may not yield the expected produce. Thus, the buyer loses. Conversely, due to favorable climatic or other conditions, the orchard may yield more produce than estimated. In this case, the seller loses from the wholesale value of their produce although they reap more than their labor's worth. In such situations, the

---

[408] Qur'an 4:29.
[409] Gülen, *Sonsuz Nur, Vol. 2 (Muhammad: The Messenger of God)*, p. 410.

Sunnah comes into action and regulates commercial transactions, that is, establishes trade principles to protect both parties. Hence, it helps commercial ethics to be established in the society. The verdict here is used by means of *qiyas* (analogy) instrument in Islamic literature, as a legal source for other areas of trade and commerce. Looking from the perspective of these explanations, the Noble Prophet followed a rational and progressive path with a delicate balance to educate the populace of the Age of Ignorance. Following the Noble Prophet's footsteps, Gülen uses a delicate method to explain things repeatedly from various perspectives (*tasrif* method) and according to the academic and intellectual level of his audience.

The Sunnah in Gülen's system of thought is an Islamic source that holds a position to impose legislation on issues where the Qur'an is silent, as a principle source of reference in jurisprudence and as an authority to interpret and explain Quranic verses. Gülen's approach complies with Dr. Beser's definition of Sunnah being an independent source. Also, according to Gülen, Sunnah began to fulfill its function with the beginning of the revelation of the Qur'an and has always been in close correlation with it. As the two complement each other, they constitute the two fundamental sources of Islam.[410] The four major Islamic schools of thought (*madhhabs*)[411] have no difference of opinion about the Qur'an and the Sunnah being the two fundamental sources.[412] Thus, the Sunnah has been regarded together with the Qur'an since the beginning. Because of this close relationship, neither the Sunnah nor the Qur'an can be isolated from the other.[413] Despite certain rationalistic thought trends that emerged in almost every age since the beginning, Sunnah holds its position as a source for the religion and religious life, a basis for scholarly and scientific research, and offers seminal presentations to scholarly and scientific researchers. Looking into Gülen's works in its entirety shows he seems to have the same considerations.

---

[410] ibid., p. 411.
[411] *Hanafite, Shafi'ite, Malikite,* and *Hanbalite.*
[412] Ahmet Kurucan, *Fikih Dunyamiz (Our World of Islamic Jurisprudence),* (Istanbul: Isik Publishing, 2011), p. 35.
[413] Canan, *Fethullah Gülen'in Sunnet Anlayisi,* p. 383.

However, another significant point to be mentioned here is that the hadiths and the Sunnah has interpreted the traditions of the Noble Prophet. According to Gülen, when the Companions applied the Sunnah into practice incorrectly due to their misunderstanding, the Noble Prophet explained the misunderstood point with another hadith. For example, a Companion, who is called Nuayman, sometimes had drunk alcohol and the Messenger would apply the provision of *fiqh* (jurisprudence) to him. This act was a sin; however, when one of the Companions condemned Nuayman for his sin, the Messenger of God frowned and said:[414] "Do not help Satan against your brother. I swear to God that he loves God and His Messenger."[415] The Noble Prophet has explained the situation of an individual being classified wrong due to his faults in the society, with a second hadith. In this way, he points out on an important rule which establishes peace in the society.

Works on Gülen's Expertise of Islamic Disciplines

There exists an abundance of works on the Hizmet (aka Gülen) Movement, a transnational social movement inspired by the ideas of Fethullah Gülen, mainly on education, tolerance, and dialogue. International conferences and symposiums organized especially during the first decade of this century produced a great number of academic-quality publications. On the other hand, despite Gülen's authorship of 77 books, there is a lack of works and research done on his intellectual qualities, Islamic identity and religious teaching methods.[416] However, the few individual attempts that have been made lately cannot be ignored. In this connection, it is beneficial to briefly mention some of the works on Gülen's knowledge of Quranic exegesis, Islamic jurisprudence and Prophetic traditions.

Suat Yildirim has written extensively on Gülen, including his views on Quranic exegesis and the Sunnah. In his work, titled *Fethullah Gülen'in Kur'an-i Hakim'e Yaklasimi (Fethullah Gülen's Approach to the Wise Qur'an)*, Yildirim deals with Gülen's distinct approach and commentaries that offer potential solutions to some contemporary so-

---

[414] Gülen, *Sonsuz Nur, Vol. 2 (Muhammad: The Messenger of God)*, pp. 302-303

[415] Bukhari, *hudud* 4-5.

[416] Ali Unal, *M. Fethullah Gülen, Bir Portre Denemesi (Fethullah Gülen: A Portrait Essay)*, (Istanbul: Nil Publishing, 2002), p.16.

cial problems. Rather than providing a traditional introduction of the Qur'an, Yildirim draws attention to Gülen's interpretation through which valuable contributions have been made to Islamic disciplines and scholarly works. In his work, Yildirim also points to one of Gülen's works on Quranic exegesis, titled *Kur'an'in Altin Ikliminde* (*In the Golden Climate of the Qur'an*) and suggests this work possesses the quality to be used as lecture notes in graduate and post-graduate programs within faculties of religious studies.[417]

Another work on Gülen's understanding of the Quranic exegesis (*Tafsir*) is Ismail Albayrak's *Fethullah Gülen Hocaefendi'nin Tefsir Anlayisi* (*Fethullah Gülen's Understanding of Quranic Exegesis*).[418] Albayrak focuses mainly on Gülen's approach to the methodology of Quranic exegesis and compares him with other important modern Muslim intellectuals. Albayrak has also edited another book regarding Gülen's exegetical, theological, mystical, legal thoughts and his approach to the Hadith discipline, titled *Mastering Knowledge in Modern Times: Fethullah Gülen as an Islamic Scholar.*[419]

Faruk Beser, a Turkish theologian, analyzed Gülen`s understanding of Islamic jurisprudence in one of his books, titled *Hocaefendi`nin Fikhini Anlamak* (*Understanding of Gülen`s Islamic Jurisprudence*).[420] Here, Beser summarizes Gülen's expertise of jurisprudence in the light of legal judgments (*fatwas*) given by Gülen since the early years of 1970s.

It is also worth mentioning that there is another book edited by Hamza Aktan, entitled *Bir Alim Portresi: Fethullah Gülen Hocaefendi* (*The Portrait of a Scholar: Fethullah Gülen*).[421] The contributors of this edited book have dealt with Gülen's expertise of Islamic disciplines from various perspectives along with some psychological and sociological analyses in their work.

---

[417] Suat Yildirim, *Fethullah Gülen'in Kur'an-i Hakim'e Yaklasimi* (*Fethullah Gülen's Approach to the Wise Qur'an*), (Istanbul: Nil Publications, 2011), p. 42.

[418] Ismail Albayrak, *Fethullah Gülen Hocaefendi'nin Tefsir Anlayisi* (Fethullah Gülen's Understanding of Quranic Exegesis), (Istanbul: Nil Publishing, 2010).

[419] Albayrak, *Mastering Knowledge in Modern Times: Fethullah Gülen as an Islamic Scholar,* (NJ: Blue Dome Press, 2012).

[420] Faruk Beser, *Hocaefendi`nin Fikhini Anlamak* (*Understanding of Gülen`s Islamic Jurisprudence,* 2 vols.) (Istanbul: Ufuk Kitap Publishing, 2006).

[421] Hamza Aktan, *Bir Alim Portresi: Fethullah Gülen Hocaefendi* (*The Portrait of a Scholar: Fethullah Gülen*), (Istanbul: Nil Publishing, 2014).

As far as the books on Gülen's understanding of the Prophetic Traditions are concerned, the first work published is Ibrahim Canan's (d. 2009) book, titled *Fethullah Gülen'in Sunnet Anlayisi* (*Fethullah Gülen's Understanding of Sunnah*). It is a noteworthy analytical work in this field, which is also very relevant to this book. In his work, Canan draws attention to an important point about Gülen's understanding and evaluation of Hadith. According to Canan, Gülen prefers to draw heavily on the practical, action-oriented aspect of the Hadith rather than the theoretical matters in the discipline.[422] Canan proposes that Gülen does not only approach Hadith as a scholar, but he also considers them as an intellectual who endeavors to discover how they should affect a Muslim's daily life. Canan's view may be assessed from the point of Gülen's selection of the hadiths, and considered as one of the reasons behind his choice of the hadiths. However, there may also be other reasons for Gülen's preference in the Prophetic reports. All of these issues will be dealt with in this work.

It should be noted that Canan confined himself to providing brief information about Gülen's acknowledgment of the importance of the discipline of Hadith and his profound knowledge on the qualities of traditionists (*muhaddiths*). He points to the characteristics of the traditionists and narrators (which is a point of focus for skeptical and critical thought), and emphasizes their qualities of learning and memorizing.[423] However, Canan falls short of presenting sufficient details on Western intellectual views about the subject and Gülen's views on non-Muslim critical thoughts on Prophetic Traditions. Nevertheless, he specifically highlights Gülen's work, titled *Sonsuz Nur-3* (*Muhammad, the Messenger of God*) as an answer to skepticism based on Hadith and Sunnah. There is a serious need for analysis and commentary to clarify and fill the gaps left by Canan.

The issue of the genre of *Rijal* (criticism of Hadith narrators and transmitters) not receiving adequate treatment may be considered as another outstanding point in Canan's work. The discipline of *Rijal* is a vital field of knowledge in the transmission of the hadiths, which is also a focal point of academic interest and criticism for scholars and intellectuals in the modern era. Gülen's knowledge in this field will

---

[422] Ibrahim Canan, *Fethullah Gülen'in Sunnet Anlayisi* (*Fethullah Gülen's Understanding of Sunnah*), pp. 67-94.

[423] Ibid., p. 84.

also be examined and analyzed in this work. Canan briefly touches on Gülen's views concerning the issue of the correlation between the Revelation and the Prophetic Practice—a subject of debate among Muslim scholars—and suggests that, according to Gülen, the Prophetic Practice (*Sunnah*) is connected to Revelation.[424] Gülen, who is an advocate of the Divine origin of the Sunnah, has been mentioned in Canan's work as being criticized for using the hadiths that are considered weak in his discourses. However, although Canan provides detailed information on the classification of the hadiths from the authenticity point of view, he does not explain why and under what circumstances Gülen resorts to such a practice.[425] This work will attempt to explore the rationale and wisdom behind Gülen's approach to the so-called weak hadiths.

In a brief assessment of Canan's work, titled *Fethullah Gülen'in Sunnet Anlayisi* (*Fethullah Gülen's Understanding of Sunnah*), Faruk Tuncer describes Gülen as a scholar with authority in the discipline of Hadith.[426] He states that Gülen is a notable Hadith critic who can analyze and evaluate a hadith from its narrators and chain of transmission perspectives, as well as from its textual point of view (*matn* critique). Tuncer emphasizes that in Gülen's works one can encounter no criticism of any one of the fundamental principles of the Hadith methodology or assertion and/or defense of any modern view contrary to Islamic tradition.[427]

In his article *"Fethullah Gülen's Theology of Peace-building"* published in *Islam and Peace-building*, Zeki Saritoprak stresses on Gülen's thoughts on the notion of peace, presenting his ideas through excerpts from his written works. Saritoprak asserts that Gülen's ideology is founded on the Qur'an and the Prophetic practices. However, he does not include quotes and comments that refer directly to the Prophetic Practice.[428]

Another book on Gülen, titled *Bir Alim Portresi* (*The Portrait of a Scholar*), has many articles from different researchers in academia. In this

---

[424] Ibid., p. 86.
[425] Ibid., pp. 117-133.
[426] The full text of this article can be accessed at www.fgulen.com.
[427] Faruk Tuncer, "Fethullah Gülen'in Sunnet Anlayisi," Book review, (2007), https://fgulen. com/tr/turk-basininda-fethullah-gulen/fethullah-gulen-hakkinda-kose-yazilari/2007-ko- se-yazilari/14324-Dr-Faruk-Tuncer-gyvorgtr-Fethullah-Gulenin-Sunnet-Anlayisi.
[428] Zeki Saritoprak, *Islam and Peacebuilding: Gülen Movement Initiatives*, *"Fethullah Gülen's Theology of Peace-building,"* (NJ: Blue Dome Press, 2010), pp. 169-187.

work, Osman Guner analyzed Gülen`s approach to the defense of Hadith. Guner's article is entitled "*Oryantalistlerin Hadis Hakkindaki Iddialarinin Kritigi: Fethullah Gülen Hocaefendi Ornegi*" (*The Critique of the Orientalists` Claims Regarding Hadith: the Exemplar of Fethullah Gülen*). Guner points out that the hadiths, according to Gülen, started to be recorded by the Prophet's Companions. As stated by Guner, Gülen expresses that the claims about hadiths being initially recorded in the aftermath are not founded on substantial sources. It is observed that whilst analyzing Gülen's views, Guner does not touch upon his efforts to prove the reliability of Sunnah through comparing it with today's scientific knowledge.

An important academic article pertaining to Gülen's teaching, "*Gülen's Teaching Methodology in His Private Circle*," has been authored by Ergun Capan and published in the work, titled *Mastering Knowledge in Modern Times: Fethullah Gülen as an Islamic Scholar*—a book compiled at academic-level with scholarly articles on Islamic disciplines. In his article, Capan cites books Gülen teaches in the areas of Quranic exegesis, Hadith, Islamic jurisprudence and its methodology, Sufism, advanced Arabic grammar and Islamic systemic theology. In addition, Capan mentions Gülen's knowledge on the Qur'an and the Hadith as well as the major works in principal Islamic disciplines (i.e. Quranic exegesis, Hadith studies, Islamic biographical literature, Islamic systematic theology, Islamic jurisprudence, and Sufism). He also explains how Gülen teaches these books to his students through a specific method.[429]

Another article on Gülen's understanding of Hadith was authored by Halim Calis in the same work. Calis draws profiles from Gülen's life and points to his influence within academic circles. For example, he cites Ali Bulac's statement, "[Gülen] exhibits a profile of intellectual-scholar,"[430] to refer to the immensity of Gülen's knowledge of both Islamic and modern sciences and his ability to combine them harmoniously.[431] In his article, while providing some general information about Hadith and Sunnah and citing the definitions of the area related

---

[429] Ergun Capan, *Mastering Knowledge in Modern Times: Fethullah Gülen as an Islamic Scholar,* "Gülen's Teaching Methodology in His Private Circle," (New York: Blue Dome Press, 2011), pp. 132-151.

[430] Scholar and writer Ali Bulac's views on Fethullah Gülen: www.fgulen.com.

[431] Halim Calis, *Mastering Knowledge in Modern Times: Fethullah Gülen as an Islamic Scholar,* "Fethullah Gülen's Thoughts on Hadith," (New Jersey: Blue Dome Press, 2011), pp. 39–63.

terms, Calis omits Gülen's views on these definitions, which is central to this work. This book will attempt to fill this gap by giving full treatment to Gülen's views on the transmission and codification of Hadith since the time of the Noble Prophet.

Calis highlights Gülen's "special interest" in the hadiths related to the prediction of events that may occur in the future. The issue of interest is to identify the motives behind Gülen's selection and interpretation of the hadiths, in particular regarding the Prophetic foreseeing of the future. Calis does not provide any explanation on the reasons behind this special interest. This work will explore the reasons behind Gülen's selection of this kind of hadiths.

Calis also investigates Gülen's modern interpretation of hadiths, his contribution to the teaching of Hadith and his approach to the problems arising in our time in the light of the Prophetic reports. Again, there is a lack of detail on what Gülen proposes in terms of resolving these problems. He also mentions Gülen's attribution of great importance to the correlation between Quranic verses and Sunnah when explaining the hadiths. This reflects Gülen's view of the Qur'an and the Hadith as two elements supplementing each other. However, Calis' article does not provide any detailed information in this regard.

In the same work, Ismail Acar analyses Gülen's understanding of Islamic jurisprudence (*Fiqh*) in his article, titled "*A Classical Scholar with a Modern Outlook: Fethullah Gülen and His Legal Thought*." Throughout this article, Acar brings clarity to Gülen's way of "independent reasoning" (*ijtihad*) and his standpoint in the field. He emphasizes Gülen's idea of a qualified committee being established to address the *fiqh*-related modern day problems yet to be resolved. In order to do this, he uses parables from Gülen's *fatwa*s; an example of which is Gülen's indication that punishing a wrongdoer does not belong to a person but rather to the legal authorities. Whilst analyzing Gülen's outlook and understanding of *fiqh*, Acar also highlights his proficiency regarding Hadith studies and the Prophetic traditions.[432]

---

[432] Ismail Acar, *Mastering Knowledge in Modern Times: Fethullah Gülen as an Islamic Scholar,* "*A Classical Scholar with a Modern Outlook: Fethullah Gülen and His Legal Thought,*" (NJ: Blue Dome Press, 2012), pp. 65-84.

In this work, Gülen's understanding of Sunnah will be analyzed in detail, especially from the point of the new elements he introduced into the teaching of Hadith. In this regard, Capan's article is of great importance as it provides an inventory of books taught by Gülen. Since Capan was a pupil of Gülen's, his article is much more than a mere academic exercise. In effect, it provides the reader an opportunity to study the views of an insider in a clear way. However, the article is not adequately analytical. Since Capan had to deal with a series of other topics along with the Hadith, he did not provide much comment relevant to the focal points in this work. As such, this work will attempt to fill in the remaining gaps. In doing so, the focus will be on Gülen's understanding of Sunnah along with his interpretations and the terminology he has used in relation to the Prophetic Traditions in his close circle and his writings.

Gülen's Knowledge in the Field of Sunnah

The levels of Gülen's knowledge and competency in the field of Sunnah constitute an important issue in terms of the correctness of his legal decisions and comments. As Sunnah is one of the main sources of reference for legal and practical rulings, proficiency in this area is the first prerequisite of Muslim scholars. Sunnah offering solutions to modern day problems is possible by means of competent scholars. For this reason, according to Gülen, upholding and safeguarding the religion in this century has been guaranteed by this hadith, "God will raise for this community at the end of every hundred years the one who will renovate[433] its religion for it."[434] In accordance with this hadith, there existed a *mujaddid*[435]—whose scholarly knowledge and competence

---

[433] According to the Islamic creed, there will come no more prophets after Prophet Muhammad, upon whom be peace and blessings. Therefore, the responsibility of protecting the religion against innovations, teaching Muslims their religion and finding solutions to modern problems rests with Muslim scholars. Competent Muslim scholars who assume these responsibilities are called *mujaddids*.

[434] Abu Dawud, *Malahim*, 1.

[435] According to Muslim scholars, the first century's *mujaddid* was 'Umar ibn 'Abd al-'Aziz, and Imam Shafi'i for the second century; and Abu al-Hasan al Ash'ari, Abu Hamid al Isfirani, and Imam al-Ghazzali for the following two centuries. (*'Awn al-Ma'bud 4/181; Kashf al-Khafa'*, 1/243).

is confirmed by their contemporaries—in every century to renovate the religion. The message of this hadith also infers that scholars with deep knowledge (*mujaddid*)[436] will emerge to preserve and revive the religion—today and in the future. At the same time, the hadith imposes the responsibility of cultivating competent scholars on the Muslim community. Otherwise, the likelihood of occurrence of a gap in the preservation of the Qur'an and the Sunnah would be very high. Therefore, the safeguarding of the religion is directly proportional to the efforts of Muslim community, although God assumes the responsibility to protect the Qur'an.[437] Despite some serious failures and degeneracies that occurred in the history of Islam, the Muslim world has the potential to fill any void related to the Qur'an and the Sunnah and to sustain its stamina.

At this juncture, some relevant questions come to mind about Gülen. Can Gülen—who is a public figure internationally—be directly associated with the term *mujaddid*; does he possess the required level of knowledge in Sunnah and related disciplines? Whether Gülen qualifies as a *mujaddid* does not have a direct relation to this subject. However, the prerequisite to qualify for the title of *mujaddid* (renovator), i.e. proficiency in the fields of the Qur'an and the Sunnah, coincides with the possibility of Gülen's possession of knowledge. Looking from this perspective necessitates dealing briefly with the subject of *mujaddid*.

Faruk Beser, who expounds on the qualities of *mujtahid* (Islamic thinker/reformer), gives Gülen a special position among present day Muslim scholars. He focuses on his scholarly qualities and considers him a *mujtahid*.[438] Beser emphasizes that his view is not binding on anyone. However, looking from the point of view of a *mujtahid's* qualities and knowledge in Sunnah, Beser—despite the possibility of being mistaken in considering him a *mujtahid*, opens a door for researchers that may lead to further studying Gülen's expertise in the discipline of Sunnah. Beser examined Gülen's level of knowledge using scientific criteria and proved

---

[436] According to Islamic literature, the most prominent characteristic of a *mujaddid* is the possession of deep knowledge and competency in the disciplines of Qur'an, the Sunnah and other Islamic sciences.

[437] Qur'an 15:9.

[438] Beser, *Fethullah Gülen Hocaefendinin Fikhini Anlamak*, p. 18.

his scholarly proficiency. Whereas, what does Gülen think about Beser's assertion and how he positions himself? Does he accept or reject these kinds of views about his stature? As mentioned earlier, the subject matter is not whether Gülen is qualified for the title of *mujaddid*, but rather his level of knowledge on and adherence to the Prophetic Tradition. In other words, the question is about whether Gülen is accepted to be an authority in the field of Sunnah.

Despite his respect for individuals and diversity of views, Gülen displays the well-known characteristic of defending the Sunnah at any cost as perceived in Islam. However, he does not hesitate to make necessary corrections when he himself is the subject matter. He believes in freedom of speech and asserts that researchers have the right to express the results of their intellectual activities without any restrictions; he does not see himself in a position to make any editorial interference. While expressing views about *mujaddid*, Gülen asserts that construing the new concepts of the era, laws of the nature, new conditions and social formations, and filling the voids in areas open to independent reasoning according to the rules of *ijtihad*[439] is the duty of the *mujaddid*. Gülen does not consider himself as possessing the required qualifications in this field, as he says, "I neither considered myself a *mujaddid* to fill that position nor a *mujtahid*."[440] He emphatically advises that all possible solutions to new problems should be discovered and necessary legal rulings issued by a council of scholars who are experts in respective Islamic sciences and other related areas, instead of the view of single *mujtahid*. This reflects the importance he attributes to this issue. The safeguarding of the religion in its pristine form would be directly proportional to the expertise of the scholars constituting this council. It is possible to infer from Gülen's view that the position of *mujtahid* in this age should be held by a juridical personality rather than a real person. However, with the non-existence of such a council and important issues needing to be solved, Gülen does not hesitate to make a choice from among existing

---

[439] Reasoning carried out by a Muslim, based on his knowledge of the Qur`an and teaching of the Noble Prophet in a matter not specified by either.

[440] Fethullah Gülen, "Ne Muceddidim ne Muctehid ne de Reformist" (March, 2006), http:// fgulen.com/tr/fethullah-gulenin-butun-eserleri/terbiye-ve-cihad/175-fgulen-com-turkce/hitabet/bamteli-cozumleri/9849-Fethullah-Gulen-Ne-Muceddidim-Ne-Mucte-hid-Ne-de-Reformist

opinions or exercise his own power of *ijtihad*.[441]

According to Beser's view, Gülen appears to be in a contradictory position vis-à-vis his own words. That is, while highlighting the necessity of a council of experts on one hand, on the other hand, he, individually, focuses on legal issues. In this situation, Gülen's issuing of legal rulings on certain issues may be considered the result of the non-existence of such a council and accomplished expert scholars. Also, these legal decisions reluctantly issued by Gülen may be motivated by his concern for the Muslim community's needs that must be satisfied, and the possibility that ignoring these needs would leave religious principles and values exposed to risks of erosion and deviation. This provides evidence of scholarly courage and expertise in Sunnah and other sources of reference when issuing legal decisions. Needless to say, issuing a legal decision requires proper understanding of all Quranic verses, the Hadith and other accumulated Islamic literature related to the subject matter. In a way, it is possible to say that Gülen acts on the principle that aiming to fill a legal void is essential to ward off social handicaps—even though there may be a chance of erring in his decision. By this action, he draws attention to the golden rule of easing the practice of the religion instead of complicating it, as recommended by the Noble Prophet, and presents rational and practical principles.

Islam, being a living and dynamic religion, will dictate the establishment of mechanisms for the issuing of legal opinions. As there were Muslim scholars serving the religion in the past, there will always be a need for equally qualified scholars who can read well the spirit of the time and assume a leadership position in the community. Beser's approaches to *mujaddid* and *mujtahid*[442]—although not accepted by Gülen—appear to be welcomed by others, because there exists no thesis put forth to counter Beser's thesis or any other arguments as rebuttal to his views. This may be seen as the acknowledgement of his high level of knowledge in the discipline of Hadith, thus recognition of the correctness of new legal decisions he issued. This acceptance, as mentioned above, may also be interpreted as viewing him as a member of an incorporeal

---

[441] Beser, *Fethullah Gülen Hocaefendinin Fikhini Anlamak*, p. 43.

[442] A legist formulating independent decision in legal or theological matters, based on interpretation and application of the main principles of derivation of Islamic law

(or incorporated) entity.

Assessing in light of the above explanations, it is possible to say that Gülen may be viewed as fitting well with Beser's definition of *mujaddid* and *mujtahid*, especially in the field of Islamic sciences, and particularly in the discipline of Hadith. This is because Gülen is well-known and recognized for his studies of the Sunnah and various Hadith collections together with other Islamic sciences, and his research on the biographies of the Noble Prophet and his Companions.[443] Gülen explains this in his own words, "I spent my whole life in investigating the Sunnah."[444] What is understood from this statement is that Gülen puts Sunnah in the center of all Islamic disciplines and looks into all other sciences from this perspective. He views Sunnah as a primary source of reference in analyzing and justifying other sciences. In addition, his understanding of Sunnah is not historical or instrumental but deeply theological.

According to Suat Yildirim,[445] the source of Gülen's scholarly career consists of the Qur'an and the Sunnah. In his research and writings, Gülen gives unique illustrations from the lives of the Companions, who represent dynamic manifestations of the Sunnah. In Gülen's narratives, analyses and new interpretations of these examples—although some date back almost 50 years—the source does not appear to have lost any vigor at all. Those who follow Gülen closely, and those who know him from his writings and speeches, can see the exceptional level of his knowledge—based on many hundreds of scholarly sources of reference—on Sunnah and the time of the Noble Prophet.[446] Here may come to mind the question of why Gülen mostly derives his proofs and evidence from the Companions, whom he estimates highly. The reason is that the Companions witnessed the most pristine form of the religion during the time of the Noble Prophet; they were directly targeted by the Qur'an and were personal representatives of the Quranic verses. Thus, they became role models as they adopted Islam as their way of life. At

---

[443] Erdogan, *Fethullah Gülen Hocaefendi, Kucuk Dunyam (Fethullah Gülen: My Small World)*, p. 45.

[444] Unal, M. *Fethullah Gülen: Bir Portre Denemesi (Fethullah Gülen: A Portrait Essay)*, p. 307.

[445] Yildirim is colleague who worked with Gülen in the Religious Affairs Department (Diyanet Isleri Baskanligi). They first met in 1964.

[446] Unal, M. *Fethullah Gülen Bir Portre Denemesi (Fethullah Gülen: A Portrait Essay)*, p. 17.

this juncture, Gülen presents the Noble Prophet's sayings, "Be cautious about my Companions, and do not say anything inappropriate to them!" and "My Companions are like stars in the sky, whichever of them you use as a guide, you will be rightly guided."[447] It may be appropriate to say that Gülen attributes more importance to knowledge on Sunnah because of these hadiths. Thus, he selects his examples from this source.

Thomas Michel questions Gülen's interpretations of Islamic sources, and seeks answers to the question of how much is known about his commentaries. Michel concludes that, in his interpretations of Islamic sources, Gülen takes the Qur'an and moral values as his fundamental basis. According to him, Gülen places the necessity of worship and the moral and personal virtues at the center of religious motives and emotions. He explains the true Islam as excellent morality. This is to say, this approach of his views the Prophetic Tradition as the spring of morality, and places the Sunnah in its center. Michel highlights Gülen's frequent usage of Hadith as a source of reference and strengthening for his views.[448] He illustrates this with the following hadith as an example, which Gülen uses in elaborating on this topic: "Islam is all about good moral values. I have been sent only to complete the good character."[449]

Furthermore, Faruk Tuncer, who carried out research on Gülen, emphasizes that Gülen is a prominent Hadith critic, who can evaluate a hadith from the point of view of its narrator and chain of narration as well as the text. In fact, Gülen is well known for his substantial volume of acquis in Hadith literature.[450] It is for this reason that Gülen uses examples he carefully selects from the body of Sunnah. Here, it is necessary to draw attention to a particular characteristic of Gülen's. He is known to be a person who does not assert himself. He explains this approach by saying, "Persistence or declaring one's views forcefully is a kind of impertinency, presumptuousness, hypocrisy and boasting."[451] However, when it comes to issues concerning the Prophetic Traditions, i.e. whether something is part of the Sunnah, he always gives clear and assertive responses

---

[447] Gülen, *Sonsuz Nur, Vol. 2 (Muhammad: The Messenger of God)*, p. 359.
[448] Thomas Michel, "Gulen as Educator and Religious Teacher," Article, (April 2002), http://fgulen.com/en/press/review/24902-gulen-as-educator-and-religious-teacher.
[449] Jalaluddin as-Suyuti, *al-Jamius Saghir*, 1/79.
[450] Tuncer, "Fethullah Gülen'in Sunnet Anlayisi".
[451] Gülen, *Umit Burcu (The Bearing of Hope), Kirik Testi series*, Vol. 4, (Istanbul: Nil Publishing, 2011), p. 57.

and argues strongly.[452] This may be judged as stemming from his serious stance and sensitivity in terms of avoiding ambiguity in matters concerning the Sunnah. When Sunnah is concerned, Gülen defends his thesis with definite information, and endeavors to prove it by detailed evidence. This aspect of him constitutes evidence for his confidence in the discipline of Sunnah and his accumulated experience in this field.

Canan, however, says the discipline of Hadith involves classifications based on certain criteria. According to this arrangement, Hadith scholars are categorized in line with their level of Hadith knowledge, such as *talib*[453] (knowledge seeker), *muhaddith*[454] (Hadith scholar), *hafidh*[455] (one who guards or memorized hadiths), *hujjah*[456] (proof), and *haqim*[457] (wise one).[458] In accordance with these definitions, Canan points that Gülen has a very good command of Hadith literature. He emphasizes that Gülen presents proofs and evidence from Sunnah to support the subjects he discusses when needed. He points out Gülen's attention to the authenticity of the Traditions, textual variations between narrations reported through different chains of transmissions and conditions of the transmitters.[459] However, despite these conclusions, Canan declines to include Gülen into any of the above categories. He appears to be unwilling to provide a clear judgment and confine Gülen's position in the field of Hadith, and leaves the verdict to experts in the area. However, his ability of bringing evidence—whenever needed—from Hadith collections together with their state of health, source and textual variations, presenting information about their transmitters and, on some issues, saying definitely, "This issue does not exist in the body

---

[452] Canan, *Fethullah Gülen'in Sunnet Anlayisi,* p. 75.

[453] *Talib:* A person who is determined to learn the science of Hadith; a Hadith student.

[454] *Muhaddith:* A scholar who has learnt the science of Hadith, memorized a sufficient number of *hadith* together with their texts, chains of transmission and narrators, and who knows the practical applications of these traditions.

[455] *Hafidh:* A scholar of Hadith who memorized approximately 100 thousand hadiths with their texts and chains of transmissions.

[456] *Hujjah:* A scholar of Hadith who memorized approximately 300 thousand hadiths with their texts and chains of transmissions.

[457] *Haqim:* A scholar who memorised the whole body of *hadith* collections—texts, chain of transmission, and so on.

[458] See more details: Aliyyu'l-Qari, *Sharhu Nuhbati'l-Fikar,* pp. 3-4; Babanzade, *Tecrid* p. 8.

[459] Canan, *Fethullah Gülen'in Sunnet Anlayisi,* p. 74.

of Sunnah; that matter does not exist in the Sunnah,"[460] constitute a reasonably solid basis for one to think that he may be a *hujjah*.

Whilst commenting on the recording of Revelations and Sunnah which attracts criticism from outsiders, Gülen always establishes a comparison between the process of recording of the primary components of Islamic juridical process. When presenting this information, he is confident of his sources. This display of confidence suggests he has scanned all major *tabaqat* books. Otherwise, Gülen's comments would be wrong. However, thoughts exhibited in his works do not collide with Islamic literature or have never been refuted.

Gülen's close interest in the lives of the Companions and his detailed knowledge on the subject were discussed in previous sections. Here, we will look at some of Gülen's comments on the characteristics of the Companions. He emphasizes that it would be highly unrealistic to claim Companions' fluency in local vernaculars when delivering the message of Islam in foreign lands. Drawing on Islamic biographical sources, Gülen informs that there were only three or four people among the Companions who could speak a foreign language and these people were always with the Noble Prophet to translate[461] his correspondence.[462] This high level of knowledge and attention to detail displayed in Gülen's works leads researchers to the conclusion that Gülen closely follows the Sunnah and the characteristics that belong to the Companions. The important point here is Gülen's knowledge of existence—or nonexistence—of an issue that is related to Sunnah and Companions in the literature. Gülen displays a difference from others by pointing out such minute details. Gülen's approach—i.e. offering detailed information in explaining historical events and constructing theses—displays his profound scholarly knowledge as well as his principle of convincingly proving his case.

Giving some examples about Gülen's emphasis on details would bring clarity to the issue. At first glance, these details may be

---

[460] ibid., p. 75.
[461] The necessity of learning foreign languages may be inferred from this practice of the Noble Prophet.
[462] Gülen, *Umit Burcu (The Bearing of Hope), Kirik Testi* series, Vol. 4, p. 194.

inconspicuous and ignored. However, they do not escape Gülen's attention and comments. This characteristic of Gülen's highlights the importance of scanning and interpreting the Sunnah and Islamic hagiography with utmost care, and points out the possibility of these details offering solutions to problems encountered in the present time. Therefore, looking into the Sunnah and the lives of the Companions needs to be made from a holistic perspective as well as in detail.

Gülen draws attention to social issues, for instance, men having long hair, which sometimes become issues of criticism. He argues that the hadith narrating that Qatadah—when he accepted Islam—was cautioned by the Noble Prophet to cut his hair is not sound. He maintains that it is highly unlikely for the Noble Prophet to say something that is not in accordance with the general principles of Islam,[463] and no such narration exists in any reliable Hadith sources. Gülen points out certain biographical works mentioning that most of the Companions had long and plaited hair. His evidence is that when some Companions tied their hair, the Noble Prophet advised them to let their hair loose so they can also benefit from blessings during *sajdah* (prostration).[464] He brings further clarity to the issue by another comment, which also indicates his high level knowledge on the Companions. For example, Gülen argues that Abu Bakr, 'Umar and 'Uthman had long hair and the Noble Prophet never ordered these three of his closest friends to cut their hair short.[465] If the narration about Qatadah was sound, the Noble Prophet would have warned his close friends—who accepted Islam before Qatadah— about their hair, and Qatadah would have already understood this sensitivity before being warned by the Noble Prophet. As can be seen by these examples, Gülen counters the report by providing answers from the body of Sunnah. On the issue of Qatadah's long hair, he proves there exists no such record in Hadith literature, thus putting forth the view that

---

[463] It is beneficial to remember that Gülen's view asserts certain Hadith scholars' dexterity to tell whether a given text—on the basis of its context and meaning—is a hadith or not. Attempting to make an inference on the basis of this piece of information would make it possible to say that Gulen—in light of his close acquaintance with the Noble Prophet and his Sunnah—possesses the ability to argue for the unlikelihood of this text being attributable to the Noble Prophet.

[464] Ahmad ibn Hanbal, *al-Musnad* 6/8, 391; Abdurrazzak, *al-Musannaf* 2/183.

[465] Gülen, *Prizma 4 (Prism)*, (Istanbul: Nil Publishing, 2010), p. 378.

men having long hair may even be considered as Sunnah—depending on the intention of the individual.[466] With this defense and proof system and by following a logical way, Gülen offers his interlocutor rational observations. He draws attention to the practicability of the Sunnah and the fact it does not clash with present day values. Thus, he places the Sunnah in a problem-solving position.

In evaluating the numbers of the Companions provided in various hadiths and biographical sources, Gülen puts forth a rather different comment. According to Ibn Hajar, there were 130 thousand Companions during the time of the Noble Prophet. Although he accepts the accuracy of this number, Gülen displays a different approach to its assessment. Providing available sources and researches as evidence, he argues that the number of Companions' graves in Medina Cemetery is less than ten thousand. Retaining his clarity of mind on this issue, he suggests that the remaining 120 thousand Companions were dispersed to different parts of the world to deliver the message of Islam.[467] This may be seen as a minor detail. However, when comparing the historical data with the actual number of graves of Companions, the value of this little detail becomes obvious. Otherwise, the data provided on the numbers of the Companions would remain unsatisfactory. It is possible to say that Gülen, while explaining his views about Companions' migration, may be inferring duty for the Hizmet Movement, whose members represent the Prophet's Companions in our time.

In his works, Gülen prefers to focus on Companions' behavior, and derive training and education rules therefrom. In this way, he focuses on the Companions and illustrates them as role models. It is noticed that Gülen is well informed regarding the sources relevant to his point of focus and draws important—and amazing—inferences. For example, emphasizing Abu Bakr and 'Umar's talking less—out of respect—in the presence of the Noble Prophet, Gülen asserts, "I would

---

[466] During his chats, Gulen sometimes gives presents to his guests. This is due to his *sunnah* understanding. During one of these gatherings, he took off his headgear and asked his assistant to give it as a gesture to a man with long hair sitting among the audience. He then added: "It is not to be though that I disapprove the long hair or reprove him; wearing long hair is *sunnah*, provided that the intention is correct" (Mustafa Erdil, April, 2008, visiting of Fethullah Gülen).

[467] Gülen, *Prizma 3 (Prism)* (Istanbul: Nil Publishing, 2010), p. 38.

argue that if all Hadith, Sirah and Maghazi books were scanned, the totality of Abu Bakr's talks in the presence of the Noble Prophet would not amount to one hundred sentences."[468] This is a striking argument concerning the Sunnah a point that can be put forth following careful research. A personality like Gülen, who is in the center of attention for his views, is normally expected not to speak baselessly on these kinds of serious matters. Gülen also argues that 'Umar's speeches in the presence of the Prophet are so few that they can be counted easily. Yet, 'Umar spent many years with the Noble Prophet.[469] Capturing this point, which can constitute a rule of manners, and commenting on it would require a serious revision of literature. Certain moral rules may be inferred from Gülen's deduction; such as, the right of speech in a gathering belongs to the most knowledgeable and experienced person, highlighting qualified people, respect for knowledge and holders of knowledge, trust and confidence in the leader (especially the Noble Prophet).

In another example, when asked about whether a hadith exists saying, "When a person drinks alcohol, his Prayer will not be accepted for forty days," Gülen answered clearly: "There exists neither an explicit Quranic verse commanding to repeat someone's Prayers offered after consuming alcohol, nor a hadith that is *mursal, marfu', da'if,* or *matruk.*"[470] Thus, he clarifies a contentious issue that can cause trouble in a community.[471] The statement, "The Prayer of one who drinks alcohol is never accepted," conflicts with fundamental principles of Islam regarding human beings. However, being affected by alcohol may diminish the quality of the Prayer (though one delays offering their obligatory Prayer until they know what they are saying) and interfere with a person's inner feelings vis-à-vis God during worship.

Commenting with regards to the idea of renouncing material wealth in Sufism (*Tasawwuf*), Gülen advises not to abandon material gains, but highlights the importance of renouncing the love of riches in the heart. He diverts attention to the Hadith corpus, saying, "In fact,

---

[468] Gülen, *Umit Burcu (The Bearing of Hope), Kirik Testi, Vol. 4*, pp. 57-58.
[469] ibid., p. 58.
[470] Gülen, *Fasildan Fasila 1 (From Chapter to Chapter, Vol. 1)*, (Istanbul: Nil Publishing, 2010), pp. 283-284.
[471] For verdicts on the consumption of alcohol (*hadd al-shurb*) see Bukhari, *Hudud*, 4; Muslim, *Hudud*, 35; Abu Dawud, 35, 36; Tirmidhi, *Hudud*, 14, 15.

it is impossible to see a statement by the Noble Prophet prohibiting, in its absolute sense, richness and possessions."[472] Deducing such a legal decision and presenting it as a "proof" (*hujjah*) would necessitate scanning the whole Hadith corpus, including weak hadiths.

Gülen also brings in some explanations concerning the dress code in Islam, which is another contentious issue presented by certain groups as a fundamental part of the religion. The issue of the *turban* (headgear for man) is one example. Gülen emphasizes that reputable Hadith compilations, i.e. Bukhari and Muslim, contain no narration from the Noble Prophet concerning wearing a turban. He mentions a narration about the Noble Prophet wearing a black turban and letting one end hang down over his back during the conquest of Mecca.[473] However, he says that narrations[474] related to receiving extra rewards for praying while wearing a turban are mentioned in secondary Hadith collections (*zawa'id*) and not main sources of Hadith (*ummahat*). Here, he highlights an important point: he believes that issues like wearing a turban come under secondary matters of Islam and insisting on them would make the practice of religion difficult.[475] Looking from a logical standpoint, one would understand that Gülen must have studied all Hadith collections classified under *ummahat* and *zawa'id* to reach this conclusion.

Up until this point, some examples illustrating Gülen's thorough knowledge and understanding of Hadith sources have been dealt with. The non-availability of any works contradicting the above examples leads to the conclusion that Gülen is correct in his thinking. The soundness of evidence Gülen presents in his works and close connections with the Sunnah render his theses strong.

Also, it is possible to say that Gülen has thorough knowledge of the lives of the Companions and Hadith narrators. The discipline of *Rijal* (narrators)[476] plays an important role in safeguarding the Sunnah, as an error committed in the chain of narrators negatively affects the authenticity of the hadiths. This is the reason why Gülen attributes special

---

[472] Gülen, *Kur'andan Idrake Yansiyanlar (Reflections on the Qur'an)*, p. 332.
[473] Muslim, *hajj* 453; Abu Dawud, *libas* 21.
[474] Al-Daylami, *al-Musnad*, 2/265; al-Sakhawi, *al-Maqasid al-Hasana*, p. 423.
[475] Gülen, *Prizma 4 (Prism Vol. 4)*, p. 121.
[476] The chain of narrators that have allowed future generations to access hadiths that can be traced back to the Noble Prophet.

importance to the discipline of *Rijal* and is passionate about teaching this science.[477] He is convinced that studies were done on *Rijal* since the time of the successors of the Companions. He argues that chains of narrators and textual criticisms were carried out during that time, important *Rijal* books were authored as well, and all these works were taken under care and protection.[478] A proper understanding of the level of Gülen's knowledge of Sunnah would require a perusal of the works he studied. This comprises numerous large volumes of Hadith works and corpuses.[479]

One may say that Gülen, with his modern Hadith comments, exhibits a different approach than his contemporaries. He is convinced that Sunnah sheds light on all kinds of problems in the past, and contemporary problems can be solved in the light of Sunnah as well. His focus on basic issues, such as individual and community education, progress in modern technologies and social events, causes him to study the Sunnah deeper and come up with new deductions and analogies. For this reason, he further trusts the Sunnah and attributes more value to it.

On the one hand, because of these characteristics, Gülen, as highlighted before, persistently refuses to accept titles, such as *mujaddid* and *mujtahid*, others give him. For this reason, the people in his immediate surroundings also reject this sort of excessive praising. On the other hand, it is possible to mention a welcome by Muslim scholars and scholars in the West. Sunnah-centered theses he put forward, evidence supporting his criticism, accuracy in his new comments and solutions exhibit his profound knowledge in the discipline of Sunnah and give Gülen a place in the Islamic sciences. What is missing is the naming of his position. Although this is not important, it may give rise to some misunderstandings and false perceptions. It may also cause divisions within the Muslim world. At this point, Gülen takes a firm stance against discord and sedition. He highlights that any disagreements within the community can be solved—as mentioned earlier—by a council of Muslim scholars to accommodate modern day needs. He draws attention to the

---

[477] Canan, *Fethullah Gülen'in Sunnet Anlayisi*, p. 82.
[478] Gülen, *Zamanin Altin Dilimi (The Golden Realm of Time)*, Cag Ve Nesil, 4 *(The Modern Age and the Contemporary Generation series*, Vol. 4), p. 182.
[479] Canan, *Fethullah Gülen'in Sunnet Anlayisi*, pp. 80, 83.

inadequacy of individual scholarly efforts and highlights the consequent problems that may result. Besides, legal decisions issued by an authoritative council with broad participation are more likely to be met with public acceptance and legitimacy. Gülen's view of the establishment of a council of *ijtihad* may stem from his own interpretation of the Noble Prophet's decision not to appoint a caliph after himself but to leave the selection of the person considered as his successor to a group of leaders among the Companions.

Revelation-Hadith Correlation

According to Muslims, Revelation (*Wahy*) is an undeniable truth, as per the following Quranic verses:

> We have revealed to you (O Messenger), as We revealed to Noah and the Prophets after him; and We revealed to Abraham, Ishmael, Isaac, Jacob and the Prophets who were raised in the tribes, and Jesus, Job, Jonah, Aaron, and Solomon; and We gave David the Psalms.[480]

> O you who believe! Believe in God and His messenger, and the Book He sent down to His messenger, and the Books He sent down before. Whoever rejects God, His angels, His Books, His messengers, and the Last Day, has strayed far in error.[481]

Revelation is a Divine law carried along by a chain of Prophets, beginning with Adam and ending with Muhammad, peace be upon them all. Also, the status of Hadith vis-à-vis Revelation is an important issue emphasized by Muslim scholars. Like scholars in the past and his contemporaries, Gülen also makes some remarks in this regard. The focus here will be on how Gülen differs from other scholars and understanding his views on Divine Revelation and its mode of advent.

      In the definition of Revelation, Gülen does not differ from other scholars; his views are identical with other Muslim theologians. *Wahy* is a piece of knowledge revealed by God—with or without an intermediary—into the hearts of His Prophets. In other words, it refers

---

[480] Qur'an 4:163.
[481] Qur'an 4:136

to spiritual words that God instills into the hearts of Prophets by some means unknown to ordinary people. In Islamic literature, the mode of Revelation differs from one Prophet to the other. However, Gülen asserts that Prophet Muhammad, upon whom be peace and blessings, received revelations in various ways and forms—he heard, perceived and experienced them at the level of "certainty gained through direct experience" (*haqq al-yaqin*).[482] This may imply the Noble Prophet was gifted with a different representative ability than other Prophets. This may also constitute evidence for his status of "The Seal of the Prophets (*Khatam al-Nabiyyin*), as mentioned in the Qur'an (33:40). Receiving Revelation in all forms and modes puts forth a further evidence for the truth that there will be no Prophet after him for all realities and forms of the Revelation are represented by him and the judgment (*hukm*) has been completed.[483] For Gülen, this characteristic of the Noble Prophet also points out his status in the sight of God Almighty.

According to Gülen—Muslim scholars also share the same view—the Noble Prophet received the Revelation in three different ways. Gülen bases his view on this Quranic verse: "*It is not for any mortal that God should speak to him unless it be by Revelation or from behind a veil, or by sending a messenger (angel) to reveal, by His leave, whatever He wills (to reveal).*"[484] According to this verse, Revelation (*Wahy*) took place by means of God talking directly to the Noble Prophet from behind a screen or sending His heavenly envoy Gabriel. Gülen explains that, according to Islamic sources, including the Qur'an and the Sunnah, *Wahy* was generally revealed[485] to Prophets in this way.[486] While commenting on the Noble Prophet's hadith, "*Ruh al-Quds* ("The Spirit of Holiness," that is Gabriel) blew into my heart,"[487] Gülen draws attention to a different mode of the reception of the Revelation. He argues that the event, with this aspect, is a spiritual exchange and the Noble Prophet kept the nature

---

[482] Gülen, *Kalbin Zumrut Tepeleri 3 (Emerald Hills of the Heart, Vol. 3)*, (Istanbul: Nil Publishing, 2011), p. 77.

[483] *"This day I have perfected for you your Religion (with all its rules, commandments and universality), completed My favor upon you"* (Qur'an 5:3).

[484] Qur'an 42:51.

[485] Bukhari, *Bad'u'l-wahy*, 3-5.

[486] Gülen, *Kalbin Zumrut Tepeleri (Emerald Hills of the Heart), Vol. 3*, p. 79.

[487] Ma'mar ibn Rashid, *al-Jami'*, p. 125; at-Tabarani, *al-Mu'jam al-Kabir*, 8/166.

of this experience a Divine secret.[488] Consequently, the content of the Revelation (*Wahy*), rather than its mode of Revelation, is emphasized and the Noble Prophet's Sunnah is highlighted. That is to say, what is essential is the content and not the container. This is because the Noble Prophet—while keeping the nature of the Revelation to himself as a Divine secret—highlights the Sunnah, which represents the Divine Revelation's practical aspect. From the present day point of view, it is important in this respect for the Divine Revelation is an event of the past; however, its products—the Qur'an and the Sunnah—are still in effect.

After this formal information and definition of *Wahy*, alongside the Qur'an—which is *Wahy al-matluw*—it is needed to focus on the Hadith qudsi (Sacred hadiths), which are represented by the Noble Prophet. Hadith qudsi represent God's message expressed in the Prophet's words.[489] In other words, a "hadith qudsi" is a hadith delivered in its meaning by Gabriel, the Archangel of Revelation, but its text is expressed by the Noble Prophet's words.[490] Here may come to mind the question of "What is the difference between *Wahy* and *Hadith qudsi?*" The most important factor that differentiates *Wahy* and *Hadith qudsi* is the wording. In *Wahy*, Gabriel delivers God's message in His words. In *Hadith qudsi*, Gabriel receives God's message in meaning and delivers this message to the Prophet. The Noble Prophet then renders this meaningful message into sentences with his own words and delivers it to people. In terms of their sacred source, Hadith qudsi and *Wahy* spring from God. However, regarding their characteristics, Hadith qudsi is not like *Wahy*, thus not included in the Qur'an.[491] The most important feature of Hadith qudsi is its wording, which belongs to the Noble Prophet. For this reason, the Hadith qudsi (sacred hadiths) do not have the miraculous eloquence that the Qur'an possesses.[492] It may be necessary to add here that it is essential not to differentiate between Hadith and Hadith qudsi. Both are

---

[488] Gülen, *Kalbin Zumrut Tepeleri (Emerald Hills of the Heart)*, Vol. 3, p. 78.

[489] Gülen, *Kendi Iklimimiz (Our Climate)*, Prism series, Vol. 5, (Istanbul: Nil Publishing, 2010), p. 152.

[490] Subhi as-Salih, *Hadis Ilimleri ve Hadis Istilahlari*, vol. 8 (Istanbul: M.U. Theology Foundation Publishing, 2009), p. 247.

[491] Talat Kocyigit, *Hadis Istilahlari (Terms of Hadith)*, vol. 2 (Ankara: Ankara University, Ilahiyat Fakultesi Publishing, 1985), pp. 123-124.

[492] Muhammad Ajjaj al-Hatib, *As-Sunnatu Kabla't-Tadwin*, (Cairo, 1963).

in the same Hadith category.[493]

In Gülen's view, the Hadith qudsi and the Prophet's statements—regardless of their form or mode of reception—are all inspired by Revelation (*Wahy*). According to him, the Noble Prophet, being the most eloquent of the Arabs, expressed in the best form and wording what is inspired into his heart as Hadith qudsi.[494] Concerning "Wahy," "Hadith qudsi" and "Hadith" stemming from the same source, Gülen shares similar views with many Muslim scholars. According to Subhi al-Salih, the Qur'an and the Hadith are identical in terms of their source, both being revealed by God, as indicated in the verse, *"That (which he conveys to you) is but a Revelation that is revealed to him."*[495] Al-Salih states that, from the *Wahy* point of view, he does not differentiate between the Qur'an and the Hadith qudsi as both were inspired into the Noble Prophet's heart.[496] Al-Shafi'i (d. 819 CE),[497] and al-Ghazzali (d. 1111 CE) highlights similar views.[498] *Wahy* and Sunnah both stem from the same source even though they are considered different from each other. At this point, Kocyigit asserts that Hadith and Hadith qudsi have the same source and are based on *Wahy*, and the majority of Muslim scholars share the same view.[499]

Gülen emphasizes that Hadith is inspired by Divine Revelation (*Wahy*). He deems the ambiguous expression *ma* (whatever) in the verse 53:3-4[500] to include everything in universe the Noble Prophet conveyed to us as *wahy ghayr al-matluw*—be it hadith qudsi or hadith.[501] Here, one may say that hesitation and drawback arise in the criticism of the Sunnah as it is inspired by *Wahy*. As *Wahy* is closed to any criticism, a critical

---

[493] Muhammad Abu Zahw, *Hadis ve Hadisciler,* trans. M. Ali Sonmez and Selman Basaran (Istanbul: Ensar Publishing, 2007), p. 38.

[494] Gülen, *Asrin Getirdigi Tereddutler,* Vol.2, (*Questions and Answers about Islam*), pp. 144-145.

[495] Qur'an 53:4.

[496] as-Salih, *Hadis Ilimleri Ve Hadis Istilahlari,* 8, p. 247.

[497] al-Shafi'i, *al-Risala,* 91-93.

[498] Ghazzali, *al-Mustasfa,* I, p.83.

[499] Kocyigit, *Hadis Istilahlari,* 2, p. 125.

[500] As the official interpreter of the Qur'an—which is *wahy al-matluw,* whatever the Noble Prophet conveyed to his Ummah is also from God. He was thus inspired by God in whatever he delivered to us—which is *wahy ghayr al-matluw,* as stated in the verses (which mean), *"He does not speak on his own, out of his own desire; that (whatever he conveys to you) is but a Revelation that is revealed to him"* (53:3-4).

[501] Gülen, *Sonsuz Nur,* Vol. 2 (*Muhammad: The Messenger of God*), p. 418.

approach to Sunnah may cause objections. However, these inferences may, at the same time, be considered as evidence to the Sunnah being a strong source of reference.

All these above views may be summed up by one question: "If the Revelation and Hadith stem from a Divine source, looking from a definition and practice point of view, what are the main points separating—and at the same time linking together—the two elements?"

In these two elements, God's words are classified as *Wahy*, and speeches and behaviors of the Noble Prophet as Sunnah. Therefore, the point where these two elements differ is very clear. As for the difference in practice, "Wahy" is the primary reference point in terms of legislation and "Sunnah" is the secondary source. However, with both stemming from the same Divine source, these two sources are always considered together in legislative processes. With its miraculous and inimitable character, *Wahy* does differ from the Sunnah. Besides, the Qur'an has been recorded in *al-Law al-Mahfuz* (the Well-Preserved Tablet), and neither the heavenly envoy who brought the Divine message, Gabriel, nor the Noble Prophet have any authority to add anything into it.[502] As mentioned in the Qur'an, *Wahy* is and will always be protected.[503] Looking from this point, *Wahy* is under God's protection. Therefore, tampering with it is out of question. It is equally important to preserve the Hadith's originality without any tampering as it is inspired by *Wahy*. At this point, the Noble Prophet prohibited false statements about himself. This prohibition aims to protect the Hadith against tampering attempts. Thus, fabrication of hadiths in later periods was warded off by this hadith.

According to Gülen, where Hadith differs from *Wahy* in terms of application, *Wahy* as the Divine command leaves its representative quality and ability to the Sunnah. What is known for sure is that *Wahy* is not represented directly by itself; its physical body and tongue is the Sunnah and the Hadith. *Wahy*, in a way, comes to life in a society through Sunnah. Representation of *Wahy* is directly proportionate with the life of the Noble Prophet, who was honored with receiving the *Wahy*.

---

[502] As-Salih, *Hadis Ilimleri ve Hadis Istilahlari*, 8, p. 247.

[503] *"Indeed it is We, We Who send down the Reminder in parts, and it is indeed We Who are its Guardian"* (Qur'an 15:9).

Gülen's Defense of Hadith

Muslim scholars link evidence supporting the originality and recording of the Sunnah back to the Noble Prophet through Hadith history and methodology. According to the scholars, evidence and other sources in this area are supported by historical records. They maintain that safeguarding these materials throughout Islamic history since the beginning of the Noble Prophet's mission is a reality. Weak hadiths have been criticized and separated from those that are sound, and their injuries and weaknesses identified in detail.

Sunnah, attracting attention with this aspect, has also entered the field of interest of non-Muslim researchers during the last few centuries. Sunnah has been, intentionally or unintentionally, subjected to criticism and questioned. This criticizing and questioning process has continued for certain periods and still continues. The ascertaining and recording of the Sunnah, and its compilation, authenticity and status as a source of reference constitute the focus of criticism. However, according to many Muslim scholars, these criticisms are based on divergent evidence, insufficient arguments and unreliable sources. Arguments on this issue—for and against—have been explained in Chapter One. In this section, Gülen's views and comments in defense of Sunnah will be examined. An attempt will be made to assess these criticisms from his perspective and analyze his approach.

Primarily, it is necessary to make it clear that, from an academic perspective, examination of the evidence of the critical views is as important as the analysis of Muslim scholars' evidence. If Muslim scholars' research and inferences are bound by a cause-aim-effect relationship, the same applies to any research concerning Sunnah. For this reason, each claimant is obliged to base their claim on concrete evidence, assert and clearly explain the reason, aim and conclusion of their thesis. Otherwise, a criticism or analysis that is not based on concrete evidence moves away from being academic. Thus, values and statements huddle around an assumption. Starting from this point, it can be said that criticism of matters deeply concerning individuals and societies require a more delicate approach. Suspicions stemming from baseless and unproven criticisms can cause handicaps and faith-based social disintegrations. Therefore, criticism of Sunnah must be based on sound and concrete evidence in connection with a cause-aim-effect relationship.

After this brief introduction, it is beneficial to deal with Gülen's approach to criticism of Sunnah. Approaching the subject with questions may be more reasonable. First of all, does Gülen have any set of criteria for criticizing and assessing Sunnah? Is criticism of Sunnah in terms of authenticity and essentiality reasonable? What is his attitude on this issue? These and similar questions will shed light on Gülen's approach to Sunnah criticism.

Gülen does not choose to be directly involved in discussions on Sunnah developed in the historical process. He refrains from asserting his views in a destructive and radical manner. In putting forth his arguments and evaluating opposing sides' arguments, he considers respect paramount even when he regards his interlocutor as being wrong. Consequently, he expects his opponent to be controlled in their criticism, and respect available sources of reference and established historical deposition. To preserve moderation in criticism and questioning, he takes certain criteria as his basis. According to Gülen, criticism exists to find out the rights and wrongs of a matter, and to determine the ideal by way of comparison. For a critic, being open to criticism is an academic principle. Furthermore, a critic should keep their thesis unblemished from personal feelings and ethnic interests. The critic's main goal should be finding the truth. Otherwise, immoderate criticism indulged in shrewdness can cause damage to the truth.[504] Also, while duly expressing views in his area of expertise, a critic should refrain from asserting views on matters outside their field of expertise; this becomes especially important in religious matters. Likewise, moderation in criticism is essential; one should steer away from destructive criticism.[505] Gülen believes healthy communication can be established and truth achieved only if these criteria are observed.

Gülen draws attention from within these criteria to Hadith being subjected to unregulated and deliberate criticism by some critics, giving

---

[504] Gülen, *Vuslat Mustusu (Glad Tidings of a Reunion)*, Kirik Testi, 8 (*The Broken Jug series*, Vol. 8), p. 279.

[505] Gülen, *Umit Burcu (The Bearing of Hope)*, Kirik Testi series, Vol. 4, p. 225.

rise to suspicions.[506] Suspicion is far away from logic and knowledge. It is based on assumption and doubt, and cannot be freed from these injuries unless proven true by real evidence. A thesis can be freed from doubt if proven by results based on strong evidence. Such facts and values, around which some doubts are created, would not lose anything from their health and continue to reserve their authority as primary sources until proven otherwise.

Analyzing Gülen's views on the criticism of Sunnah, Canan draws attention to a point. According to him, Gülen, with his work entitled *Sonsuz Nur*, does not criticize works written in the past, complement any missing elements, or come up with an alternative Hadith methodology. In this work, he prefers to deal with the hadiths that have been subjected to criticism rather than the authentic (*sahih*) hadiths, and express, in his peculiar way, his views about their soundness.[507] The hadiths and comments carefully selected for this work are seen in the nature of answers to the opponents of Sunnah and to the criticism of Hadith.[508] In his work, Gülen chooses to give, in his unique style, encyclopedic information to his addressee. Also, he selects issues subjected to criticism during times when adherence to Sunnah becomes weak, and draws attention to the status of these hadiths in the society. Being in line with present day values and offering solutions to problems will automatically remove question marks from Hadith. Thus, the Hadith will have proven itself. With this thinking, Gülen offers de facto and empirical answers to criticisms. The Sunnah, with its practicability being a subject of debate, proves its own health and presents answers to doubts. A Hadith reality, whose correctness in this field has been proven, means its origin and connection to the main source has been strengthened and doubts have been removed.

According to Canan, Gülen, with this concise work, has explained criticisms in a way that is understandable by all segments of the society. Gülen's work holds a significant place with regard to proving the determination and codification of the Hadith.[509] This work, in fact, provides crucial information although it is not authored to defend the

---

[506] Gülen, *Prizma 4 (Prism series*, Vol. 4), p. 195.
[507] Canan, *Fethullah Gülen'in Sunnet Anlayisi*, p. 109.
[508] ibid., p. 96.
[509] ibid., p. 102.

Sunnah. This may be deemed as Gülen's stance in the defense of Sunnah, which stems from his confidence in Sunnah.

Gülen's Response to Non-Muslim Scholars

When and how did criticism and doubts on Hadith and Sunnah begin and how has the Muslim world been influenced by them? What is Gülen's attitude vis-à-vis these criticisms and uncertainties? Has Gülen authored an independent work to specifically defend Hadith and answer the related criticisms? What are his views about works published in this area and what are his recommendations? Are Muslim scholars' and intellectuals' defense and evidence adequate? What should be done regarding the defense of Hadith? The answers to these questions reveal Gülen's stance against Sunnah criticism.

Gülen is seriously concerned about Sunnah criticism within the Muslim as well as the non-Muslim world. For a clear understanding of the subject, it must be stressed that the essence of Islam allows all views and thoughts—which do not stem from the Revelation—to be questioned and criticized in the name of finding the truth. This is one of the fundamental principles of Islam, and prepares the ground for the production of ideas and theories. Thus, the Qur'an and the Sunnah guarantee the freedom of scholarly and academic/scholarly research, and also encourage constructive criticism and questioning. At this point, Gülen sets limitations to criticism by saying, "In Islam, there is self-criticism. Everything that is not verified by *Wahy* (i.e. anything other than the Qur'an and the Sunnah) has been questioned among the Muslims."[510] The case of a woman criticizing Caliph 'Umar, while he was delivering a sermon, by saying, "O 'Umar! What you have said is wrong. The truth of the matter is such and such,"[511] is an anecdote illustrating a good example for the pursuit of the truth. Due to these and other similar examples, freely discussing Islamic issues among jurists and theologians has become possible during later periods. There exist countless voluminous works and examples about this. In Islamic sciences, thoughts and theories have been vigorously criticized, and

---

[510] Gülen, *Mefkure Yolculuğu (A Journey into Noble Ideals),* (Istanbul: Nil Publishing, 2014), pp. 409-417.

[511] Bayhaqi, *al-Sunan al-Kubra* 7/233; Ajluni, *Kashf al-Khafa* 1/317.

these criticisms tolerated to a certain extent.[512] All these debates and discussions were not aimed at criticizing the essence of the Revelation or the Sunnah, but were focused on the soundness of inferences derived from them. These efforts, in one way, reflect the positive side of the questioning. What is essential here is fairness and justice.

Gülen is apprehensive that negative and destructive criticisms—especially questioning of some of the prominent Hadith narrators like Abu Hurayrah, Anas ibn Malik, 'Abdu'llah ibn 'Umar—would pave the way for disparaging criticism of the Noble Prophet. The questioning of the Noble Prophet, the bearer of the Divine Revelation, will soon evolve—in the eyes of a superstitious sect—into the questioning of Gabriel, the Archangel Revelation.[513] At this stage, questioning Gabriel's legitimacy would unavoidably mean questioning the existence of the Creator, the owner of the Revelation. Criticisms and questionings arising in such an environment would trespass all boundaries and give rise to a rationale that everything can be questioned and criticized. In this situation, everyone, regardless of being qualified or not, will chose to deduce rules according to their own opinion and the fundamentals of the religion will be damaged. Thus, doubts over the primary sources, the Qur'an and the Sunnah, would become inevitable. Because of these kinds of justifiable concerns, Gülen voluntarily assumed the duty of defending the Sunnah against these movements and disparaging questionings. Gülen, due to his belief, is known as a personality who depicts serious caution and shows sensitivity to safeguarding the essence of the religion.

In Gülen's view, this kind of questioning began during the period when Muslims were first acquainted with Neoplatonic Greek philosophy.[514] These thoughts finding place in the Muslim world through

---

[512] Gülen, "Fethullah Gülen Elestiriye Kapali mi? Kendisini Elestiriden Muaf mi Goruyor?" (Is Fethullah Gulen closed to critique? Does he consider himself exempt from criticism?) https://fgulen.com/tr/fethullah-gulen-kimdir/gulen-hakkinda/sorularla-fethullah-gulen/15387-fethullah-gulen-elestiriye-kapali-mi-kendisini-elestiriden-muaf-mi-goruyor.

[513] Gülen, *Sonsuz Nur, Vol. 2 (Muhammad: The Messenger of God)*, pp. 388-389.

[514] "Philosophy is considered in two parts. The first part—philosophy and wisdom—serves the social life of humankind, its morality and maturity, and the development of arts. This part of philosophy is in reconciliation with the Qur'an and religious sciences, and serves the Qur'an and its wisdom. The second part of philosophy is conducive to heresy, atheism and lowering people into the quagmire of "mother nature," and gives way to hedonism, sinful pleasures, heedlessness and misguidance. This part is in opposition to the Qur'an and reli-

philosophy highlights a vacuum of faith experienced during that period. This, in a way, can also be interpreted as differing thoughts finding their place in the social body due to interaction between communities. These thoughts entered Islamic cultural and scientific life through books during the time of Abbasid Caliph Ma'mun (reigned 813-833 CE). These thoughts—which initially focused on debates of the Qur'an's creation— with the influence of Greek philosophy, were later directed towards criticism of the Sunnah. Gülen holds that these approaches and the idea of criticizing were not seen among Sunni scholars, but were rather prevalent among the Mu'tazilite followers who indulged in philosophy.[515] With the introduction of philosophical thought currents among the Muslims, he indicates the emergence of various sects, such as *Mu'tazilah*, *Jabriyyah*,[516] *Murji'ah*[517] and *Mushabbihah*[518] among Muslims. He denotes that the followers of these sects chose to fabricate hadiths to support their arguments and criticized the Prophet's Companions who narrated hadith(s) that do not conform with their view.[519] In fact, views of these schools of thought were criticized and refuted by Sunni scholars with strong evidence during their respective periods. However, the roots of intellectual approaches among the Muslims that appear lately are likely to go back to these periods, and their views may be considered stemming therefrom. Re-emergence of criticisms—which has already been responded and refuted—and advocacy of these views among Muslims suggest the faith gap experienced in the past is also valid in present day.

Remaining silent against criticisms of Sunnah stemming

---

gious values." Quoted from Nursi, *Asa-yi Musa* (The Staff of Moses), (Istanbul: Sahdamar Publishing, 2007), p. 4.

[515] Gülen, *Yol Mulahazalari (Contemplating the Journey), Prizma* series, Vol. 6, pp. 186-187.

[516] A school of thought established by Ma'bad ibn Khalid al-Juhani (d. 85/704). Ma'bad argued against predestination and maintained that man has absolute freedom in his actions and thoughts.

[517] The *Murji'ah* sect first emerged during the tumultuous period of 'Uthman, the third caliph. The main pillar of this theological school of thought is that sins would not damage the faith, and good deeds while in disbelief would not render any benefit. In other words, if someone believed in Islam and adopted its way, their violation of Islamic rules is not important. A believer committing grave sins would remain Muslim and be eligible for Paradise as long as they remained faithful.

[518] *Mushabbihah* is a theological school of thought that likens the creation with God: anthropomorphism in Islam.

[519] Gülen, *Sonsuz Nur*, Vol. 2 *(Muhammad: The Messenger of God)*, p. 546.

from *Mu'tazilah* and other sects is not possible for Gülen. It should be noted that Gülen is a very strong believer of Sunni Islam. From Gülen's perspective anything outside this circle is problematic. Moreover, he is known to closely follow current issues and opposing thoughts concerning the Sunnah. His arguments in this regard are clearly visible in his various works. As mentioned earlier, Gülen maintains that the view that claims "The writing down of hadiths began upon 'Umar ibn 'Abd al-'Aziz's decree, and not before,"[520] is not based on valid reasons. He emphatically bases his argument on original works authored during early periods. Pointing out numerous books and other sources in this field, he draws attention to the presence of necessary answers. In a way, he argues that these sources are not studied carefully and deemed non-existent. This way, he highlights academic inadequacy in the Muslim world and moving away from original sources. For that reason, shallowness in scholarly research leads researchers to copying the thoughts and views of the past.

At this point, this may come to mind: since Gülen is so sensitive about and closely follows the Sunnah, why did he not author a specific and independent book to refute critics of Sunnah? This may be viewed as a legitimate expectation of Gülen's readers and followers. At the same time, his neglect of authoring an independent work may be seen as a deficiency. Naturally, the reasons behind this neglect should be discussed and questioned. As such, Gülen leaves an open door for comments about his views and himself.

Approaching this issue from Gülen's epistemological point of view, he emphasizes that knowledge is not the exclusive property of an individual or nation; therefore, no one can claim exclusive ownership of it.[521] Development of thoughts and ideas in academic studies, and achieving results, can only be possible with the contributions of everyone who has an idea in the relevant area. For this reason, Gülen perhaps did not choose to narrow the field by authoring a work on an important discipline such as Sunnah. Whereas, by mentioning Sunnah in his works often and keeping the sensitivity in this area always current, it is

---

520   ibid., p. 518.
521   Unal, *M. Fethullah Gülen: Bir Portre Denemesi* (Fethullah Gülen: A Portrait Essay), p. 406.

possible to say that he may have endeavored to call Muslim scholars and intellectuals to take up their responsibilities on this issue. In addition, he might prefer to focus on more concrete issues for the revival of Islamic understanding rather than wasting his time in discussing delicate and academic problems which have no benefit for lay people.

Looking from another angle, Gülen is known to have adopted Sunnah in his daily life. He may be emphasizing the importance of Sunnah simply by applying it in his own practical life. Sunnah, whose principles are interpreted and applied in real life, would thus be defended in a more reasonable way. Adherents of Sunnah would more diligently study the discipline they practice and find answers to arising criticisms. This, consequently, would increase awareness of Sunnah among Muslims. Gülen's preference of practical hadiths has been highlighted at the beginning of this chapter.

Sunnah, like the Qur'an, caters to all times and is open to new interpretations. Focusing on Gülen's omission of authoring an independent work dedicated to answering criticisms on Sunnah, his unwillingness to restrict the defense of Sunnah within a certain period of time may be deemed justifiable. Also, according to Gülen, the Sunnah is prevalent and part of life. Therefore, Sunnah should not be treated as a phenomenon about which authoring a one-off publication would be enough. This may also be perceived in such a way that doubts and criticisms manufactured about Sunnah did not begin and end during a certain period of time in the past; this is an ongoing continuum. In this continuum, Sunnah must be defended perpetually as well as its aspect open to new interpretations must be investigated. In one aspect, interpreting hadiths in the context of present times and bringing in reasonable answers to new problems would, in fact, constitute factual evidence to the soundness of Sunnah. At this point, one may say that Gülen invites meticulous researchers to be vigilant about the Sunnah.

In addition, Gülen—by his natural disposition—prefers to stay away from the grounds of controversy, and more particularly refuses to render a religious source, such as Hadith or Sunnah, a subject of contention. For this reason, he may have chosen to put forth his views on Sunnah step by step when necessary instead of collecting them in a separate work with a limited capacity. Along with these considerations, however, it would not be an overstatement to say that Gülen's work, titled *Sonsuz Nur*, practically presents its readers with solid answers supported by concrete evidence while explaining the Noble Prophet's life and his Sunnah. According to Yildirim, this work is about the Noble Prophet's attributes, his mission, his teachings, and lessons derived from his Sunnah, and constitutes a source of reference for the discipline of *Fiqh al-Sunnah* (the understanding of the philosophy of Prophetic Traditions). Many scholars such as late Ramadan al-Buti and Abdul Fatah Abu Ghuddah have the same opinion.[522] Also, the last part of the second volume of the work is a kind of response especially to the determination and recording of the Sunnah and its status as a primary source of reference. Besides his concise presentation in this way, Gülen prefers to leave the hard work to competent researchers.

Gülen also closely follows works authored for the defense of Sunnah and puts forth his views about them. Moreover, he uses these works to support his views. Evaluating from this aspect, Gülen's approach constitutes evidence to his thesis that every owner of a view must assume some responsibility for it. According to Gülen, anti-Sunnah movements induced by critical non-Muslim scholarship first appeared in Egypt and India and received their first refutation from there. The first contemporary work authored in the defense of Sunnah is *al-Sunnah wa Makanatuha fi al-Tashri' al-Islami* by Mustafa al-Siba'i (1915-1964 CE). Similarly, *Hujjiyah al-Sunnah*, which was co-authored by 'Abd al-Ghani and 'Abd al-Khalio, and *al-Sunnah Qabla al-Tadwin* and *Abu Hurayrah: Rawiyat al-Islam* by Muhammad 'Ajjaj al-Khatib, are other major works authored initially to defend Sunnah.[523] By studying and investigating these works, Gülen confirms once more that, as mentioned above, efforts about Sunnah cannot be attributed to an individual or a nation. Thus, he underlines the fact that the responsibility of defending Sunnah belongs to everyone who is qualified. In addition, Gülen's acceptance and investigation of these works is a sign of their reliability and the expression of the importance he attributes to the issue.

In light of the results of investigations and evidence presented in these works, Gülen draws attention to refutations against doubts that

---

[522] ibid., p. 17.
[523] Gülen, *Yol Mulahazalari (Contemplating the Journey), Prizma 6 (Prism series*, Vol. 6), p. 190.

have been raised about Sunnah. He argues that volumes of books have been written on issues of debate, such as the authenticity of the hadiths, reconciliation of contradictions and eliminating fabricated narrations, and most disputes have been resolved. Gülen opines that Abu Ja'far ibn Muhammad al-Tahawi (843-935 CE) allocated two of his works, *Mushkil al-Athar* and *Sharh Ma'ani al-Athar*, to the authenticity of the Sunnah and its status as a primary source of reference. Gülen points out that reading these thick volumes of books would require quite a long time; however, he says they contain detailed information related to the solution of all problems in the field of Hadith.[524] The abundance of these kinds of publications, which provide necessary evidence besides their large size and detailed contents, may be shown as another reason behind Gülen's unwillingness to write an independent book on Sunnah. He usually bases his thoughts and evidence on these works, and gives weight to the introduction of these works to present times.

Gülen can be seen, in this regard, as giving satisfactory answers to points some critics stumbled on. He claims the narration that goes, "We asked for the Prophet's permission to write down [hadith], he did not permit us to do so,"[525] which is accepted as evidence by Ignaz Goldziher and his followers, is considered not worthy of mentioning by Hadith experts. While pointing out the reliability of the hadith upon which Goldziher based his views, Gülen argues that the source with regard to the prohibition of recording hadiths is a different one. According to him, the hadith, which constitutes evidence for this issue, is the one reported by Abu Sa'id al-Khudri and recorded in *Sahih Muslim*—a famous and reliable source:[526] By establishing his argument in this way, Gülen asserts that Goldziher and his followers made an incorrect choice of hadith for their evidence, and based their arguments on carelessly chosen unreliable sources. Thus, he presents indirect proofs to highlight the inconsistency in their theses. Here, **Gülen appears to have shown a reference contrary to** the thesis for the recording of hadiths. However, the evidence justifying the recording of hadiths that he presented is already mentioned in Chapter One. If the readers do not pay attention

---

[524] ibid., p. 191.
[525] Tirmidhi, *ilm*, 11; Hatib al-Baghdadi, *Takyid al-Ilm*, 32-33.
[526] Gülen, *Sonsuz Nur, Vol. 2 (Muhammad: The Messenger of God)*, p. 511.

and fail to investigate thoroughly, they may fall into contradictions about Gülen. The point he stresses is the unreliability of the hadith source used by Goldziher. For this reason, Gülen's views on the defense of Hadith should be sorted and compiled in a separate work. Even if Gülen had not authored such a work and has no intention of doing so in the future, the publishing of such a dedicated work appears to be necessary. Otherwise, access to accurate information by scanning through all his works will require a painstaking effort. This is a necessary endeavor to make Gülen's mission understood.

Continuing with the subject, Gülen emphasizes the reliability of evidence and sources that Goldziher and his followers refer to. Gülen argues that these critics use *al-'Iqd al-Farid*[527] and *Kitab al-Aghani* as sources of reference to their views,[528] which can only be referred to as sources of poetry and general Arabic literature, and not of Hadith.[529] This is for this reason Gülen emphasizes the necessity for Goldziher's followers to take extra care about their sources before asserting any view on an Islamic issue. They are in his view not a legitimate religious source of reference. Calling to mind Goldziher's reference to hadiths as "some Arab proverbs," the probability of his sources being these works Gülen pointed out dramatically increases. This prospect strengthens Gülen's thesis. At the same time, a situation like this arises: Goldziher and his followers, being fixated on the idea of discovering a fault in Hadith, intentionally choose weaker sources for reference rather than the healthier ones. Nevertheless, to understand exact frame of Goldziher sources, one need more extensive research on his various works.

Highlighting contradictions by Goldziher and other critics, Gülen draws attention to mistakes they make in scanning sources. Goldziher comments on political bias, citing that Ibn Kathir, in his *al-Bidayah wa al-Nihayah*, blames Abu Hurayrah for taking sides with Mu'awiyyah against 'Ali. However, Gülen points out Ibn Kathir says the

---

[527] *al-'Iqd al-Farid ("The Unique Necklace")*, a work that belongs to Ibn 'Abd Rabbih and lead him to fame. It covers the history of the Umayyads of al-Andalus from 'Abd al-Rahman I (750-788 CE) to 'Abd al-Rahman III (912-961 CE). Some sections contain Arab proverbs and other sections deal with morality and religious piety.

[528] A book of poetry and literature by Abu Faraj al-'Ali ibn al-Husayn ibn Muhammad ibn Ahmad al-Quraishi al-Isfahani (d. 356/967).

[529] Gülen, *Sonsuz Nur, Vol. 2 (Muhammad: The Messenger of God)*, pp. 555, 589.

exact opposite of what they claim in his book,[530] and emphasizes Ibn Kathir's establishing Abu Hurayrah's position against Umayyads, not supporting them.[531] According to Gülen, Abu Hurayrah is a cockshy for Orientalists. He is a Hadith narrator on whom they produce arguments to discredit in any case; Abu Hurayrah never forgot the hadiths he once heard from the Noble Prophet and transmitted this legacy of the Noble Prophet to the next generations.[532]

According to Gülen, Goldziher and similar academics are known to be researchers well-versed in Islam.[533] As mentioned earlier, the majority of Western researchers have a good knowledge of Islam. However, this brings to mind Gülen's remark, "Their sources mostly are works of poetry and literature." This consequently suggests Gülen falls into contradictions in his examples and criticisms. That is, on one hand, declaring their sources unreliable, but on the other hand, recognizing their proficiency in Islamic sciences. At this point, questions must be raised about either the Islamic knowledge of Goldziher and his followers or the objectivity of their theses. Only one of the two options can prove to be true because accurate knowledge leads to correct outcome and has little chance of misleading. Either the thesis attributing deficiency to their Islamic knowledge and usage of sources is justifiable, or Gülen's assertion of their proficiency is incorrect. Or, as another possibility, perhaps Gülen is right in his views, but Goldziher and others are prejudiced and subjective although their Islamic knowledge is complete. For this reason, they intentionally look for their supporting evidence in wrong sources to justify their biased views. At this point, Gülen's thought that they are not sincere in their intention prevails. For this reason, Gülen argues that those who are preoccupied with focusing their attention on criticizing and questioning the Sunnah, are, in fact, in an Endeavour to turn the truth upside-down.[534] Therefore, they do not hesitate to look into wrong sources, hoping to find evidence to support their twisted views, although they have quite a good knowledge of Islam. It is exactly for this

---

[530] Ibn Kathir, *al-Bidaya wa al-Nihaya*, 8/108-114.
[531] Gülen, *Sonsuz Nur, Vol. 2 (Muhammad: The Messenger of God)*, p. 556.
[532] ibid., p. 503.
[533] Gülen, *Fasildan Fasila 1(From Chapter to Chapter, Vol.)*, p. 59.
[534] Gülen, *Sonsuz Nur, Vol. 2 (Muhammad: The Messenger of God)*, p. 555.

reason that Gülen focuses on their sources of reference, and asserts, as mentioned before, that they are not consistent in the choice of resources.

Illustrating this with an example, Gülen draws attention to the method and resources they employed in their effort to discredit Ibn Shihab al-Zuhri (d. 742 CE).[535] According to Gülen, Ya'qubi, a Shiite historian, is the first person who accused al-Zuhri for fabricating hadiths. As said by Ya'qubi, to prevent Muslims from circumambulating the Ka'bah, Abd al-Malik ibn Marwan (d. 705 CE)[536] had Masjid al-Aqsa repaired and pleaded with al-Zuhri (d. 1154) to fabricate a hadith to encourage Muslims for its circumambulation. Ya'qubi claims that al-Zuhri "coined"[537] the following hadith, which is mentioned in reputable Hadith compilations such as Bukhari, Muslim and Ibn Hanbal: "Do not set out on a sole journey to visit a mosque except for three masjids: al-Masjid al-Haram, my masjid (al-Masjid al-Nabawi), and al-Masjid al-Aqsa."[538] From this point onward, Gülen highlights Ya'qubi's inconsistencies in his sources. Firstly, since there exists no single provision or topic mentioning "circumambulation of al-Masjid al-Aqsa," similar to the Ka'bah, in the history of Islam, Christianity or Judaism, how could it be possible for the Noble Prophet to emphatically advise people to do so? Such advice would be inconsistent with the Sunnah and the Quranic verse, *"From wherever you go out (for journeying), turn your face (O Messenger) towards the Sacred Mosque (in the Prayer)."*[539]

Al-Masjid al-Aqsa is a sacred mosque for Muslims and not only itself but also its surroundings are declared sacred in the Qur'an.[540] Therefore, the abovementioned hadith is not fabricated; on the contrary, it is an authentic hadith indicating the value and importance of al-Masjid al-Aqsa along with al-Masjid al-Haram and al-Masjid al-Nabawi.[541] Hence, al-Masjid al-Aqsa was repaired and restored not only by 'Abd

---

[535] According to Gülen, Ibn Shihab al-Zuhri is an expert *hadith* scholar. He received *hadith* from tens of Companions, and reported them to hundreds of followers and the generation that followed them. He started the official compilation process of *hadith* by Caliph 'Umar ibn 'Abd al-'Aziz's decree. Ibid., p. 590.

[536] 'Abd al-Malik ibn Marwan (646-705), the fifth Umayyad Caliph.

[537] Gülen, *Sonsuz Nur, Vol. 2 (Muhammad: The Messenger of God)*, pp. 587-588.

[538] Bukhari, *sawm*, 67; *tatawwu*, 14; Muslim, *hajj* 511.

[539] Qur'an 2:150.

[540] Gülen, *Sonsuz Nur, Vol. 2 (Muhammad: The Messenger of God)*, p. 588.

[541] ibid., p. 484.

al-Malik, but also by Prophet Dawud and his son Prophet Sulayman, peace be upon them, Caliph 'Umar, Nur al-Din Zangi and Salah al-Din Ayyubi. Looking from this perspective, Ya'qubi's claiming an authentic (*sahih*) hadith as "fabricated" does not appear to be reasonable. On the other hand, according to historical records, Imam al-Zuhri (d. 742 CE) never met 'Abd al-Malik during the hadith reporting period. At that time, he was only a baby in his mother's arms. Another important point is that Ya'qubi's approaches and assertions are not mentioned in any other Islamic source. Yet, judging by the timing, this event coincides with a period, i.e. the time of successors of the Companions, when there existed thousands of Hadith scholars. None of the scholars from among the Companions' successors mentioned this event in their works. That is, Ya'qubi's assumption and his thesis claiming Imam al-Zuhri fabricated a hadith is totally unfounded. Gülen argues that Goldziher's and his followers' leaving the main Hadith sources and choosing Ya'qubi as their reference and using unfounded events as evidence is worrisome.[542] In this situation, the view of premeditation in Hadith criticisms gains strength.

Thus, it becomes clear that certain thought movements have a premeditated approach to Sunnah, persistently make Hadith a subject of criticism, and intentionally portray many authentic and healthy hadiths as weak or fabricated.[543] Starting from Gülen's remarks, displaying his respect for all religions and their value systems, it is safe to say that the standard in criticism and evaluation must be based on fairness. Criticism should be focused on the detection of the wrong, and care must be taken when criticizing sensitive issues on religious values that have been already solved and become "matters decided," or *res judicata* (*al-qadiyyah al-muhkamah*).

Criticisms and uncertainties that have been raised about Sunnah are based on the assumption that Hadith collections are false and the process of hadith fabrication began during the time of the successors of the Companions. Gülen argues that Orientalists' claim of writing down of hadiths began upon 'Umar ibn 'Abd al-Aziz's decree 100 years after the Noble Prophet is not correct; this is the beginning of

---

[542] ibid., pp. 588-589.
[543] ibid., p. 470.

the official compilation of hadiths, and as shown by concrete evidence, the Sunnah has been memorized and written down since the early days of the Prophetic mission. In addition to other evidence he provided to support his thesis, Gülen refers to the heritage left behind by the Prophet's Companions Jabir ibn 'Abdu'llah and Ibn Mas'ud, which consists of a significant number of written hadiths approved by the Noble Prophet and his Companions.[544] **Gülen argues that, despite all this strong evidence, there is an attempt to underestimate the** Sunnah—even negate it—in order to leave the Qur'an alone and open to freehand interpretations, and these Sunnah criticism efforts are far from being objective or constructive.[545] He stresses the impossibility of achieving good results by this kind of a critical approach.

Gülen also draws attention to certain sensitive points on studies Muslims carry out in the name of defending Hadith. He reminds that not only the Sunnah, but also the Companions are unfortunately subjected to criticism and discredit because, according to Gülen, the religion has been brought to the present day thanks to the serious efforts and meticulousness of the Companions. Thus, criticizing the Companions means criticizing the religious value system they represent. In Gülen's view, the Companions, by their strict adherence to the rules, circulated the representation of the religion to future generations, and the representation of the Sunnah in our age rests on the shoulders of Muslims. Therefore, Muslims have a responsibility to safeguard the Sunnah and other religious values, and refute unfounded and incoherent criticisms directed at these values.[546] In light of Gülen's thoughts and views, it is possible to infer that he should support the defense of Sunnah by authoring a separate work entirely dedicated to this issue.

At this point, the share of responsibility that falls on Muslims is to respect opponents' religious values while defending their own, to avoid unnecessary arguments and debates on religious matters, and to maintain their solemnity at all times. Conversely, arguing about religious values, using harsh rhetoric and criticism will make both parties lose, and consequently, impede dialogue efforts between members of

---

[544] ibid., p. 518.
[545] ibid., p. 594.
[546] ibid., p. 546.

different religions and lead to social and cultural polarizations.[547] What is imperative is to be able to accept every thought in their respective position.

Based on this reason, in his conferences, sermons, talks, and written works, Gülen appears to keep away from debates and negative criticisms. As for Sunnah criticism, he usually makes his comments without naming names and prefers to present positive, concrete evidence to answer criticisms. He does not give names when he uses terms such as "Western intellectuals." This is Gülen's usual style of expression. However, he occasionally mentions the names of certain intellectuals like Goldziher when analyzing their views. However, the reason behind violating his own principles is not known. Also, he mentions the names of certain Muslim intellectuals that subscribe to Goldziher's views, such as Ahmad Amin, Abu Rayyah and 'Ali 'Abd al-Raziq. Gülen's not explaining the reason behind mentioning these names opens the door for certain questions. It is possible to say that, in a way, he may have intended to draw attention to the current they started. Thus, he may have implied whom he intended to indicate by using the term "Orientalists." Besides this point, the usage of a blanket term like "Orientalists" in a pejorative sense may put under suspicion many other non-Muslims who objectively investigate Islam. This may be the reason why he mentions the names of a few leading antagonists. In addition, wherever Gülen uses the term "Orientalists," he also mentions their respective views, thus avoiding ambiguity about the sense in which the term "Orientalists" is being used.

Gülen argues that certain Orientalists' destructive criticisms may become an important factor in discouraging advocates involved in Christian-Muslim dialogue.[548] Whereas, starting from the Quranic verse, *"Say (to them, O Messenger): 'O People of the Book, come to a word common between us and you, that we worship none but God, and associate none as partner with Him, and that none of us take others for Lords, apart from God.' If they (still) turn away, then say: 'Bear witness that we are*

---

[547] Gülen, *Hosgoru Ve Diyalog (Tolerance and Dialogue)*, (Istanbul, Turkey: Merkur Publishing, 1999), p.10.

[548] ibid., p. 10.

Muslims (submitted to Him exclusively)," [549] Gülen takes dialogue as his basis for the exchange of ideas. He endeavors for the continuation of this dialogue.

Gülen demonstrates a firm and determined stance in the defense of Sunnah. In this stance, he endorses intellectual and basic moral principles, and recommends positive thinking and positive action. If repetition is needed, he gives answers—together with rational and textual evidence—to the critique which asserts the view that Hadith and Sunnah are no more than customs prevalent during the time of the Prophet whose adoption in modern days are not possible. Thus, he strives to revive the Sunnah, which is battered by suspicions, and bring it back to the lives of Muslims.

Response to Muslim Intellectuals

What is Gülen's approach to Hadith criticisms raised by Muslim intellectuals? How does he comment on their shortcomings and how does he answer them with his own Hadith interpretations? We will attempt to find answers to these and similar questions in this section.

Primarily, Gülen presents rational, psychological and intellectual explanations to doubts and questions raised by Muslim intellectuals who are influenced by Hadith criticism. His approach and answers to Muslim intellectuals show similarity to those he adopts toward non-Muslim researchers. In his presentations, as mentioned earlier, he abstains from unnecessary debates and chooses not to use expressions that may give rise to dispute or close the door to dialogue. Discussing a problem in an environment of dispute may close the path of reconciliation and even carries the risk of bringing in theological tremors among Muslims. Besides these concerns, Gülen draws attention to impasses Muslim intellectuals fall into and prefers to focus on supporting evidence and rectifying their mistakes. At the same time, he concentrates his attention on the process and reasons for this kind of Hadith criticism spreading among Muslims.

As mentioned earlier, the first doubts about Hadith in the Muslim world were raised by the adherents of the *Mu'tazilah* school

---

[549]   Qur'an 3:64.

of theology. The *Mu'tazilah* school, which is prominent for its reason- and rational thought-based theology, attributes exceeding functions to human intellect and accepts reason as the most important arbiter in all religious matters. This school accepts the intellect as the second primary source among "the proofs of Islamic Law" (*al-adillah al-shar'iyyah*) after Divine Revelation.[550] That is, reason, on account of its functions, holds a status next to the Qur'an while the Hadith have been dropped in rank. Further, there is a stance against Hadith. However, in Islam, intellect is a tool to understand and analyze Divine commands and derive new rulings. The Qur'an, the Hadith and the human intellect are factors that complement each other if they are used properly in their respective places. Deeming intellect as an independent value means tearing it out of its original source. In this case, the intellect alone is not enough to solve problems.[551]

It is because of their replacement of Sunnah with rational values that this school of thought adopts views prevalent in our days such as "Hadiths have been collected and written in the third century AH; and not everything has been preserved in its originality."[552] This thought has been accepted by some modern Muslim intellectuals who follow *Mu'tazilite* line as the foundation of their thought system. Although he values rational thoughts, Gülen defines these interpretations and approaches as "neo-*Mu'tazilah*."[553] By considering rational thought as valuable, Gülen demonstrates a relative proximity to the *Mu'tazilah* school; however, he differs from *Mu'tazilah* on the point of seeing intellect as the final arbiter and discarding the Sunnah. In contrast to *Mu'tazilah*, he places intellect as a value next to the Sunnah.

Especially at this point, he draws attention to an important issue. By the time *Mu'tazilah* put forth their views on Hadith, Hadith collections had already been sifted and criticized using scientific methods by Hadith scholars—in a way that leaves no room for objection—and published in large volumes of books. As the time when the *Mu'tazilah*

---

[550] Gülen, *Yasatma Ideali (So That Others May Live)*, (Istanbul: Nil Publishing, 2012), p. 73.
[551] Gülen, *Kalbin Zumrut Tepeleri 3 (Emerald Hills of the Heart, Vol. 3)*, pp. 211–214.
[552] Gülen, *Yol Mulahazalari (Contemplating the Journey), Prizma 6 (Prism series, Vol. 6)*, p.188.
[553] ibid.

views developed coincides with the period the Hadith works were taking place, as mentioned by Gülen, the *Mu'tazilah* arguments are answered by this concurrence. Therefore, *Mu'tazilah* follows a different path while the Sunnah preceded them. This is akin to substituting Sunnah with different considerations and, naturally, gives rise to questions about the integrity of their views. Why search for a different way in spite of Sunnah? Is the reason behind this situation mistrust or lack of confidence in Sunnah, or instituting a new thought system? Analyzing the views of this school of thought is outside the scope of this work. The subject matter here is the criticism directed at the Sunnah by this school's conception. It is possible to see the followers or sympathizers of this school involved in the criticism of Sunnah in our days. In fact, their views appear to be unchanged since the beginning and they are steadfast in their opinions. The present day followers of this school must be questioned about this solid resoluteness and how this thought has been preserved. The explanation they may give to the preservation of their views in the course of the history would, through a similar rationale, explain the preservation of the Sunnah by a similar recording process.

Gülen clarifies this point by his remark, "However, objections to Hadith and Sunnah are nothing more than efforts to confuse minds by repeating some outdated information (already determined as wrong) as original."[554] **Gülen's explanation suggests that certain happenings are put on the agenda on purpose to keep them alive. Gülen stresses that certain Muslim intellectuals take** Hadith criticisms believing they are new, make them the subject matter of their books and give rise to doubts and suspicions about the Sunnah. Yet, most of the objections they take as their source of reference were answered during the time of Ibn Qutaybah (d. 889 CE) with theses and incongruous claims refuted as they were put forth.[555] Based on this information, Gülen puts forward his own thesis, asserting that *Mu'tazilah*, *Murji'ah* and *Mushabbihah* prepare the groundwork for lies about Hadith. According to him, those who attribute lies against the Companions, their followers and the generation that followed them by claiming that hadiths were

---

[554] ibid., p. 190.
[555] ibid., p. 191.

not written down during the time of the Noble Prophet are—without realizing—taking part in Hadith criticism and acting like Hadith critics' representatives. Thus, Gülen goes further and says that they fall into lies and academic plagiarism.[556] Looking from a rational point of view, in a situation where the Companions and their successors are criticized and information coming through this channel are negated, what kind of religious source of reference can be considered healthy? The Qur'an, for example, with all the arguments about whether it was created or not, was also made a subject of debate during that time. In the case of the Sunnah being negated, the whole value system established by Islam will have to be presented as a dead culture. At this juncture, critics can be seen in conflict with values the Qur'an and Sunnah may offer for the present and future eras.

Further, Gülen draws attention to some Hadith critics other than the followers of *Mu'tazilah*. In his view, Muhammad ibn 'Abd al-Wahhab (1701-1793 CE), besides his weakness in Hadith knowledge, is of those who exceeded the limits in criticizing early period Muslim scholars. A careful study of his books reveals that 'Abd al-Wahhab has drawn heavily—in the form of abridgement—on authors like Ibn Taymiyya, Ibn Kathir, Ibn al-Qayyim al-Jawziyyah and Shawkani, and cherry-picked hadiths to serve his purpose. Those who are influenced by his views consider many acts of Sunnah, such as visiting graves, reciting *Surah al-Fatihah* for the dead and using prayer beads, as *shirk* (ascribing partners placed beside God).[557] Their approach to Sunnah may be regarded as shallow rather than completely rejecting the Sunnah.

According to Gülen, Muslim intellectuals who blindly follow their imam (*taqlid*) are unacquainted with the fundamental sources of Hadith and consequently their knowledge in this discipline is next to nothing. For this reason, they have no idea about the Hadith discipline, the criteria employed in relevant works and stages accomplished in the choice of hadiths—such as subjecting hadiths to stringent tests from textual and chain of narration points of view.[558] Moreover, they do not feel the need to study works authored against Hadith criticism. Whereas,

---

[556] Gülen, *Sonsuz Nur, Vol. 2 (Muhammad: The Messenger of God)*, pp. 543–544.
[557] Gülen, *Yol Mulahazalari (Contemplating the Journey), Prizma 6*, p. 149.
[558] ibid., p. 192.

works like Zaheed al-Kawthari's (1879-1952) *Maqalat* or Mustafa Sabri's *Mawqif al-'Aql wa al-'Ilm wa al-'Alam min Rabb al-'Alamin* and some other new research papers and articles provide satisfactory information. These works produce sound evidence and shut all doors against Hadith criticism.[559] Clearly, Gülen is keen in preserving his Ottoman heritage to refute Hadith criticism. It is also worth noting that besides some rational and textual argument, some of his arguments go beyond them and seems religious or confessional in nature.

Gülen emphasizes that some Muslim intellectuals' offensive statements like "The Prophet also was a human-being, and naturally, he made mistakes,"[560] cannot be regarded as innocent. In his view, these remarks stem from condescending statements like "They were human-beings, so we are,"[561] about Muslims jurists. Negative criticism is like fire—once it is started, no one can predict where it will stop. Defaming prominent Sunni scholars, like Abu Hanifah and Imam Shafi'i, would extend to the questioning of the Companions and even the Noble Prophet. Looking from this point of view, the Qur'an is being questioned with the help of the projection of this idea in our age and a spiritual breakdown in society effected with regard to faith.[562] For this reason, and based upon his concern that a small deviation may lead to a drastic heresy, Gülen feels the need to caution Muslim intellectuals and amend their thoughts. Clearly, Gülen is very sensitive but also quite apologetic to protect the innocence of the first Muslim generations.

As mentioned above, Gülen approaches thoughts about the Sunnah using psychological analysis and exposes the claimants' mental situation. He asserts that this approach stems from a lack of knowledge and, consequently, falling into an identity crisis. He explains that Muslim intellectuals attempt to question the Sunnah because of this identity problem.[563] In fact, Gülen points out, in this questioning of the Sunnah, they compare themselves to reputable Muslim scholars because of their lack of knowledge. Setting themselves as the standard of the truth, they

---

[559] ibid., p. 149.
[560] Gülen, *Prizma 2, (Prism, Vol. 2)*, (Istanbul: Nil Publishing, 2010), p. 64.
[561] ibid.
[562] ibid.
[563] Gülen, *Sonsuz Nur, Vol. 2 (Muhammad: The Messenger of God)*, p. 411.

declare some authentic hadiths "weak" without taking into consideration early period Muslim scholars' judgments.

At this point, to further clarify the matter, we will focus on some authentic (*sahih*) hadith evaluations to which certain non-Muslim thinkers and Muslim intellectuals objected. Taking into account the originality of the hadith subjected to criticism and their agreement with present day scientific realities, the appropriateness of Gülen's evaluations and advice can be understood. With his comments on Hadith, Gülen presents some answers and brings scientific explanations to arguments, which opponents use as material for their criticism. For example: Gülen focuses on a hadith—reported by Bukhari, Muslim, Tirmidhi, Abu Dawud, Nasa'i, Ibn Majah and Ibn Hanbal—through which the Noble Prophet addresses a health issue that throws light on present day medical facts. The hadith in question is: "The purification of the vessel of one of you, if a dog licks it, is to wash it seven times, the first time with soil." Some variations of this hadith go like this: "When a dog drinks from your vessel..."[564] with the influence of rationalist thought, this hadith has been rejected by some Muslim intellectuals who considered its content irrational. Gülen indicates that Abu Hurayrah's name being mentioned in the chain of narration is the primary reason for the rejection of this hadith. He opines that the name of this narrator triggers an automatic reflex to take an opposing stand. Looking into the evaluation of this hadith from Gülen's point of view, Hanafite jurists interpret the word "seven" in the hadith as an allusion to "multiplicity" and decide that washing the vessel three times would suffice.[565] Starting from this point, Gülen presents answers to the owners of thought who act impatiently from the medical science perspective. He builds his arguments on the basis of medical research and emphasizes the existence of some diseases that can be transmitted from dogs to humans. In Gülen's view, this hadith indicates, in the name of hygiene and sanitation, the presence of viruses and microbes that can cause diseases in dogs and people. This hadith proves itself to be a miraculous admonition and warning about these microbes' ability to survive comfortably in both bodies (dog and

---

[564] Bukhari, *Wudu'* 33; Muslim, *Taharah* 90-91; Tirmidhi, *Taharah* 68; Abu Dawud, *Taharah* 37; Nasa'i, *Taharah* 50; Ibn Majah, *Taharah* 31; Ibn Hanbal, *al-Musnad* 2/245, 253, 460.

[565] Sarakhsi, *al-Mabsut* 1/48; Kashani, *Badaiu al-Sanai'* 1/64; Marghinani, *al-Hidaya* 1/23.

human). In this age, it is possible to come across numerous results and research papers in scientific publications.[566] **Gülen's approach on issues pertaining to hadith**s of this kind is to refute the opponents' theses by giving answers based on their own tenets, i.e. rational and scientific data. By adopting this approach, he, on the one hand, draws attention to Hadith interpretations applicable in present-day conditions and, on the other hand, gives examples, in a rational plan, from Hadith collections to those who follow a thought system based on intellect and reason. Clearly, Gülen speaks the same language as his opponents.

Once again, Gülen responds through scientific arguments to denials raised against another hadith. In a hadith reported by Abu Hurayrah, the Noble Prophet said: "If a fly falls into the drink of any one of you, he should dunk it all the way in and then remove it." The hadith continues, "Because on one of its wings is disease and on the other is its cure."[567] The literal meaning of the hadith is irreconcilable with intellect and reason. According to Gülen, *Mu'tazilah* criticizes and rejects this hadith because of these rational reasons. For the same reasons, in our day, Gülen argues that Maurice Bucaille, who acted hastily in commenting and attributing defect to this hadith, failed in his view. The situation described in the hadith has been attributed to ignorance of Muslims and ridiculed. Again, the presence of Abu Hurayrah's name in the chain of narrators is the main cause of this reaction and the hadith has been logically rejected and derided. Gülen argues that criticizing this hadith because of the chain of narrators is not possible because it is mentioned in many major Hadith collections, such as Bukhari, Abu Dawud, Nasa'i, Darimi and Ibn Hanbal. Besides, neither the Companions nor Hadith experts imply doubt about this hadith.[568] Emphasizing the authenticity of the hadith, Gülen assures Muslims they should not have any suspicion in their mind.

Gülen makes some comments and scientific explanations about the characteristics of flies employing medical language. In the first part of the hadith, the Noble Prophet draws attention to the microbe-carrying characteristic of the fly. The second part emphasizes

---

[566] Gülen, *Sonsuz Nur, Vol. 2 (Muhammad: The Messenger of God)*, p. 481.
[567] Bukhari, *tib* 58; *badu'l-halq* 17; Abu Dawud, *at'ima* 48; Nasai, *al-Fara' wa'l-atira* 11; Ibn Majah, *tib* 31; Darimi, *at'ima* 12; Ibn Hanbal, *al-Musnad* 2/229, 246.
[568] Gülen, *Sonsuz Nur, Vol. 2 (Muhammad: The Messenger of God)*, p. 482.

the presence of disease on one side of the fly and remedy on the other side. The term mentioned in the hadith "side of the fly" (*janah*) refers to the wings. Modern research has brought to light that the fly carries a microbe on one side and a cytoplasm containing a sterilizing agent on the other side.[569] Therefore, a hasty rejection of the hadith—without proper investigation—which throws light into modern day medical science, cannot be explained in any other way than the manifestation of prejudice. Moreover, this characteristic is not unique to the fly; it has been scientifically established today that the scorpion, honeybee and some species of snakes also have the same characteristic. Researchers need to evaluate the hadith in question from every aspect and then make their own comments. Bringing these kinds of arguments in defense of Hadith through his style of approach, Gülen gives new dimensions to Hadith criticism. Furthermore, establishing the strength and health of the Hadith highlights the fact of its validity for all ages.

Gülen points out, as example, a particular hadith that was made a subject of mockery and rejected due to a lack of understanding of its import. At this point, he emphasizes his opponents' lack of sensitive criteria for evaluation. Gülen says the Noble Prophet stating, "When one of you wakes up from sleep, he must not dip his hand into a utensil until he washes it three times, for indeed none of you knows where his hand spent the night,"[570] has been made a subject of ridicule, especially by Goldziher and some Muslim intellectuals who follow him. Ahmad Amin (1886-1954)—the author of books *Fajr al-Islam*, *Duha al-Islam* and *Zuhr al-Islam*—ridicules this hadith by saying, "How can a person not know where his hands were?"[571] Abu Rayyah also ridicules this hadith on the same basis. However, Gülen presents them answers through a distinct interpretation. Gülen argues that a sleeping person may scratch some parts of his body—including the private parts—due to some ailments, such as allergy, because the consciousness is partly closed down during sleep and movements of limbs cannot be controlled. The presence of millions of germs under the fingernails is a known fact of the medical science in our days. Unsurprisingly, a person who scratches any dirty part

---

[569] Ibid., pp. 482–484.
[570] Bukhari, *Wudu* 26; Muslim, *Taharah* 87-88; Abu Dawud, *Taharah* 50; Tirmidhi, *Taharah* 19 (text from Abu Dawud).
[571] Gülen, *Sonsuz Nur, Vol. 2 (Muhammad: The Messenger of God)*, p. 488.

of their body will have those germs lodged under their fingernails and touching food without washing the hands will transfer these germs first to the food and then into the body, potentially causing diseases. A hadith or warning—which is not contradictory to scientific findings—being rejected due to being reported by the Companions who lived in a period where medical science was not so advanced is a serious predicament for some Muslim intellectuals.[572] Faced with modern scientific data, this situation causes them to fall into psychological guilt.

As can be seen, Gülen stands against the flat out rejection of the hadith based on prejudice or without proper investigation of all their aspects relevant to our time. Emphasizing their difficulty in explaining the hadith's compatibility with modern data, Gülen argues that these rejections are no more than mere repetition of old objections without any serious underlying research. With this aspect, Gülen advises the owners of pure conjecture to thoroughly investigate the said hadith and their sources to avoid an embarrassing situation vis-à-vis modern scientific data.

With his examples, Gülen offers Muslim intellectuals comments based on current scientific data. The dominance of psychological, sociological and scientific comments in Gülen's analyses demonstrates his ability in keeping with the spirit of the contemporary age. Through these kinds of interpretations, he brings hadiths closer to present day understanding and reveals their compatibility with scientific data. This may be perceived as his unique teaching and persuasion method.

Gülen believes there is an intended target and design to be achieved by Hadith criticism in the Muslim world. Through his analyses he concludes that questioning the primary sources of the religion, i.e. Hadith and Sunnah, prepare the groundwork for the spread of various ideologies. He argues that discrediting the Sunnah would leave the Qur'an alone and exposed to free-hand interpretations. Ultimately, this would create a vacuum of faith—a fertile environment for the development of diverse ideologies. The fact is that human nature (*fitrah*) does not accept a vacuum. According to Gülen, strict communism was an alternative offered to fill a gap, but failed because it was not compatible with natural

---

[572] Ibid., pp. 488–489.

human disposition. Besides this, thought movements like spiritualism and reincarnation are also being propagated. At this point, Gülen reacts to Muslim intellectuals who are caught up with these currents and their efforts to inject them into Islam, and emphasizes that what they are doing is not compatible with Islamic sources and a scholarly approach. He stresses the difficulty of understanding their persistent questioning and criticism of the Sunnah.[573]

As understood from Gülen's assessments, Hadith criticism creates suspicions on authentic hadiths and gives rise to debates about Hadith criteria. He does not believe that Hadith critics have any chance to arrive to a positive outcome due to their lack of knowledge and wrong psychological approach. Instead, the most valuable contribution they could make in this era would be the protection and dissemination of the huge amount of information so far collected in the field of Hadith, using all available means and techniques. In other words, Hadith literature, which has been recorded and safeguarded through traditional methods since the early period, must be transformed into a digital environment. Digital data on the internet facilitates rapid and widespread dissemination of information. As much as various events taking place in the world affect each other in some way, scientific progress and research also interact and huge amounts of information are shared rapidly on a global scale.[574] At this point, according to Gülen, it is essential to leave the job to the experts. Gülen, despite the fact he has been studying Hadith with postgraduate students for more than thirty years, states he has mastered only one-twentieth of this discipline. In his view, the discipline of Hadith is not a branch of science one can claim to have mastered just by saying so.[575] Hadith is a field of knowledge, which requires exceptional scientific depth. Criticizing Hadith by shallow considerations will not suffice to achieve correct results.

Gülen supports his views in the defense of Hadith by basing them on a Prophetic tradition:

---

[573] Gülen, *Sonsuz Nur, Vol. 2 (Muhammad: The Messenger of God)*, p. 388.
[574] Gülen, *Insanin Ozundeki Sevgi*, (Toward a Global Civilization of *Love and Tolerance*), (Istanbul: Da Publishing, 2003), p. 195.
[575] Gülen, *Yol Mulahazalari (Contemplating the Journey)*, Prism series, Vol. 6, p. 150.

There will be a man to whom my hadith will reach him, while he is sitting comfortably, and he will say, "There is only the Book of God between me and you; whatever we find in it that is lawful we will make it lawful, and whatever we find in it unlawful we will make it unlawful." (Then, the Noble Prophet stated the following:) Whatever the Messenger of God has made unlawful is as if God has made it unlawful.[576]

According to Gülen, the Sunnah is just this in the sight of God and His Messenger. To those Muslim intellectuals who criticize and degrade the Sunnah despite this hadith and their insufficient knowledge of Arabic language and to those who attempt to bring solutions to all issues only by the help of a Qur'an translation, Gülen asks this question: "Where do you think you're going?"[577] The Qur'an cannot stand alone without the Sunnah and neither can the Sunnah stand without the Qur'an – they complement each other. If this fact is disregarded, deriving correct knowledge from either of these two sources would be impossible. Gülen's proposal with regard to the council of jurisprudence (*fiqh*) can be considered also for safeguarding and defending the Hadith. Such a scholarly committee to be formed at global level can produce satisfactory answers to all questions and criticisms raised against the Sunnah.

---

[576] Tirmidhi, *'Ilm*, 10; Abu Dawud, *Sunnah*, 5; Ibn Majah, *Muqaddimah*, 2.
[577] Gülen, *Sonsuz Nur-2 (Muhammad: The Messenger of God, Vol. 2)*, pp. 593–594

Chapter Four

Gülen's Usage and Interpretation of Sunnah

Gülen's Application of Sunnah in His Own Life

G ülen's level of knowledge in the field of Sunnah has been explained in the chapter, titled Gülen's understanding of Sunnah.
At this point, the practical aspect of his Hadith knowledge
and how this shaped his lifestyle will be expounded. How much of his
knowledge of Hadith and Sunnah reflects on his daily life? What is his
Sunnah-centered representation of the message of Islam and self-accountability, and how does it affect social life? Seeking answers to these
questions may reveal valuable ideas and information about Gülen's life
and his mission.

Being closely related to this subject, it is appropriate to have a
brief discussion on the relationship between faith (*iman*) and practice
(*'amal*) in Islam. These two elements constitute complementary aspects
of Islam. That is, a human being can attain the level of perfection through
the agency of knowledge-faith and good, righteous deeds. Once faith
comes into the heart, a believer seeks ways to become a true servant
and closeness to the Creator as a necessity of their faith. This idea is the
natural result of the cause-and-effect relationship between knowledge,
faith and worship. The human intellect reaching the knowledge of its
Creator through the teachings of God's Prophets looks into practical,
individual and social events with the eyes of the Prophetic teachings. The
aim is to achieve the perfection required by the Creator. In the Islamic
concept, the way to perfection (becoming a mature, perfect human being)
is through applying the rules stipulated by Divine decrees and moral
values into practical life. For this reason, a proper understanding of the
values concerning morality and worship is closely related to adherence
to Prophets who represent these values. The Noble Prophet confirmed
this by saying, "I was sent to complete the best of character."[578] The
Qur'an also draws attention to this characteristic of the Noble Prophet:
*"You are surely of a sublime character, and do act by a sublime pattern of
conduct"* (Qur'an, 68:4).

Many researchers such as Canan highlight Gülen's sensitivity on
this matter. Therefore, it is inconceivable to think he would disregard
knowledge, practice and religious principles. A quick look into the

---

[578] Muwatta, *Husn al-Khulq*, 8; Ibn Hanbal, 2/381.

works he authored or his talks that have been compiled into book form reveals how much emphasis he puts on Sunnah, worship—and especially the pillars of Islam, such as daily ritual prayers, fasting, almsgiving and pilgrimage—and the level of his sensitivity on morality and good character.

Worship in Islam is an element of the religion that comes immediately after knowledge and faith, and occupies an important place in Gülen's life. He perceives this as perfect servitude to the Almighty God. According to him, there exists a mystery of servitude (*sirr ubudiyyah*) in inclining to God (*tawajjuh*), worship and prayers. Believers may not understand the true meanings attributed to these values, but act with the consciousness of servitude and perform these duties simply because they are ordered by God.[579] In Gülen's view, the factor that brings a human being to this level of consciousness is nothing less than the Qur'an. The Noble Prophet, through his Sunnah, is the representative of the Qur'an. Thus, loyalty to God and His Prophet manifests itself as a philosophy of life in Gülen.

Looking with this understanding in mind, worship, according to Gülen, is practicing one's religion for the sake of God without expecting anything in return. He bases his understanding of obligatory and optional duties on this principle. Furthermore, Gülen maintains that, not only the obligatory duties, but also the principles related to individual, familial and social life have a devotional aspect. For this reason, a servant attains pure servitude by connecting the flow of his everyday life to devotional considerations. Gülen uses Bediüzzaman Said Nursi's thoughts to support this view.[580] According to Nursi, "If a person performs his everyday tasks for the pleasure of God, and adheres sincerely to the Prophetic Traditions—i.e. eats, sits, stands up like him and takes him as a role model in all his routines—he will have converted his habits into worshipping."[581] Due to his total agreement with this view, Gülen's life manifests as a system that is full with reflections from the Sunnah. Gülen also believes Nursi's view stating the three major

---

[579] Canan, *Fethullah Gülen'in Sunnet Anlayisi*, p. 31.
[580] Gülen, *Kirik Testi-1(The Broken Jug series*, Vol. 1), pp. 31–32.
[581] Bediüzzaman Said Nursi, *The Flashes Collection*, The Eleventh Flash, First Point (Istanbul: Sozler Publishing, 2006), p. 64.

obstacles or enemies—i.e. ignorance, poverty and discord—that affect individual and community life may be overcome by adopting the faith and Sunnah into people's daily lives. This is the reason why he accepts individual and family education as the primary element in social development. He attaches a particular importance to school education for the cultivation of the members of the society.[582] He considers this as a form of devotional thought in terms of adherence to the Sunnah because there exists a sampling of educational processes in the Noble Prophet's life, which began in Mecca and evolved into a formal school status in Medina. It is possible to see many examples of one-to-one interaction and individual training in the Prophetic Sunnah.

For this reason, not contending himself with defending the Sunnah, Gülen puts his focus on practical interpretations of the Sunnah. The priority in this context, according to him, is to attain maturity and perfection in worshipping and renewal (*tajdid*). Highlighting the role of worship in training individuals, he focuses on cultivating a model community. Keeping his emphases at the highest level on this issue, he encourages individuals to bring vitality to their worship. He often says:

> In fact, we are experiencing fatigue in our servitude. There are virtually fatigue and frustration in our devotion. We are looking into Islam vulgarly. We are narrowing and shallowing it in our hearts. We have become the victims of acquaintances. Our values have become dull in our eyes; they do not create a stir anymore. Why is there no excitement?[583]

Gülen emphasizes that each individual should look for this renewal in the liaison between his Lord and his own self because any form of renewal not starting from this point would not be a *tajdid* in its true sense. Gülen sees devotion not just in terms of formal injunctions, but rather an ontological issue, and for this reason, places them on top of the list of individual and social revival. Believing that current perceptions of worship are completely built upon routines, Gülen

---

[582] Zeki Sarıtoprak, "Fethullah Gülen and His Theology of Social Responsibility," *Mastering Knowledge in Modern Times: Fethullah Gülen as an Islamic Scholar*, Ismail Albayrak (ed.), (Clifton, NJ: Blue Dome Press, 2012), p. 91.

[583] Gülen, *Kirik Testi-1 (The Broken Jug, Vol. 1)*, p. 36.

criticizes contemporary Muslims with very harsh language. He believes that modern Muslims have failed to internalize the truths of the Qur'an and the Sunnah, and this is why faith and worship have been perceived shallowly as traditions and customs inherited from the family. Shallowness in thought, knowledge and faith can be counted as some of the reasons behind this failure, which hinder the understanding of the essence of worship. For example, the issue that the Quranic verse "*When they rise to do the Prayer, they rise lazily,*"[584] deals with is employed by Gülen according to a rather different argument. According to Gülen, worship that is not genuinely internalized can turn, in time, into fatigue, boredom and laziness, and loses its original purity.[585] Consequently, a serious degeneration emerges in society due to religious values losing their effect. In this case, the survival of the society becomes difficult.

In this environment of corruption, Gülen judges individuals by their devotional aspect. He analyses the perfect human portrait psychologically on the criteria of sincerity in devotion. In his analyses, he does not neglect giving examples from the Sunnah and providing new perspectives upon it. According to Gülen, Prayer is a human behavior. It is a Divine command shaped particularly for human beings. Its form and essence were taught to the Noble Prophet personally by Gabriel, the Archangel of Revelation.[586] From this point of view, the ritual aspect of the Prayer has a Divine origin. Prayer—due to these characteristics—should be performed as best as it can be in the human dimension. Gülen perceives the performance of the Prayers without proper consciousness as an escape from duty. This escape from sincere worship may also be seen as running away from other responsibilities in life. Failure in internalizing Divine commands may reflect in one's life as an inadequate development of the sense of individual responsibility. He presents these inferences by way of new interpretations he introduced into Hadith. In his view, if worship is not performed in its peculiar spiritual atmosphere, the formal postures

---

[584] Qur'an 4:142.
[585] Gülen, *Kirik Testi-1 (The Broken Jug, Vol. 1)*, p. 43.
[586] Muslim, *Janaidh*, 1; Tirmidhi, *Imam*, 18; *Jihad*, 32; Suyuti, *Miftah*, 29; *Musnad*, II, 85, 160; Bukhari, *Adab*, 28; Muslim, 1, 140; Abu Dawud, *Manasiq*, 24, 27; Tirmidhi, *Hajj*, 14; Abu Dawud, *Salat*, 2; Bukhari, *Badu'l-Halq*, 6; Abu Dawud, *Sunnah*, 9; *Musnad*, I, 191; Ibn Hihsam, *Sira*, III, 101–102.

and acts are considered outside natural human behavior.[587] That is, they turn into instinctive animal movements.

Starting from this point and drawing attention to similes in hadiths, Gülen presents contemporary Muslims with the reality and essence of the Prayer. For example, the condition of a worshipper who moves into the bowing position (*ruku'*) before the imam has been described as: "Would you like God to turn your faces into that of a donkey's when you are rising from the bowing position?"[588] In the context of the hadith, moving in anticipation of the movements of the imam leading the Prayer means going out of the line of servitude. Here, it is possible to infer that Gülen, by pointing out the obedience to the person in authority as required by individual and social morality, communalizes devotions and establishes rules in community training. Continuing again, it is said, "When one of you goes into the prostration (*sajda*) position, you should not do it like a rooster picking the grain."[589] This has also been interpreted as an animal behavior. The worshipper is being invited to live the feeling and cordiality while performing prostration. Explanation of the wisdom behind performing the prostration by "not sitting on the haunches like a dog"[590] during the Prayer, implements paradigms to prevent vulgarization of individuals.

Gülen emphasizes that an individual can only achieve progress in human values parallel to the level of his contact with God Almighty because one of the characteristics of the Divine laws is to directly affect people's behaviors and lives. This can be seen as conforming to the view asserting that religion represents material and spiritual integrity.

The abovementioned hadith highlights the characteristics of a human being during worship and differentiates between the human on the one hand, and the animal that has no intellect or judgment on the other. While inviting people to an orderly social life, it also builds a solid and healthy value system for the community. In a way, it puts forth the thesis that worship is the most prominent difference between humans

---

[587]   Gülen, *Kirik Testi-1 (The Broken Jug,* Vol. 1), pp. 43–44.
[588]   ibid.
[589]   ibid.
[590]   ibid.

and other living creatures, thus justifying humans' worthiness of being subject to Divine addressing.

Suleyman Sargin describes Gülen's worship consciousness as in perfect accordance with the target set in the above hadith. He connects Gülen's sensitivity on worship to his proper interpretation of the Sunnah and the Noble Prophet. In Gülen's view, the prostration (*sajdah*) represents the pinnacle of worship and is the ground for thanking God for the gifts and rewards that come with the Prayer.[591] **Gülen also interprets the state of** prostration as the summit of convergence with the Prayer.[592] His comment on the following Quranic verse with regard to the Noble Prophet's way of performing his Prayer gives tips on Gülen's worship consciousness:

> He Who sees you when you rise (in the Prayer, and in readiness to carry out Our commands), as well as your strenuous efforts in prostration among those who prostrate (to be able to fulfill your duty of servanthood and help the believers to reform their lives).[593]

According to him, this verse—besides describing how the Noble Prophet prays—explains the reality of perfect devotion. Thus, Gülen concludes that—as mentioned in the hadith, "Perform your Prayer as you see me praying"[594]—Muslims are responsible to perform their Prayers exactly the same way the Noble Prophet did.[595] For this reason, a self-accountability that questions Gülen's personal worship is perceived. Stressing frequently the expression of gratitude to God through worship for all the blessings He bestowed upon us, he advises a perpetual intellectual and devotional vivacity.[596] The modality should reflect this inner sincerity on the outward appearance and the hadith points out this aspect of the worship. A devotion performed at this level of consciousness would normally represent the purpose of the creation.[597]

---

[591] Suleyman Sargin, "Namazi sanki secde etmek icin kiliyor," *Zaman daily,* October, 4, 2013.
[592] Gülen, *Kirik Testi-1 (The Broken Jug,* Vol. 1), p. 48.
[593] Qur'an 26:218–219.
[594] Bukhari, *Adhan,* 18; *Adab,* 27; Darimi, *Salat,* 42; Ibn Hanbal, *Musnad,* 5/53).
[595] Gülen, *Fasildan Fasila 1 (From Chapter to Chapter,* Vol. 1), p. 61.
[596] ibid., 86.
[597] ibid., 99.

The perfection in servitude finds its place with superior Divine values and Sunnah offered by Islam. Through these values, the Creator shows the nurturing method to individuals. For this reason, Gülen mainly focuses on the nurturing and devotional aspect of Sunnah. He endeavors to have the nurturing function of devotion work at individual and community levels. For this reason, he begins with questioning his own self. He focuses on the scarcity of his own worship and the qualitative deficiency of his inner-formation vis-à-vis God's power of creation.[598] By his comments, Gülen draws attention to the material and spiritual substance of worship and highlights the necessity of addressing the issue in a holistic manner. According to him, in worship, matter and spirit are in a position where they cannot be distinguished from one another.

Gülen interprets modality related metaphors mentioned in the hadith as the causes of disorders in physical behaviors and, thus, lack of discipline in life. In fact, he draws attention to the correlation between the physical body and soul. Between body and soul there exists an uninterrupted liaison that can be felt and sensed by experience. A disorder or discipline in the physical body has a similar effect on the soul. As a negative thought system can cause anxiety and stress, positive plans, projects and worship lead to development of the soul.[599] While these thoughts and behaviors somehow affect the soul, at the same time, they become instrumental in forming and clarifying human nature. The modality mentioned in the hadith points out the soul although it appears to be related to outward appearance. Corruption of the inner being is thus reflected on outward appearance and this has been compared in form to animal behaviors. Conversely, the outward deformation and resemblance to an animal may be seen as the cause of a serious degeneration of the inner being. Thus, the hadith deals with man's inward-outward unity and educates him. Otherwise, looking at man from only one aspect would be similar to the situation of an airplane with only one wing.

Believing that a believer's psychology of guilt and sin in individual and family life can be overcome by the Prayer, Gülen explains his thesis by "seeking forgiveness from God (*istighfar*). According

---

[598] Unal, *M. Fethullah Gülen: Bir Portre Denemesi (Fethullah Gulen: A Portrait Essay)*, p. 497.
[599] Gülen, *Kalbin Zumrut Tepeleri 3 (Emerald Hills of the Heart, Vol. 3)*, pp. 219–220.

to him, the prescribed Prayer—as mentioned in many hadiths—is a means of purification from sins because the Prayer is an effective factor in evolving repentance into a state of consciousness. That is, a prayer that is performed according to its prescribed acts and manners is a leavening agent of consciousness to an individual.[600] Because of this state of consciousness, individuals can heal themselves psychologically and attain a state of grace. A careful study of Gülen's works discloses that his sensitivity about the Prayer is also valid for each and every truth revealed by the Qur'an and the Sunnah. According to him, no form of worship has any superiority over another in terms of practicing devotion and adherence to the Sunnah. All forms of worship and values of the Prophetic Traditions have their own weight relative to their status.

Besides worship, Gülen approaches the Noble Prophet's actions from two different points: delivery of the Divine message (*tabligh*) and representation, or setting himself up as a role model (*tamthil*). As mentioned by his beloved wife 'A'ishah, the Noble Prophet, through his actions, put into practical life the superior morality the Qur'an brought to humankind. The Muslim community was ordered with adherence to the Sunnah because of this reality of representation.[601] This is why Gülen emphatically advises the Sunnah to become a way of life. According to him, the verse, "*Assuredly you have in God's Messenger an excellent example to follow for whoever looks forward to God and the Last Day, and remembers and mentions God much*" (33:21), points directly to the Noble Prophet's representative mission.[602] It is because of these reasons that Gülen, on account of his mission, ascribes the upbringing of future generations to a Sunnah-centered representative ability. Therefore, he focuses on the generations (*alperens*) to bring, by representation, what they believe into life because the dullness would be removed by means of representation from Islamic understanding and its original purity reinstated. Generations with these qualities will be able to perform their mission of "bringing peace and harmony to humanity."[603] **Gülen, who**

---

[600] Gülen, *Fasildan Fasila 1(From Chapter to Chapter,* Vol. 1), p.162.
[601] Qur'an, 4:59; 33:36; 59:7; 16:44–64; 3:31–32.
[602] Canan, *Fethullah Gülen'in Sunnet Anlayisi (Fethullah Gülen's Understanding of Sunnah),* p. 107.
[603] ibid.

firmly believes in this, emphasizes that representation (*tamthil*) in the Prophet's mission had priority and importance over the presentation of the message (*tabligh*)—as he says in his own words, "always one step ahead of the *tabligh* circumstance."[604] According to him, with his representative ability, God's Messenger constitutes a role model for humankind. Thus, the Noble Prophet gave priority to the representation of the Quranic verses over their delivery; that is, put "representation" one step ahead of "presentation."[605] Briefly, for Gülen, understanding of Sunnah, internalizing the values in it and finally practicing it is a project of civilization. In Gülen's thought, not only Muslims but all humankind needs Sunnah oriented life.

Muslims' failure in interpreting and representing the Qur'an and the Sunnah properly may be counted among the reasons for their falling behind in certain areas because Muslims were seen to rise during the times when their representative ability reached the highest level. For example, progress was successfully sustained during the time of the Noble Prophet and the first four Rightly Guided Caliphs, and in some other Muslim states that followed.[606] This progress trend in Islam can be interpreted as the result of adherence to the principle of steadfastness (*istiqamah*) in representation.[607] Upholding steadfastness is a quality that can maintain the vivacity in representation. At this point, putting his focus on representation (*tamthil*) and steadfastness (*istiqamah*), Gülen exposes his own self-accountability. He concentrates on the questions of "how" and "why" with regard to the failure in representing Islam.[608] He presents the way out of the problem and the means of achieving the aim by inculcating his interlocutor with inner accountability along with *tamthil* and *istiqamah*.

With these considerations, Gülen points out the qualities of a genuine believer and draws a picture of his representative ability. He discusses the views that the believer is under God's control in their attitude and behavior. So, as he points out, caution and vigilance

---

[604] ibid.
[605] ibid., 107–108.
[606] Gülen, *Prizma 4 (Prism series*, Vol. 4), p. 81.
[607] Gülen, *Fasildan Fasila 3 (From Chapter to Chapter*, Vol. 3), p. 76.
[608] Gülen, *Kirik Testi-1 (The Broken Jug*, Vol. 1), pp. 118–119.

constitute indispensable principles of life.[609] **Gülen implements serious strict disciplinary measures in the application of** Sunnah; he draws attention to the significance of these characteristics in the training and education of the target generation. In defining and executing these implementations, Gülen has not neglected drawing disciplinary principles directly from Sunnah.

In light of this information, drawing attention to another matter, a true spiritual guide (*murshid*)—even though they are well-equipped on the horizon of *'ilm-ma'rifah* (knowledge-intuitive knowledge of God)—must take into account their audience's level of cognizance, thoughts and feelings when speaking or writing.[610] This will help avoid any confusion or misunderstanding in the mind of their interlocutor. This approach of Gülen's conforms to the Prophetic report: "Speak to people according to their level of understanding, and not your level of knowledge."[611] He takes moderation and gradualism as his principle and shows, once again, his strict adherence to the Prophetic Practice (*Sunnah*).

Gülen also points out the importance of presentation (*tabligh*), which is a dimension of representation (*tamthil*). While highlighting this aspect of Gülen's, Unal draws attention to his life being intertwined with Sunnah. Unal takes some examples from the Qur'an and the Sunnah to support his view about this quality of Gülen's. He explains the Noble Prophet's stress about people's unwillingness in entering in Islamic faith by the Quranic verse, "*Yet it may be that you (O Muhammad) will torment yourself to death with grief, following after them, if they do not believe in this Message.*"[612] The verse expresses the Noble Prophet's eagerness in making people accept his message. On one hand, the verse highlights the Prophet's compassion and, on the other hand, he is cautioned about his eagerness. The Noble Prophet is not responsible for people's faith; his mission is just to deliver the message. After these examples, Unal points out Gülen's eagerness in adopting the Sunnah. According to Unal, Gülen views the Noble Prophet's eagerness as the pinnacle of the mission's

---

[609] Gülen, *Kalp İbresi (The Heart's Cursor)*, (Istanbul: Nil Publishing, 2010), p. 94.

[610] ibid., 28.

[611] Al-Munawi, *Fayd al-Qadr*, Cairo, 1356, Vol. III, p. 378/ v. IV, 299; Abu Nu'aym al-Asfahani, *Hilyat al-Awliya'*, Beirut, 1405, Vol. II, p. 300; Ibn Hajar Abu al-Fadl al-Askalani al-Shafi'i, *Lisan al-Midhan*, Beirut, 1406/1986, Vol. VI, p. 274.

[612] Qur'an 18:6.

understanding and representation. Therefore, Gülen sets the Sunnah as his target. It is possible to say that Gülen has been influenced by his contemporary Nursi's commentaries and developed a new thought system for his own commentaries because Gülen frequently uses Nursi's works as his source of reference and recommends his followers also to do so.

His Criteria for the Selection and Usage of Hadith

The main theme of this section is Gülen's priorities and criteria for selection, usage and presentation of Hadith; what type of hadiths he selects and for what purpose he uses them in his works? Answers to these questions will provide important information about Gülen's dialogue with Sunnah and the objective he wants to achieve.

Science and Faith-based Action

Gülen's energetic character may be a good starting point to arrive at the right conclusion on this matter. With his thought and vision, he displays the characteristic of a man of action. However, it is necessary to emphasize that the term "action" here should not be understood in the sense of *jihad* or similar activities. Nowadays, *jihad* is being brought to the fore as an action in the name of Islam; values such as faith, contemplation, affection, tolerance and dialogue are left in the background.

According to Gülen, action, unlike physical reactions, is a person's ability to engage in the ontological analysis of existence and to read the book of the universe in detail. Regarding the study and understanding of the universe, he accepts as his guide the Noble Prophet, and his Sunnah, who encourages[613] his followers to seek knowledge.[614] This approach of Gülen demonstrates a close relation with the command of the first Quranic verse revealed, "*Read!*"[615] Reading results in thinking, analysis and synthesis. The very first verse of the Qur'an presents the universe in a book form and leaves its analysis to humankind. At this point, the Qur'an appoints the Noble Prophet to the position of the delivery and

---

[613] "Whoever goes out seeking knowledge is in the path of God until he returns." Tirmidhi, *'Ilm* 2, (2649); Ibn Majah, *Muqaddimah* 17, (227).

[614] Gülen, *Ruhumuzun Heykelini Dikerken 1 (The Statue of Our Souls)*, pp. 65-66.

[615] "*Read in and with the Name of your Lord, Who has created...*" (Qur'an 96:1).

representation of the message, and links the way to reach God to reading (reflection, analysis, study) and to the understanding of the Prophetic messages. Necip Fazil Kisakurek, at this juncture, demonstrates a similar approach to Gülen's and places the Noble Prophet in a central position for the understanding of the book of the universe, and explains it as the main purpose of God's art.[616] It is difficult to talk about a very strong influence of Kisakurek on Gülen; however, it is also not difficult to say that there is no influence at all. According to Gülen's thought, the first step in faith is linked to thought based action. That is, the book of the universe (physics, astrophysics and other sciences) is being examined and synthesized in the shade of the Sunnah. These two action-oriented thoughts deal with the thesis that man can reach the truth through reflection, discernment and analysis. For instance, Kisakurek voices that God—in order to be recognized and known—placed humankind in a faraway place, and put the universe, with all its knowledge and sciences, at their disposition.[617] And, Gülen appears to have taken this action-oriented spirit one step further in his personal life and mission.

From these approaches of Gülen's, it is possible to conclude that he is convinced that the world of the future will be shaped by thought, faith, knowledge and the spirit of action. For this reason, Gülen draws attention to the importance of the foundation stones being supplied by the Sunnah. According to him, the architects of the future need to reinterpret the Book, the Sunnah and the legal opinions (*ijtihad*) of the pious predecessors (*salaf al-salihin*) in a manner consistent with the perception, style and understanding of the time by taking the advantage of the flexibility and universality of the religious-societal dynamics.[618] Essentially, at the foundation of historical dynamics, a healthy society and scientific progress lays the proper reading of these principles in accordance with the spirit of the time.

The rationality of knowledge, experience and research with Gülen is, in fact, hidden within these abovementioned dynamics. This means that a new impetus and energy will also be possible by the help

---

[616] Necip Fazil Kisakurek, *Cile*, vol. 18, *Siirlerim ve Sairligim* (Istanbul: Buyuk Dogu Publishing, 1992).

[617] ibid.42

[618] Gülen, *Ruhumuzun Heykelini Dikerken 1 (The Statue of Our Soul)*, p. 67.

of these dynamics. Inculcating aspiration and commitment to learning in individuals will be possible with the interpretation of the Sunnah in accordance with the necessities of the time. Therefore, he directly turns to the Sunnah and starts analyzing this key element. This is the reason why his samplings, analyses and comparisons are Sunnah-related. Inspired by the hadith, "Whoever follows a path to seek knowledge, Allah will make the path to paradise easy for them,"[619] he focuses on knowledge and tries to convince his interlocutor.[620] Mobilizing the power of the Sunnah behind him in order to achieve his goal, Gülen enters into a variety of presentations and defenses. While showing thus the efficacy of the Sunnah, he is actually aiming for a generation with the ability to think and analyze with it.

Gülen comes up with rather original comments on the abovementioned hadith in order to motivate his mission and followers. Thus, he draws attention to "following a path to seek knowledge" becoming more and more important for scientific researches. He is of the view that the achievement of successful decisions and interpretations by the architects of the future will depend on the proper analysis and knowledge of the global world, and on the reading and closely following of technological progress. Failure to understand and follow the scientific world, and inability to synthesize the obtained data, will result in certain losses for humanity. He believes in this reality and tries to convince his interlocutor of its existence.[621]

Gülen highlights the potential danger that in remaining isolated from the world, a researcher may consequently feel trapped in his own small reality and, therefore, limit his ability. Conversely, he believes that being informed of scientific developments would be promising for the progress of science and the future of humanity.[622] While emphasizing that his educational mission—with the help of the above hadith and similar others—would result in new perspectives arising in Turkey, Gülen prepares the groundwork for expansions in diverse geographical parts of the world. Also, while he encourages knowledge-seeking

---

[619] Muslim, *Dhikr* 38; Tirmidhi, *Hudud* 3, *Birr* 19, *Qira'ah* 3.
[620] Gülen, *Kalp Ibresi (The Heart's Cursor)*, pp. 239-240.
[621] ibid., p. 245.
[622] ibid., p. 246.

through these hadiths, he does not neglect the furnishing of finances to (or from) businessmen for the realization of his mission. By adopting this method, he prefers to solve problems through education; he rightly believes that scientific progress depends on this, and likes to convince others of the same. Due to the same considerations, he points out the necessity of closely following those who exceed in scientific research and developments.[623] From this perspective, Gülen views scientific works and progress as a philosophy of life and as elements encouraging the study of Sunnah and Hadith.

It is beneficial here to draw attention to one particular quality of Gülen: in the selection of hadiths, he generally leaves the secondary and theoretical matters out of his agenda. He considers these matters as belonging to the field of experts, *muhaddith*.[624] For example, works in the technical areas of Hadith literature in modern period by Muslim experts such as Talat Kocyigit, Ismail Lutfi Cakan, Muhammad Abu Zahw, Muhammad Mustafa al-A'zami, Mustafa Asim Koksal, Gurm Allah al-Dumayni, Subhi al-Salih, Ibrahim Canan et al. may be considered satisfactory—both quantitatively and qualitatively. However, the action-oriented aspect of the Hadith like reflection, faith and science/knowledge has not received due consideration. But in all honesty, works published in the fields of Hadith methodology and terminology and their role in the defense of Hadith cannot be ignored.

Belief and Examples from Sunnah

Gülen attributes a great importance to regaining the energy and action lost at individual and community level—most particularly the faith and spirituality element. A revival and action at this point would result in other factors starting to progress. The first impetus and example for this is the Sunnah, which was empirically tested, and the Prophet's Companions. According to Gülen, the first step the Noble Prophet took during the Meccan period was faith-based action.[625] This action constitutes the first and the most important stage of rebuilding individuals and the community. This is establishing a new way of life and demonstrating

---

[623] Gülen, *Yenilenme Cehdi (Endeavor for Renewal), Kirik Testi* series, Vol. 12, p. 94.
[624] Canan, *Fethullah Gülen'in Sunnet Anlayisi (Fethullah Gülen's Understanding of Sunnah)*, p. 93.
[625] Gülen, *Sonsuz Nur-2 (Muhammad: The Messenger of God, Vol. 2)*, p. 241.

human dignity. This is also the first step towards solving the problems amassed during the Age of Ignorance. The Noble Prophet's one-to-one dialogues with individuals and solidarity between the faithful under all circumstances are the most salient feature of this period. At this point, Gülen also sets his focus on one-to-one education and the training of individuals. Looking at the mission represented by Gülen from this perspective, all that could be seen at the nascence of the Hizmet Movement were no more than a few students, a house and a dormitory. The objective was the individuals' education and training, and equipping them with material and spiritual action-oriented qualities, i.e. thought, faith, knowledge and delivery-representation. In this regard, the Meccan period of the Prophet's mission (delivery of the message) was taken as an example by Gülen. For instance, in drawing attention to the Prophet's compassion for his Companions, he says, "Throughout his life, the Noble Prophet did not close eyes and had a comfortable sleep once,"[626] and brings him to the present time as a role model. This way, Gülen endeavors to help make his interlocutor envisage the Noble Prophet and his Sunnah, and aims at intriguing a move in the spiritual life of the individual. Gülen compares the present day social structure with the Mecca period, and concludes that the method of dealing with the people of that time can be adopted in our days. This is because problems experienced in the area of faith in this age show a close resemblance with those that prevailed during the Meccan period. And this is the reason why Gülen sets his focus on the fact that the solution needs to begin with "faith."[627] Therefore, for nurturing a dynamic community and individuals, he bases his *Hizmet* philosophy on a faith system.[628] In brief, on the one hand Gülen theologizes (kalamizes) Sunnah at individual level; on the other hand, he socializes Sunnah at community level.

---

[626] ibid.240.

[627] Gülen, *Umit Burcu (The Bearing of Hope), Kirik Testi* series, Vol. 4, pp. 131-133.

[628] Kate Kirk, Yusuf Alan and Gurkan Celik, "Modern Ideals and Muslim Identity: Harmony or Contradiction? A Text Linguistic Analysis of Gülen's Teachings and the Movement," (October 25, 2007), http://fgulen.com/en/gulen-movement/conference-papers/contributions-of-the-gulen-movement/25828-modern-ideals-and-muslim-identity-harmony-or-contradiction-a-text-linguistic-analysis-of-gulens-teachings-and-movement?highlight=WyJmYWl0aCliYXNlZCJd&hitcount=0.

Interest in Every Member of the Community

Gülen considers paying attention to and meeting all layers of society—children, youth, elderly and leaders—as essential, and bases this view on narrations transmitted from ʿAli ibn Abi Talib.[629] He draws attention to the Noble Prophet who, in delivering his message, did not differentiate between the poor and the rich, and between ordinary people and intellectuals. In this way, he based his mission on premises intended to eradicate the class difference in society in a de facto manner. Thus, the Noble Prophet recognizes the human factor with all its realities and diversities (poor, rich, white, black, free, slave, uneducated, intellectual, etc.) as his partner. And he accepts equality between human-beings as a reality. This practice of the Noble Prophet resulted in his speedy welcome among the lower classes in his society although he was still frowned upon by the higher classes.[630] With this approach, the Messenger of God proves that there is neither a cast system in Islam nor any kind of negative nationalism.[631] Starting from these criteria, Gülen turns towards the individual and community training system. He focuses on the material and spiritual equipment of the new generation he had in mind, and endeavors to develop it to such a level so as to be accepted as a real role model.

He views the members of society—student, teacher, businessman, and so on—all together as a whole, and aims at the establishment of a strong bond of love between them. For this reason, he strives to meet the needs of people from all thoughts and beliefs,[632] and does this within a family environment in a way similar to the relationship between parents and children. Moving this core structure a little further, he views all nations of the world—Muslim or non-Muslim—and their needs, as one big family. He bases the realization of this objective on the action-oriented Sunnah, and puts forward the illustrious example

---

[629] The Noble Prophet asked the leaders of Quraysh: "Who among you is going to help me?" ʿAli, who was barely a teenager, placed on the ground the water pitcher he was holding and said: 'O Messenger of God! I am!'" Ibn Hanbal, *al-Musnad* 1/159.

[630] Historical evidences show that these people who were considered as lower class learnt how to read and write in a short period of time and become role models for other communities.

[631] Gülen, *Sonsuz Nur-1 (Muhammad: The Messenger of God,* Vol. 1), p. 242.

[632] Cihan News Agency, "Gülen Offers Condolences for Slain Istanbul Resident Shot at Protest," *Today's Zaman daily,* May, 24, 2014.

of the Noble Prophet's wife Khadijah's spending all her wealth for this cause.[633] **Gülen chooses to use this core structure that he put together within Turkey as leaven for diverse nations and cultures. Besides this, another important point that should be highlighted is that, in Gülen's education and training method, it is essential to accept and respect every nation with their own socio-cultural values.** The "core structure" that is being offered for education and training is, in fact, to be established on the distinctive universal values of the nations. It is possible, in a way, to view this phenomenon as a mutual give-and-take process. This practice of Gülen's can also be considered as being based on the example of the Noble Prophet's art of cohabitation with people from diverse ethnic and religious backgrounds.

Staying Away from Expectations

Gülen cautions his followers particularly to stay away from all kinds of expectations while turning this mission into reality.[634] According to Gülen, the mission of representation remaining untainted from all suspicions and doubts is due to the Noble Prophet's unwavering stance against temptations. Gülen points out that the Noble Prophet's abstinence from expectation is clearly mentioned in the Qur'an: "*I ask of you no wage for that (for conveying God's Message); my wage is due only from the Lord of the worlds.*"[635] This Quranic verse, in fact, clarifies the matter beyond any doubt. According to Gülen, as mentioned above, Khadijah, the Prophet's beloved wife, spent all her wealth for the sake of his mission. However, the Noble Prophet did not request anything from anyone—even from his wife—for his own self. During the migration from Mecca to Medina, he accepted the mount, which Abu Bakr prepared for him, only after he paid the cost of the animal.[636] With these inferences of his, Gülen, while protecting the representatives and the office of the representation from suspicions, actually offers them an exemplary ascetic life. Primarily, his personal decency stems from the Sunnah, and he presents the Sunnah—which he adopted as a lifestyle—as a means of treatment for diseases arising in this era.

---

[633] Gülen, *Sonsuz Nur-1 (Muhammad: The Messenger of God,* Vol. 1), pp. 241-267.
[634] Gülen, *Vuslat Mustusu (Glad Tidings of a Reunion), Kirik Testi* series, Vol. 8, pp. 68-69.
[635] Qur'an 26:109
[636] Gülen, *Sonsuz Nur-1 (Muhammad: The Messenger of God,* Vol. 1), p. 267.

Gülen imagines the same consciousness of non-expectation—which he endeavors to instill into individuals and the community—also for the administrative bureaucracy that represents the state. He emphatically highlights that greed and expectation would cause corruption and injustice in the governance, and, ultimately result in degeneration in the society.[637] Looking into this aspect, he imagines a secure and healthy social structure within the triangle of an individual-society-state. A social structure that achieves its maturity in this manner will certainly be able to continue strongly into the future.

Gülen seeing the solution in the Sunnah and his selection of hadiths to fit into this paradigm can be seen as an established disposition in him. His way of finding solutions in line with the Sunnah to all problems, demonstrates a way of life hand in glove with Sunnah. Therefore, his solving theological and other problems with ease within the Prophetic moral context should not be considered strange. In contrast to classical understanding of the status of Sunnah which is primarily sources for jurists is not the way which Gülen follows. In other words, while classical scholars see the people who dealt with Sunnah as pharmacist, the jurist were doctors. Gülen, however, sees the expertise of Sunnah as a real doctorship. Within this mindset, solutions he offers for individual and social improvements are generally accurate. This situation may also be interpreted as the energy he receives from the Sunnah. Otherwise, decline and corruption within individuals and the society is inevitable. This is the reason why a spirit based on faith and no expectation is one of Gülen's main objectives.

Hijrah Dimension of the Sunnah

Gülen designates new targets like *hijrah* to the individuals and the society that he wrought and molded into consistency and coherence through the spirit of knowledge, belief, action, self-sacrifice and non-expectation. Therefore, he associates dynamic life and maintaining vigor to an altruistic philosophy of life. Using the migration rationale, he strives to explore ways to establishing bridges of dialogue between diverse cultures and nations.

---

[637] *Yeseren Dusunceler (Reflorishing Thoughts), Cag Ve Nesil series, Vol. 6* (Istanbul: Nil Publishing, 2011), pp. 105-107.

According to him, the Companions' going out of the Arabian Peninsula during and after the time of the Noble Prophet is one of the most striking examples to illustrate this. Migration from Mecca to Abyssinia (present-day Ethiopia) and Medina are the first examples of migration for the sake of religion in Islam. The Noble Prophet's saying, "...he whose migration is for God and His Messenger, his migration is for God and His Messenger... "[638] highlights specifically the pure intention in the migration.[639] With the energy he receives from these values, Gülen emphatically highlights the act of migration, and seeks to bring into present-day a vigor and vitality similar to that of the Companions. This indicates that the Sunnah can be adopted in the present-day with the same functionality. Therefore, he asserts that, in this day and age, the spirit of action accompanied with the Companions' mentality—and without expectation—does and will realize the hijrah phenomenon.[640] Looking from this perspective, Gülen studies both periods ('*Asr al-Sa'adah* – "Age of Bliss" and contemporary time) together, and, by comparing them highlights the similarities between the two. In this way, he proves that hadiths can be practiced again in the light of the Sunnah, and thus constitute a significant source of reference and a striking example of the Noble Prophet's time. It is also important to note that Gülen's appeal to the Companions and the Prophetic Traditions are very different from modern day salafi interpretation of Islam. Main difference lies in their contextualization of this period. Shortly, while Gülen tries to bring early period of Islamic understanding with some amendments to today, the hardcore salafi approaches try to take contemporary Muslims to the early period of Islam without any change. Thus, Gülen takes the early history and modern society into consideration while the salafis look at the issue quite ahistorical manner.

Examples of God Consciousness and Self-examination from Sunnah

Gülen prefers to turn subjective belief into practice as much as he can through good, righteous deeds and representation. Starting from this

---

[638] Bukhari, *Bad al-Wahy 1; Ayman 23; Muslim, Imarah 155; Abu Dawud, Talaq 10.*

[639] Gülen, *Sonsuz Nur-1 (Muhammad: The Messenger of God,* Vol. 1), p. 308.

[640] Gülen, *Ornekleri Kendinden Bir Hareket (A Movement with Inherent Exemplars), Cag Ve Nesil series,* Vol. 8 (Istanbul: Nil Publishing, 2010), p. 113.

fact, Gülen puts forth and attempts to prove that the sense of God consciousness (*taqwa*)—which is an important factor in establishing public security as well as disciplining an individual's life—is a principle that can be applied into everyday life. According to him, humankind ontologically possesses a negative aspect which is open to evil temptations. This deleterious characteristic in humans—unless cultivated and disciplined—can cause anarchy and all sorts of other problems in society. Therefore, there is a need for a self-control mechanism to cultivate and discipline this destructive potential in human beings. At this point, Gülen focuses on the individual's mental-moral discipline, and tends to the one-to-one training of individuals. Although human cultivation is a long and difficult process, the yield is worthy, and no trace of anarchy can be seen in communities made of people well disciplined. Even though the deterrence of law can be reasonably effective to some extent, the loss of control after a certain point is unavoidable. At this juncture, Gülen selects certain recipes from the Sunnah and proposes them for the establishment of public security and peace. According to him, God consciousness and fear of God (*taqwa-makhafatu'llah*) is an important denominator in nurturing individuals. The person who represents this culminating point is none other than the Noble Prophet himself. He knitted the concept of God consciousness in all his own attitudes and behaviors and in the lives of his Companions.[641] And in this way, the Noble Prophet protected every member of his community from unfair practices. When mentioning the deterrent effect of the fear of God against the oppressive potential in human-beings, Gülen uses an important hadith as evidence:[642] "Two eyes will not be touched by Hellfire: an eye that cries from the fear of God, and an eye that spent the night in a guard post in the way of God."[643] God's existence and His constant watching and questioning of human beings will restrain their tendency for wrong-doing. Eventually, a portrait of a trustworthy human being—both in spirit and matter—will emerge. For this reason, Gülen draws the picture of the true believer as a person who firmly placed the faith in the heart, who is constantly in fear of God—like the

---

[641]   Gülen, *Sonsuz Nur-2 (Muhammad: The Messenger of God,* Vol. 2), pp. 572-573
[642]   ibid., p. 411
[643]   Tirmidhi, *Fada'il al-Jihad* 12.

Noble Prophet's Companions—resisting temptations, and questioning. Of course a society made of people with these qualities would be free from insecurity. Therefore, dignity and security will be established in the community in the light of the hadith, "…a rider will be able to travel from San'a' to Hadramawt fearing none but God […] and wolves against his sheep..."[644] As can be seen from this, Gülen uses constructively and decisively the hadith's arguments in line with the exemplary way of life that he aims to establish.

Gülen asserts that there exists a direct link between protecting individual and state rights and the fear of God—and belief in the Hereafter—that lays the foundation for self-examination. An individual who has the habit of self-examination (*muhasaba*) is less likely to be inclined to crime. In case of crime, his conscience would lead him to admission of his guilt. With serious moral training, the Sunnah moulds an individual into a trustworthy human being and brings about a safe and secure society.[645] **Gülen strives to prove the upbringing characteristic of the** Sunnah through certain examples from the time of the Noble Prophet. A case in point is that of Ma'iz and a lady from the tribe of al-Ghamidiyyah who committed adultery and went to the Noble Prophet and confessed their crime due to the fear of God and conscientious self-examination.[646] Although confessing this shameful act in front of the Noble Prophet and the Companions created an embarrassing situation, it is also possible to mention here an internalized faith. Based on this hadith, Gülen highlights a rather different point. He presents the repentance (*tawbah*) element as a moral norm, which has an important function in individual and social life.[647] Through repentance, he shows ways to ward off the fear of hopelessness and losing, points it out as a means of psychological healing. He particularly emphasizes the corrective function of repentance.[648] Through these examples, Gülen illustrates the Noble Prophet's progressive methodology and his step-by-

---

[644] *Sahih al-Bukhari*, 3426, 6544.

[645] Gülen, *Enginligi Ile Bizim Dunyamiz, Iktisadi Mulahazalar (Our World in Depth, Economic Contemplations)*, p. 310.

[646] Muslim, *Hudud*, 22; al-Shawkani, *Nayl al-Awtar*, VII, 95,109; al-Zayla'i, *Nasb al-Rayah*, III, 314.

[647] Gülen, *Kur'an'nin Altin Ikliminde (In the Light of the Qur'an's Golden Climate)*, pp. 332, 336.

[648] Gülen, "Yolsuzluk," http://www.herkul.org/herkul-nagme/401-nagme-yolsuzluk/.

step journey from a community of ignorance towards a civilized society made of individuals who became role models for generations to come.[649] He analyses the Noble Prophet's putting forth and finalizing all ways and methods of education with an amazing patience during a period of 23 years. He strives with great enthusiasm to bring to our days all aspects of portraits from the lives of the Companions.

The global human portrait, which Gülen aims at through these examples, will represent the peace and security with all his qualities. That is, he is endeavoring to see and show others the human portrait described in the hadith: "A true Muslim is the one from whose tongue and hand other Muslims stay safe."[650] For this reason, he prefers to see the Sunnah being adopted as a norm at all levels.

Some Interpretations Regarding Women's Issues

The Sunnah in the historical process has been discussed and interpreted according to the needs and problems of each period. Therefore, some critical issues such as women's rights that require new interpretations can be examined by Muslim scholars under the lens of the Sunnah: What is the status of women in different cultures? What kind of status does the Sunnah give to women? These are the major questions that need to be addressed, and Gülen's comments will constitute the main theme of this chapter. Also, the status of women in Islam is an issue that is most frequently asked and criticized. Therefore, Gülen's views will be discussed and analyzed in this chapter.

According to Gülen, the closed aspects of the Sunnah—not yet opened—should be interpreted according to the needs of the time, but always within the framework of its fundamental principles. These interpretations are, in fact, a requirement of the modern age.[651] Reading the messages stemming from the Sunnah and making inferences therefrom according to the context of the time would be a significant work. With the help of these new elucidations, some social events, uncertain issues and the needs of the modern era would be solved. Real, satisfactory and accurate interpretations in this area will re-establish

---

[649] Gülen, *Sonsuz Nur-2 (Muhammad: The Messenger of God,* Vol. 2), pp. 89-90.

[650] Bukhari, *Iman* 4; *Abu Dawud, Jihad* 2

[651] Gülen, *Fikir Atlası (The Atlas of Ideas), Fasildan Fasila* series, Vol. 5, p. 65.

the Sunnah's value and trustworthiness; hence, removing doubts and suspicions arisen about the Sunnah will be possible.

After this brief introduction, it would be appropriate to look into some of the most discussed issues in our days from Gülen's perspective. Firstly, the issue of "woman and her status in Sunnah"—an issue, in a way, subject to the most debate and suspicion—will be discussed in the light of Gülen's approaches. Why does Gülen feel the need of defending the women's rights so persistently? What is really understood from Sunnah with regard to equality between man and woman? What do the Qur'an and the Sunnah say about women's headscarf and polygamy? Gülen's comments about these issues are a subject of interest.

A proper understanding of the rights and status of women in all cultures, and their acceptance in social environments primarily depends on viewing the picture as a whole. Attempting to assess an existing situation without knowing the conditions before the change, and its positive and negative aspects, may lead to biased and inappropriate results. This necessitates looking into women's status in pre-Islamic Arabian Peninsula and in other cultures. It is only in the light of this information that the value Islam attributes to women can be understood appropriately.

Women in Pre-Islamic Era

In the Arabian Peninsula during the Age of Ignorance, a woman's birth, childhood development and marriage were a complete tragedy. During that time, a girl's existence in the family was a burden, considered as a cause of shame, and, in certain areas, they were even buried alive as soon as they were born.[652] The Qur'an clearly explains this pre-Islamic circumstance in the following verse:

> When any of them is given news of the birth of a girl, his face becomes overcast, and he is (as if choking inwardly) with suppressed anger. He hides himself from the people because of the evil (as he wrongly supposes it) of what he has had news of. (So he debates within himself) Shall he keep her with dishonor, or bury her in earth? Look now! How evil is the judgment they make![653]

---

[652] Gülen, *Beyan (Speech and Power of Expression)* (Istanbul: Nil Publishing, 2011), pp. 73-74.
[653] Qur'an 16:58-59

This verse points out a moral value prevalent during the Age of Ignorance, and strictly prohibits an unjust killing of women. The verse highlights woman's freedom and right to life, and safeguards her rights. The Noble Prophet did not only draw attention to the unjustness of the pre-Islamic approach but also made himself pursuer of the Quranic injunction prohibiting killing. Then, he establishes an important social principle by his statement: "He who is involved (in the responsibility) of bringing up daughters, and he is benevolent towards them, they would become protection for him against Hell-fire."[654]

At this point, it is necessary to call to mind the thesis claiming that Islam enslaves women and usurps their rights.[655] According to this thesis, women are in a status where they have no right to life, and considered as men's slaves. Therefore, the thesis argues that women were free before Islam, and lost their freedom with the advent of Islam. However, historical facts prove otherwise, and demonstrate that women gained their full freedom thanks to the value system Islam introduced.

This fact necessitates looking into moral foundations of the family structure before Islam. This period was marked by the fact that women and girl children had no value at all.[656]

Women in Different Civilizations and in the Modern Era

While this was the status of women in pre-Islamic Arabian Peninsula, the situation was not much different in certain other civilizations. During ancient Greek and Roman times, the prevalent view was that "woman is the gateway to Hell." This view has entered into historical records as the philosophy of Plato (427-347 BCE). Also, according to a thought attributed to Aristotle (384-322 BCE), women were viewed as "unfinished men." Cicero (106-43 BCE) said: "Women were created to hinder men achieving great things. If they were not created, men could be deified."[657] Women are defined as obstacles by these approaches.

---

[654] Bukhari, *Adab*, 24
[655] n.a, "Kadin nasil kolelestirildi? Nasil ozgurlesecek?," http://devrimkurtulus.forums3.com/devrimci-kadin-f70/kadin-nas-kolele-tirildi-nas-ozgurle-ecek-t281.html.
[656] Salih Akdemir, "Tarih Boyunca ve Kur'an-i Kerim'de Kadin" (Women through the History and in the Qur'an), *Islami Arastirmalar* 4, (Ankara, 1991), p. 263.
[657] Gülen, *Beyan (Speech and Power of Expression)*, pp. 73-74

Saint Augustine (354-430 CE) was quoted to have said: "If women were resurrected with sexual desire in the Hereafter, I am afraid they would seduce men even there." Similar thoughts and approaches concerning women have also been witnessed during later periods. John Milton (1608-1674), the author of *Paradise Lost*, viewed women as "a creation error."[658] In ancient Chinese civilization, the situation was even worse as women had no name and were called by numbers.

In contemporary time, certain thoughts about women are being observed relatively similar to earlier periods. For example, Nietzsche's (1844-1900) maxim, "When you go to woman, take the whip along," classifies women a gender to be tamed by beating. Leo Tolstoy (1828-1910) who first said, "Happy to be married," can be seen to have later deviated from his views as he labeled woman striving to lower and vulgarize her husband's soul because she is common and vulgar.[659] As these views belong to leading intellectuals of various societies, it will not be wrong to assume that they were welcomed by many of their followers.

Here, this reality should not be ignored: As every individual man has his own peculiar moral character, women-folk also have moral values and characteristics changing from one individual to another. Therefore, problems stemming from the character defects of a certain gender cannot be generalized to all. Some intellectuals mirroring the negative female image in their family or social environment into the wider community can be considered as projecting their subjective views on women generally. How can attributing one individual's peculiarities to a whole society be seen as an objective view? Yet, presenting such a peculiar case as a characteristic of a nation or civilization may result in even more grave consequences. Again, it is not reasonable to blame all Arabs for the despicable custom of certain desert tribes burying new born baby girls alive in pre-Islamic Arabian Peninsula or any other nation. Otherwise the Arab nation would be extinct in one generation. It is not the case, and moreover, there are many wealthy businesswomen and top female executives in Arab societies. With its principle of right to life, the Qur'an highlights the repugnance of such a custom, which

---

[658] ibid., p. 74.
[659] ibid.

was practiced only among a few desert tribes.[660] Even today, it can be witnessed in some uneducated societies that the girl children are viewed as detestable and shameful. This, at the same time, demonstrates the universality of the Quranic verses. What was occurring in the past—due to ignorance—is still occurring today, and will occur in the future so long as ignorance is prevalent in society.

Women in Islam

After this brief overview of the status of women in the course of history, Islam's approach to women in general—and particularly that of the Sunnah—needs to be examined. Reading and analyzing the Sunnah's value system regarding women essentially through Gülen's comments would be appropriate. Taking into consideration the value attributed to women in pre-Islamic Arab Peninsula and certain other civilizations, Gülen demonstrates important approaches. According to him, Islam reinstituted women's rights previously usurped by the society, and took them under protection by instituting firm rules in this regard.[661] The Qur'an's declaration, "...*According to customary good and religiously approvable practice, women have rights similar to those against them (that men have), but men (in respect of their heavier duty and responsibility) have a degree above them (which they must not abuse). And God is All-Glorious with irresistible might, All-Wise,*"[662] clearly emphasizes the rights of women, and elevates them to their ontological position consistent with the plan of creation.[663] According to Gülen, this verse gives women all their rights, including the right to divorce, and highlights that women have natural rights. This view of Gülen's is in perfect accordance with Sunni scholars' views. Gülen asserts that the Noble Prophet's "Farewell Speech" established an important principle, and argues that this alone constitutes evidence regarding women's rights. Looking from this angle, his views appear to be somewhat an interpretation of the abovementioned

---

[660] "It is because of this that We ordained for (all humankind, but particularly for) the Children of Israel: He who kills a soul unless it be (in legal punishment) for murder or for causing disorder and corruption on the earth will be as if he had killed all humankind; and he who saves a life will be as if he had saved the lives of all humankind..." (Qur'an 5:32).

[661] Gülen, *Beyan* (Speech and Power of Expression), pp. 75-76

[662] Qur'an 2:228

[663] Gülen, *Beyan* (Speech and Power of Expression), p. 75.

Quranic verse. By his statement, "Fear God concerning women, for you have taken them on the security of God and have made their persons lawful to you by words of God,"[664] the Noble Prophet, in fact, takes women under protection and security. The Noble Prophet's elevation of women's status to a respectful position is a historical event for all women, indeed. The responsibility of the protection of women—relatively weaker gender in terms of physical strength—has been put on the shoulders of men as their custodians. The role of the custodian here is in the sense of holding women as a trust of God, and ensuring the safeguarding of all their rights. According to Gülen, women have been emancipated from all forms of oppressions by the rulings of the Qur'an and the Sunnah. A clear emphasis on women's rights and status in the Qur'an and the Sunnah, and to their name a Quranic chapter's title being dedicated are viewed as the emancipation of women by Islam.[665] It should be noted that Gülen approaches the issue of women and their rights in Islam from a different perspective. He considers the issue as a matter of oppression and victimization. The "human" factor, in his understanding, is the most honorable of the creation, whose rights cannot be violated. Looking from this perspective, Gülen takes the side of wronged people, regardless of their gender. In the light of women's status in the Age of Ignorance, this approach of Gülen's may be considered reasonable. At the same time, he is reacting to prejudicial views labeling women as being oppressed in Islam. In this regard, Gülen refutes unjust criticisms directed to Islam and Sunnah, and, at the same time, protects women who have been subjected to discredit, and elevate them to their rightful status. Gülen supports his approaches with L. E. Obbald's views which have been quoted as stating, "Freeing women from slavery and reinstating their usurped rights have only been possible by the advent of Islam."[666] This means that women found their identity, and took their place in the society as a name and a value thanks to the Qur'an and the Sunnah. And the rationale that Gülen highlights and defends must be nothing but this. This approach of a researcher with a different cultural and religious background, i.e. L. E.

---

[664] Muslim, *Hajj* 147; Abu Dawud, *Manasiq* 55.
[665] Gülen, *Beyan (Speech and Power of Expression)*, p.75.
[666] ibid., 75.

Obbald, draws attention to the inadequacy of comments and inferences presently made in that cultural environment.

Gülen strives to make his arguments more convincing by supporting them with some researchers' thesis from Europe such as G. Demombyne and Stanley Lane-Pole (1854-1931).[667] What is noteworthy in these statements—which should not be understood in the sense that the currently existing civil laws are not adequate—is the necessity of women's issues to be addressed by a more comprehensive and inclusive method. It is also important to note that Gülen is trying to respond implicitly to many criticisms raised by non-Muslim scholars by quoting positive remarks from Western scholars.

Particularly in response to the spreading misconception of women being imprisoned in her house in Islam, Gülen offers various comments from the Age of Bliss and the Sunnah.[668] Gülen argues that, unless approached with prejudice, it is very clear to see in all major Islamic resources and exemplary practices of the pious predecessors (*al-salaf al-salihin*) that the Muslim woman has never been a prisoner in her house. According to him, the ignorance of this fact and various misconceptions are possibly the results of the misunderstandings and wrong practices stemming from customs all along the history being attributed to Islam.[669]

In Islam, women hold a position where they can ask questions, make queries, and be conferred with. In this civilization and the practical Sunnah of the Noble Prophet, womenfolk constitute a community who requests from the Noble Prophet, and obtains, a specific time slot to be set aside for their education, and who forms knowledge platforms of their own. They also hold a position where they could go to war and fight against the enemy when needed. They were also in the commerce as business people. Besides all these, women are also known as educationists-pedagogues who are in charge of rearing children.[670] Disregarding all these facts results in impeding the recognition of the true position of

---

[667] ibid.

[668] "Paradise is under the feet of mothers." (Nasa'i, *Jihad*, 6)

[669] Gülen, *Olumsuzluk Iksiri (The Potion for Immortality), Kirik Testi* series, Vol. 7, (Istanbul: Nil Publication, 2011), p. 45.

[670] ibid., pp. 47-57

women in the Sunnah and in making way for the emergence of one-sided opinions. Or, the failure of in-depth understanding of matters explained in hadiths brings about only a superficial view of reality. After the Hudaybiyyah Treaty, due to the slow response by his Companions to his order to slaughter their sacrificial animals and end the state of *ihram*, the Noble Prophet went to his wife Umm Salamah, and consulted with her. She said to him: "O Messenger of God, would you like them to obey your order? Go out and do not speak to anyone of them until you slaughter your camel and call out to your barber to cut your hair (and thus end the consecrated state of *ihram*)."[671] The Noble Prophet accepted her advice, did as she suggested and prevented an undesirable event from happening.[672]

Women in Our Days According to Gülen

While providing examples from the time of the Companions and later periods, Gülen does not hesitate to question the status of women in modern societies, or to make various criticisms. He draws attention to the necessity of women being active in the society, and puts forth certain arguments. He takes a serious stand against the insistence on maintaining in practice, in our days, thoughts and views stemming from customs and cultures. He stresses that women are being subjected to restrictions and limitations in both social and professional life all over the world, including countries that are supposed to be modern democracies. And he asks certain questions: How many modern countries have female presidents today? How many countries have high ranked female officers in their armies? In how many parliaments women are represented proportionally? How many female spiritual leaders and religious representatives do exist among the world religions?[673] Are the numbers of women employed in the Courts of Justice, government offices, police forces approaching anywhere near their male counterparts? He directs the same questions to Turkey and continues: How many female presidents exist in the history of the modern Turkish Republic (none)? Is

---

[671] Bukhari, *Shurut* 15; Ibn Hanbal, *al-Musnad* 4/330
[672] Gülen, *Kalb Ibresi (Heart's Cursor), Kirik Testi series, Vol. 9*, p. 205.
[673] It is noteworthy to remember here female scholars and sufis such as 'A'ishah, the Noble Prophet's wife.

this the view that is dominant that a female president would compromise the administration due to her mental weakness? Why is it that the numbers of female ministers are nowhere near their male counterparts? Why has no woman been appointed as the chief of joint forces or as a chief of any force?[674] With these queries, Gülen, in a way, turns to the feminist movements—which never stop talking about women's rights and which appear to be their advocates—and expects some satisfactory answers from them.[675] With these questions, in fact, he points out the need for those who claim that the Sunnah restricts the rights of women to question their own social structures. At this point, when he evaluates the wide circle drawn by the Sunnah, he does not insist on the absolute necessity of the questions he asked. However, looking from the point of Sunnah, he opines that women taking their parts in various fields and occupying positions would not pose any problem. He expresses his view that women have the ability to fill those positions mentioned.[676] The questions that Gülen raised are important in the name of finding answers to perplexing questions about the relationship between Sunnah and women in modern days. A thorough research of historical records will reveal answers to the abovementioned question in due course.

According to Gülen, a woman is a legally free and independent individual. The quality of being a woman does not, in any way, restrict or remove any of the competences she possesses. According to the Sunnah, women, like anyone else, have the freedom of expression. Legally, there exists no difference between men and women in this respect. A case in point in this matter is the following example from the Sunnah: A woman discussed with the Noble Prophet the issue of *zihar*[677] between her husband and herself so persistently that a revelation came down, setting the Divine ruling. The Quranic chapter that contains these verses was

---

[674] Gülen, *Olumsuzluk Iksiri (The Potion for Immortality)*, *Kirik Testi* series, Vol. 7, p. 47.

[675] ibid. 46.

[676] ibid.48.

[677] A pre-Islamic custom practised during the Age of Ignorance. This was a form of divorce proffered by a husband upon his wife, which likens her to the back of his mother, which makes her prohibited for himself for ever. But he would not actually divorce his wife. This would violate wife's rights. Islam prohibited this unjust practice (58:2), and introduced some sanctions for those who continued to practise it (58:3).

named after this event, *al-Mujadilah* (She That Disputed or the Pleading Woman). This story of a woman's seeking justice is an important evidence and reliable reference to the freedom of expression for women and the rule of the Law in Islam. This and similar events helped the Prophet's Companions to develop the sense of seeking justice and questioning as a natural behavior. The courage emanating from the Qur'an and the Sunnah acts as an important function in the representation of the Law. For example, when Caliph 'Umar suggested to set up an upper limit to the amount of *mahr* (dowry paid to the bride) in order to ease the financial burden on people who want to get married, an old woman objected to the Caliph's view and said: "O Umar, is there a Quranic verse or hadith on this issue that you know and we do not? The Qur'an commands, *'But if you still decide to dispense with a wife and marry another, and you have given the former (even so much as amounts to) a treasure, do not take back anything thereof,'* (4:20) thus not setting a limit to the amount of bridal dues." And Caliph 'Umar said aloud to himself, 'O 'Umar, you do not know your religion even as much as an old woman,'[678] and accepted the correctness of this objection.[679] Women, whose name and existence had been a subject of controversy, were elevated by the help of the teaching of the Qur'an and the Sunnah to a level where they could teach a law lesson to 'Umar, the head of the state. This, in fact, highlights the education of women regardless of their age. An elderly woman's knowledge of the Qur'an and the Sunnah and her ability to directly deduce rulings therefrom demonstrates the level of her education. Also, such an action by an elderly woman—considered to be beyond the age of marriage in her society—who reacts with such a sensitivity and passion carries important messages in the name of standing up to defend the rights of younger women. This and similar events constitute a good example to show the level of the sense of justice and sensitivity in the society.

Women's Right to Education and Status as Educators

Starting from the abovementioned historical events, Gülen makes important inferences about the status and scientific competency of

---

678 al-Bayhaqi, *al-Sunan al-Kubra*, 7/233
679 Gülen, *Olumsuzluk Iksiri (The Potion for Immortality)*, Kirik Testi series, Vol. 7, pp. 55-56

women in Islam. The wide range of rights and freedoms provided by the Sunnah are among the most important factors that positively affect and encourages seeking of knowledge and education among women. Although the level of education was very poor and literacy among women was very low during the early years of the Meccan Period, this situation changed during the Medinan Period, and literacy and education showed a dramatic upward improvement. The effect of the female Companions' commitment to and involvement in knowledge and education become an exemplary model for the future generations. Besides, the Noble Prophet's wives—each one acting as a female mentor—guided the leading Islamic scholars. For example, scholars such as Masruq ibn Ajda', Tawus ibn Kaysan (d. 725 CE), Ata ibn Abi Rabah (d. 115 AH), al-Aswad ibn Yazid al-Nakha'i took lessons from the Noble Prophet's wives; especially 'A'ishah is known to be a prodigy in the discipline of *fiqh* in Islam.[680]

As can be seen in the historical records, women in Islam, especially the Noble Prophet's wives, are holding a position of teacher/ trainer, and the men also benefited from their lessons. Thus, the limits of the dialogue between men and women with regard to education are being drawn. Looking from this point of view, theses arguing that women's right to education have been violated in Islam in modern days are lacking a basis. These theses have been refuted by historical Muslim women's portraits from the early period. The reason for raising this issue in our days, as inferred by Gülen also, may be the association of some cultural residues falsely with Islam, and certainly not Islam itself. As can be observed in certain cultures, usurping women's right to education and keeping them only in their houses can never possibly be associated with the Prophetic Practice. It is understood that mentalities of this kind prevail in cultures where the principles and sensitivities of the Sunnah were failed to be understood properly. Starting from this point, it is rather impossible to talk about proper understanding of and adherence to the Sunnah in communities where women's right to education has been usurped. And this illustrates a good example of the lack of education in a society. In fact, the application of the authentic Sunnah proves to be the exact opposite of this practice. Gülen's starting from these points and

---

[680]   ibid., p. 56.

beginning his movement of reconstructing individuals-communities and the Islamic world with education may be considered an appropriate and meaningful thesis.

Equality between Genders and Gülen's View

Equality between genders is another impasse for women in this century. Gülen's comments on the issue of equality demonstrate a different approach than his contemporaries. He expresses his views based on the Quranic verse, "*And all things We have created in pairs, so that you may reflect and be mindful.*"[681] According to him, the word "pair" mentioned in the verse refers to gender difference (male-female) between all particles in the nature, plants, animals and human beings, and these opposite genders are interdependent and complete each other. Perhaps there exist more "pairs" in the nature not yet discovered and can only be known by advance of the science and technology. Electron with proton, the Earth with sky, night with day and man with woman form interdependently a unity. Therefore, man and woman cannot be equal as electron and proton or negative and positive are not equal. This is an unchangeable law of the creation. As nothing has been created as complete and "perfect" (perfectness in its absolute sense can only be attributed to God alone), everything that exists is in need of its opposite in order to form a "whole" and to subsist.[682] Gülen substantiates this view of his by the hadith, saying: "Women are the other halves of men,"[683] and makes reasonable comments on the hadith. He explains that the word *shaqiq* (half) mentioned in the above hadith refers to one half of a whole divided into two through the middle. In other words, each one of the two equal halves of a whole is the *shaqiq* of the other half. In this sense, a man and a woman both represent two equal halves. But neither one is the same as the other. This means, their inherent dispositions and psycho-spiritual qualities are completely different; thus, in this sense, they are not equal. Gender difference is a fact of life and human-beings cannot interfere with the creation. This fact necessitates everyone, believers and non-believers, to abandon this dream of equality between genders and

---

[681] Qur'an 51:49.
[682] Gülen, *Prizma (Prism* series, Vol. 1), (Istanbul: Nil Publishing, 2011), pp. 139-140
[683] Abu Dawud, *Taharah*, 94; Ibn Hanbal, 6/377.

consider both man and woman in their own status.[684] In fact, man and woman are like one soul in two bodies; in other words, they represent the two different aspects of one reality. Over time, deterioration of this integrity resulted in turning the balances upside down, and degeneration of family and social orders.[685] Drawing on Hammudah 'Abd al-'Ati's article on the status of woman in Islam, Abdulkadir Suphandagi writes: "Man and woman are not the exact same of each other. By their superior and lesser qualities they mutually complete each other in terms of rights and responsibilities in life."[686]

In addition, Gülen elaborates on the Quranic verse[687] assigning men a higher status over women—a point, which appears to be in contradiction with what has been mentioned above. Gülen views the attribute of "*authority*" mentioned in the verse beginning with "*... inasmuch as [men having] greater capacity than [women]...*" as the status of man in the capacity of head of the family and the responsibility that comes with it.[688] Inasmuch as the division of labor is necessary in all aspects of life, the same is the case also in the family. Here, the bigger part of the burden such as the responsibility for providing for the family has been bestowed upon men, and women have been exonerated from such high responsibility duties.[689] This, in fact, is the manifestation of respect and protection of women. As to the man's responsibilities towards his family, Gülen's views are in line with many Sunni Muslim scholars' approach to this issue. To put it more clearly, the division of labor mentioned here does not mean that women cannot take a role in the world of business. On the contrary, women can be as productive as they can in their fields of competence. The verse is emphasizing the

---

[684] Gülen, *Prizma (Prism)*, Vol. I, p. 140.

[685] Gülen, *Beyan (Speech and Power of Expression)*, pp. 73-76.

[686] Abdulkadir Suphandagi, "Kadindan Israrla Esirgenen Bagimsiz Sahsiyeti, Islam 14 Asir Once Vermis," *Zaman* daily, May 21, 2005.

[687] "*Men (those who are able to carry out their responsibilities) are the protectors and maintainers of women inasmuch as God has endowed some of people (in some respects) with greater capacity than others, and inasmuch as they (the men) spend of their wealth (for the family's maintenance). Good, righteous women are the devoted ones (to God) and observant (of their husbands' rights), who guard the secrets (family honour and property, their chastity, and their husband's rights, especially where there is none to see them, and in the absence of men,) as God guards and keeps undisclosed (what should be guarded and private)*" (Qur'an 4:34).

[688] With this interpretation, Gülen shares the same view with Sunni scholars.

[689] Gülen, *Olumsuzluk Iksiri (Potion for Immortality)*, Kirik Testi series, Vol. 7, pp. 51-52

women's exemption from providing for the family rather than limiting their right to participate in the workforce. However, women would like to work, and therefore the jobs must be appropriate for their physical abilities and psychological disposition. Offering women inappropriate jobs cannot be reconciled with the principle of equality; on the contrary, this would mean usurping their rights. Similarly, forcing men to work in jobs against their nature would also constitute violation of their rights.

Gülen demonstrates a rather different approach based on the necessity of proper physical conditions that are suitable to the natural disposition. In nature, everything has been created in certain measure and balance, and placed and positioned appropriately. Therefore, maintaining this natural balance will remove injustice. For example, this hadith illustrates the wisdom of creation: "A cow which was yoked turned to its master and said: 'I was not created for this kind of works!'"[690] Gülen selects this kind of hadiths carefully in connection with the subject matter, and strives to explain his views to people from all walks of life. By this approach, Gülen makes even the farm field laborers fit into his target audience. He employs examples that they can easily understand. Inasmuch as saying, "Every creature must be employed according to its ability and purpose of creation so that the true justice be established,"[691] Gülen interprets the hadith from a different perspective. Day and night or the sun and the moon cannot be considered equal in physical creation or have the same purpose. They complete each other although they are not equal.

It needs to be mentioned here that an absolute equality is non-existent not only between different species but also between the same species. Obvious contrasts can be seen between creatures of the same kind. However, women being different in their natural disposition do in no way make them less human. Conversely, women seeing men as less human can only help to generate a negative energy, which ultimately result in an unnecessary conflict. Therefore, instead of dissociating individuals and communities from each other, all differences should essentially be accepted in their own relative positions and treated as a

---

[690]   Bukhari, *Hars* 4; Muslim, *Fadail al-Sahabah*, 13; Tirmidhi, *Manaqib* 16.
[691]   Gülen, *Prizma (Prism)*, Vol. 1, p. 142.

common wealth. The Quranic statement, "*The believers, both men and women: they are guardians, confidants, and helpers of one another*,"[692] encourages mutual support rather than conflict, and highlights the complementary factor.

Gülen's Approach to Islamic Dress Code

The most frequently asked question and a subject of debate in the modern era is the issue of *tasattur* (Islamic dress code), more specifically women's headscarf.[693] The issue of the headscarf[694] has been clearly enjoined by the Qur'an and the Sunnah. Covering the head is not only a Divine order in Islam but also in many other religious traditions:

> Every man praying or prophesying, having his head covered, dishonoureth his head. But every woman that prayeth or prophesieth with her head uncovered dishonoureth her head: for that is even all one as if she were shaven. For if the woman be not covered, let her also be shorn: but if it be a shame for a woman to be shorn or shaven, let her be covered.[695]

As can be seen in the above Biblical verses, the New Testament commands women to cover their head. It is also possible to see similar remarks in the Old Testament.[696]

What is understood from the above passages is that covering up for women was a norm in society. Also, references to women's clothing such as muffler, bonnet, mantle, wimple, hood and veil can be seen in other parts of the Old Testament.[697] It can thus be said that all three monotheistic religions highlight the same fundamental issues.

Covering up for women is a legal obligation agreed by almost

---

[692] Qur'an 9:71.

[693] *Tasattur* is an Islamic term, which means to cover the parts of the body that have to be covered as required by the Qur'an and the *sunnah*. This Islamic dress code applies to both men and women. However, in the Muslim world, the term is generally used to indicate women's covering themselves in modest clothing, and more specifically the headscarf.

[694] Qur'an 24:31.

[695] I Corinthians 11:4-6.

[696] "And Rebekah lifted up her eyes, and when she saw Isaac, she lighted off the camel. For she had said unto the servant, what man is this that walketh in the field to meet us? And the servant had said, It is my master: therefore she took a veil, and covered herself" (Genesis 24:64-65).

[697] See Isaiah 3:16-23.

all exegetes, jurists and Hadith scholars all along the history of Islam. However, this issue has been a subject of criticism like Sunnah, and took its place among the popular topics of debate in our days. It is rather difficult to understand certain theologians' attitude against the headscarf despite all clear evidences in the Qur'an and the Sunnah and Muslim women's practices since the time of the Noble Prophet.[698] Some religious researchers argue that the headscarf is not mentioned in the Qur'an, and the meanings of the verses related to the issue have been distorted. Zekeriya Beyaz, Yasar Nuri Ozturk, Sahin Filiz, Ihsan Eliacik can be mentioned among the contemporary representatives of this view in Turkey. However, there is no shred of evidence to support this view in the Islamic literature since the early days of Islam. The Divine command for the head cover is clear, and has never been understood otherwise. However, Feyza Bilgin asserts that the reference to the head cover in the Qur'an is in the context of moral code; therefore, this phraseology is not consistent with "command" form but is rather an advisory form.[699] Salih Akdemir shares the same view and affirms that the said verse should be understood in the sense of advice instead of order. Akdemir also emphasizes that the verses in question are about the Noble Prophet's wives, daughters and "married women."[700] However, statements in those verses such as *"They should restrain their gaze [from what is prohibited],"* *"Guard their private parts and chastity,"*[701] *"They should not display their charms,"* and *"Let them draw their veils over their bosoms,"*[702] are consistent with decisive command form rather than a simple advice. This clear Divine command comes in a relatively moderate style suitable for women's natural psychological disposition. Viewing this command of wearing headscarf in an advisory context would create obvious contradictions within the verse; statements such as *"They should restrain their gaze"* and *"guard their private parts and chastity,"* which clearly prohibit certain acts would become meaningless, and those illegal acts would be seen as legal. Applying the same rationale to the whole Qur'an

---

[698] Gülen, *Vuslat Mustusu (Glad Tidings of a Reunion), Kirik Testi* series, Vol. 8, pp. 193-196.
[699] Feyza Bilgin, "Basortusu bir tavsiyedir vazgeçilmez bir dini emir degil," *Sabah daily* (October 02, 2006).
[700] Gercek Gundem, "Ilahiyatcidan Turban Cikisi," *Gercek Gundem* daily, December 04, 2007.
[701] Qur'an 24:31.
[702] Qur'an 24:31.

would, in fact, render the Word of God into a bundle of contradictions. Therefore, the approach adopted by Bilgin and Akdemir is objectionable. Whether Bilgin and Akdemir accept or reject the Sunnah as a source of reference is another matter. But, an authentic hadith clearly explains that the abovementioned verse orders women to cover their charms. Bukhari transmits the Prophet's beloved wife 'A'isha's words in this respect: "May God have mercy on the early immigrant women. When the verse '*That they should draw their veils over their bosoms*' was revealed, they tore their thick outer garments and made veils from them."[703]

As it can be seen from above, the criticism of the Sunnah goes along with questioning of the Islamic values without reliable evidence and/or sources. The verdict of the Sunnah, which expounds Quranic verses regarding to the headscarf, is unequivocally clear. However, the Sunnah itself being a subject of questioning, its verdicts are automatically disregarded. Inasmuch as the great majority of people are unable or, for some reason, unwilling to retrieve detailed information/instruction directly from the Qur'an, the thoughts and views of the scholars and researchers play a major role in the religious education of the populace. Average individuals are generally satisfied with the piece of information they receive from "knowledgeable" people whom they trust. This may result in very strong evidence being considered "weak" in the hands of a weak researcher or vice versa.[704] Therefore, it is the duty of jurists and theology experts to identify correctly the values and principles of the Sunnah, and the Hadith and Sunnah literature. Failure to do so may affect the lives of many average individuals.

Looking from this perspective into Gülen's views on the issue of headscarf, it is clearly visible that he shares the same views with the scholars of the past as mentioned in the traditional Sunni literature. That is, he strongly defends the headscarf and, by virtue of its importance, he insistently dwells upon the issue. However, he takes a different approach from his contemporaries. Gülen explains that the command of wearing headscarf is among the "furu'at"[705] (*furu' al-fiqh*: lit. branches of jurisprudence) of Islam, and draws attention

---

[703] Wahba al-Zuhayli, *Tafsir al-Munir* (24:31).

[704] Bediüzzaman Said Nursi, *Mektubat (The Letters)*, (Istanbul: Envar Publishing, 1995), p. 370.

[705] One of the major genres of juristic literature, which deals with issues open to *ijtihad*.

to the need that it should not be made a subject of constant debate, giving it priority over the matters of faith, in this day and age. Here, he points to an important detail of jurisprudence, and emphasizes that headscarf is not a matter of faith, which constitutes the essential of Islam. That is, headscarf is included among neither the pillars of Islam nor the fundamentals of faith. Therefore, an Islamic practice, which is among the interpersonal transactions (*muamalat*), cannot be elevated to the same level with the pillars of faith, such as the testimony of faith (*kalimah al-shahadah*). This testimony is the first and foremost pillar of the faith—an essential part of the faith. Inasmuch as the headscarf is not an essential part of the faith but is among the compulsory (*fardh*) acts that come under interpersonal transactions (*mu'amalat*), failing to cover the head is a sin; however, women who commit this sin are still within the fold of Islam.[706] It is possible to say that with this approach, Gülen showed a way out of the dilemma that female students were facing in some extremely secular countries, such as Turkey and France. In this contemporary age, he offered a solution to a serious problem that was forcing young believing girls to choose between two difficult options: abandoning their dream of education or rejecting a command of God.

Polygamy in Islam and Gülen's Perspective

Gülen elaborates on the polygamy in Islam, which is an issue that has been much criticized and exploited. The criticisms are concentrated especially on two issues. Firstly, there are attempts to condemn Islam for the number of wives the Noble Prophet had. Secondly, the focus is drawn on the permission for a Muslim man to marry up to four wives. To begin with, Gülen offers reasonable comments on the issue of the Noble Prophet's polygamy. These comments are mainly based on the Sunnah and *sirah*. The arguments he put forth on this issue are very convincing and no refutation has been published to this date. In fact, his arguments are not new; they can be easily analyzed, and a close study would disclose its consistency with rationale. For this reason, Gülen opines that there is an ulterior motive behind making this issue—which

---

[706] Gülen, *Vuslat Mustusu (The Glad Tiding of Reunion)*, Kirik Testi series, Vol. 8, pp. 198-199.

is very clear—a subject of debate, and concludes that it is the result of the serious lack of knowledge in the field of *sirah*. Gülen draws attention to the fact that, looking from an analytical research perspective, answers to this issue can easily be found in the Prophetic biography (*maghazi* and *sirah*) literatures.[707] Gülen attributes a special care and importance to the Noble Prophet's chastity and modesty. At this point, he prefers to meet his interlocutor on a reasonable ground. In a hot climate area where the age of marriage, which at the time was as low as the early teenage years, the Noble Prophet's remaining bachelor up to the age of 25 years and being known and respected for his modesty is strikingly noteworthy. Thus, even his harshest critics could not find a shred of evidence to support their claims. Should they had been able to find any evidence, they would have used them most effectively to discredit the Noble Prophet's reputation. Even the Meccan people, who were staunchly opposed to his Prophetic mission, maintained their respect for his honor and modesty. The Noble Prophet's first marriage was to Khadijah, at that time a 40 years old widow, when he was only 25. And this happy marriage lasted 23 years monogamously.[708] At this point, the critics need to be called to reason. Living a chaste bachelor life until he was 25 and then marrying a widow who was 15 years older than him, instead of a young maiden, poses a serious question to be answered by the critics who claim that sexual lust was the main motive behind the Noble Prophet's marriages. Another point to be noted is that there was again a bachelor period of five long years after the death of his beloved wife Khadijah. After this second bachelor period, the Noble Prophet reached the age of 53, which is an age when a man's sexual desire begins to decline. Gülen draws attention specifically to the fact that the Noble Prophet's other marriages took place in this age period when the need for marriage diminishes. He made his second marriage at the age of 53 to Sawdah bint Zam'ah who was then 55 years old.[709] Most of his marriages after this age are directly related to his Prophetic mission. Keeping in mind that he died at the age of 63, the last ten years of his mission coincides with his old-

---

[707] Gülen, *Inancin Golgesinde -2 (Essentials of the Islamic Faith,* Vol. 2), (Istanbul: Nil Publishing, 2009), p. 103.

[708] ibid., pp. 104-115.

[709] Akgul, *Ezvac-i Tahirat* (The Pure Wives of the Noble Prophet), p. 44.

age. Marriages that take place during this age period are less likely to be motivated by sexual desire. It is also noteworthy to mention here that critics highlighting especially the Noble Prophet's polygamous family life, and persistently disregarding the culture of polygamy that was prevalent in the pre-Islamic Arabian Peninsula, and the fact that women were being bought and sold like a commodity is a striking deficiency of objectivity.

Gülen asserts that polygamy is not contrary to the spirit of the Prophethood, and argues that polygamy did not begin with the Noble Prophet; the Prophets before him also used this practice as part of their mission. The following can be listed among the reasons behind the Noble Prophet's polygamous practice: educating and training female teachers and role models for Muslim women; need to address and record specific issues for women of all ages; representation of the Prophetic mission by establishing kinship between various nations and tribes; and the individual cases of some of the Prophet's wives.[710] Also, the Noble Prophet's private family life needed to be clearly explained to the public so that they could find answers to their questions regarding their own private and family lives. Otherwise, many aspects of Islam would be obscured—in this case Islam could not be seen as a universal religion. Therefore, the message delivered by a Prophet and his private life must be known in minute detail, including women-specific issues pertaining to all age groups.[711] And the Noble Prophet's wives from different cultures, age groups and tribes continuously transmitted the details of the Prophet's private and family life to their people from their own perspectives and answered their questions.

Some of the Noble Prophet's marriages are politically motivated. His marriages established kinships and ended enmities between certain tribes. The Noble Prophet's marriages to Juwayriyyah bint al-Harith, Safiyyah bint Huyayy and Ramlah bint Abi Sufyan are of this kind. The fathers of Juwayriyyah and Safiyyah were leaders of the Jewish community. The Prophet's marriages to these two ladies established kinship and

---

[710] Gülen, *Asrin Getirdigi Tereddutler -1 (Questions and Answers about Islam*, Vol. 1), pp. 92-104.

[711] Muhittin Akgul, "Peygamberimizin Hanimlari Ve Evliliklerindeki Hikmetler-2" *Yeni Ümit*, Issue 47, (January- March 2000).

close relationship with the Jews of Medina. Similarly, his marriage to Abi Sufyan's daughter Ramlah ended the Meccan Chieftain Abi Sufyan's enmity against Islam. This marriage also resulted in establishing affinity with the Umayyads in the later years.[712] This practice of the Noble Prophet's establishing relationship with various communities through marriage became a model for state-to-state relationships during later periods.

As can be seen from above, the Noble Prophet's polygamous family life was reflecting some other aspects of his Prophethood rather than his carnal desires. Also, polygamy being practiced by the Noble Prophet himself was in fact the application of the Islamic Law into practice. For example, Zayd ibn Harithah is known to be the Prophet's adopted son. According to Arab customs at that time, such a child was regarded as a son enjoying the same legal status as biological children, who is not required to observe familial privacy, and his wife treated as daughter-in-law. The Qur'an abolished this practice through the intermediary of the Noble Prophet[713] and established that Zayd ibn Harithah was not his son and thus Zayd's wife not his daughter-in-law. After her divorce, Zaynab bint Jahsh married the Noble Prophet by Divine command. With the wording of the Prophet's beloved wife 'A'ishah, "If God's Messenger were to conceal anything (of the Divine Revelation), he would have concealed this verse (regarding the Prophet's marriage to Zaynab bint Harithah),"[714]

---

[712] ibid.

[713] In Islam, taking care of an orphan or any other child in need is one of the most righteous, good deeds provided that the guardians do neither conceal the names of the child's biological parents, if they are known, nor attribute the child to themselves as if there is "a biological relationship." In the pre-Islamic period, an adopted child was regarded as enjoying the same legal status as a biological child. God Almighty abolished this grounded "legal" fiction with the verses 33:4-5. When the child is old enough to understand, they should be informed with wisdom about the reality so that they retain their own family identity without assuming that of the guardians.
The pre-Islamic custom also dictated that the child hold the same status within the forbidden degrees of marriage (*mahram*) as a biological child. In Islamic law, a *mahram* is limited with those with whom marriage is permanently forbidden because of the blood ties, breastfeeding or marriage ties. Accordingly, the former spouse of a guardian or an adopted child is legally considered a *non-mahram* – someone with whom marriage is not prohibited. With the revelation of the verse 33:37, God Almighty willed that this grounded pre-Islamic custom of prohibiting a guardian, or a foster child, from marrying a *non-mahram*, someone with whom marriage is not legally prohibited, be abolished and first put into effect through His Messenger's actions.

[714] Bukhari, *Tawhid* 22; Muslim, *Iman* 288: Ibn Hanbal, 2/5.

because this was a very heavy burden on the Noble Prophet.[715] This demonstrates that Divine commands take effect regardless of the Noble Prophet's social status or psychological conditions. The true status of an adopted child established by an exemplary case involving the Noble Prophet himself, and an old irrational custom thus abolished. Also, this historical event throws light on the wisdom behind the Noble Prophet's marriages.

But besides this, the abovementioned verse clearly lays down provisions for polygamy, which is another important issue. In case of necessity, God leaves the doors open for a man to marry up to four wives;[716] however, in case of failing to maintain justice between wives, advises to be content with monogamous family life.[717] Examining polygamy from modern civil laws perspective, Beser concludes that monogamy is more reasonable.[718]

If it needs to be mentioned here, polygamy was not introduced or enjoined or advised by Islam. God gradually reduced this pre-Islamic Age of Ignorance practice of polygamy (sometimes powerful men could marry dozens of women) down to limiting it to four wives, and highlighted the superiority of the monogamous family life. Another one of these pre-Islamic customs is *mut'ah* (temporary contractual sexual relationship) that has been prohibited by the Noble Prophet during the Medinan period. It is unlawful according to Sunni Islam, however still practiced in the Shiite world.

Historical records show that the practice of polygamy was not limited to Muslim lands only; it was also customary in other cultures and

---

[715] Gülen, *Sonsuz Nur-2 (Muhammad: The Messenger of God, Vol. 2)*, p. 198.

[716] *"If you fear that you will not be able to observe their rights with exact fairness when you marry the orphan girls (in your custody), you can marry, from among other women (who are permitted to you in marriage and) who seem good to you, two, or three, or four. However, if you fear that (in your marital obligations) you will not be able to observe justice among them, then content yourselves with only one, or the captives that your right hands possess. Doing so, it is more likely that you will not act rebelliously"* (Qur'an 4:3).

[717] *"You will never be able to deal between your wives with absolute equality (in respect of love and emotional attachment), however much you may desire to do so. But do not turn away altogether (from any one of them), so as to leave her in a dangling state (uncertain if she has or does not have a husband). If you act righteously (between them) and act in piety (fearful of doing any deliberate wrong to any of them), then surely God is All-Forgiving, All-Compassionate"* (Qur'an 4:129).

[718] Faruk Beser, *Hanimlara Ozel Ilmihal*, (Istanbul: Nun Publishing, 2010), pp. 36-41.

parts of the world. Also, extramarital relationships—which are basically another form of polygamy—taking place in modern days all over the world necessitate an examination of this social phenomenon more closely. Nevertheless, the Sunnah allows polygamy under certain conditions, e.g. a high number of women becoming widows without any support due to wars, etc., and in such cases, maintaining justice between wives is paramount. The Qur'an strongly warns those who fail to do so.[719] At this point, the Qur'an insistently emphasizes the impossibility of maintaining justice between wives. Yet, considering the economic reasons also makes the impossibility of the justice more clear. The Noble Prophet comments on the Quranic principles regarding this issue as he says: "A man who has *two wives* and who is completely inclined to one and who ignores the other emerges with one side of his body paralyzed on the Day of Judgment."[720] Although this hadith justifies the practice of *rukhsah* (an exception to a general rule in *shari'ah*, or permission for opting for the easier way in contrast to *azimah* or determination), it draws attention to difficulties and serious obligations associated with polygamy. Also, the hadith charges men with the responsibility of protecting the rights of women and maintaining justice between them. The caution expressed in the Qur'an with regard to being content with one wife (monogamy) and the issue of upholding justice highlighted by this hadith are in perfect conformity with each other. In a sense, attentions are drawn to the rigors of the matter and the impossibility of justice. According to the verse and the hadith, Gülen stresses that justice is the main significant point for second marriage. This justice point is difficult for the man to follow. That's why Gülen emphasizes that marriage with only one wife is *wajib* (necessary) in Islam.[721] He insistently does not advice second marriage and bans it implicitly. While pointing out the fact that the practice of polygamy is considered *mubah*[722] in Islam, Ahmet Kurucan[723] stresses that this is so under certain conditions and the government holds the power to ban polygamy whenever it deems necessary. For example, the

---

[719] Halime Demiresik, "İslam'da çok evlilik," *Şebnem Kadın ve Aile Magazine,* Issue 6 (2003).
[720] Ibn Majah, *Nikah,* 47.
[721] Zahw, *Hadis ve Hadisciler.*
[722] *Mubah* is an Islamic term denoting an action as religiously neutral, i.e. neither forbidden nor recommended.
[723] Pupil of Fethullah Gülen

codification of *Hukuk-u Aile Kararnamesi* (*Decree on Family Law*) 1917 prohibited polygamy in the Ottoman Empire (modern civil laws do not permit polygamy). Unfortunately, many people are unaware of the fact that such social issues are matters of *ijtihad*, and this permission (*rukhsah*) is being wantonly used by a few. Evidences are clearly visible in the Islamic Law for judgments with regards to the state's power to outlaw polygamy.[724] Therefore, when this permission is being abused it can easily be revoked by the state.

An important point here is that a wife has the right to enforce monogamy upon her husband simply by stipulating a clause in their marriage contact. This is because the consent of both parties is essential for the validity of a marriage act in Islam. The wife automatically gains the right to divorce her husband if he fails to honor the marriage contract, i.e. he attempts to marry another woman.[725] Hence, there is no way for a man to marry another woman without first obtaining the permission of his lawfully married wife. Any shrewd way of bypassing the civil law would result in the second "wife" being deprived of all her legal rights and a great injustice against both women. Keeping all this in mind, it is clear that polygamy brings in a lot of drawbacks and is widely open to abuse especially in this day and age when the norms are set by modern civil laws.

A study of Gülen's written works fails to show any remarks on this issue. However, in view of his high esteem for individual and social justice, and especially for women's rights, it is possible to conclude that he would not approve of this kind of injustice against women because Kurucan's explanations—possibly as he learned from Gülen, his mentor—shows that the issue is open to abuse. Therefore, presenting a practice—which is *mubah*—at the same degree of obligation evokes different thoughts. According to Gülen, if it needs to be stated here, the Noble Prophet advised marriage to a single woman (neither did he close the path to marriage nor did he order his followers to curtail their carnal feelings). Carnal feelings that are an ontological part of human nature have been directed to a lawful path, i.e. marriage. The Noble

---

[724] Ahmet Kurucan, "Ilan Edilmemis Nikah Olur Mu?" *Zaman daily*, September 15, 2011.
[725] Demiresik, "Islam'da Cok Evlilik."

Prophet's art of nurturing had been in the framework of directing the natural human disposition to the positive direction and in line with the teleological purpose.[726] Consequently, keeping in mind the Noble Prophet's sensitivities for the welfare and goodness of his community, it is possible to conclude that the practice of polygamy is not judicious— although *mubah*—as it causes injustice to both sexes.

In conclusion, it is possible to say that women, as human beings, are created equal to men and have the same normative legal values. Their rights, which had been usurped in the course of history of civilizations have been reinstated by the Almighty Creator and safeguarded by the Divine Law. Thus, Islam reformed false customs and practices, which were prevalent before its advent, and introduced new social and moral norms for the benefit of humanity. The Noble Prophet moved his Companions from the Age of Ignorance to an exemplary position for the future generations. Both men and women find their respective position and status in this picture with perfect demarcation between sexes. All necessary laws and principles for individual and social requirements have been implemented by the Noble Prophet himself during a short period of time such as 23 years, and no point was omitted. While being deprived of a name during the Age of Ignorance, women become a value as a result of the laws and lifestyle imposed by the Qur'an and the Sunnah. Today the dialectic, which argues that Islam turned women into slaves and rendered them as commodities vulnerable to abuse, either blatantly disregards the pre-Islamic Age of Ignorance and the injustices that women were subjected to in other cultures, or suffers from lack of knowledge about Islam and its sources (Qur'an and Sunnah). Because for Gülen, there are no loopholes in the Qur'an, the Sunnah or the body of Islamic literature based on them that can be used to abuse women; both sexes have been appropriately positioned and evaluated. The following Quranic verses lay down the foundation stones of the family and community structures: "The believers, both men and women: they are guardians, confidants, and helpers of one another..."[727] The verse makes both man and woman responsible for promoting the good and

---

[726] Gülen, *Sonsuz Nur-2 (Muhammad: The Messenger of God*, Vol. 2), pp. 72-73.
[727] Qur'an 9:71

preventing the evil, and considers them helpers of each other in this field. Again, all other rights of women, e.g. privacy, marriage, freedom of speech, and so on, have been firmly established and guaranteed by the Qur'an and the Sunnah. Nevertheless, Gülen does not completely disregard the misdeeds of many Muslims today who act in the name of God. So his main criticism should be read not only in the light of non-Muslims' attack against Islam but also in the light of mistakes made by Muslims. Thus, one cannot see Gülen's approach as an attempt to reconcile Islam with liberal values of contemporary time. Clearly, his analysis of women issues is from time to time legally conservative and apologetic. Nevertheless, in certain issues he does not hesitate to go beyond classical framework. Finally, it is also important to note that the number of young women in Gülen (Hizmet) Movement is increasing, and they are actively participating in many social and cultural projects. Comparing with status of many women in various religious communities, because of Gülen's powerful appeal to their active participation in the society, women in the movement are doing far more better than others.

The Notion of Tolerance and Dialogue and Gülen's Thoughts

Tolerance is a doctrine of the Divine religions and a starting point for people and civilizations to meet and be acquainted with each other. In the Sunnah literature, the basis for tolerance is outlined in terms of forgiveness, compassion, understanding and respect. The positive impact of tolerance in inter-cultural/religious relations and world peace has been widely accepted, and its examination from the Hadith point of view in Gülen's thoughts represents an important point. In this section, an answer will be sought to the question of the extent to which tolerance has been handled in the Hadith literature. Also, tolerance and dialogue are the most popular issues in the society and people needs in this contemporary time. It will, therefore, be focused in this chapter.

There are many examples of intercultural and interfaith dialogues in Islamic literature. For instance, Mawlana Jalal al-Din al-Rumi (d. 1273) evaluates the human being from both material and spiritual aspects, and puts forth a portrait of love and tolerance for humanity. In this Sunnah-based teaching, Muslims view humankind as the most honorable creature of God, and consider tolerance as a moral due. During the 13th Century CE, like Mawlana Jalaluddin Rumi, Yunus Emre with his maxim, "Love the created for the sake of the Creator," also highlights the theme of tolerance in Islam and thus relates it to the gist of the value system of the Sunnah. For the foundations of these two Muslim sages' teachings, which transcend centuries, are based on the Sunnah.[728] The Noble Prophet's mission during both the Meccan and Medinan periods focused on tolerance—the Prophet's telling his Companions not to interfere with a desert Bedouin urinating in the mosque[729] and similar examples—may be viewed as the main factor shaping many great Muslim scholars' understanding of tolerance.

Tolerance and dialogue, according to Gülen, means turning a blind eye to mistakes as in the case of the above hadith; showing respect and understanding to divergent views; being forgiving, not seeking justice for oneself even when fully justifiable; displaying a soft approach in the face of roughest thoughts and views by adopting, in his own words, the formula of *kalb-i layyin, hal-i layyin, tavr-i layyin* ("being soft-hearted and mild-mannered and having soft attitude") and an immense heart that can view the most dissident thoughts as useful.[730] Gülen views tolerance as a prerequisite for one to be a Muslim. Also, in his view, the Sunnah—which is the source of the religion—necessitates tolerance and dialogue.[731] A quick comparison shows an interesting similarity between Gülen's thought and that of many philosophers. The rationale of respect for thoughts and status along with them delivers important messages with regard to seeking solutions to human problems. In the final analysis, it is possible to say that different groups come close when it comes to understanding—and listening to—humankind, although they have differing views on the definition of tolerance. In fact, thinkers

---

[728] Mehmet Aydin, "Mevlana Humanizminin Boyutlari" (The Dimensions of Rumi's Humanism), *Turk-Islam Medeniyeti Akademik Arastirmalar Magazine*, Mevlana *special issue* (2007), p. 53.

[729] Narrated by Bukhari: "A Bedouin stood up and started making water in the mosque. The people caught him but the Noble Prophet ordered them to leave him and to pour a bucket or a tumbler of water over the place where he had passed the urine. The Noble Prophet then said, 'You have been sent to make things easy and not to make them difficult.'" (Bukhari, *wudu'* 57; Muslim, *taharah* 98-100).

[730] Gülen, *Yeseren Dusunceler (Reflorishing Thoughts)*, Cag Ve Nesil series, Vol. 6, p. 29.

[731] Unal, *Advocate of Dialogue: Fethullah Gülen* (Fairfax: The Fountain, 2000), pp. 193-194.

such as John Stuart Mill, John Locke, Spinoza, Gandhi, Rumi, Yunus Emre and Gülen give priority to the human factor and weave values like tolerance around it.

It is well known that Islam enjoins tolerance through principles such as affection, respect, mercy, acquaintance and security. Nowadays, however, a wrong perception is being created about the Sunnah, which is the main source of these values. Tolerance and interfaith dialogue hold a position that can be an important cornerstone to overcome this wrong perception. Doubts in thoughts can thus be eliminated; affection and principles of peace will prevail. The Qur'an presents these tolerance principles as the Noble Prophet's personal behavior and way of life: "*It was by a mercy from God that (at the time of the setback), you (O Messenger) were lenient with them (your Companions). Had you been harsh and hard-hearted, they would surely have scattered away from about you...*"[732] This Divine commandment has been interpreted by the Noble Prophet as follows: "A Muslim is the one who avoids harming Muslims with his tongue and hands. And an immigrant (*muhajir*) is the one who abandons all what God has forbidden."[733]

As can be seen, tolerance is considered one of the basic principles of Divine religions. Therefore, it is the source of nutrition for problem solving. Also, it is necessary to mention here that believing in the previous Divine messages is among the principles of the Islamic creed. Hence, Gülen approaches all Divine religions and other world religions with tolerance as dictated by his own faith.[734] And through this way he presents a peaceful world proposal where it would be possible to live in harmony under the teachings of Divine religions and all faith traditions.

According to Gülen, it is not possible to talk about collective thoughts and consciousness in nations and communities where there exists no tolerance between individuals. In such an environment, thoughts go after each other and fall one after the other in a web of bickering and quarrelling. Thus, intellectuals' thoughts become

---

[732] Qur'an 3:159.
[733] Bukhari, *Iman*, 4.
[734] Gülen, *Toward a Global Civilization of Love and Tolerance* (New Jersey: The Light Publishing, 2004), pp. 75-76.

worthless, and the administrative structures based on solid power move away from the populace. It is not possible to think that genuine freedom of speech and religion can be established in such a situation. Again, a government system bereft of tolerance cannot be considered a "state of law."[735] Looking into historical events would reveal that intolerant organizations had driven themselves and their communities into insoluble dilemmas. The tyrannical administration of the pharaoh with its prohibition of the freedom of religion, belief and speech, had been noted down into history. As for today, it is not possible to talk about the freedom of press, independent academic thought or cultural activities in communities deprived of the principle of tolerance. Such a social structure would hinder the survival of non-governmental organizations, and prevent the state from reaching the capillaries of the society.

It is also impossible to talk about compassion, which establishes peace, in an intolerant society. Gülen asserts that a hadith[736] heralds that on the Day of Judgment, the Almighty will order His angels to show tolerance to those who showed mercy and tolerance to others in this world. While highlighting the importance of this point, Gülen points out the metaphysical repercussions of this Divine message and the Sunnah, and establishes correlations between the physical world and the spiritual realm. Due to manners he received through the Sunnah, he emphasizes the importance of kindness towards animals alongside human beings. He illustrates as an example the case of a sinful woman receiving salvation for her kind act of giving water to a thirsty dog,[737] and, as mentioned in another hadith,[738] the exit from atrocity psychosis of a murderer who killed 99 people.[739] With the help of these kinds of illustrations, Gülen prepares the groundwork for compassion and tolerance to become a moral norm in individual and social lives, and the fact that he introduces training methods.

---

[735] Gülen, *Yeseren Dusunceler (Reflorishing Thoughts)*, Cag ve Nesil series, Vol. 6, p. 32.
[736] Ahmad ibn Hanbal, I, 5.
[737] Muslim, *Tawbah* 155; Ibn Hanbal, *al-Musnad* 2/507.
[738] al-Tabarani, *al-Mu'jam al-Kabir* 2/222.
[739] Gülen, *Yeseren Dusunceler (Reflorishing Thoughts)*, Cag ve Nesil series, Vol. 6, p. 30.

Dialogue and Gülen's Proposed Solutions to the Problems

Gülen's tolerance of and dialogue with different faiths had been outlined previously. In this section, Gülen's proposed solutions to problems will be analyzed on an academic level in terms of dialogue.

Gülen proposes some solutions during the meeting with Pope John Paul II on behalf of dialogue between religions. Gülen's first proposal regarding the field of academia is remarkable. He proposes a series of conferences in collaboration with the leaders of three heavenly religions for the identification of determined and deliberated commonalities and differences between the religions; the first was in Washington, DC, which included the participation of scholars in various world capitals.[740] This opportunity has provided new resolutions for issues and problems through analysis, which had not been discussed and had accumulated until today. The second proposal included students of different levels of social science and science discussing their knowledge with students of religious sciences. Through this, differences would enrich the knowledge shared and make it easier to comprehend.[741] Hence, academicians of various religions studying together would also establish close relationships between community members sharing the same beliefs. Gülen's third proposal was the constructing of a school of theology in Harran, Urfa, where Prophet Abraham – who is accepted as the father of the three heavenly religions – was born.[742] A similar offer had been made by Bediüzzaman Said Nursi, who had recommended for a university called "Madrasatu'z-Zahra" to be established in the city of Van, aiming to have profound impact on solving the Kurdish issue in Turkey.[743] He proposed the education at the university to be offered in Arabic, Kurdish and Turkish languages, and labeled them as "the must, the licit and the requisite" respectively.[744] It is remarkable for all three proposals of Gülen to be

---

[740] Gülen, *Insanın Ozundeki Sevgi (Towards a Global Civilization of Love and Tolerance)*, pp. 186-188.

[741] ibid.

[742] ibid.

[743] Bediüzzaman Said Nursi, *Sualar (The Rays)*, (Istanbul: Sozler Nesriyat, 2009), p. 482.

[744] Tugba Kaplan, "Kurt Sorununu Cozecek 105 Yıllık Proje: Medresetu'z-Zehra," *Zaman daily* (August 25, 2013).

education-driven. Hence, it can be seen that he considers education as a vital part of solving issues of the current day.

Hadi Uluengin accepts Gülen's recommendations as projects that will be able to sooth stereotypes, solve problems and establish healthy dialogue between countries.[745] Similarly, Ahmet Tezcan draws attention to the fact that the dialogue between religions will smooth the harsh edges of patriotism and fanaticism and minimize their harmful consequences. According to him, making Harran the base of science for all three heavenly religions will not only significantly contribute to global peace, but will also be of great assistance in ending terrorism in Turkey's Southeast.[746] The results of both Nursi's proposed university and Gülen's aspirations about Harran are capable of presenting profound solutions to current affairs.

Along with these proposals, upon his request for the reopening of the Christian seminary on Istanbul's Heybeli Island (Heybeli Ruhban School) during their meetings, Gülen asked Patriarch Bartholomew I to use his identity to ask the government of Greece for the permission of a Turkish school in the Greek port city of Salonika.[747] This suggestion is a project that holds important outcomes for both sides; the reestablishment of the Christian seminary would be of ecumenical profit for the Patriarchate, whilst helping the school's former graduates gain a global reputation. It will also contribute to international education and cultures.

In addition to these, interfaith dialogue and suggestions similar to those discussed have the power to enlighten the path of current global problems. Different nations, cultures, races and religions sharing the same atmosphere whilst holding true to their own beliefs will naturally diminish many problems. Steps to be taken in achieving such peace will further transform the world shrunken by technology into a global village and further yet, a neighborhood. Furthermore, Gülen's suggestion of a school of theology in Harran, Urfa can ultimately be carried out in a way that will render it a project capable of tending to the needs of three

---

[745] Gülen, *Hosgoru Ve Diyalog (Tolerance and Dialogue)*, (Istanbul, Turkey: Merkur Publishing, 1999).

[746] ibid.

[747] Unal, *M. Fethullah Gülen: Bir Portre Denemesi (Fethullah Gülen: A Portrait Essay)*, p. 389.

religions, and an independent university with a far-reaching curriculum. Although these may seem like impassable tasks, they are definitely not unattainable.

Works of Tolerance Based on Sunnah

While discussing the constructive effect of the moral values such as tolerance, affection, compassion and forgiveness in the society, Thomas Michel gives examples from the Gülen-inspired schools that are projects as part of the mission based on Sunnah. He illustrates the friendly relations between Christian and Muslim children and their parents and a peaceful environment in a school in the middle of a region in Philippines where heavy armed conflicts are taking place between Christians and Muslims. Besides providing high-standard education, the school is conducive to solidarity among students/parents from diverse ethnic and religious backgrounds.[748] In case of offering good educational and toleration values together, it becomes possible to minimize the problems, and establish small inter-national/inter-religious peace oases.

The Sunnah-based toleration practices demonstrated by Gülen are an important key to peace and security in society.[749] Acceptance of diverse color,[750] religion, culture and ideology of individuals, communities and nations, and putting humanity at the forefront is an important achievement in terms of solving problems.

Here, it is important to mention this: in our days, the Sunnah-based toleration and dialogue activities are not read and understood properly by certain researchers. Tolerance and dialogue meetings and fast-breaking (*iftar*) dinners organized by Gülen and his followers are

---

[748] Thomas Michel, "Gülen as Educator and Religious Teacher," (February 05, 2002), http://fgulen.com/en/press/review/24902-gulen-as-educator-and-religious-teacher?highlight=WyJ0aG9tYXMiLCJtaWNoZWwiLCJ0aG9tYXMgbWljaGVsIl0=&hitcount=0.

[749] Heydar Shadi, "Interfaith Dialogue and Religious Tolerance in Contemporary Islamic Thought: A Comparative Study of Fethullah Gülen and Abdul Karim Soroush," (November 22, 2007), http://fgulen.com/en/gulen-movement/conference-papers/peaceful-co-existence/25870-interfaith-dialogue-and-religious-tolerance-in-contemporary-islamic-thought-a-comparative-study-of-fethullah-gulen-and-abdul-karim-soroush?highlight=WyJ0b2xlcmFuY2UiLCJkkaWFsb2d1ZSJd.

[750] Taking into account the fact that Bilal al-Habashi, the first *mu'adhdhin* (caller to the Prayer) in Islam, was a black slave would help to understand better the all-embracing character of the Sunnah.

being questioned and criticized. For example, Deniz Arman does not view *iftar* programs organized by Muslims being shared with various religious communities such as Armenian, Orthodox, Protestant, Jewish as rational-ethical. In a way, he considers this as a shame for the Muslim.[751] It is obvious that Arman has no idea about the Sunnah and *sirah* literatures. His statements like "I do not know," "I do not understand" in his article do, in fact, support this conclusion. We can count some of the lucid examples from the Noble Prophet's tradition clearly showing his innumerable contacts with people from all religious backgrounds since the beginning of his Prophetic mission, and his repeated conversations with 'Amr ibn Hisham (Abu Jahl) and 'Abd al-'Uzza ibn 'Abd al-Muttalib (Abu Lahab, the Prophet's uncle) and his kind treatment of them despite the fact that they were strongly against him and Islam. His dialogues with all these people, his affinity with his uncle Abu Talib, his contact with the King of Abyssinia, his negotiations with the Jews of Medina and agreement on a common ground, and so on should all these and similar events be considered shameful according to Arman's approach? If all these acts constitute a shame on the part of the Noble Prophet and his Sunnah, what is the right way of dealing with people? When the Qur'an says, "*You have your religion (with whatever it will bring you), and I have my religion (with whatever it will bring me)*"[752] it does not prohibit people from coming together with people, on the contrary, it advises them to come together on a common ground and share core human values. In this connection, Armenian Patrick Mesrob Mutafyan demonstrated his appreciation by his statement on the occasion of an *iftar* invitation, "Up until a short while ago, even people from the same religion could not come together in this country, now people from different religions sat at the same dinner table." Patrick Mutafyan highlighted the plausibility of the interfaith dialogue and tolerance in the Noble Prophet's Sunnah by saying, "What brings different religions together at the same dinner table is Fethullah Gülen and the [GYV] foundation of which he is the honorary president. Now we follow his path."[753] In the meantime, Gülen emphasizes

---

[751] Deniz Arman, "Benim dinim bana, senin dinin sana," *Vatan daily*, November 14, 2003.

[752] Qur'an 109:6.

[753] Mesrob Mutafyan, "Hocaefendi'nin Actigi Yoldan Yuruyoruz," *Zaman daily*, October 28, 2003.

that interfaith dialogue and tolerance has been misunderstood by certain sections of the community, and feels the need to make some explanation in order to point out the principles of the dialogue: "This is a dialogue between followers of religions. You cannot mix religions together and obtain something syncretic."[754] So, according to the Sunnah, values, principles and understandings of each religion belong to itself. All in all, the Noble Prophet did not only deliver his message during the Meccan and Medina periods, he by no means ridiculed the religious values of his opponents. The meaning of dialogue and tolerance is accepting everyone in their own status and to create a peaceful environment.

One could say that the Noble Prophet took as a basis for his Sunnah tolerance and dialogue. The first Christian-Muslim contact took place during the fifth year of the Prophetic mission, in 615 CE, by the migration of a group of 15 Muslims to Abyssinia. A similar situation can be observed during the Medina period where the Noble Prophet established a brotherhood tie between Ansar ("the Helpers"; residents of Medina) and Muhajir ("the Immigrants" from Mecca). The long lasting fight between the two Meccan tribes of Aws and Khazraj had been settled by peace and brotherhood. Also, a treaty was signed by the Noble Prophet with the Jewish tribes of Medina. Containing 47 clauses, this treaty agreement, which is also known as the "Medina Document," was based on peace, security, mutual trust and respect.[755] With these steps taken, the Noble Prophet first ensures the peace and security in the land, and accepts everyone in their own position. Historical documents show no record of any problems caused by the Muslim delegation sent to Abyssinia although they spent many years in this land of different religion and culture. Historical records witness the establishment of a peaceful environment rather than problems in Medina. Starting from this point, it is possible to comfortably say that Gülen's mission—in its opening to the world through its education and dialogue services—follows the same path. Members of the Hizmet Movement are seen representing peace, tolerance and mutual understanding in every country they go to. No

---

[754] Gülen, *Hosgoru ve Diyalog (Tolerance and Dialogue)*, (Istanbul, Turkey: Merkur Publishing, 1999).

[755] Yusuf Celik, "Peygamberimizin Ehl-i Kitapla Munasebetleri" *Yeni Umit, Issue 78*, (January-March 2007).

official report has been made regarding the "volunteers" who represent the movement causing any clashes with the people or the state, or any complaints reported, where the schools operate since their opening outside of Turkey, in 1991. On the contrary, expressions of gratitude and welcome are offered by the locals, and as a result, the Hizmet Movement is now active in 160 countries.

In conclusion, it is possible to say that the world is becoming a global community composed of people adhering to diverse religions, beliefs and cultures. In this global village, relations between people from diverse cultural and religious backgrounds are of even greater importance. It is for this reason that Gülen's tolerance stemming from the teaching of Sunnah is being charged with a greater mission. The Prophetic Practice built a safe and secure environment and established good relations and cooperation between members of various religions and cultures. For instance, the Noble Prophet's armor was still pawned with a Jewish merchant when he died, and recovered only after the Companions paid his debt. This incident shows the extent of the relations between communities from commerce to finances. The application of the Sunnah presents important messages to the present day and future Muslims. The world of the future is projecting a support for a real and modern understanding integrated with global values through tolerance rather than an introverted society. The most important criterion here is the acceptance of all individuals in their own status regardless of their creed, color, culture and language. It is none other than this reality that is needed in this century and that will be needed in the future. The insurance for the salvation of the humanity—for the present and the future—is, in a single word, Sunnah-based tolerance and dialogue. It should also be noted that Gülen easily negates many insiders' (Muslims) criticism against his pro-interfaith-dialogue activities by referencing to Sunnah. Bringing countless anecdotes from the life of the Noble Prophet regarding inter-religious dialogue, he silences some opponents to go further in their criticism. In addition, as mentioned above, Gülen is not dogmatic or just theoretical person but put his ideas and views into practice. As Saritoprak has highlighted, Gülen socializes the theology by creating many areas and fields to implement his opinions. He is a unique

Muslim in the contemporary world putting the theological notion of social responsibility into practice in more than 160 countries.

Interpretations Regarding Terrorism and Suicide Bombers

This section will be focusing on Islam and its stance against terror and violence, taking into account Gülen's approach and evaluation of the Prophetic Practice against terrorism. The main theme will be constructed through topics that touch upon the prohibition of the acts of terror and violence in Islam, the place of suicide bombers in the Sunnah, and the methods illustrated by the Sunnah to solve problems.

The Definition of Jihad in Islam and Gülen's Approach

Many Islamic terms are frequently used out of context by different mediums to describe the supposed "violent" fundamentals of the religion. With the term *jihad* taking the lead, some of the Islamic values being used as slogans by terrorists and some biased groups cause Islam to be frequently mentioned and associated with terrorism. Terrorists and terrorist groups feel the need to rely on religious entities in order to build on valid or well-founded grounds and express themselves visibly.[756] Therefore, convincing militants with "Islamist" rhetoric becomes a simpler task. It is especially easier for an uneducated individual who was not raised with or sustained by religious resources to be convinced to take part in terrorist acts. Hence, if the term "Islamist" is going to be used to describe a devout Muslim who is well grounded in the Islamic resources, it should be considered that according to Islamic values, a person with such consciousness cannot be a terrorist.

In addition, it is not possible to associate the acts of terror and violence with the Qur'an and the Sunnah. Despite the term being misused to define terror, attacks and barbarity, *jihad* in the Islamic literature is explained as "striving in the way of God."[757] Therefore, *jihad* is the name of every religious, scholarly or financial struggle undertaken to share the beliefs and values of Islam with humankind. This includes the efforts

---

[756] Hamza Aktan, "Kur'an Ve Sunnet Isiginda Teror Ve Intihar Eylemleri," *Yeni Umit*, Issue 63, (January-March 2004).

[757] Gülen, "What is Jihad," (September 13, 2001), http://fgulen.com/en/fethullah-gulens-works/faith/questions-and-answers/24522-what-is-jihad?highlight=WyJqaWWhhZCJd.

of the lettered and knowledgeable to educate others, the generosity the wealthy display, the energy the healthy exert to serve humankind, and even the intrinsic battle one experiences to appease his carnal desires.[758] If the time and place requires so, *jihad* could also be defined as any written or verbal disagreement with or endeavors against disbelief, including evidence-oriented arguments, seminars, conferences and articles.[759] Further expanding on his explanation, Gülen says: "*Jihad* is not the method or approach used by terrorists who threaten people and generate fright and terror to the society. It is also not the name of the method of crude people such as bandits. *Jihad* is the lifestyle of people who are in a constant struggle to nourish their beliefs and improve it to a state that is loved and appreciated by God."[760] "It is the definition of achieving a higher rank in God's eyes by introducing and familiarizing humankind with Him using a soft and insightful manner."[761] Furthermore, *jihad* is any attempt of an individual to prevent and clear barriers that might harm the personal bond created between him and God. It is making belief a natural and vital part of one's life.

Considering the above clarifications of the term, it could be said that the approach of Gülen and many other thinkers is in correspondence with the following hadith: "Perform *jihad* against disbelievers with speech and representation of your beliefs."[762] When the issue is examined from this perspective, it can be seen that *jihad* is the name given to the more spiritual dimension of Sunnah, and hence claimed that it is impossible for acts of terror to be derived from or rooted in the Sunnah.

Gülen believes that weapons, tyranny and provoking terror will neither aid in communicating ideas, nor will it be effective in solving problems. According to him, the path to global harmony or the domination of peace passes through embracing the spirit of dialogue, faith and belief. If people are forced to say, "At your service" with armed

---

[758] Aktan, "Kur'an Ve Sunnet Isiginda Teror Ve Intihar Eylemleri," *Yeni Umit*, Issue 63, (January-March 2004).

[759] Sukran Vahide, "Said Nursi'nin Cihat Yorumu," (1970), http://www.ufkumuz.com/said-nursinin-cihat-yorumu-2708h.htm.

[760] Gülen, *Hitap Cicekleri (Blossoms of Declamation)*, (Istanbul: Nil Publishing, 1995), p.105.

[761] Ibid., *Asrin Getirdigi Tereddutler -3 (Questions and Answers about Islam, Vol. 3)*, (Istanbul: Nil Publishing, 2010), pp. 194-198.

[762] Abu Dawud, *Jihad*," 18 (2504); Nasa'i, "*Jihad*," 1 (6,7), *Kutub al-Sittah*, v, 67.

forces, nuclear power, electronic system control or invasions, this cannot be considered a victory.[763] On the contrary, it will curtain the values of Islam and build barriers against inter-faith dialogue. In an atmosphere that does not allow faith to become intrinsic and people to be truly convinced and satisfied with reasoning, enmity will only fade to resurface at a later stage.

Gülen's thought on jihad is also seen to be closely related with a hadith narrated by Abu Dharr. Upon asking the Noble Prophet which deed is more virtuous, this Companion receives the following answer[764]: "*Jihad* in the sense of believing in God, and striving to spread His religion and your faith with speech and representation."[765] Therefore, the Sunnah shows *jihad* as the maturation and spreading of knowledge through reflections it has on one's good character and manners.

Terrorism and the Approach of the Qur'an and the Sunnah to Jihad

There is no concurrency between the Qur'an and the ongoing acts of terrorism and assassinations that are "equated" with *jihad*. In the Holy Qur'an, God Almighty says, "*It is because of this that We ordained for (all humankind, but particularly for) the Children of Israel: He who kills a soul unless it be (in legal punishment) for murder or for causing disorder and corruption on the earth will be as if he had killed all humankind; and he who saves a life will be as if he had saved the lives of all humankind...*"[766] God does not permit the intentional killing of a person by any individual. If anything, He encourages people to live by principles that help them live their own lives whilst sustaining the lives of others. Even if an individual is legally deserving of a severe punishment, the above verse of the Qur'an only licenses the justice system with a right to practice harsh penalties. It therefore prevents chaos or events of terror that may break out between individuals or societies as a whole.

Along with this, it is observed that permission for physical *jihad* – only within circumstances of self-defense – was given after the Noble

---

[763] Gülen, *Hitap Cicekleri (Blossoms of Declamation)*, p. 106.
[764] ibid., p. 106.
[765] Bukhari, *adab* 1.
[766] Qur'an 5:32.

Prophet's migration to Medina thirteen years after the commencement of his Prophethood: "*The believers against whom war is waged are given permission to fight in response, for they have been wronged. Surely, God has full power to help them to victory.*"[767] As can be drawn from the verse, the concept of war in Islam can only be constructed on the need for defense; even within this system, the decision for self-defense and war can only be made by the willpower of the government that the society is ruled by.

According to Gülen, individuals do not have the right to announce physical *jihad* based on their own personal interests.[768] It is also against Islamic law for an individual to declare war on his own accord.[769] This could only be called an act of terror. Hence, it is impossible for Islam to be truly associated with any expressions of terrorism.

Just as every other nation or community, Muslims have the right to defend themselves and protect their dignity by eliminating threats posed by intelligence and military attacks. The number of major and minor campaigns and military actions Prophet Muhammad, upon whom be peace and blessings, commanded himself or appointed commanders for from amongst his Companions exceeds sixty. However, he was never the attacking party in any of these situations.[770] This means that he had never attacked a tribe of idol-worshippers or unbelievers due to their values; his attempts were always aimed at self defense and predicting attacks to render them futile before they developed into larger threats.

During the Meccan period, the faith in one-and-only God, representation and speech aspects of *jihad* seem to have been more prominent. Throughout this thirteen year long Meccan period, the religion was lived and represented by the Noble Prophet and his Companions. In this contemporary age, the lifestyle that Gülen encourages today's Muslims to adopt is one that resembles the Noble

---

[767] Qur'an 22:39

[768] Gülen, *Yenilenme Cehdi (Endeavor for Renewal)*, Kirik Testi series, Vol. 12, p. 267.

[769] Nuriye Akman, *Gurbette Fethullah Gülen*, Fethullah Gülen Terore Panzehir Sunuyor *(Gülen in a Foreign Land: Fethullah Gulen Presents the Antidote against Terror)*, (Istanbul: Zaman Kitap, 2004).

[770] Aktan, "Kur'an Ve Sunnet Isiginda Teror Ve Intihar Eylemleri," *Yeni Umit, Issue* 63, (January-y-March 2004).

Prophet's practice during his time in Mecca. What was intrinsic during the Meccan period was "the Dar al-Arqam service," which was a system of houses in which the Noble Prophet gave lessons to his Companions by speaking of and representing his knowledge in order to furnish their souls and raise awareness of the religion revealed.[771] In exchange for an educated Muslim who is capable of thinking, contemplating and questioning, it is important for such a system to be implemented and regarded as a necessary value by the society. During the Meccan period, it was essential neither to show fear nor to reciprocate violence when exposed to threats and attacks. As related by his daughter Fatima, the exemplary patience the Noble Prophet showed when the polytheist Meccans placed tripe on his head during the Prayer, when they stoned him on the streets or threw soil at him[772] was an aspect of this reality.[773]

Attention should be drawn on the fact that such actions were done to provoke the Noble Prophet and his Companions and would have caused civil war in case of any retaliation. Either case of victory or defeat might have damaged the Noble Prophet's mission of spreading the Divine religion; at such an early age, defeat would have diminished the values Muslims held due to their small numbers, and a victory would have eliminated the polytheists' willpower and imprisoned their freedom of thought to dominion.

Suicide, Suicide Bombings and the Approach of the Sunnah

According to Gülen, committing suicide or suicide attacks equates to disbelief. A person who commits suicide is considered to have tortured the life that was given to him as a trust from God, for humankind is expected to protect his life to the best of their abilities.[774] The Noble Prophet draws attention to this fact with the comment he makes about Quzman, who committed suicide during the battle of Uhud: "He is of the people of Hellfire!"[775] Some scholars consider people who have

---

[771] Gülen, *Hitap Cicekleri (Blossoms of Declamation)*, p. 105.
[772] Bukhari, *Wudu* 69; Muslim, *Jihad*, 107-108.
[773] Gülen, *Hitap Cicekleri (Blossoms of Declamation)*, pp. 105-106.
[774] Gülen, *Yenilenme Cehdi (Endeavor for Renewal)*, Kirik Testi series, Vol. 12, p. 263.
[775] at-Tabari, *Tarikhu'l-Umam wa'l-Muluk*, 2/73.

committed suicide as those who abandoned their faith and thus declare that the Funeral Prayer for them cannot be performed.[776]

Gülen believes that a person with deep-seated faith can neither commit suicide nor become a suicide bomber. In this case, one who takes his own or another's life will have a thin line between disbelief and himself, and will be face to face with a high risk of losing his faith. His characteristics will no longer allow an attribution to his Islamic beliefs. Thereby, a person who dies as a suicide bomber and causes the death of others cannot be a true Muslim.[777]

This individual is not a believer at the time of murder; one who commits this sin with such a state of mind, spiritual condition, plan and fantasy cannot be called a "Muslim." The Sunnah defines these borders with the following truths: "A servant of God is not a true believer in the instant of adultery ... and is not a believer when he is taking the life of another."[778] All these act as the principles in setting the cornerstones of peace in a society.

Gülen states that the crimes committed by a suicide bomber who has caused the death of many innocent can in no way be linked with the Islamic faith.[779] According to him, although nations such as Palestine have faced many hardships, the suicide bombings they have organized cannot be acceptable. Proceeding an attack without a specific target, mounting bombs onto oneself with an intention of killing and pulling the dowel amongst innocent people cannot be classified as an act with Islamic motives. Islam has set rules regarding how to battle against the enemy even during the most violent moments of war. For there is no verdict in Islam that allows the killing of civilians – any people, including children, men and women who are not actually participants of the ongoing war.[780] Every individual's right to live is under protection with the Islamic law. The Noble Prophet's orders during the conquest of

---

[776] Gülen, *Yenilenme Cehdi (Endeavor for Renewal)*, *Kirik Testi* series, Vol. 12, p. 265.

[777] Gülen, "A Real Muslim cannot be a Terrorist," (October 5, 2004), https://www.fgulen.com/en/fethullah-gulens-works/toward-a-global-civilization-of-love-and-tolerance/jihad-ter-rorism-human-rights/25259-real-muslims-cannot-be-terrorists.

[778] Nasai, *Qasama* 48, 49, *Qat' al-Sariq* 1; Abd al-Razzaq, *al-Musannaf* 7/415; Ibn Abi Shayba, *al-Musannaf* 6/169.

[779] Gülen, *Yenilenme Cehdi (Endeavor for Renewal)*, *Kirik Testi* series, Vol. 12, p. 267.

[780] Gülen, *Gurbet Ufuklari (Horizons of Foreign Land)*, *Kirik Testi* series, Vol. 3, p. 179.

Mecca can be appraised within the same sphere: "You are not to battle with or kill anyone as long as you are not faced with violent resistance and attacks!"[781]

The principles that Islam has on the matter of bloodshed are remarkable in every aspect. A father has the right to disown and deprive of inheritance a child who is a murderer or a terrorist.[782] En masse, these morals illustrated by the Qur'an and the Sunnah are important factors in maintaining communal peace.

When asked whether it was the desire for heaven that encouraged Muslims to become suicide commandos, Gülen replied: "If people are acting with such deliberations, it means they have guided themselves rather wrongly. For whoever attempts such a crime will find himself falling into Hell, not Heaven."[783] According to Gülen, these types of people are murderers who are unaware of the essence of the religion. Whilst committing a deed that belongs to Hell by killing themselves, they are held accountable for the deaths of the children, men and women – Muslims and non-Muslims alike – and will be asked to pay the price by God in the Hereafter.[784] Speaking on the grounds of such contemplation, Gülen claims, "One of the people I despise most and hold contempt against in this world is Osama Bin Laden for he has stained the luminous face of Islam,"[785] and condemns the 9/11 attacks with the following words: "No terrorist can be a Muslim, and no true Muslim can be a terrorist."[786] When his works are examined, it can be seen that due to his moral standing, Gülen does not make statements about public figures, and that it is only towards this name that he uses words of contempt. Gülen also poses his disapproving attitude of Bin Laden and his followers by stating: "No organization or individual can decide on *jihad* on their own accord."[787] Considering Gülen's unswerving

---

[781] Ibn Hisham, *Sirah*, Vol. 4, p. 51.

[782] Gülen, *Fasildan Fasila-1 (From Chapter to Chapter*, Vol. 1), p. 278.

[783] Gülen, *Yenilenme Cehdi (Endeavor for Renewal)*, Kirik Testi series, Vol. 12, p. 268.

[784] ibid., p. 267.

[785] Gülen, "A Real Muslim cannot be a Terrorist."

[786] ibid.

[787] Nuh Gonultas (ed.), *Gurbette Fethullah Gülen, Türkiye'nin Baska Fethullah Gülen'i Yok (Gülen in a Foreign Land: Turkey Does Not Have Another Gülen)*, (Istanbul: Zaman Kitap 2004), p. 117.

approach to the issue, it could be said that the Sunnah does not leave any doors ajar to terrorism or the forming of a terrorist group in any way.[788]

It is verified through historical records that even whilst enduring the toughest oppression in Mecca, Prophet Muhammad, upon whom be peace and blessings, always advised patience and was an embodiment of peace and compromise. He always preferred refraining from being the side that provoked or caused disputes. Hence, the famous poet of the Age of Ignorance, Imru'l-Qays' modality becomes of use in shedding light on the issue: "There are two things that you cannot halt at your will once you ignite them: fire and war!"[789]

The Sunnah's Influence on Conflict Resolution

According to Gülen, the Sunnah ascribes every individual with the responsibility of preventing possible harm. In situations where physical intervention is not an option in stopping a wrongdoing, it is advised that one must approach the issue with wise words and counsel. If intervention by the tongue is also not possible, one must at least despise the act by heart and show no affirmation. Issues should be looked to be handled from this triangle, for the Noble Prophet says: "When one of you witnesses wrongdoing, he should make it right with his hands. If he cannot achieve this, he should advise that the act is wrong and try to prevent the harm. If he is not able to carry this out either, he must at least feel the weight of the misdoing in his conscience and be able to lament; for this last one is the lowest degree of faith."[790] With this principle, Prophet Muhammad, upon whom be peace and blessings, is seen to bring measures to what individuals can do to prevent damage.[791]

Putting forward the first segment of the hadith about "physical intervention" as enough verification, some may begin a quest to establish their own ways of justice. Thus, Gülen brings clarity to this crucial point in his work. As claimed by Islamic scholars, the right to the power of physical

---

[788] Gülen, *Yasatma Ideali* (So That Others May Live), pp. 212-213.
[789] Gülen, *Vuslat Mustusu*, *Kirik Testi* series, Vol. 8, p. 229.
[790] Muslim, *iman* 78; *Tirmidhi*, *fitan* 11; Abu Dawud, *salat* 239.
[791] M. Fethullah Gülen, *Dirilis Cagrisi* (A Call to Revival), *Kirik Testi* series, Vol. 6, (Istanbul: Nil Publishing, 2011), p. 38.

intervention belongs to the government;[792] every individual is obligated to consult the government regarding this point. However, Gülen's take of this facet of the hadith is more interesting. He places more importance on being a powerful nation that owns a potent justice system, instead of confining oneself to being a third class community that accepts living under the rules of a nondescript regime. Hence, he believes in assigning responsibilities to every citizen for their country to earn an important global status.[793] A government that is constructed by communities well-founded in and equipped with knowledge and spirituality will be a system in which violence and terror will find no opportunity to surface. In view of this, Gülen stresses that all the problems humanity faces can be resolved with proper education. In a sense, he points to education as the perpetrator and says: "It is the fault of poor education. Education was the instrument that could have prevented these matters. That is to say, Islamic education has thus far not reached its potential and has been a failure. We have not been able to teach humankind how to refrain from evil and adopt kindness for the sake of God."[794]

With this comment, Gülen shows his persistence about the necessity of sparing time for education although it may take a long period of time. This also illustrates that the focal point of his mission is education. He says, "Retaliating to acts of terror within the society with similar tactics will only intensify the ongoing violence and increase the friction."[795] However, it is not possible to speak of such violence amongst a society that is made up of properly educated individuals.

Gülen draws attention to the fact that under the condition of protecting public dignity, those with opposing views could be communicated with in order to solve problems, bring about peace, and prevent terror.[796] According to him, the paths to peace should be founded and framed to maintain harmony between nations and countries. Thus, he states: "The good lays in peace and peace is always beneficial,"[797]

---

[792] ibid.
[793] ibid.
[794] Akman, *Gurbette Fethullah Gülen (Gülen in a Foreign Land)*, (Istanbul: Zaman Kitap, 2004).
[795] Gülen, *Sonsuz Nur-2* (Muhammad: The Messenger of God, Vol. 2), p. 123.
[796] Gülen, *Vuslat Mustusu (Glad Tidings of a Reunion), Kirik Testi* series, Vol. 8, p. 230.
[797] Gülen, "Sulh Hayirdir, Hayir Sulhtadir," herkul.org, http://www.herkul.org/herkul-nag-me/195-nagme-sulh-hayirdir/.

commenting on the Quranic verse, *"Peace brings goodness (and certainly, it is the greatest of goodness.)"*[798]

Based on Gülen's commentary, it could be understood that compromise is seen as a principle in establishing communal harmony; it is the only way to ease all-encompassing peace. At this point, the Noble Prophet's excellent character and Sunnah serve as important resources in shaping Gülen's ideology.[799] To him, these two resources contain veritable parameters in the name of solving problems for the safety of humankind.

Throughout history, disputes, war and terror have never been a useful part of any equation assembled to solve the problems of the society. They have always brought about unrest and division, diminishing any values that could have coexisted and destroying any bridges that could have been the meeting point of different nations and cultures.

It is not possible for any argument or rationale put forward by terrorist groups formed under the name of *jihad* to fall back on examples from the Sunnah. There are no loopholes in the fundamental Hadith collections that could be utilized as the breeding grounds of terrorism. However, the methods put forward to solve problems through education, dialogue, respect and religious morals are innumerable in Prophetic Practice. These values have formed and are still forming "oases of peace" for those truly seeking peace.

---

[798] Qur'an 4:128
[799] Gülen, *Sonsuz Nur-2 (Muhammad: The Messenger of God,* Vol. 2), p.123.

CHAPTER FIVE

GÜLEN AS A STUDENT OF HADITH

Gülen's Teachers and His Works

The previous sections of this work focused on examining the Sunnah and Gülen's understanding of the Sunnah in both classical and modern framework. In this chapter, attention will be drawn to the background that influenced Gülen's acquisition in Hadith science, and the figures and reasons that encouraged him to follow the Sunnah. This objective will assist in introducing the Gülen ideology that has motivated a large- scale community to take action upon approaches presented to resolve the issues of the modern era. At this juncture, the portrait of the profiles that Gülen seeks to represent with his works will be faintly illustrated, as the factors and methods that motivate Gülen to take action have the potency to set cornerstones for the Sunnah- oriented education of future generations.

Along with this, the books and theories that Gülen follows regarding the learning and teaching of the Sunnah will also be focused on. This will enable one to detect and take note of techniques of teaching the Sunnah that may be suitable for the current era.

Gülen's Teachers

Firstly, it is important to understand the exemplary human profile that also influenced Gülen's life. Some of his remarks may be considered as descriptive of the profile he seeks to see. The following comment is an example that points to the human prototype he aims for: "A person is of value the further he stands from harboring negative feelings... The physical facet of good manners can be observed by anyone; the main point is to nurture your thoughts and feelings to elevate your true character."[800] When his activities are carefully examined, it can be seen that this criterion becomes an embodiment, and is an answer to the type of exemplary person he imagines. When viewed from this point, it can be said that the factors that influence him in both a spiritual and scholarly sense are the Sunnah, moral figures and his teachers.

Growing up to listen to the lives of his grandfathers recounted by his elders has had a large impact on the wisdom and morale of Gülen. His great grandfather Molla Ahmed, his grandfather Samil Agha and

---

[800] Gülen, *Olcu Ve Yoldaki Isiklar (Pearls of Wisdom)*, p. 167

his grandmother Munise Hanim are symbols of righteousness with a religious lifestyle that has reflected on Gülen's own life. The respect that his father Ramiz Efendi had towards scholars and the Sunnah has also left permanent impressions on Gülen's manners and spiritual life. He remembers his father as one who constantly occupied himself with worship and knowledge.[801] His father's two-year retreat away from his village to do further study and earn fluency in Arabic and Persian was also a significant impact on Gülen's eagerness to learn. Along with this, his mother Refia Hanim's efforts to help him learn how to read the Qur'an at the age of four despite the restrictive and deterring rules of the ultra-secular Turkish government has evidently settled in his conscience.[802] Being the first teacher in his life, Gülen's mother draws attention to his outstanding memory, claiming that even during his early childhood, he would be able to memories a section of a book after reading it once or twice.[803]

It could be said that Gülen's interest and enthusiasm towards Islamic studies were further triggered by the pressure of the prohibitions set by the ultra-secular government against religious education. Due to this, Gülen showed effort to further prosper with every scholar that visited his home; and with the negative societal and governmental structure that surrounded him throughout his adolescence, it could be claimed that he naturally developed an idea of a new community that revolved around the axis of the Sunnah.

As mentioned before, alongside the discipline and manners he acquired from his family, Gülen's childhood and youth were also influenced by various scholarly figures. Mehmed Lutfi Afandi, the Imam of Alvar, and his elder brother Vehbi Afandi as well as Sirri Afandi and Shahabaddin Afandi, the two sheiks of Tagh, Halil Hoja and Harun Afandi are amongst the characters that Gülen has benefited from.[804]

---

[801] fgulen.com, "Years of Education," (September 15, 2001), http://fgulen.com/en/fethul-lah-gulens-life/1304-biography/24652-years-of-education?hitcount=0.

[802] Erdogan, *Fethullah Gülen Hocaefendi, Kucuk Dunyam (Fethullah Gulen: My Small World)*.

[803] fgulen.com, "Fethullah Gülen'in Mualla Validesi Merhume Refia Gülen," fgulen.com, http://fgulen.com/tr/fethullah-gulen-kimdir/gulen-hakkinda/fethullah-guleni-taniyan-lardan/166-fgulen-com-Fethullah-Gulenin-Mualla-Validesi-Merhume-Refia-Gulen?hit-count=0.

[804] Erdogan, *Fethullah Gülen Hocaefendi: Kucuk Dunyam (Fethullah Gulen: My Small World)*.

However, Gülen refers to Mehmed Lutfi Afandi of Alvar (d. 1956), as the person from whom he received the foundations of his spiritual and scholarly sustenance until the age of 16. His unshakable adherence to the Sunnah and the Noble Prophet's Companions was also ingrained by this figure in his life.[805] The following words of Mehmed Lutfi Afandi of Alvar seem to mark the beginning of a revival in Gülen: "Heedlessness is the biggest disaster to fall upon humanity"[806] Such expressions of the scholar have given rise to Gülen's desire to restore the Noble Prophet's Sunnah as a lifestyle. Gülen frequently cites his teacher throughout his works, presenting him as an exemplary figure. With this approach, he aims to keep historical personas alive in the memories of communities.

Works That Gülen Has Read

Written works that Gülen reads can be classified into two groups: "positive" knowledge, which relates to an accumulation of great encyclopedic wisdom, and knowledge of Islamic disciplines, which encompasses books about Arabic morphology, syntax and eloquence, Quranic exegesis, Hadith, and Islamic jurisprudence. Some of the works he studied during his youth on the morphology of Arabic words include *al-Amthila, al-Bina, al-Maqsud, al-Izzi* and *al-Marah*; and a collection of books he studied about the syntax and grammar include *al-Awamil, al-Kafiya, Izhar,* and *Mulla Jami*. Of these, it is known that he has memorized *al-Awamil, al-Kafiya*.[807] Besides practice, memorizing is observed to be the most efficient method of learning the Arabic language, and this method shows similarity to the way the Prophet's Companions kept record of the hadiths they heard. Being used by Gülen to also keep a mental note of hadiths, this method has a high chance of having originated from the Sunnah, as speech and the learning of a language is dependent on practice rather than memory.[808]

---

[805] Unal, *M. Fethullah Gülen, Bir Portre Denemesi* (*M. Fethullah Gülen: A Portrait Essay*), p. 495.

[806] ibid., p. 121.

[807] Cemal Turk and Ergun Capan, "Fethullah Gülen Hocaefendi'nin Bilinmeyen Bir Yonu: Ders Ve Tedris Metodu," *Yeni Umit*, Issue 89, (July-September 2010).

[808] Discussion with Fethullah Gülen's student Cuma Ordu: *Reflection of Gülen's Thoughts on Academia*, July 26, 2014.

During his earlier education, Gülen also studied *Multaqa al-Abhur* and *Mir'at al-Usul* on Islamic jurisprudence, *Talkhis, Mukhtasar al-Ma'ani* and *Majma' al-Mutun* on eloquence, and Ushi's *Bad' al-Amali* and Qadi Baydawi's *Tawali' al-Anvar* on scholastic theology. From amongst these masterpieces, he has memorized the texts of *Talkhis* and *Bad' al Amali*. Alongside these, he studied Qadi Baydawi's *Anwar al-Tanzil* and *Tafsir al-Jalalayn* on Quranic exegesis, *Mughni al-Tullab* on logic, and memorized Imam Busiri's *Qasidat al-Burda*, the ode of praise for the Noble Prophet. Regarding Hadith science, he has read majority of the books to be mentioned in the following sections.[809] When it is considered that he learnt how to read the Qur'an at the age of 4, and had memorized it by the age of 12, a conviction about Gülen's healthy analysis of Islamic sciences could be established. It is possible to reach this conclusion about a great pool of knowledge that was first formed at an early age and updated consistently.

It is known that alongside his extensive background in Islamic knowledge, Gülen has also read majority of the Turkish, Western and world literary masterpieces. In addition, his ability to compare different perspectives on history, philosophy and social sciences with his detailed knowledge of the fields is outstanding.[810]

Gülen as a Teacher of Hadith and His Teaching Methods

In order to comprehend Gülen's understanding of the Prophetic reports (*Hadith*) and the Prophetic Practice (*Sunnah*), it is important to educate and be educated by the wisdom of the Sunnah, to understand issues like the role of teachers and students, and to examine Gülen's approach to all of these. Hence, it is important to analyze **Gülen's perspective on such issues before examining his method of teaching the** Sunnah.

A Scholar in the Islamic Tradition According to Gülen

Due to the manners he was brought up by, Gülen considers the Noble Prophet's Sunnah as a role model for educators. In Gülen's approach, the

---

[809] Cemal Turk and Ergun Capan, "Fethullah Gülen Hocaefendi'nin Bilinmeyen bir Yonu: Ders ve Tedris Metodu."

[810] Muhammad Sarkawi, "Klasik ve Modern Ilimleri Sentezleyen Alim" (A Scholar Who Have Synthesized the Classical and Modern Sciences), *Zaman Daily,* July 1, 2014.

Noble Prophet is a teacher whose manners are cultivated by God's.[811] He is an educator who is able to respond to every individual and community's needs accurately.[812] He is also one of God's Messengers who is able to channel wisdom and knowledge to people through representation. Therefore, it is possible to find doctrines and principles of education that apply to people of every level in the Noble Prophet's methods.[813] When this angle is examined, it could be concluded that teachers are the people who could raise and protect an orderly community.[814] An educator is one who teaches manners through representing them, using love, compassion, tolerance and respect as educational criteria. The cultivation of one's character is an affair that has long been addressed and studied by people competent in the field of Sufism.[815] Today, it is considered the most important aspect of education, and **Gülen is in a constant struggle to represent this affair through methods resourced from the** Sunnah. A teacher is one who strives to elevate student's potential to make them useful to humanity throughout a programmed time. If this matter is to be one's journey through education, this would manifest in all education levels. A teacher needs to be able to foresee this time course and prepare the student for events that they may come across throughout their lives.[816] In this instance, one remembers the Noble Prophet's devotion towards his Muslim community and hence his agility towards protecting and educating them by warning them of incidents that may take place in the future (therefore, the news he has given about future events should always be taken into account). This also strengthens the possibility that the importance Gülen places the focus on improving a student's chastity throughout his education roots in the Sunnah.

Through his following statement, Gülen aims to imply that a teacher should also be an educator: "Teaching is different from educating. Anyone can become a teacher if they wish, but only a minority will be able

---

[811] "My God cultivated me, and goodly cultivated," Ali al-Muttaqi, *Kanz al-Ummal*, 11/406.
[812] Gülen, *Cag Ve Nesil 1* (The Modern Age and the Contemporary Generation, Vol. 1), (Istanbul: Nil Publishing, 2009), p. 122.
[813] ibid., p. 123.
[814] ibid., p. 114.
[815] Gülen, *Yol Mulahazalari (Contemplating the Journey)*, Prism series, Vol. 6, p. 135.
[816] Gülen, *Kirik Testi-1 (The Broken Jug series*, Vol. 1*)*. p, 135.

to earn the title of an educator."[817] In short, Gülen believes that the term "teacher" should also be able to carry the essence of an educator for, in the implementation of the Sunnah, the Noble Prophet played the role of both a teacher and an educator that guided, protected and watched over his Companions and community. According to Gülen, a teacher is a guide who is able to encourage, teach and lead to what is right with patience and persistence.[818] Hence, Gülen holds teachers and educators equal and encourages unity.[819] Herewith, by adopting the essence of an educator, a teacher would be able to conquer the hearts of students and create an atmosphere they could seek refuge in when they encounter difficulties. In an environment as such, problems will not find ground that will allow them to develop any further.

In the modern period, the learning tools and technologies such as newspapers, books, radio, television and the internet are accepted as educational resources that can contribute to some extent. However, it is the educator as an only resource who works on improving his student's mental and spiritual welfare with love and respect. Nothing could healthily replace the role of such a figure.[820] It is with this understanding that an educational institution can be transformed into a place where physics, science and social studies are tools in reading the book of the universe. Otherwise, it cannot be said that the institution and its teachers will function to fulfill expectations, as the students will only be fed with theoretical information.[821] When closely examined, it is seen that Gülen strives to enrich the principles of education by emphasizing the importance of love and sincerity. He searches for ways to solve the problems and approach the spirituality of students who are thrown into self-centeredness and solitude with the materialism surrounding them. Hence, he has belief that problems can be solved through a relationship between teachers and students constructed on mutual love and respect. When this ideology is evaluated through the following hadith, it is certain that Gülen's method of cultivating the manners of a person is

---

[817] Gülen, *Olcu Ve Yoldaki Isiklar* (Pearls of Wisdom), p. 169.
[818] Gülen, *Buhranlar Anaforunda Insan (Humankind within a Whirlpool of Crises)*, Cag ve Nesil series, Vol. 2, (Istanbul: Nil Publishing, 2011), p. 104.
[819] Gülen, *Olcu Ve Yoldaki Isiklar (Pearls of Wisdom)*, p. 169.
[820] Gülen, *Cag Ve Nesil* series, Vol. 1, p. 115.
[821] ibid., p. 91.

founded by his reliance on the ways of the Noble Prophet: "He who does not show affection towards youth and he who does not show respect towards the elderly is not of us."[822]

Along with this, within the system of education he has woven, Gülen does not neglect people of different religions and cultures, and tries to relate to them by presenting them with examples that concern their native values. As a result, growing familiar with the values of the community he was raised in assists a student in discovering his own identity. An example of Gülen's tolerance and respect is his belief in and his adoption of the principles of Prophet Jesus, upon whom be peace. According to Gülen, Prophet Jesus advised patience and gentleness to his disciples even at the time of the attempt for his crucifixion, and has thus displayed a righteous mission.[823] Through such tolerance he shows towards different beliefs and faith traditions, Gülen proves that he does not agree with having any boundaries in the criteria set for both providing and receiving an education, and that he is ready to be accepting of positive values regardless of which culture they originate from. Although it is a weak narration when evaluated with the Hadith criteria, Gülen is seen to point to the following saying frequently: "Seek knowledge even if you have to go as far as China."[824] It is possible that Gülen's values have been influenced by similar hadiths. During the time of Prophet Muhammad, upon whom be peace and blessings, tribes living in the geography of present-day China held beliefs such as Buddhism, Hinduism, Brahmanism and Shintoism. However, due to the respect he had towards these tribes and their religions, he does not show nearby provinces as a target in the previous hadith, but points to a land then unknown to them for the most part.[825] Hence, he accepts every culture and religion with its own essence, and emphasizes the knowledge and wisdom to be learnt from each. A teacher with the characteristics of an educator will be capable of finding ways of teaching the right kind of knowledge whilst keeping his respect towards other perspectives intact.

---

[822] Tirmidhi, *Birr*, 15; Abu Dawud, *Sunan*, Adab, 66
[823] Gülen, *Cag Ve Nesil* series, Vol. 1, p. 115.
[824] al-Bayhaqi, *Shuab al-Iman* 2/253; Ibn Abd al-Barr, *Jami' Bayan al-Ilm*, p. 9; Jami' al-Saghir, 1/310, Hadith No: 640.
[825] Gülen, *Kalp Ibresi (The Heart's Cursor)*, pp. 240-241

Gülen's Teaching Methods

Which method does Gülen, who summarizes education by defining the difference between an educator and a teacher, use to teach his personal students? Does his approach share similarities or show differences to known methods?

Gülen's lessons to exclusive circles of students started within his first year of working as an imam (prayer leader) in Edirne. Keeping within the boundaries of the Sunnah, he prefers keeping track of his students and meeting their needs personally. Despite his old age (b. 1941), Gülen has not abandoned this approach. Within this understanding of education, the numbers of Gülen's students are subject to change every year and are usually a group of 10-18 people. Elected students are usually graduates of theology[826] who are proficient in Islamic sciences as Gülen's lessons are of a structure that further master and expand on the details of content learnt at the faculty. After undertaking the studies for a certain period of time (which differs between 1-4 years), students who are willing to raise their own pupils or undertake further study in a field of research are permitted to leave the circle.

Daily discussions are held for three hours in the early and productive hours of each morning. During the remaining times of the day, the students review the lectures given and prepare for the content of the next lesson. The time is also utilized by reading the books recommended by Gülen and researching about any progress made in the world of science.[827] The fact that students mostly reside in the same location as Gülen is comparable to the traditional madrasah education, whilst the atmosphere established with the daily routines evoke the culture of a dervish lodge.[828] Hence, the system followed by Gülen shares many similarities with long-established methods of education. At this point, it is also important to indicate that Gülen spares 3-4 minutes for prayer before each lesson, spiritually preparing his students for the session.[829] When such elements of his work are taken into account, it is

---

[826] Gülen sometimes allowed graduates of science to attend his lessons. He asked for their professional opinions whilst interpreting a *hadith*.

[827] Interview with Gülen's student Recep Dogan regarding *Fethullah Gülen's Teaching Methods in Islamic Science,* July 2, 2014.

[828] A place where sessions of prayers, dhikr and religious or scientific discussions are held.

[829] *Reflection of Gülen's Thoughts on Academia.*

seen that Gülen considers the Noble Prophet and his Companions as his main resource and role model. Throughout the books he has authored, Gülen frequently expresses that he intends to persevere with the teaching system that he has established under the light of the Sunnah.

During his Hadith lessons, Gülen opts to examine masterpieces written on Hadith and elaborate on aspects that concern the contemporary time. In conjunction with this, he concentrates on the teaching of *Rijal* (a study of the reporters of Hadith), which is an Islamic discipline he finds to be important in comprehending the science of Hadith. Although it is a field that has been abandoned by researchers today, Gülen persists on educating his students on this matter and discusses every reporter of Hadith mentioned in the chain. In order to achieve this and make his students well versed in the field, Gülen emphasizes the main characteristics of each narrator of every hadith.[830] Along with this, a hadith is studied closely and its authenticity or weakness (due to the discontinuity in the chain of its narrators or the lack of integrity of its transmitters) as well as the commentaries made regarding it and the decrees that have been or may be drawn from it are all analyzed before new commentaries are made on the hadith. Gülen also adds assumptions of what the hadith may have implied for its own era to his evaluations.[831]

It is also important to mention that Gülen chooses different books to study with different groups of students for every new period of instruction and hence makes it possible to cover all the written works that have been recorded under the field of Hadith or any other Islamic sciences.[832] The books that Gülen has thus far utilized as resources whilst teaching the Hadith science can be another research area.

Lesson Preparations

It is a common practice for teachers today to encourage students to prepare for the class before they attend. Although it is difficult to enforce this upon large classes in short amounts of time, it is still considered to be a method that is the key to success. This practice also stands out amongst Gülen's method of teaching. The exclusive circles of students

---

[830] Canan, *Fethullah Gülen'in Sunnet Anlayisi*, p. 82.
[831] *Reflection of Gülen's Thoughts on Academia.*
[832] ibid.

taking his lessons get prepared beforehand for the content to be studied in the next class. Some of these preparations include learning the meanings, pronunciations and characteristics of each and every word in a text.[833] In essence, it is important for the students to have understood the context of situation and be able to generate questions. This allows them to contribute effectively, saving them from being dependent only upon the passed-down knowledge and, hence, the ground for new and revised commentary is established.

On the other hand, the student reads aloud the notes he makes prior to the lesson and Gülen makes explanations wherever he sees the need to. The topic is also compared to other relevant masterpieces. For example, Bukhari's books of commentary are read during Hadith classes and their characteristics are discussed in detail.[834] Questions asked during this time avail in benefiting from new and unique commentary made by Gülen.[835]

As mentioned before, this method that Gülen applies shares similarities with methods practiced by the traditional education system, demonstrating that the system he was raised by is still applicable for today's age. Unlike this system, however, Gülen does not place the main focus on memorizing the rules of the science of Arabic grammar but rather prefers to concentrate on its vital sections.[836] By means of this, the quick-wit of the students is challenged to improve, and the wasting of time that memorizing usually causes is prevented. Hence, Gülen strives to follow a more efficient way of teaching whilst ensuring that his students have the competency to study an extensive range of topics. As this encourages his pupils to practice perseverance, it creates a more resourceful system of education that is constructed under the light of traditions.

Summarizing

Another method Gülen practices is summarizing, which is seen to be influenced by examples from the Qur'an and manner of the Sunnah

---

[833] Canan, Fethullah Gülen'in Sunnet Anlayisi, p. 79.
[834] Ergun Capan, "Fethullah Gülen Hocaefendi'nin Bilinmeyen Bir Yonu: Ders Ve Tedris Metodu."
[835] Canan, *Fethullah Gülen'in Sunnet Anlayisi*, p. 79.
[836] *Regarding Fethullah Gülen's Teaching Methods in Islamic Sciences*

(which is expressing the ultimate with minimal wording). On the one hand, the Almighty God taught Prophet Adam, upon whom be peace, the necessary knowledge and wisdom in summary and Gülen draws attention to the fact that whilst knowledge of sciences was also given to Prophet Muhammad, upon whom be peace and blessings, in brief, the Sunnah was responsible for explanations of the details where relevant.[837] On the other hand, it could be seen that Prophet Adam presenting the angels with a summary of the universe by teaching them the names of creations (with God's permission) meant he was acquainted with extensive knowledge condensed with essentials.[838] Hence, Gülen decides that learning something with its abstract is of underestimated value. Summarizing also hastens intellectual development and the ability to reason, whilst preventing mental inertia.

With this way of thought, Gülen draws attention to the impossibility of reading all the written masterpieces and the ease offered by learning with summaries. Hence, he encourages every student to summaries the book given to one twentieth.[839] By doing this, Gülen aims to achieve a collective understanding of the topic being taught, which in turn also aids in utilizing time effectively and prevents waste of time. By this means, a result that is not mutually or collectively achieved can be abandoned for the better.

In order to raise students well versed in science, Gülen recommends for every book in the relevant fields to be made available to students and be distributed evenly to small groups. This aims to summaries, analyze and hence recompose large numbers of written works.[840] This procedure being followed by every student and the summaries being discussed by large groups of people leaves a door ajar to rejuvenated commentary and ideologies. This method, for example, is not a practice that was common for the traditional system of education

---

[837] Gülen, Kur'an'nin Altin Ikliminde (In the Light of the Qur'an's Golden Climate), (Istanbul: Nil Publishing, 2011), p. 30.

[838] Gülen, *Asrin Getirdigi Tereddutler (Questions and Answers about Islam*, Vol. 2), pp. 174-179.

[839] Ergun Capan, "Fethullah Gülen Hocaefendi›nin Bilinmeyen bir Yonu: Ders Ve Tedris Metodu."

[840] Gülen, *Yasatma Ideali (So That Others May Live)*, p. 93.

and this demonstrates that the educational disciplines adopted by Gülen are influenced by paradigms in the Qur'an and the Sunnah.

Gülen supports his theory by giving Said Nursi as an example. According to him, Nursi was able to raise a large number of students due to the fact that he summarized the books of the *Risale-i Nur* collection as he taught them. Gülen considers this method to be significantly effective, as the student being able to compose summarized answers to "what have I gathered from this?" after every discussion is of unparalleled benefit.[841] Students schooled by him agree that Gülen has been practicing this method for a long time and that is indeed rewarding.[842]

Since it is impossible to mention all the books summarized[843] by them, it is beneficial to name a few.[844]

Comparing, Discussing and Commenting

Gülen's students express that the lessons he conducts are constructed upon following different notions from different books, hence illustrating a method of learning aided by comparison. He is able to establish new and original commentaries by analyzing the correlation between the knowledge acquired by previous eras and the science accepted today, the science of Hadith being the leading link of the chain. This also inspires the students to advance in their abilities to criticize and make remarks. In order to avoid discrepancy in the comments made, Gülen ensures that the main resource is read and weighed carefully, whilst its content is evaluated according to the aspects that concern today's age.[845] At this point, it is necessary to indicate that Gülen does not use definite or conclusive statements when deliberating and commenting on Hadith. Rather, he focuses on possibilities and leaves doors open to further remarks by making statements like, "This hadith could be understood in

---

[841] Gülen, *Kirik Testi series*, Vol. 1.
[842] *Regarding Fethullah Gülen's Teaching Methods in Islamic Sciences*
[843] Ergun Capan, "Fethullah Gülen Hocaefendi'nin Bilinmeyen Bir Yonu: Ders Ve Tedris Metodu."
[844] Mustafa Sabri, *Mawqif al-Aql wa al-Ilm wa al-Alam min Rabb al-Alamin wa Rasulihi*; Shurnubi, *Hikam-i Ataiya-Sharhi*; M. Ajjaj al-Khatib, *al-Sunnat Qabla al-Tadwin*; M. Tahir ibn Ashur, *Maqasid al-Sharia al-Islamiyya*; Izz al-Din Abd al-Aziz ibn Abd al-Salam, *Qawa'id al-Ahkam fi Masalih al-Anam*.
[845] *Regarding Fethullah Gülen's Teaching Methods in Islamic Sciences*

this way" or "The following meaning could be derived from this hadith." In this way, he does not limit the applicability the essence of the hadith could have for different eras. An example of this is Noble Prophet's words about a creature that is said to emerge before Doomsday: "*Dabbat al-ard* is going to appear, roam the universe and will be visible from every angle." Whilst some Islamic thinkers claim that this hadith foreshadowed AIDS, Gülen points out that it is not plausible to interpret it so and place a definite label on the underlying meaning of the Noble Prophet's words.[846]

Similar to the Qur'an, Gülen highlights that Hadith also speak to and address different eras. If AIDS was to be labeled as *Dabbat al-ard* and a cure was to be found for it, the Noble Prophet's interpretation would be found unreasonable and the credibility of the Sunnah would be damaged. Hence, the real *Dabbat al-ard* to emerge before Judgment Day would not be recognized, and the implication of the Noble Prophet's words would never be discovered. Consequently, it is not appropriate to make conclusive statements when commenting on hadiths, and claiming to have discovered the meaning of the Prophet's interpretation. The matter requires being approached with possibilities and left with question marks.[847] Along with this, Gülen renders his comments regarding *Dabbat al-ard* and other portents of the Hour by reflecting upon the tidings given in different hadiths at different times.[848] For example, many hadiths indicate that *Dabbat* is an incident that will occur before Judgment Day and that immediately after, there will be no believers left to channel belief onto others. However, there is also a hadith stating that the Noble Prophet's message will be heard of and accepted on every land that witnesses the sunrise and sunset.[849] Considering that this glad tiding has not yet surfaced, accepting that *Dabbat al-ard* is AIDS will impoverish the hopes of believers.[850] Thereby, discrepancy between the hadiths will be formed, and their applicability to

---

[846] Gülen, *Questions and Answers about Islam*, (New Jersey: Tughra Books, 2010), pp. 103-112.
[847] ibid.
[848] ibid.
[849] Muslim, *fitan* 19; Abu Dawud, *fitan* 1; Tirmidhi, *fitan* 14; Ibn Hanbal, *al-Musnad* 4/123, 5/278.
[850] Gülen, *Questions and Answers About Islam*, pp. 103-112.

different ages will be questioned. The tidings given in the first hadith enlighten humanity about incidents to take place before Judgment Day; however, its scope cannot be confined to one definite meaning. This approach of Gülen could also mean that he opposes any kind of conclusive attitude towards a matter.

In addition to this, Gülen takes care to discuss the content of Hadith and Sunnah in conjunction with various branches of science.[851] By doing this, he draws attention to the points of intersection between Hadith and today's fields of science, enabling himself and others to construct a scientific commentary; in one respect, this produces a notion unique to him. Herein, it is important to express that during extensive discussions of the topics, Gülen does not take the footnotes into consideration with all their details.[852] Hence, on the one hand, he prevents the wasting of time by focusing especially on the aspects of sections that concern the current age. On the other hand, keeping within the boundaries of respect, Gülen does not abstain from criticizing old commentaries. At points where he considers certain commentaries inappropriate, Gülen expresses that in respect of the specific era it was written in, he would have phrased his remarks differently. When evaluating hadith in accordance with today's age, Gülen weaves his opinion by frequently stating, "It might be more appropriate if this hadith was interpreted in this way for its applicability to our time."[853] Whilst his approach demonstrates that he accepts the Sunnah as a solution, it also implies that individuals competent in the field of Hadith science can make certain contributions to commentaries.

The Question and Answer Method

The most effective method that Gülen uses in both his lessons and public sermons is the question and answer method. During the lessons, questions asked by students having difficulty are all answered by Gülen and, if need be, questions are also asked by Gülen himself.[854] Whilst applying this method, Gülen does not permit time loss by answering questions that

---

[851] *Regarding Fethullah Gülen's Teaching Methods in Islamic Sciences*
[852] ibid.
[853] *Reflection of Gülen's Thoughts on Academia*
[854] *Regarding Fethullah Gülen's Teaching Methods in Islamic Sciences*

have been answered before, and he bases[855] this on examples of the Sunnah.[856] Throughout his lifetime, Gülen used this method at mosques, coffee houses and during sermons. He currently practices it with the students he raises.[857]

Using Technology for Educational Purposes

Gülen consistently pursues every progress made with regard to studying the Sunnah, and encourages his students to do the same with any and every kind of technical facility. When Gülen compares today's circumstances with that of the Prophet's Companions, he emphasizes that with facilities such as computers, the internet and television that allow scientific data to be collected and distributed effortlessly, believers should be able to reach the immaculate level of performance that the Companions had demonstrated.[858] With this, Gülen gives his students goals that will constantly renew themselves, and presents humanity with a research method that will involve following up with new developments and commentaries regarding the Sunnah with technical fluency. By the practicing of this method, Gülen aims to establish sound archives of resources, easy access to these and hence utilize time effectively.

The Islamic Sources Taught by Gülen

It is sufficient to touch upon a few of the fundamental resources in the field of Hadith without discussing the books followed by Gülen in detail. These resources are highly regarded and followed by Gülen as

---

[855] M.Fethullah Gülen, "Dogru Yer ve Zamanda Dogru Sorular Sorulmali," (March 3, 2006), http://fgulen.com/tr/fethullah-gulenin-kursu-akademi-yazilari/fethullah-gulen-2006-kursuleri/12007-Fethullah-Gulen-Zaman-Dogru-Yer-ve-Zamanda-Dogru-Sorular-Sorulmali?highlight=WyJzb3J1bGGFyIl0=.

[856] One of the lucid examples of the Prophetic Practice was when Angel Gabriel had appeared in human form to the Noble Prophet and his Companions, asking questions to the Prophet about iman, Islam, benevolence and the Hereafter. The Noble Prophet answered them, thus enlightening his Companions (Bukhari; Muslim; Abu Dawud; Tirmidhi; Ibn Majah).

[857] Gülen, "Soru-Cevaplar Uzerine," (May 20, 2008), http://fgulen.com/tr/fethullah-gulenin-butun-eserleri/prizma-serisi/fethullah-gulen-zihin-harmani/15518-Fethullah-Gulen-Soru-Cevaplar-Uzerine.

[858] Gülen, *Yasatma Ideali (So That Others May Live)*, (Istanbul: Nil Publications, 2010), pp. 201-202.

they shelter the topical aspects of Hadith.[859] He is consistently in an Endeavour to ensure his students are raised as competent individuals in their knowledge of these resources. By following this path, he aims to carry both historical and modern collections to the future, preserving the original whilst relaying modernized commentary to the next generations. The following are some of the books that he reads and encourages his students to read to gain knowledge on the field of Hadith:

a) The *Sahih al-Bukhari* collection by Muhammad ibn Ismail al-Bukhari: After the Qur'an, it is regarded as the second most valid book. Gülen ensures the voluminous *Sahih al-Bukhari* is read along with the following commentaries:

    i. *Irshad as-Sari fi Sharh Sahih Al-Bukhari* by al-Qastallani (d. 1517 CE).

    ii. *Umdat al-Qari Sharh Sahih al-Bukhari* (20 Vols). It is one of the most important commentaries based on *Sahih al-Bukhari* by Badr al-Din al-Ayni (d. 1453 CE).

    iii. *Fath al-Bari fi Sharh Sahih al-Bukhari* by Ibn Hajar al-Asqalani (d. 1448 CE).

b) *Sahih Muslim,* which was later, named *al-Musnad al-Sahih* (5 vols) by Imam Abul-Husain Muslim ibn Hajjaj (d. 874 CE).

c) *Sunan* (4 Vols) written by Abu Dawud al-Sijistani (d. 888 CE).

    i. *Badhl al-Majhud fi Hall Sunan Abi Dawud* (10 vols) is a commentary written by Khalil Ahmad Saharanpuri (d. 1927 CE).

    ii. *Al-Manhal al-Adhb al-Mawrud Sharh Sunan Abi Dawud* (10 vols) written by Mahmud ibn Muhammad Khattab as-Subki (d. 1933 CE).

d) *Jami' at-Tirmidhi* by Abu `Isa Muhammad ibn `Isa at-Tirmidhi. (d. 892 CE).

e) *Al-Muwatta* (2 vols) by Malik ibn Anas (d. 795 CE).

f) *Sunan* (2 vols) written by Ahmad ibn Shu`ayb ibn Ali ibn Sinan Abu `Abd ar-Rahman al-Nasa'i (d. 915 CE).

g) *Kitab at-Taj al-Jami* (5 vols) written by M. Ali Nasif.

[859] Ergun Capan, "Fethullah Gülen Hocaefendi'nin Bilinmeyen Bir Yonu: Ders Ve Tedris Metodu."

h) *'Uqud al-Jawahir al-Munifa* (2 vols) written by al-Murtada al-Husayni al-Zabidi (d. 1790 CE).

i) *Kanz al-Ummal* (16 vols) by Ali al-Muttaqi (d. 1567 CE).

j) *Riyad al-Salihin min Kalam Sayyid al-Mursalin* by Zakariyya an-Nawawi (d. 1277 CE).

k) *Ash-Shifa bi Ta'rif Huquq al-Mustafa* (2 vols) by Qadhi Iyadh (d. 1149 CE).

l) *Al Lu'lu Wa'l-Marjan* (2 vols) by Muhammad Fuad Abdul Baqi (d. 1968 CE).

m) *Uqud al-Jawahir al-Munifa* (2 vols) by Imam Az-Zabidi (d. 1790 CE).[860]

When the total amount of the books that Gülen teaches is considered, it is seen that he is right in his claims of having spent his entire life studying the Sunnah. If it is recognized that each of these volumes of books were read and revised several times, the key to Gülen's insistence on writing about the Sunnah in detail throughout his own works would be better understood. When his methods of education are examined, it is seen that Gülen is strongly affiliated with these traditional resources, and is in an attempt to generate their essence to the future as well. With this stance, he aims to preserve the values of Sunnah and take lessons from them that concern today's age whilst staying in search of new methods to develop his notion. In a way, this also aids in preventing the gradual apathy too much familiarity with a specific method may bring about, and preserves the vividness of the Sunnah.

How Do Gülen's Opinions Reflect on Academia

How does the education system and ideology followed by Gülen contribute to the novelty of academia? This question is one of the topics that are most anticipated. The painting portrays a Gülen who started his journey as a Muslim cleric preaching, teaching and leading the Prayers at various mosques, who influenced societies with his education principles globally and about whom seminars, conferences, symposiums and academic research are being held. Although he does not hold a diploma from an official school, Gülen has attracted the attention of many who

---

[860] ibid.

specialize in various fields of study by being a steadfast autodidact in fields of science including medicine, biology and astronomy. The fruits of this accumulation of knowledge can be observed in the books and articles authored by him.[861] Gülen is a prolific thinker who has close to 70 books and a vast range of audio and video recordings in his native Turkish, which are also available in various world languages.

Some Perspectives on Gülen's Educational Practices

Researchers of different universities have made Gülen's contributions to education their field of research. John L. Esposito indicates that it would be more plausible to recognize the success of the schools, universities and organizations established under Gülen's influence rather than scrutinize controversies regarding his ideas. According to him, Gülen has proved that Islam can coexist with modernity and science and aid a change for the better, and has already shown countries such as the USA the effect of this with the schools he inspired.[862] Gülen supports his ideas about education and makes them tangible with the action he takes to achieve them. He is also in an effort to substantiate that Sunnah-oriented practice is able to walk the same lane as modern educational theories. Almazbek Beishenaliev offers a different perspective, and claims that by presenting science with values such as the heart, soul, and manners, Gülen evaluates a person as a whole and hence aims for a communal build founded upon humanistic values. According to Beishanaliev, teachers who are raised by Gülen's views abide by universal notions such as love, friendship, affection and tolerance as criteria for teaching science.[863] Similarly, Loye Ashton argues that love plays the largest role in Gülen's reasoning of education.[864] With such values being adopted, the relationship between teachers and students develop and the school

---

[861] Unal, *M. Fethullah Gülen: Bir Portre Denemesi (Fethullah Gülen: A Portrait Essay)*, p. 17.

[862] John L. Esposito, "The Gülen Movement: Paradigms, Projects, and Aspirations" (paper presented at the Gulen Movement Conference, International House at University of Chicago, November 11-13, 2010).

[863] Almazbek Beishenaliev, *Pedagogical Ideas of F. Gulen and Hizmet Movement on Education*, (Johns Hopkins University, December 4, 2013).

[864] Loye Ashton, "Defending Religious Diversity and Tolerance in America Today: Lessons from Fethullah Gülen," (November 12, 2005), http://fgulen.com/en/gulen-movement/conference-papers/1338-the-fethullah-gulen-movement-i/25503-defending-religious-diversity-and-tolerance-in-america-today-lessons-from-fethullah-gulen?hitcount=0.

becomes a family environment. Loye agrees that according to Gülen, ambitious teachers are ones who pay heed to human beings regardless of the physical and monetary difficulties they experience, and are able to bring together students of different cultures, religions and races to form an atmosphere of peace. Whilst doing so, these teachers are also able to respect the governmental structure, culture and religion of the country they reside in.[865]

Another researcher, Eileen Eppig points to the discovery that there is a strong relationship between Gülen's portrayal of astronomy and the Qur'an. According to her, Gülen accepts the Qur'an as the main source in deciphering the universe and provides tangible evidence to prove that these two are indeed complementary.[866] From Eppig's approach, it is understood that Gülen studies science such as physics laws in conjunction with the Qur'an and the Sunnah, and that knowledge from previous eras can be carried on to the present day, for Gülen believes that the Sunnah plays the role of a guard in protecting philosophical, medical, scientific and mental knowledge. With this insight, Gülen presents a unique approach to the connections between God, human beings and the universe.[867]

The Logic of Reasoning and Researching in Theology

Gülen strives to establish a new format of thinking and calls for academicians in the field of theology to focus on branches of science. To him, besides being well versed in the Qur'an and the Sunnah, a theologian should also become familiar with physics, chemistry, mathematics, anthropology and astronomy.[868] Hence, specialists of theology would be equipped to answer questions posed by people of different sections of society and possess strong theories. Herein, Gülen criticizes the schools of theology in Turkey that have their doors tightly closed on the acquiring of scientific knowledge in conjunction with religious values.[869]

---

[865] Beishenaliev, *Pedagogical Ideas of F. Gulen and Hizmet Movement on Education.*

[866] Eileen Eppig, *Fethullah Gülen's Care for All Creation as a Means to Nonviolence,* (University of Maryland, Oct. 29, 2009).

[867] Gülen, *Kendi Dunyamiza Dogru (Towards Our Own World),* (Istanbul: Nil Publishing, 2011), pp. 66-67.

[868] Gülen, *Yasatma Ideali (So That Others May Live),* p. 116

[869] Unal, *M. Fethullah Gülen Bir Portre Denemesi (Fethullah Gülen: A Portrait Essay),* p. 109.

He believes that this situation is contradictory to both the spiritual and conceptual system of Islam.

It could be said that Said Nursi has had great influence on Gülen's way of thought. Scientific explanations can be found woven along religious narratives throughout Nursi's works. According to Gülen, studying the compatibility the Quranic verses and the Sunnah have with scientific data poses injustice towards those values,[870] for the Qur'an and the Sunnah are regarded as guides and testimonials by researchers. Gülen believes that God's Prophets did not attain scientific results by neither research nor experimental methods, but were granted wisdom and knowledge by God through Divine revelations. Modern science has only recently begun to discover the humankind-universe-God truth that Prophets had advised thousands of years ago. Due to the ambiguous nature of experiments, science is a body that continuously questions itself and searches for innovation. It is constantly in an attempt to safeguard its discoveries with the hypotheses developed and is usually not able to step out of the circle that contains the already proven. However, besides this are the modern laboratories that study scientific data with advanced technology under the light of Prophetic messages.[871] At this point, Gülen rightfully despises the neglecting of religious resources and encourages them to be regarded as of higher importance. With his mindset, he does not aim to undervalue science, but rather to highlight the synergy between them.

The following conclusion could also be made after considering Gülen's approaches: with his proposal to Turkey's faculties of theology, Gülen is also calling for academicians of the science field to tend to his ideas. He is inviting them to question theories based on an axis of the Qur'an and the Sunnah, hoping to reconstruct the severed bond between religion and science.[872] Gülen hence advises the educational foundations he recommends Turkey to establish to teach science in conjunction with Islamic studies, and strives to create grounds on which this could be achieved.[873]

---

[870] Gülen, *Inancin Golgesinde -2 (Essentials of the Islamic Faith, Vol. 2)*, pp. 159-160.
[871] Gülen, *Kendi Dunyamiza Dogru (Towards Our Own World)*, pp. 141-143.
[872] ibid., p. 86.
[873] Discussion with Fethullah Gülen's student Ibrahim Kocabiyik, *Islam and Science*, July 11, 2014.

It could be drawn from Gülen's ideas that the faculties of theology in Turkey are in need of a reconstructed curriculum. This method will allow the faculty of theology with a curriculum devoid of science to gain depth, create a harmonious bridge between scientific and Islamic studies and establish a wide ranging association between the two branches.

Gülen's proposal to study theology with science holds the power to unify these two different worlds of wisdom and build ground on which research can reach its summit. This situation will revive the belief that the Qur'an and the Sunnah are indeed the main resources of science, and people will thus be on quests to rediscover the vast number of libraries or archives both in Turkey and around the world. Hence, scientific discoveries of previous eras are going to be recognized once more and these historical masterpieces are going to be of great acquisition to the country's cultural values. Besides this, the repeating of mistakes made in the past is also going to be easier to avoid.

Along with his discussed approach, Gülen also takes care to point out to some of the differences between Islamic and prevalent philosophy, and compares the resources of both. According to him, non-Islamic philosophy does not take divinity into account and attributes its theories to human beings, objects and events. It narrows the path of knowledge by giving intelligence priority over belief and accepting observations and discoveries as the fruits of scientific data. As opposed to this, Islamic culture leaves doors open to new commentaries by studying matters under the light of the Qur'an and the Sunnah, using their own intelligence along with scientific perspectives.[874] By touching upon the difference between these two, Gülen presents the Qur'an and the Sunnah as the source of scientific thinking and thus introduces his proposal, preparing ground for the harmony between philosophy, science and religion.

Gülen's discussed proposals could be said to have been influenced by the *madrasa* system of education. According to him, *madrasas*–which literally mean "spaces where lessons are given"–are not places at which one only acquires religious knowledge, but discusses different fields of science

---

[874] Gülen, *Kendi Dunyamiza Dogru* (Towards Our Own World), p. 86.

along with it.[875] Gülen sees the neglecting of science by the *madrasas* of more recent centuries as a detrimental mistake.[876] Islam's understanding and appreciation of science had been proven and a golden age had been lived with these institutions supporting the unity of sciences. However, the neglecting of this system with the centuries that followed caused bigotry and controversy, and mysticism paralyzed any developments that arose.[877]

Gülen believes the great Islamic higher education institutions (*madrasas*) should emerge in the world of academia once more and contribute to education as a system of its own. Along with this, he does not oversee the need for a wider range of Islamic resources to be taught at these institutions, and adds new commentaries and books written on Hadith and Quranic exegesis in the recent years to his list. During discussions held on Quranic exegesis, Gülen claims it a must for at least 20 *tafsir* resources to be found and discussed for each Quranic verse.[878] Gülen presents his own thoughts after sieving them through discussions on and analyses of 20 different books.[879] Hence, this method offers a promising and effective innovation for aspiring theologians. Gülen also recommends the field of *tafsir* to adopt the "science committee" he had proposed for the area of *fiqh* (Islamic jurisprudence), which comprises of individuals with different fields of expertise that are able to verify Quranic verses with current scientific discoveries. He believes that through this, a credible commentary addressing today's matters can be established.[880]

In addition to this, Gülen strongly urges[881] his students to become fluent in 3-4 languages.[882] This demonstrates that he is in an attempt to help theologians studying religion gain different perspectives, for it is important for every masterpiece to be read and studied in its

---

[875] Gülen, *Fasildan Fasila 3* (From Chapter to Chapter, Vol. 3), p. 116.

[876] Unal, *M. Fethullah Gülen Bir Portre Denemesi* (Fethullah Gülen: A Portrait Essay), p. 109.

[877] ibid., pp. 109-110.

[878] Every student attending the lessons would follow at least one or two books about *tafsir* and present the contents' summary to Gülen and his peers during the lessons. As a result, he would contribute to the formation of new and fresh perspectives.

[879] *Reflection of Gülen's Thoughts on Academia.*

[880] Gülen, *Journey to Noble Ideals* (Clifton: Tughra Books, 2014), pp. 94-95.

[881] *Reflection of Gülen's Thoughts on Academia.*

[882] It is known that Gülen is well acquainted with the Ottoman Turkish, Arabic and Persian.

original language. Through this, academicians are better able to integrate with a range of civilizations and cultures. This approach of Gülen shows similarity to the Noble Prophet's advice to his Companions about learning foreign languages. Besides this, Gülen also encourages his students to utilize their time in America by continuing their university education with Masters or PhD degrees in various fields.[883] Such an approach evokes an understanding influenced by Mevlana Jalaluddin Rumi, as his wisdom, spirituality and love oriented thinking can be seen to have reflected on today's affairs by Gülen. It could be claimed that these methods carried out by Gülen will continuously refresh the goals and aspirations of the world of academia, helping it maintain its contemporary nature.

Gülen's enheartening of his students well-versed in theology to study their PhD in different fields also contributes to a vivid sphere of education. For instance, a physics graduate studying his PhD in theology and a graduate of theology doing a PhD on physics may help in constructing a promising bridge between branches of science.[884] This could be understood by comparing the situation to the necessity of performing an angio on a patient with blood clots in his vascular veins so as to prevent further damage.

In order to train them efficiently, Gülen assigns tasks of research about specific topics to his students, and discusses the results with them. For example, topics such as music in Islam, insurance systems, economy, banking and international law are analyzed with consideration of varying perspectives, and a vast range of resources are read to attain the best results.[885] An applied example of the previously discussed academic committee[886] recommended by Gülen can be observed in this method.

Another one of Gülen's significant contributions to theology is having brought back the science of *"rijal"* to the curriculum of Hadith

---

[883] *Reflection of Gülen's Thoughts on Academia.*
[884] During a conference in the USA, we witnessed an academician/researcher in the field of physics who had completed his PhD in theology by evaluating information/data he had come across in the Qur'an and the *Sunnah,* (March 2013).
[885] *Reflection of Gülen's Thoughts on Academia.*
[886] This suggestion of Gülen has been put into practice on a small scale in Istanbul; for now, academicians with expertise in theology are doing the research. However, as conditions allow it, academicians of different fields will be invited to contribute in the future.

science today. Cuma Ordu, a pupil of Gülen, emphasizes that this field had been neglected and forgotten about for several years, and that Gülen has made a great calling of reviving its significance. Ordu claims that whilst Talat Kocyigit–an intellectual renowned in Hadith science–points to the difficulty of becoming learned about the Hadith collection of *Kutub al-Sittah*, he highlights that Gülen has memorized the collection along with its *"rijal."*[887] In addition to this, Canan has further accentuated the importance of the issue by stating: "Unfortunately, the science of *rijal* is a matter that is overlooked in Turkey. I wonder if any corner of the Islamic world has been able to recognize it as something important and apply it as well as Gülen has. I personally do not know, but believe in the necessity of doing so."[888]

The Sensitivity in Making Provision of Islamic Science

Gülen draws attention to the problems in different fields that are issues of expertise in finding a solution to new interpretation and jurisprudence. And he gives meticulous attention to the falsification of religious values and the denial of misjudgment. This is because an error in the center will give rise to considerable misunderstanding and interpretation in the greater society. If jurisprudence and expertise criteria are not taken as the base, the provisions of religion may not come out by authorities and individuals. Furthermore, the Noble Prophet will be spoken by personal thoughts and judgments and the most important values could be made open to unqualified comments.[889]

Due to his calculated hesitations in changing conditions on matters of jurisprudence to be solved in the century, Gülen draws attention to the formation of a committee and assembly.[890] With this, the intention is for the Islamic world to meet in the commonalities and *ijtihad* of the issues of Islamic jurisprudence. Thereby, he prefers to open a new door to unity and togetherness in the Islamic world. According to Gülen, the committee should be formed with the participation of experts and academics in social science, religion and science from every

---

[887] *Reflection of Gülen's Thoughts on Academia.*
[888] Canan, *Fethullah Gülen'in Sunnet Anlayisi*, p. 79.
[889] Gülen, *Mefkure Yolculugu (A Journey into the Ideals)*, p. 156.
[890] Gülen, *Ruhumuzun Heykelini Dikerken 1 (The Statue of Our Souls)*, pp. 58-63

corner of the Islamic geography. In these considerations, he encourages symposiums and conferences to be organized. He sends attestation messages to such programs that he will not be able to attend.[891] For instance, he attended with a message to the "Conferencing and Collective Consciousness" symposium in which the renowned scholars Muhammed Yusuf Niyazi (from Afghanistan), Muhammad Imarah (from Egypt), Rashid al-Ghannushi (from Tunisia), Isam al-Bashir (from Sudan), Muhammadu Sa'ad Ababakar (from Nigeria), Muhammad Mukhtar ash-Shinqitee (from Qatar), Ahmad Abbadi (from Morocco), Muhammad Babaammi (from Algeria) and many other leading Islamic scholars from many different countries participated.[892] At the same time, Gülen draws attention to an important point in the functioning of the committee. *Shura* (consultation and assembly) is a natural right for the administrators and participants of the committee. In the exercise of this right, there is no supremacy of one side against the other as God highlights equality with the following verse (which means): *"...and whose affairs are by consultation among themselves."*[893] In this case everyone will have equal terms whilst resolving the problems of Muslims. Therefore, conflicts such as leadership will not be given the opportunity to arise.

Gülen stresses that consultation "is the first condition for the success of a decision made on any issue" and that it must be a juridical personality, rather than the person of a *mujtahid*, to be consulted on every matter, affair, or problem on which a Divine decree was not revealed. He highlights that the most important mission and duty of resolving affairs concerning the individual and the community, the people and the state, science and knowledge, and economics and sociology belongs to such a consultative personality, unless of course there is a Divine decree – a verse of the Qur'an or a command from the Prophet, decisive on these matters. Following the Prophetic Practice, Gülen underlines that today's councils of consultation would be nothing more or less than a simple continuation of the consultation and council that we see in the Prophet's

---

[891] Gülen, "Fethullah Gülen's Message to the International Symposium, Ijtihad and Qiyas: The richness of Islam" (2014), http://fgulen.com/en/press/messages/44412-fethullah-gulens-message-to-the-international-symposium-ijtihad-and-qiyas-the-richness-of-islam?hitcount=0.

[892] http://ortakyolicma.org/sempozyum/ingilizcecontent.

[893] Qur'an 42:38.

model. He says, "The legal decisions issued by such an authoritative council with broad participation are more likely to be met with public acceptance and legitimacy." He further stresses that the conduct and the composition of such a consultative body might change according to different circumstances and eras, but the qualifications and the attributes of those select people, such as people from knowledge, justice, social education and experience, wisdom, and sagacity, should never change.

> Since the matters presented for deliberation require a great degree of knowledge, experience, and expertise, a consultation committee must comprise people who are distinguished for such qualities. This can only be a committee of people of high caliber, who are able to resolve many matters. Especially today, as life has become more intricate and complicated, as the world has globalized, and every problem has become an all-encompassing, planetary problem, it is vital that those competent in natural sciences, engineering, and technology, which are most of the time considered to be good and proper by Muslims, should participate alongside those men of high caliber who know Islamic essence, reality, spirit, and sciences.[894]

Therefore, this committee must be constructed with the coexistence of social science, religion and science experts[895] as their knowledge will be needed for the provision of religious diagnosis and identification. For example, the opinions of economic experts will be needed on matters of public concern such as Islamic banking, insurance and credit use.[896] Gülen points out that there should be professional economists alongside theologians in the committee for an exchange of views. Neither extensive expertise nor religious proficiency will be sufficient as one may not be able to find a solid answer through an analysis of vastly differing opinions. In most cases, there are no committee-driven verdicts on such issues; therefore, incorrect or false views are bound to arise, and provisions will be disregarded, leading to Muslims individually striving to come to their own judgments from their interpretations of the Sunnah. At the same time, consistent and

---

[894]   Gülen, *The Statue of Our Souls*, p. 55.
[895]   *Reflection of Gülen's Thoughts on Academia.*
[896]   *Reflection of Gülen's Thoughts on Academia.*

accurate solutions to social issues will not be present to tend to the needs of the community.

In short, Gülen draws attention to the inadequacy of individual scholarly efforts and highlights the consequent problems that may result. He says, "Even if a person has a superior nature and outstanding intellect, if he is content with his own opinion and is not receptive and respectful to the opinions of others, then he is more prone to make mistakes and errors than the average person." Hence, he stresses that solutions to problems should not be left to the decision of one person, stating that any disagreements within the society can be solved by a council of scholars to accommodate modern day needs. He further states that the advisory decisions of a consultative body "need to be supervised by the religious authorities for compatibility or accord of what they suggest with Islam." He also puts forward that since consultation is left to such a consultative body, "the prescription of the way of performing it in accordance with different times, circumstances, and states of affairs also falls within their scope." Taking the historical applications into consideration, he states, "Throughout history, it is possible to see differences in the performance and application of consultation corresponding to the different eras and particular circumstances. Sometimes in small circles or among small groups, and sometimes in wide circles or among larger groups, sometimes among civilians, and sometimes by opening its gates to the sciences and the military, the understanding of consultation itself has exhibited quite considerable change and differences."[897] He finally underlines that this change in consultation practice is not because it is a rule subject to being altered, but because of its flexibility and the universality of its practicability in every time and place.

---

[897]   Gülen, *The Statue of Our Souls*, p. 55.

BIBLIOGRAPHY

Abdullah, Muhammad and Muhammad Akram Sajid. "Muhammad" by Maxime Rodinson (an Analytical Study)." *Jihat al-Islam, Lahore-Pakistan* 4, issues 1 and 2, (July-December 2010 / January-June 2011).

Acar, Ismail, *Mastering Knowledge in Modern Times: Fethullah Gülen as an Islamic Scholar*, "A Classical Scholar with a Modern Outlook: Fethullah Gülen and His Legal Thought," (NJ: Blue Dome Press, 2012), pp. 65-84.

Ajjaj al-Hatib, Muhammad "Sunnetin Tesbiti," in "Harun Karipcin," (2010), http://www.herkul.org/kitap-ozetleri/suennetin-tesbiti/.

Agitoglu, Nurullah. "Hadislerin Tedvini," *Yeni Ümit*, Issue 85 (September, 2009).

Akdemir, Salih. "Tarih Boyunca Ve Kur'an-i Kerim'de Kadin," *Islami Arastirmalar*, 5/4 (Ankara, 1991), pp. 260-270.

Akgul, Muhittin. "Peygamberimizin Hanimlari Ve Evliliklerindeki Hikmetler-2," *Yeni Ümit*, Issue 47 (January-February-March 2000).

Akgul, Saliha. *Ezvac-i Tahirat*. Istanbul: Gul Yurdu Publishing, 2007.

Akin, Nimetullah. "Hadislerin Yazili Kaydi Ve Literatur Esasli Bir Disiplin Olma Sureci: A. Sprenger, I. Goldziher Ve G. Schoeler'in Yaklasimlari," *Hadis Tetkikleri Dergisi (Journal of Hadith Studies)*, VI/1 (2008): 54, 55.

Akman, Nuriye. *Gurbette Fethullah Gülen*. Türkiye'nin Baska Fethullah Gülen'i Yok. edited by Nuh Gonultas, Istanbul: Zaman Kitap, 2004.

———. *Gurbette Fethullah Gülen*. Fethullah Gülen Terore Panzehir Sunuyor. Istanbul: Zaman Kitap, 2004.

———. "A Real Muslim Cannot Be a Terrorist." (March 23, 2004). https://www.fgulen.com/en/fethullah-gulens-works/toward-a-global-civilization-of-love-and-tolerance/jihad-terrorism-human-rights/25259-real-muslims-cannot-be-terrorists

Aktan, Hamza. *Bir Alim Portresi: Fethullah Gülen Hocaefendi (The Portrait of a Scholar: Fethullah Gülen)*, (Istanbul: Nil Publishing, 2014).

———."Kur'an Ve Sunnet Isiginda Teror Ve Intihar Eylemleri" (Terrorist Acts and Suicide Attacks in the Light of the Qur'an and the Sunnah), *Yeni Umit*, Issue 63 (January-March 2004).

Akyildiz, Osman. "Dinde Reformcu Yaklasimlar Veya Dini Modernizmin Yukselisi" (The Reformist Approaches in the Religion or the Rise of Religious Modernism), *Akademya magazine*, Issue 1, (September-December, 2010), pp. 94-108.

Albayrak, Ismail. *Fethullah Gülen Hocaefendi'nin Tefsir Anlayisi* (*Fethullah Gülen's Understanding of Quranic Exegesis*), Istanbul: Nil Publishing, 2010.

———. *Mastering Knowledge in Modern Times, Fethullah Gülen as an Islamic Scholar* (ed.), (Clifton, NJ: Blue Dome Press, 2012).

Arman, Deniz. "Benim Dinim Bana, Senin Dinin Sana." *Vatan Newspaper*, November 14, 2003.

Ashton, Loye. "Defending Religious Diversity and Tolerance in America Today: Lessons from Fethullah Gülen." (November 12, 2005). http://fgulen.com/en/gulen-movement/conference-papers/1338-the-fethullah-gulen-movement-i/25503-defending-religious-diversity-and-tolerance-in-america-today-lessons-from-fethullah-gulen?hitcount=0.

Aveder, Mahmut. "Hadis Ilmi." (2008).

Aydin, Mehmet. "Mevlana Humanizminin Boyutlari." *Turk-Islam Medeniyeti Akademik Arastirmalar Dergisi, Rumi special issue*, (2007), 53.

al-Azami, M. Mustafa. *Studies in Hadith Methodology and Literature*. Plainfield, USA: American Trust Publications, 1997.

Bakar, Osman (ed). *Sagduyu Cagrisi*. Fethullah Gülen'in Din Ve Bilim Yorumu: Din Bilimsel Yaklasim, Istanbul: Isik Publishing, 2005.

Beishenaliev, Almazbek. *Pedagogical Ideas of F. Gulen and Hizmet Movement on Education*. Johns Hopkins University, December 4, 2013.

Berelson, B. *Content Analysis in Communication Research*. New York: Free Press, 1952.

Beser, Faruk. *Fethullah Gülen Hocaefendinin Fikhini Anlamak*. 2 vols. Istanbul: Ufuk Kitap Publishing, 2006.

————. *Hanımlara Ozel Ilmihal.* Istanbul: Nun Publishing, 2010.

Bilgin, Feyza. "Basortusu Bir Tavsiyedir Vazgecilmez Bir Dini Emir Degil." *Sabah Newspaper* (October 2, 2006).

Brown, Daniel W. *Rethinking Tradition in Modern Islamic Thought.* Vol. 1, Cambridge: Cambridge University Press, 1996.

Cakan, Ismail Lutfi. *Hadis Edebiyati.* Istanbul: Marmara University, The Foundation of Faculty of Theology, 1997.

Calis, Halim. *Mastering Knowledge in Modern Times, Fethullah Gülen as an Islamic Scholar.* Fethullah Gülen's Thoughts on Hadith. New York: Blue Dome Press, 2011.

Canan, Ibrahim. *Fethullah Gülen'in Sunnet Anlayisi.* Istanbul: Ufuk Kitap Publishing, 2007.

Capan, Ergun. *Mastering Knowledge in Modern Times, Fethullah Gülen as an Islamic Scholar,* Gülen's Teaching Methodology in His Private Circle. New York: Blue Dome Press, 2011.

Celik, Gurkan, Kate Kirk and Yusuf Alan. "Modern Ideals and Muslim Identity: Harmony or Contradiction? A Text Linguistic Analysis of Gülen's Teachings and Movement." (October 25, 2007). http://fgulen.com/en/gulen-movement/conference-papers/contributions-of-the-gulen-movement/25828-modern-ideals-and-muslim-identity-harmony-or-contradiction-a-text-linguistic-analysis-of-gulens-teachings-and-movement?highlight=WyJmYWl0aC1iYXNlZCJd&hitcount=0.

Celik, Yusuf. "Peygamber'imizin (S.A.V) Ehl-i Kitapla Munasebetleri." *Yeni Umit, Issue* 78 (January, February, March 2007).

Cerrahoglu, Ismail. "Oryantalizm Ve Batida Kur'an Ve Kur'an Ilimleri Uzerine Arastirmalar." *Ankara University, Journal of Faculty of Theology,* XXXI (1989): 105-16.

————. "Tefsir Ve Hadis Kitabetine Karsi Peygamber Ve Sahabenin Durumu." *Ankara University, The Journal of Faculty of Theology* 9 (1962): 43.

Cihan, News Agency. "Gülen Offers Condolences for Slain Istanbul Resident Shot at Protest." *Today's Zaman,* May 24, 2014.

Contentanalysis.org. "Content Analysis and Communication through the Written Language." http://www.contentanalysis.org/.

Darulkitap. "Hadis Risaleleri." http://www.darulkitap.com/oku/hadis/muhtelif-kitaplar/hadisrisaleleri/islam/2.htm.

Demiresik, Halime. "Islam'da Cok Evlilik." *Sebnem Kadin ve Aile Dergisi* 6 (2003).

Demirpolat, Enver. "Islam Felsefesinin Bati Dusuncesine Etkisi." *Selcuk University, Journal of Institute of Social Science* 9 (2003): 431-32.

al-Dhahabi, Imam Shamsudin Muhammad ibn Ahmad, *Siyar A'lam Al-Nubala*, Vol. 12, (Beirut: Mu'assassat al-Risalah, 2014).

Dikici, Erkan. "Dogu-Batı Ayrimi Ekseninde Oryantalizm Ve Emperyalizm (Journal of History Culture and Art Research)." [In Turkish]. *Tarih Kultur ve Sanat Arastirmalari Dergisi, Karabuk University*, 3 (June 2014).

Doi, Abdur Rahman I. *Hadith: an Introduction.* USA: Kazi Publications, 1980.

Donmez, Mustafa. "Islam Dunyasinda Hadis Inkarcilari Ve Gorusleri." https://dusuncetarihi.files.wordpress.com/2010/01/islam-dunyasinda-hadis-inkarcilari-ve-gorusleri.pdf.

———. "Oryantalist James Robson'un Sunnet Ve Hadis Konusundaki Goruslerinin Tenkidi." Bursa Uludag Universitesi: Temel Islam Bilimler Bolumu, Hadis Ana Bilim Dalı, 1999.

Dumayni, M. G. *Hadis'te Metin Tenkidi Metodları.* Istanbul: Kitabevi Publications, 1997.

Eppig, Eileen. *Fethullah Gülen's Care for All Creation as a Means to Nonviolence.* University of Maryland, Oct. 29, 2009.

Erdil, Mustafa. Discussion with Fethullah Gülen's Student Ibrahim Kocabiyik. *On Islam and Science*, July 11, 2014.

———. Discussion with Fethullah Gülen's Student Cuma Ordu. *Reflection of Gülen's Thoughts on Academia*, July 26, 2014.

———. Interview with Fethullah Gülen's student Recep Dogan. *Regarding Fethullah Gülen's Teaching Methods in Islamic Science* July 2, 2014.

Erdogan, Latif. *Fethullah Gülen Hocaefendi, Kucuk Dunyam.* Istanbul: Ufuk Publishing, 2006.

Ergun Capan, Cemal Turk "Fethullah Gülen Hocaefendi'nin Bilinmeyen Bir Yonu: Ders Ve Tedris Metodu." *Yeni Umit, Issue* 89, (Temmuz-Ağustos-Eylül 2010).

Esposito, John L. "The Gülen Movement: Paradigms, Projects, and Aspirations." Paper presented at the Gulen Movement conference, International House at University of Chicago, November 11-13, 2010.

Ezer, Bekir. "Alman Oryantalistlerin Hz. Muhammed, Sunnet Ve Hadis Hakkindaki Calismalari (1900–1950)." Erciyes Universitesi, 2007.

Falahi, Ghulam Nabi. "Development of Hadith: A Concise Introduction of Early Hadith Literature." (n.d). http://muqith.files.wordpress.com/2010/10/development-of-hadith.pdf.

al-Fayyumi, Ahmad ibn Muhammad al-Muqri. "Al-Misbah al-Munir Fi Gharib al-Sharh al-Kabir," (2009). http://art.thewalters.org/files/pdf/W590.pdf

Fazlurrahman. *Tarih Boyunca Islami Metodoloji Sorunu (Islamic Methodology in History)*. Ankara: Ankara School's Publications, 1995.

Genc, Mustafa. "Vahiy Sunnet Iliskisi." Konya, Selcuk University. Theology Faculty, 2005.

Goldziher, Ignaz. *Muslim Studies*. Translated by C.R. Barber and S.M. Stern. London: Allen and Unwin, 1971.

Gülen, Fethullah. *Toward a Global Civilization of Love and Tolerance*. New Jersey: The Light Publishing, 2004.

———. "Yolsuzluk." http://www.herkul.org/herkul-nagme/401-nagme-yolsuzluk/.

———. "Sulh Hayırdır, Hayır Sulhtadır." herkul.org, http://www.herkul.org/herkul-nagme/195-nagme-sulh-hayirdir/.

———. *Asrin Getirdigi Tereddutler (Questions and Answers about Islam) Vol. 1*. Istanbul: Nil Publishing, 2010.

———. *Asrin Getirdigi Tereddutler (Questions and Answers about Islam) Vol. 2*. Istanbul: Nil Publishing, 2010.

———. *Asrin Getirdigi Tereddutler (Questions and Answers about Islam) Vol. 3*. Istanbul: Nil Publishing, 2010.

———. *Beyan (Speech and Power of Expression)*. Istanbul: Nil Publishing, 2011.

———. *Buhranlar Anaforunda Insan, Cag Ve Nesil, Vol. 2*. Istanbul: Nil Publishing, 2011.

———. *Cag Ve Nesil (Modern Age and the Contemporary Generation)* Vol. 1. Istanbul: Nil Publishing, 2009.

———. *Dirilis Cagrisi, Kirik Testi (The Broken Jug series) Vol. 6.* Istanbul: Nil Publishing, 2011.

———. *Enginligi Ile Bizim Dunyamiz (Our World with Its Immensity), Iktisadi Mulahazalar.* Istanbul: Nil Publishing, 2011.

———. *Fasildan Fasila (From Chapter to Chapter), Vol. 1.* Istanbul: Nil Publishing, 2010.

———. *Fasildan Fasila, Vol. 2.* Istanbul: Nil Publishing, 2011.

———. *Fasildan Fasila, Vol. 3.* Istanbul: Nil Publishing, 2010.

———. *Fasildan Fasila, Vol. 4.* Istanbul: Nil Publishing, 2011.

———. *Fatiha Uzerine Mulahazalar (The Opening: Al-Fatiha, A Commentary on the First Chapter of the Qur'an).* Istanbul: Nil Publishing, 2011.

———."Fethullah Gülen's message to the International symposium "Ijtihad and Qiyas: The richness of Islam" (2014), http://fgulen.com/en/press/messages/44412-fethullah-gulens-message-to-the-international-symposium-ijtihad-and-qiyas-the-richness-of-islam?hitcount=0

———. *Fikir Atlasi (The Atlas of Ideas),* Istanbul: Nil Publishing, 2006.

———. *Gurbet Ufuklari, Kırık Testi series, Vol. 3.* Istanbul: Nil Publishing, 2011.

———. *Hitap Cicekleri.* Istanbul: Nil Publishing, 1995.

———. *Inancin Golgesinde (Essentials of the Islamic Faith) Vol. 2.* Istanbul: Nil Publishing, 2009.

———. *Insanın Ozündeki Sevgi (Towards the Global Civilization of Love and Tolerance),* Vol. 16, Istanbul: Da Publishing, 2003.

———. *Sonsuz Nur (Muhammad: The Messenger of God), Vol. 1* Istanbul: Nil Publishing, 2010.

———.*Sonsuz Nur (Muhammad: The Messenger of God), Vol. 2.* Istanbul: Nil Publishing, 2010.

———. *Sonsuz Nur (Muhammad: The Messenger of God), Vol. 3.* Istanbul: Nil Publishing, 2010.

———. *Irsad Ekseni.* Istanbul: Nil Publishing, 2011.

———. *Kalb Ibresi (Heart's Cursor), Kirik Testi series, Vol. 9.* Istanbul: Nil Publishing, 2010.

————. *Kalbin Zumrut Tepeleri (Emerald Hills of the Heart), Vol. 3.* Istanbul: Nil Publishing, 2011.

————. *Kendi Dunyamıza Dogru (Towards Our Own World).* Istanbul: Nil Publishing, 2011.

————. *Kendi Iklimimiz, Prizma (Prism series, Vol. 5).* Istanbul: Nil Publishing, 2010.

————. *Kirik Testi (The Broken Jug), Vol. 1.* Istanbul: Nil Publishing, 2010.

————. *Kur'an'nin Altin Ikliminde (In the Golden Climate of the Qur'an).* Istanbul: Nil Publication, 2010.

————. *Kur'andan Idrake Yansiyanlar (Reflections on the Qur'an).* Istanbul: Nil Publishing, 2009.

————. *Muhammad, the Messenger of God: An Analysis of the Prophet's Life.* Trans. by Ali Unal. New Jersey: Tughra Books, 2005.

————. *Olcu Ve Yoldaki Isiklar (Pearls of Wisdom).* Istanbul: Nil Publishing, 2011.

————. *Olumsuzluk Iksiri (Potion for Immortality), Kirik Testi series, Vol. 7.* Istanbul: Nil Publication, 2011.

————. *Ornekleri Kendinden Bir Hareket (A Movement with Inherent Exemplars), Cag Ve Nesil series, Vol. 8.* Istanbul: Nil Publishing, 2010.

————. *Prizma (Prism) Vol. 1.* Istanbul: Nil Publishing, 2011.

————. *Prizma (Prism) Vol. 2.* Istanbul: Nil Publishing, 2010.

————. *Prizma (Prism) Vol. 3.* Istanbul: Nil Publishing, 2010.

————. *Prizma (Prism) Vol. 4.* Istanbul: Nil Publishing, 2010.

————. *Questions and Answers About Islam.* Trans. by Muhammed Cetin. New Jersey: Tughra Books, 2010.

————. *Ruhumuzun Heykelini Dikerken (The Statue of Our Souls), Vol. 1.* Istanbul: Nil publishing, 2011.

————. *Sunnetin Tespiti Ve Tesrideki Yeri.* Izmir: Nil Publications, 1994.

————. *Umit Burcu (The Bearing of Hope), Kirik Testi series, Vol. 4.* Istanbul: Nil Publishing, 2011.

————. *Vuslat Mustusu (Glad Tidings of a Reunion), Kirik Testi series, Vol.8.* Istanbul: Nil Publishing, 2011.

————. *Yenilenme Cehdi (Endeavor for Renewal), Kirik Testi series, Vol. 12.* Istanbul: Nil Publishing, 2012.

———. *Yeseren Dusunceler (Reflorishing Thoughts)*, Cag Ve Nesil series, Vol. 6. Istanbul: Nil Publishing, 2011.

———. *Yol Mulahazalari, Prizma series, Vol. 6.* Istanbul: Nil Publishing, 2007.

———. *Zamanin Altin Dilimi, Cag Ve Nesil series, Vol. 4.* Istanbul: Nil Publishing, 2011.

———. "Dogru Yer Ve Zamanda Dogru Sorular Sorulmali." (3. Mart. 2006). http://fgulen.com/tr/fethullah-gulenin-kursu-aka-demi-yazilari/fethullah-gulen-2006-kursuleri/12007-Fethul-lah-Gulen-Zaman-Dogru-Yer-ve-Zamanda-Dogru-Soru-lar-Sorulmali?highlight=WyJzb3J1bGFyI10=.

———. *Hosgoru Ve Diyalog*. Istanbul, Turkey: Merkur Publishing, 1999.

———. *Journey to Noble Ideals*. Clifton, USA: Tughra Publishing, 2014.

———. *Mefkure Yolculugu*. Istanbul: Nil Publishing, 2014.

———. "Ne Muceddidim Ne Muctehid Ne De Reformist!" http://tr.f-gulen.com/content/view/9849/10/.

———. "Soru-Cevaplar Uzerine ", (May 20, 2008). http://fgulen.com/tr/fethullah-gulenin-butun-eserleri/prizma-serisi/fethul-lah-gulen-zihin-harmani/15518-Fethullah-Gulen-Soru-Ceva-plar-Uzerine?hitcount=0

———. "What Is Jihad." (September 13, 2001). http://fgulen.com/en/fethullah-gulens-works/faith/questions-and-an-swers/24522-what-is-jihad?highlight=WyJqaWhhZCJd.

———. *Yasatma Ideali (So That Others May Live)*. Istanbul: Nil Publishing, 2012.

fgulen.com. "Fethullah Gülen'in Mualla Validesi Merhume Refia Gülen." fgulen.com, http://fgulen.com/tr/fethullah-gulen-kim-dir/gulen-hakkinda/fethullah-guleni-taniyanlardan/166-fgu-len-com-Fethullah-Gulenin-Mualla-Validesi-Merhume-Re-fia-Gulen?hitcount=0.

———. "Years of Education." (September 15, 2001). http://fgulen.com/en/fethullah-gulens-life/1304-biography/24652-years-of-edu-cation?hitcount=0.

Gundem, Gercek. "Ilahiyatcidan 'Turban' Cikisi," *Gercek Gundem daily*, December 4, 2007.

al-Hatib, Muhammad Ajjaj. *As-Sunnatu Kabla't-Tadwin*. Cairo, 1963.

Hatiboglu, M. Said. *Hadis Tedkikleri (Hadith Analyses)*, Ankara: Ozkan Matbaacilik, 2009.

Hitti, Philip K. *Islam Tarihi (Islamic History), Vol. I*, Trans. by Salih Tug. Istanbul: Kitap Yurdu Publication, 2011.

Huseyin, Zuheyr. "Muhammed Abduh Kimdir (1849-1905)" in " M. Hilmi Bas" (2015), http://www.islamdusuncesi.net/muhammed-abduh-1849-1905-187h.htm

Irwin, R. *Oryantalistler Ve Dusmanlari, (For Lust of Knowing: the Orientalists and Their Enemies)*. Trans. by Bahar Tirnakci. Istanbul: Yapı Kredi Publications, 2008.

Juynboll, G. H. A. *The Authenticity of the Tradition Literature*. Leiden, Netherlands: Brill Archive, 1969.

Juynboll, G.H.A. *Oryantalistik Hadis Arastirmalari, Makaleler*. Vol. 1, Ankara: Ankara Okulu Yayinlari, 2001.

Kahraman, Abdullah. "Fikhi Hadislerin Doğru Anlasilip Yorumlanmasi Hususunda Bazi Esaslar." *Eski Dergi* (n.d). http://eskidergi.cumhuriyet.edu.tr/makale/316.pdf.

Kaplan, Tugba. "Kurt Sorununu Cozecek 105 Yillik Proje: Medresetu'z-Zehra." *Zaman daily* (August 25, 2013).

Kara, Seyfullah. "Hz.Peygamber'e Karsi Oryantalist Bakis Ve Bu Bakisin Kirilmasinda Metodolojik Yaklasimin Onemi." *Ataturk University, Journal of Theology Faculty* 23 (2005).

Karaman, Hayrettin. "Islam Hukukunda Zaruret Hali." http://www.hayrettinkaraman.net/kitap/meseleler/0177.htm.

Kisakurek, Necip Fazil. *Cile*. Siirlerim Ve Sairligim. Vol. 18, Istanbul: Buyuk Dogu Publication, 1992.

Kizil, Fatma. "Oryantalistlerin Hadis Literaturu Hakkindaki Gorusleri." (2009). http://sonpeygamber.info/oryantalistlerin-hadis-literaturu-hakkindaki-gorusleri.

Kockuzu, Ali Osman. *Rivayet Ilimlerinde Haber-i Vahitlerin Itikat Ve Tesri Yonlerinden Degeri*. Ankara: Religious Affairs Directorate Publications, 1988.

Kocyigit, Talat. *Hadis Usulu*. Ankara: Ankara University Publishing House, 1987.

———. *Hadis Tarihi*. Ankara: Ankara University Publications, 1988.

———. *Hadis Istilahlari*. Vol. 2, Ankara: Ankara University, Ilahiyat Fakultesi Publishing, 1985.

Koksal, M. Asim. *Mustesrik Caetani'nin Yazdigi Islam Tarihindeki Isnad Ve Iftiralara Reddiye*. Ankara: Diyanet Isleri Baskanligi, 1986.

Kurucan, Ahmet. *Fikih Dunyamız*. Istanbul: Isik Publishing, 2011.

———. "Ilan Edilmemis Nikah Olur Mu?" *Zaman daily*, September 15, 2011.

Lewis, Bernard. *Islamin Siyasal Soylemi*. Trans. by Fatih Tasar. Istanbul: Phoenix Publication, 1992.

M., Abu Zahw. *Hadis Ve Hadisciler*. Istanbul: Ensar Publications, 2007.

Matar, Nabil. *Islam in Britain, 1558-1685*, Vol. 1: Cambridge University Press, January 7, 2008.

Michel, Thomas. "Gulen as Educator and Religious Teacher," (April 2001). http://en.fgulen.com/press-room/review/1054-gulen-as-educator-and-religious-teacher.

———. "Gülen as Educator and Religious Teacher." (February 2002). http://fgulen.com/en/press/review/24902-gulen-as-educator-and-religious-teacher?highlight=WyJ0aG9tYXMiLCJtaW-NoZWwiLCJ0aG9tYXMgbWljaGVsIl0=&hitcount=0.

Mutafyan, Mesrob. "Hocaefendi'nin Actigi Yoldan Yuruyoruz." *Zaman daily*, October 28, 2003.

n.a. "Kadin Nasil Kolelestirildi? Nasil Ozgurlesecek?" http://devrim-kurtulus.forumo.de/devrimci-kadin-f70/kadin-nas-kolele-tiril-di-nas-ozgurle-ecek-t281.html.

Nevo, J. Koren and Y. D. *Methodological Approaches to Islamic Studies*. Amherst NY: Der Islam, 1991.

Nursi, Bediuzzaman Said. *The Flashes Collection*. The Eleventh Flash, First Point. Istanbul: Sozler Publication, 2006.

———. *Asa-yi Musa*. Istanbul: Sahdamar Publishing, 2007.

———. *Lemalar*. Istanbul: Sahdamar Publishing, 2007.

———. *Mektubat*. Istanbul: Envar Publishing, 1995.

———. *Sualar*. Istanbul: Sozler Publishing, 2009.

Ozturk, Yasar Nuri. *Kur'an'daki Islam*. Istanbul: Sidre Publication, 1992.

Qutaybah, M. A. M. *Ta'wilu Muhtalafi'l-Hadith*, Beirut: Daru'l-Kutu-bi'l- Ilmiyya, n.d.

Palabiyik, M. Hanefi. "Cahiliye Donemi ve Islam'ın Ilk Yillarinda Oku-ma-Yazma Faaliyetleri," *The Journal of Ataturk University, Theology Faculty, Vol. 27*, (2007).

Rodinson, M. *Muhammad, Yeni Bir Dunyanin, Dinin Ve Silahli Bir Peygamberin Dogusu*. Trans. by Attila Tokatli. Istanbul: Gocebe Publication, 1968.

as-Salih, Subhi. *Hadis Ilimleri Ve Hadis Istilahlari*. Vol. 8, Istanbul: M.U. Ilahiyat Vakfi Publishing, 2009.

Sargin, Suleyman. "Namazi Sanki Secde Etmek Icin Kiliyor." *Zaman daily*, October 4, 2013.

Saritoprak, Zeki. *Mastering Knowledge in Modern Times, Fethullah Gülen as an Islamic Scholar*. "Fethullah Gülen and His Theology of Social Responsibility," (Clifton, NJ: Blue Dome Press, 2012), pp. 85-96.

Shadi, Heydar. "Interfaith Dialogue and Religious Tolerance in Contemporary Islamic Thought: A Comparative Study of Fethullah Gülen and Abdul Karim Soroush." (November 22, 2007). http://fgulen.com/en/gulen-movement/conference-papers/peaceful-coexistence/25870-interfaith-dialogue-and-religious-tolerance-in-contemporary-islamic-thought-a-comparative-study-of-fethullah-gulen-and-abdul-karim-soroush?highlight=WyJ0b2xlcmFuY2UiLCJkaWWFsb2d1ZSJd.

Shahba, Muhammad Abu. *Hadis Mudafaasi, Vol. 1*. Mehmet Gormez, M. Emin Ozafsar, Foreword, Ankara: Rehber Publishing, 1990.

al-Shahrazuri, Ibn al-Salah. *An Introduction to the Science of the Hadith*. Translated by Eerik Dickinson. UK: Garnet Publishing Limited, 2006.

Sharkawi, Muhammad. "Klasik Ve Modern Ilimleri Sentezleyen Alim." *Zaman daily*, Temmuz 1, 2014.

Suphandağı, Abdulkadir. "Kadindan Israrla Esirgenen Bagimsiz Sahsiyeti, Islam 14 Asir Once Vermis." *Zaman daily*, May 21, 2005.

as-Suyuti, J. *Tadribu'r-Rawi Fi Sharhi Takribi'n Nawawi*. Cairo: Daru'l-Hadith, 2004.

Tuncer, Faruk. "Fethullah Gülen'in Sunnet Anlayisi" (Fethullah Gülen's Understanding of Sunnah), (2007). http://tr.fgulen.com/content/view/14324/12/.

———. *Fethullah Gülen, Insanın Ozundeki Sevgi.* 16 vols, Istanbul: Ufuk Kitap Publishing, 2004.

———. *Fethullah Gülen Hocaefendi'nin Fikhini Anlamak,* Istanbul: Ufuk Kitap Publishing, 2006.

Unal, Ali. *Advocate of Dialogue: Fethullah Gülen.* Fairfax: The Fountain, 2000.

———. *M. Fethullah Gülen: Bir Portre Denemesi (Fethullah Gülen: A Portrait Essay),* Istanbul: Nil Publishing, 2002.

Uraler, Aynur. "Sahabe Uygulaması Olarak Sunnete Baglilik." *Yeni Umit,* Issue 51 (2001).

Vahide, Sukran. "Said Nursi'nin Cihat Yorumu" (Said Nursi's Interpretation of Jihad), (1970). http://www.ufkumuz.com/said-nursi-nin-cihat-yorumu-2708h.htm

Wilhelm, F. Johann. *The Role of Traditional in Islam, Studies in Islam.* New York, 1981.

Yildirim, Muhammed Emin. "Daru'l Erkam'da Okuma Yazma Orani." http://www.siyerarastirmalari.org/darul-erkam-da-okuma-yazma-orani/.

Yildirim, Suat. *Kuran-i Hakim Ve Aciklamali Meali (The Wise Qur'an and Its Annotated Interpretation).* Istanbul: Isik Publications, 2006.

———. *Fethullah Gülen'in Kur'an-i Hakim'e Yaklasimi (Fethullah Gülen's Approach to the Wise Qur'an).* Istanbul: Nil Publications, 2011.

Yucel, Ahmet. *Hadis Istilahlarinin Dogusu Ve Gelisimi (The Emergence and Development of the Terms of Hadith Science).* Istanbul: Marmara University, Faculty of Theology Publications, 1996.

Yusuf, S. M. *The Sunnah, Its Development and Revision, Hadith and Sunnah.* Malaysia: Percetakan Zafar Sdn. Bhd. (Co.No. 97878-H), 2008.

Zahw, Muhammad Abu. *Hadis Ve Hadisciler (The Hadith and the Muhaddiths).* Trans. by M. Ali Sonmez, Selman Basaran. Istanbul: Ensar Nesriyat, 2007.

al-Zarqani, As-Shaykh Muhammad 'Abd al-'Azim. *Manahil al-Irfan Fi Ulum al-Qur'an.* Vol. 2, Beirut-Lebanon: Dar al-Ma'rifah, 2001.

Zubayr, Siddiqi Muhammad. *Hadith Literature, Its Origin, Development and Special Features.* Cambridge: The Islamic Text Society, 1993.

Electronic Sources

The following websites provide information on Gülen and contain his works, views and what others think of him.

- http://www.fgulen.com/en/
- http://www.fethullahgulen.org/tr/
- http://www.youtube.com/FGülenTR
- www.asringetirdigitereddutler.net
- www.cagvenesil.com
- www.fasildanfasila.net
- www.fgulen.com
- www.herkul.org
- www.herkul.org/this-week/
- www.inancingolgesinde.net
- www.infinitelight.org
- www.irsadekseni.com
- www.kalbinzumruttepeleri.com
- www.kirikmizrap.net
- www.kurandanidrakeyansiyanlar.com
- www.mquran.org
- www.olcuveyayoldakiisiklar.com
- www.pearls.org
- www.pmuhammad.com
- www.ruhumuzunheykelinidikerken.com
- www.sonsuznur.net

Index